DEMOCRACY IN DEFAULT

DEMOCRACY IN DEFAULT

FINANCE AND THE RISE OF NEOLIBERALISM IN AMERICA

BRIAN JUDGE

Columbia University Press   *New York*

Columbia University Press
Publishers Since 1893
New York   Chichester, West Sussex
cup.columbia.edu

Copyright © 2024 Columbia University Press
All rights reserved

Library of Congress Cataloging-in-Publication Data
Names: Judge, Brian, author.
Title: Democracy in Default : Finance and the Rise of
Neoliberalism in America / Brian Judge.
Description: New York : Columbia University Press, [2024] |
Includes bibliographical references and index.
Identifiers: LCCN 2023031342 | ISBN 9780231213981 (hardback) |
ISBN 9780231213998 (trade paperback) | ISBN 9780231560139 (ebook)
Subjects: LCSH: Neoliberalism—Economic aspects—United States. |
Capitalism—Political aspects—United States. |
Finance—Political aspects—United States. |
United States—Economic policy.
Classification: LCC HC103 .J83 2024 | DDC 338.973—dc23/eng/20230721
LC record available at https://lccn.loc.gov/2023031342

Cover design: Noah Arlow
Cover image: Justin Sullivan/Getty Images

To all my teachers

CONTENTS

Introduction 1
1 Liberalism and Distributive Conflict 21
2 The Crisis of Inflation 66
3 The Financialization of Liberalism 108
4 Growth Machine Politics 135
5 Democracy and Finance in California 165
6 The Crisis of Finance 201
Epilogue: Finance or Democracy? 243

Notes 253
Index 313

DEMOCRACY IN DEFAULT

INTRODUCTION

If they can get you asking the wrong questions, they don't have to worry about the answers.
                                            —Thomas Pynchon

California [is a case] not provided for in the Manifesto. . . . We shall have to allow for this.
                                            —Friedrich Engels

When we browse the pages of our recent history, we find few great events in the last four decades that have not turned to the profit of the market. From education to child-rearing to politics, nearly every domain of human life has been coopted by market logic, market imperatives, and market valuation. Action increasingly becomes value-maximizing investment; things become assets; people become human capital. At the same time, life in liberal democracies has become more insecure, unequal, and devalued as money, markets, and morals have steadily replaced public goods, public things, and public concerns. Accordingly, profit and capital appreciation have become the lodestars of what remains of political life, itself marketized yet also increasingly obsolete in a world governed by global market forces. These developments have been captured under the heading of "neoliberalism," both as a ubiquitous term of art in the critical scholarship and a colloquial swear word cursing an unlivable present.

How did we get here? There is one conventional story told with two opposing political inflections.

In the now-distant postwar Golden Age, the American state played an active role in the direction of the national economy and in securing the economic well-being of the white middle class. Massive government projects, a booming postwar economy, progressive taxation, and a tightly regulated financial system generated a period of unprecedented income growth, investment in public goods, and modestly shared prosperity. In the 1970s, however, things fell apart. Rising inflation and unemployment combined with a falling rate of profit symptomatized contradictions in the prevailing regime that could no longer be contained or managed. A conservative counter-revolution that had been gestating for three decades at the University of Chicago, on the slopes of Mont Pèlerin, and in the subdivisions of Orange County seized on the crisis. The white middle class and big business both sought emancipation from the grasping hands of a state creeping toward a modestly egalitarian and inclusive economic, racial, sexual, and environmental order. Their savior appeared in the form of General Electric spokesman, Hollywood actor, and California governor Ronald Reagan.

For proponents of "free market conservatism," Reagan's program of tax cuts, deregulation, austerity, privatization, and union busting, alongside the reassertion of traditional morality, countered the threat posed by big government liberalism. Growth returned, unemployment fell, and it was morning in America. For critics of "neoliberalism," this same program unleashed capital, intensified inequality, defanged labor, and buried the postwar consensus that the state has a constructive role to play in the economic life of the nation. For the Left, these developments were particularly worrying. Not only was the premise that government was a necessary corrective to economic power under attack, it lost in a landslide. Even worse, when Bill Clinton and Tony Blair finally retook power on behalf of the loyal opposition, they continued the same basic program of Reagan and Margaret Thatcher while softening some of the rougher edges.[1]

Neoliberalism, the common story goes, was enacted *by design*.[2] The world dreamed up by neoliberal intellectuals was actualized by neoliberal politicians, activists, and fellow travelers: the state was successfully redeployed to insulate the economy from democracy and restore the conditions for unfettered capital accumulation. Some celebrate, while others mourn. Figures like F. A. Hayek and Milton Friedman provided the intellectual ammunition for the battle of ideas and subsequent seizure of the state.[3] Neoliberal politicians won over the polity with freedom talk and subsequently enacted a wide-ranging program to free capital from its postwar shackles and retake what was lost in the New Deal.[4] Faith in markets replaced faith in the collective capacity to solve collective problems. The rise of neoliberalism marked the intensification of capitalism after a brief social democratic detour.

In this vein, David Harvey canonically defines neoliberalism as a "political project to re-establish the conditions for capital accumulation and to restore the power of economic elites."[5] Harvey explains that "neoliberalism as a potential antidote to threats to the capitalist social order" was cooked up by the Mont Pèlerin Society, disseminated through academic economists and Washington think tanks, and consolidated as a "new economic orthodoxy regulating public policy at the state level."[6] The avowed neoliberals, especially those associated with the Mont Pèlerin Society, promoted a positive program for the liberal state as the enforcer of a system of markets and market conduct extending across all of society. Unlike classical liberalism, neoliberalism is a theory of the state requiring active measures to ensure the market mechanism works unimpeded by social and political demands: the strong state ensures the free society.[7] Neoliberalism, therefore, theorizes the state as constructing, enforcing, and overseeing a social order governed by competitive markets. The state must become an iron maiden of liberty keeping disorderly demands for justice, equality, and sustainability safely at bay.

From this perspective, neoliberalism is explained as an intentional policy paradigm serving the material interests of capital deployed to defuse rising labor militancy and reverse declining rates of profit (hence the moniker "neoliberalism by design").[8] The crisis of the 1970s was the occasion for implementing this far-reaching vision for the transformation of state, society, and economy. For a while, it delivered the goods. But after three decades at the end of history, the bubble finally popped, precipitating the 2008 global financial crisis and ushering in a new era of populist backlash and social unrest.[9] Capital scored a decisive victory in its war against the postwar consensus in the late 1970s, but in so doing, it sowed the seeds of its own near-destruction in 2008.

There are at least five major problems with this account.

First, neoliberalism by design acquiesces to the neoliberal diagnosis of the antecedent crisis: interest rate hikes, labor discipline, tax cuts, and deregulation are explained as successfully taming inflation where Keynesian demand management and social democratic regulation failed. Harvey, for instance, argues that "the reduction and control of inflation is the only systematic success neoliberalization can claim," thereby accepting the hodgepodge of empirical claims at the heart of the neoliberal project.[10] Yet, if neoliberal ideology was only thin cover for the material interests of capital, then it is surprising that it seemed to offer both the correct diagnosis and prescription for the terminal contradictions in the postwar order. Indeed, it is surprising that the political thesis advanced by the neoliberals—that inflation was the necessary and inevitable manifestation of the attempt to subordinate markets to social demands—remains uncontested by scholars ostensibly critiquing the neoliberal turn. This presumption opens the door to readily dismissing the inegalitarian and de-democratizing effects of neoliberalism as the necessary price for taming inflation: there was no alternative.[11]

Second, neoliberalism by design cannot explain the massively increased role and importance of finance—what scholars have termed "financialization"—over the same period.[12] In brief, financialization encompasses developments such as corporate profit-making and investment increasingly shifting to financial channels, "shareholder value" emerging as the dominant corporate governance paradigm, the rise of the shadow banking system, and the proliferation of new financial instruments ensnaring previously insulated domains in the circuits of global capital. However, financialization was not part of the revolutionary agenda: it was neither theorized directly by neoliberal intellectuals nor the intended goal of neoliberal policymakers.[13] As neoliberalism replaced political control with market control, the American economy was also undergoing a fundamental shift that was neither identical with neoliberalism nor radically independent of it. The coincidence between financialization and neoliberalism is generally conceptualized as a happy accident in which the explosion of financial assets, profits, and practices softened the blow from public retrenchment. At best, the conventional account treats financialization as an accidental offshoot of neoliberal deregulation run amok. Consequently, the theoretical and historical relationship between financialization and neoliberalism remains underspecified at best and fundamentally incoherent at worst.

Third, neoliberalism by design cannot explain the seemingly limitless and totalizing reach of neoliberalism from the commanding heights of national political economy to the intimate lives of individuals and families. State policy alone cannot explain the distinctive and encompassing *political rationality* of neoliberalism or cases of neoliberal transformation that occur in the absence of neoliberal actors or ideology.[14] Neoliberalism does not simply convert everything into a market, but submits all forms of life to economic rationality and the rubrics of market conduct. Subjects and publics have been thoroughly transformed into competitive pools of human capital endlessly striving to maximize their portfolio value—"all the way down and all the way in"—beyond what state repression or ideological reconfiguration alone can explain.[15] Neoliberalism operates as a ubiquitous form of governance that frustrates traditional conceptual vocabularies. Critics of neoliberalism as a critical paradigm make a related point from a different angle by observing how the supposed productions of "neoliberalism" vastly exceed the reach of the state.[16]

Fourth, neoliberalism by design misses the crucial role of democracy in supporting the neoliberal agenda. By implicitly adopting an explanatory frame centered on "capitalism" in which mass electoral politics is famously absent, political agency is instead monopolized by "the ruling class," "the state," and/or "structural forces."[17] But none of these delivered 520 electoral votes to Richard Nixon in 1972, 525 electoral votes to Reagan in 1984, or the House of Representatives to Newt Gingrich in 1994.[18] Reagan's legislative agenda passed a House of Representatives controlled by the Democratic Party. The fracture of the New Deal coalition and breakdown of the postwar social consensus—the political soil of neoliberalism in America—cannot be explained solely by the reawakened class consciousness of capital. Wolfgang Streeck argues that the "postwar settlement [was] abandoned by capital in response to a global profit squeeze."[19] It was also abandoned by the white middle class.[20]

Fifth, neoliberalism by design struggles to explain what Colin Crouch termed the "strange non-death of neoliberalism" in the aftermath of the 2008 financial crisis.[21] The presumptive supremacy of unregulated markets precipitated a global financial crisis, generating an intense popular backlash to the neoliberal project itself.[22] After a twenty-five-year hegemony, in which the efficiency and normative desirability of markets went largely unquestioned, many neoliberal policies were abruptly abandoned and Keynesianism was raised from the dead in a desperate attempt to prevent the collapse of the financial system and world economy.[23] However, neoliberalism easily survived: the rule of markets and morals was extended and intensified despite the promise of hope and change.[24] Although the crisis was a cataclysm for neoliberalism as an explicit theoretical and policy paradigm—its ideology and political partisans were widely discredited, and popular anger across the political spectrum arose against the incumbent political economic order—the neoliberal consumption of democracy marched on.

What explains the political economic transformations of the last four decades, if not only the capture of the state and subsequent deployment of a coherent ideological and political program?

* * *

In its most compressed form, this book argues that finance is empowered by liberal democracy to depoliticize distributive conflict and that finance, in turn, transforms everything it touches around the imperative to generate monetary return.[25] The cumulative and compounding consequences of financial risk taken in response to distributive conflict explain much of what we now call "neoliberalism" in the American context.

I follow the familiar account of neoliberalism's ascendance but use this historical plot to tell an unfamiliar theoretical story, one that shifts from an inherently crisis-prone capitalism to a liberalism requiring definite preconditions and reliant on certain tactics of depoliticization. In place of capital and ideology, my approach centers on depoliticizing discourses and growth regimes responding to the liberal imperative of neutralizing distributive conflict.[26] To explain this overtaking of liberal democracy by finance, the book charts how finance enters particular political settings, fundamentally transforms the parameters of government, and ensnares everyone and everything as its agents.

Neoliberalism canonically manifests as an encroachment by "the economic" on "the political." I begin by briefly sketching how these domains were originally constituted within the liberal tradition. Then I will chart at both the theoretical and concrete levels how finance changes the map.

* * *

Liberalism, like capitalism, is a formation that is neither unified nor stable.[27] However, a number of defining features can be identified.[28] In Michael Walzer's characterization, liberalism is "a world of walls, and each one creates a new liberty."[29] The preceding order of monarchical absolutism, as the frontispiece of Thomas Hobbes's *Leviathan* illustrates, saw only an "undifferentiated land mass" over which it was master. Liberalism separates this terrain into autonomous spheres and limits where the sovereign may legitimately intrude. For Walzer, these distinctive separations define liberalism as a "certain way of drawing the map of the social and political world."[30] The separation of church and state creates religious liberty. The separation of civil society and the state creates economic liberty. These separations give rise to the familiar vision of liberalism as a world of autonomous, separable domains.

John Rawls argues that liberalism begins with the Reformation. In response to two centuries of religious wars, religion was gradually expelled from liberal public life. A precarious truce replaced the constant and bloody struggle for religious domination. Under this truce, religion was freed from the state and the state was freed from religion. This regime, which would come to be called "secularism," maintains political order through the depoliticization of religious conflict. In this condition, religious power was forbidden from governing publicly, and the state was formally forbidden from governing religiously. We are familiar with and generally sanguine about the resulting regime of tolerance, beginning with religious conflict and extending in secular modernity to every axis of social identity. Marked differences and social hierarchies are not abolished by this regime but depoliticized and shunted into a domain of private, and privately deployed, social power. The liberal state remains above the fray by proclaiming its formal neutrality.

But conflict in liberal orders is not limited to religion: like any other political order, liberalism exists in a condition of material scarcity that requires making decisions about the production and division of resources. The potential for *distributive conflict* arising from these decisions poses special difficulties for liberalism. An absolutist regime can tax, spend, expropriate, and persecute without an account or explanation. Indeed, economic life in the age of absolutism was dictated by the state through caps on interest rates, compulsory feasts and religious celebrations, regulations on wages and hours, prohibitions on speculation, and an elaborate system of clerical taxation. Managing such decisions politically requires the kinds of politically determined valuation and state control forbidden by the new order of autonomous spheres of liberty that Walzer identifies with liberalism. Much like politically dictating sacraments or suppressing certain religious minorities, politically dictating production quotas or distributive shares invites destabilizing conflicts. Nevertheless, such decisions must be made. How can production and distribution take place outside of the state while also generating a stable and consensual political order?

The answer we see in canonical liberal theorists is the relocation of distribution to an autonomous sphere outside the liberal state that enables decentralized coordination without centralized state coercion. An "invisible hand" or "spontaneous order" beyond the liberal state is supposed to impartially and efficiently mediate humanity's complex interdependence. Distribution is removed from the sphere of legitimate political contestation and thus "depoliticized," creating the familiar separation of "politics" and "the economy," "the state" and "the market." Simultaneously, canonical liberals make clear that growth and rising living standards, and not only the free circulation of capital and labor, secure popular investment in this regime. Resolving conflicts over resources such as oil, housing, pension benefits, or city budgets politically would require exactly what liberalism is founded to oppose: the tactical deployment of sovereign power in accordance with public values. Fortunately, "the market" is able to transmute conflicting private interests into collectively beneficial outcomes without requiring a single public vote.

From the early Marx, we know that liberal depoliticization—wherein the liberal state disavows and disinvests from social conflict through the declaration of formal equality—actually presupposes the regime of social powers generating and governing these conflicts.[31] Marx's insight is that the bestowal of liberal freedoms presumes unequal positioning within the powers toward which the liberal state declares its neutrality or indifference. Liberal freedom solely grants subjects equal rights within these powers. Removing the object of conflict from politics does not remove the object from the lives of liberal subjects. Depoliticization therefore presumes inequality as it insulates these privatized powers from public authority. The liberal state emancipates the abstract, universal, and ultimately imaginary citizen from these particularizing forces of civil society rather than the real human beings subject to them. This "political emancipation" *depoliticizes* the conflicts arising from these forces, absolving the state of responsibility for their particular and particularizing effects. However, the liberal state only claims universality through adopting formal neutrality toward these particular conflicts, abolishing what Marx calls their "political significance." The state cannot (and does not) remain neutral on the forces themselves.

Although Marx's heuristic is religious conflict, the same logic can be applied to distributive conflict. To rephrase Marx, "the political suppression of *distributive conflicts* not only does not abolish *distributive conflicts*; it actually presupposes their existence."[32] When, like religion, the liberal state withdraws from distribution, the result is not equality, efficiency, or equilibrium but the depoliticized rule of social power. Just like religion, abolishing the political character and denying the political standing of distributive conflicts does nothing to free society from such conflicts: instead, they are shunted into another domain of government, newly free to manifest its own nature in response.

I use the term *distributive conflict* to denote the open political contestation of distributive shares. Definitionally, distributive conflict marks the breakdown of some prior regime that enjoyed a minimum level of popular support. Examples of distributive conflict include anything from bread riots to anti-austerity protests.³³ Distributive conflict encompasses more than the familiar category of class conflict because it occurs along multiple intersecting, overlapping, and even contradicting axes of social power. These include, among others, race, gender, nationality, immigration status, geography, education, income, credit score, occupation, and homeownership. Class conflict between owners and workers does not exhaust the range of conflict in liberal orders. Conflict—and the sense of scarcity and insecurity generating it, as Hobbes reminds us—is a general condition. As we will see, one crucial fulcrum of distributive conflict during the rise and consolidation of neoliberalism was between taxpayers and beneficiaries, categories that are irreducible to purely class terms.

Liberalism resolves the problem of distributive conflict by relocating it from the political sphere (under Tudor monarchy) to the realm of privatized social powers or "the economy" (under liberal democracy). When, as with religion, the liberal state withdraws from the economic sphere, liberal subjects do not magically transform into the figure idealized in liberal theory, equal and free. Instead, they are beholden to newly depoliticized social power. The liberal state, again borrowing from Marx, is "premised on that which it pretends to transcend" and "requires what it claims to abolish" by transferring, translating, and transposing distributive questions to this realm of privatized powers: what we now call "the economy" or "the market." Through depoliticization, the liberal state solidifies its dependence on what it disavows politically as it leaves liberal subjects to navigate these forces individually: "there alone rule Freedom, Equality and Bentham."³⁴

In liberal orders, the process of producing and distributing the material requirements of human life is imagined to be governed by "the market," which ensures both fairness and efficiency and obviates overt political valuation, contestation, or control.³⁵ The designation and ideological separation of "the economic" and "the political" sequester distributive conflict in an allegedly natural order spontaneously producing efficiency and equilibrium. The inhuman and antidemocratic consequences of private social power and unlimited individual license are thereby metabolized as the necessary consequences of freedom and efficiency. Intrinsic nature, and not political agency, political will, or political power, is imagined to govern the liberal economy. But in contrast to the happy image of depoliticized fairness and efficiency, liberal civil society harbors powers that make it unequal, insecure, violent, and predatory.

Marx's fundamental insight is that liberal depoliticization frees the state, not us, from social power.[36] Liberal subjects become, in Marx's words, "the plaything of alien powers" as official liberal discourses trumpet the rule of right and reason. Like religion and religious conflict, the depoliticization of distributive conflict creates latent tensions that must be constantly finessed and that lurk beneath the placid surface of universalistic liberal discourse. Liberalism institutionally secures and discursively consecrates this condition in the name of freedom, individual rights, and state neutrality. In this way, conflict and domination do not vanish but are instead prevented from manifesting politically or being the subject of public deliberation, decision-making, and authority. Distributive conflict is not abolished but depoliticized, a depoliticization that is an essential yet unavowed premise of liberal government.

* * *

This book explains financialization as a political strategy to "re-depoliticize" distributive conflict that in turn deploys neoliberalism. When distributive conflict reemerges in the postwar era—whether in the form of inflation, tax revolt, or austerity—finance provides immediate relief. Internal political obligations to constituents and citizens are met with external supply from creditors and counterparties. Contentious political questions of relative need and desert are replaced with the formal parameters of proper technocratic management. Political provision of public goods based on public values is replaced with financial provision based on market values. The good might itself remain unchanged—public employee pensions, wastewater treatment, electricity, housing—but its provision is now contingent on upholding the terms of the financial contract.

The effects of this transformation are profound. Financialization once again depoliticizes distribution but at a price: bond covenants must be upheld, interest payments must be made, and financial claims by lenders must supersede political claims by constituents.[37] Once the deal has closed, there is no alternative. Financialization enacts a far-reaching transformation in the conduct of liberal government and political rule: portfolio value replaces political equality, private maximization replaces public-mindedness, and care of creditors replaces care of citizens. The state removes itself from its overt role in structuring distribution and instead abdicates to finance: what was once managed politically is now managed financially. Finance extends growth, temporarily restoring the necessary liberal condition of distributive depoliticization, but transforming liberal government around market valuation and market imperatives in the process. The liberal state capitulates to dismantling democracy on behalf of finance because of its foundational inability to manage distributive conflict politically. *Finance deploys neoliberalism.*

From this vantage, the neoliberal eclipse of social democracy and popular sovereignty originated not from the masterplan of the Mont Pèlerin Society or the Powell memo calling for government to favor business, but from the liberal imperative to depoliticize distributive conflict. Financialization was not the culmination of the decades-long ideological program to remake state and society, but a seemingly obvious solution to pressing political crisis. Elected officials, regardless of party affiliation, willingly embraced financial solutions to their political problems—a decision that presents as being nonideological, nonpartisan, and pragmatic. Finance, like the Trojan Horse, enters through the front door of liberal democratic politics by promising to break a seemingly intractable political impasse.

My argument is not that intentional neoliberal policies like the Volcker shock, Reagan tax cuts, and general economic deregulation are unimportant or unrelated, but rather that these policies alone do not explain the triumph of neoliberalism.[38] There can be no doubt neoliberal actors capitalized on the crisis of inflation and its financial resolution. However, neoliberal ideology *exploits* but does not *explain* how this process unfolds: neoliberalism discursively neutralizes the problem of distributive conflict while financialization works beneath and behind these discourses to secure a new regime of distributive depoliticization. The neoliberal vision of a society run based on perfect market efficiency is politically captivating precisely because it appears amid the failure of the previous regime of distributive depoliticization.[39] However, financialization enables much of neoliberalism's apparent success. Neoliberal reformers did not create the imagined utopia of a competitive market order but the depoliticized rule of finance. I will argue that financialization is not simply a companion to neoliberalism, a betrayal by a captured political class, or a cunning of late Fordist capitalism, but a modular political strategy for "re-depoliticizing" distributive conflict in liberal orders. Although neoliberalism as a policymaking ideology clearly sought to sever democracy from the levers of political and economic power, we must also account for the role of liberal democratic politics in aiding this transformation.

Financialization generates new powers, new inequalities, and new limits on the capacity to govern democratically. Unless we have a theory of financialization grounded in liberal democratic politics, we will keep acting as if we are in the old liberal building of neatly separable spheres and will remain blind to how finance has fundamentally transformed the parameters and possibilities of liberal democracy itself. Finance capitalizes on a deep structural feature of liberal democratic politics that must be understood before any serious "alternative to neoliberalism" can be contemplated. We must first understand why liberal democracies place the financial yoke around their neck.

Explaining this process requires going deep into the liberal tradition in order to locate how finance attaches itself to liberalism, reorients everything it touches around the imperatives of maximizing monetary return, and subsequently erodes both the division between "political" and "economic" and the possibility of democratic self-rule. To see this, we will not enter what Marx called "the hidden abode of production" but the open City Hall chamber, where decisions about financialization and their new constraints on governing are both on full display.

* * *

Before proceeding, I must make four points about the nature of the argument.

First, liberalism, democracy, financialization, and neoliberalism as the key terms in this account will be stipulated in more detail but will not be crudely defined. They are all huge and contested terms yet have accepted colloquial and scholarly meanings I will largely accept. My purpose is not to radically redefine any of these terms but rather to rearrange the relationship among them.

Second, my argument is emphatically not one of conventional determinism. The structural features of liberalism this book charts, in my estimation, do not entail inevitable outcomes. The point is not that there is "no alternative" to financialization (and thus neoliberalism) but rather that the political dynamics and processes generating financialization must be squarely confronted. Potential alternatives would require identifying and enacting political strategies for avoiding or reversing financialization. Structural obstacles should not be mistaken for impossibility: people make their own history but not as they please.

Third, it is not the first to link distributive conflict to financialization. Both Greta Krippner and Wolfgang Streeck argue that finance forestalls the eruption of distributive conflict. Krippner argues that financialization was the "unexpected resolution to the various policy dilemmas they confronted in the guise of social crisis, fiscal crisis and legitimation crisis of the state."[40] Policymakers turned to "domestic and global capital markets to resolve domestic political dilemmas."[41] Financialization was thus the "unintended consequence" of policymakers' attempts to extricate themselves from interlinked crises of the 1970s. Streeck also argues that pushing distributive conflict off with debt "buys time" by "generating mass allegiance to the neoliberal social project dressed up as a consumption project." Inflation, public debt, and private debt revitalized "late capitalism" in a way that "the theory of late capitalism could never have imagined."[42] Both, in different ways, extend arguments developed by Daniel Bell and Lester Thurow in the late 1970s about the inability of governments to resolve problems requiring explicit distributional choices and the role of economic growth in avoiding such occasions.[43] Democracies, Thurow argues, are especially incapable of resolving "zero sum" distributional conflict. I build on these accounts by identifying a theoretical grounding of distributive conflict within liberalism, linking financialization to the subsequent deployment of neoliberalism, and charting how finance transforms the parameters of democratic governance.

Fourth, it is an American story. I focus on California because of its unique role as a land of experimentation and a forerunner of national developments: what happened in California didn't stay in California. Reagan is such an important figure not because he imposes a particular political economic orthodoxy, but because his rise manifests the deeper tensions and limitations of liberal government articulated in the theoretical chapters. The California story parallels the more familiar history of the last forty years. However, the experience of financialization and neoliberalism outside of the United States, especially in the Global South, is importantly distinct and must be theorized accordingly.[44] In these cases, financialization was not chosen politically but imposed externally. Such limitations must be stated clearly at the outset.

***

The book begins by exploring the ways that liberal political doctrine disavows and depoliticizes the problem of distributive conflict. It then revisits the rise of neoliberalism in terms of this problem, showing how finance both responds to renewed conflicts and enacts a fundamental transformation in liberal democratic governance. The second half of the book presents three intersecting case studies in which one sees vividly how governing for the people, while never fully realized in liberal democracies, was radically displaced by the shift to financial market constituencies: the bankruptcy of Stockton, California; the investment strategy of the California Public Employees' Retirement System (CalPERS); and the 2008 financial crisis.

The first chapter introduces distributive conflict as a constitutive problem of liberal government through an examination of the political thought of John Locke, John Stuart Mill, and John Rawls. The chapter recovers how "the market" and growth together prevent the bald disclosure of the constitutive inequalities that liberalism secures. The lines between "the political" and "the economic" do not express some ontological truth but are drawn by liberal discourse itself to depoliticize distributive conflict. Only by recovering liberalism's disavowal of distributive conflict—and liberalism's tacit solution to that conflict—can we understand the distinctively liberal origins of financialization and neoliberalism.

From the perspective of the theoretical framework developed in chapter 1, the second chapter revisits the crisis of inflation in the 1970s that served as the political antecedent for the turn to neoliberalism. The neoliberal diagnosis of inflation continues to frame the crisis in neoliberal terms. Although theories like monetarism and supply-side economics, as subsets of the broader neoliberal program, were essential for justifying radical changes to the postwar political economy, they were abandoned almost immediately as guides to actual policy and fail as empirical explanations of both the antecedent inflationary crisis and subsequent development of finance capital and financial political rule. The chapter reframes inflation as manifesting the breakdown of embedded liberalism and traces how financialization—a radical departure from the state's careful control of money and finance—emerges to "re-depoliticize" distribution in the wake of these renewed social conflicts.

The third chapter charts how financialization reconfigures liberalism in the distinctly neoliberal mold. As a depoliticizing response to distributive conflict, finance infiltrates and redirects the forms of power composing actually existing liberal orders. For this explanation, I use the analytic grid developed by Michel Foucault to explain how finance operates as a form of power in liberal orders. Though he never studied finance, Foucault's account of modern power—decentralized and operating through networks, practices, and rationalities—is enormously helpful in understanding its political force. Most importantly, this framework for understanding political power offers a systematic alternative to inherited liberal schemas focusing on autonomous dynamics of the economy or intentional state actions. Equipped with a Foucauldian-inflected theory of finance and liberalism, I return to the Marxian thesis of liberal depoliticization. I look to Marx not for the dynamics of capitalism nor to Foucault for the specifics of neoliberalism but to recover a problematic and sketch a field of power that spans liberalism's apparent separation between "the political" and "the economic." The chapter then charts the consequences of the financialization of liberalism through this theoretical grid.

The fourth chapter presents a case study of Stockton, California. Over the past two decades, Stockton underwent a typical neoliberal transformation: public employment and spending were nearly halved, political discourse was reoriented around the virtues of entrepreneurialism, and concern for financial creditors replaced care for political constituents. Yet conservative activists, market ideologues, business interests, and other agents central to existing accounts of neoliberalism did not drive these changes. Instead, I show how Stockton assumed financial risk through a variety of deals designed to augment the distributive rewards of economic growth. In the aftermath of the subprime housing market collapse, these latent financial risks became concrete fiscal imperatives that demanded priority over other claims. Austerity and market-oriented reorganization were imposed in an effort to generate positive cash flow to meet these obligations. Stockton provides a stark example of how distributive conflict and financial depoliticization unfold.

The fifth chapter explores the recent history of CalPERS, the largest public pension fund in the United States. I chart how the State of California came to rely on investment returns to supplement public employee compensation in the aftermath of the tax revolt in the late 1970s (itself a crucial precursor to the Reagan Revolution). This reliance, in turn, led CalPERS to seed financial asset classes like venture capital and private equity, transform corporate governance around "shareholder value," and invest in subprime mortgages in an effort to generate the required rates of return. The chapter traces how CalPERS is used as a relief valve for distributive conflicts at the state level and how, despite its nominal democratic control, it contributes to the wider rollout of neoliberalism over the last several decades.

The sixth chapter explains how the 2008 financial crisis manifested the limits of the financial growth regime installed in response to the previous crisis of inflation. The crisis was not only the result of free market ideology, gross capture, and malign neglect but also of the foundational imperative for depoliticization at the heart of liberal government. The financial reforms undertaken to soothe spiraling social conflict nearly three decades prior were the product of a nearly spontaneous, self-evident, and bipartisan political consensus. The central mechanisms of the 2008 crisis—mortgage-backed securities, credit default swaps, and the wider "shadow banking system"—initially took root as an expedient solution to this earlier political crisis. For this reason, the financial crisis cannot be explained solely as a textbook crisis of capitalism enabled by an ideologically captured regulatory apparatus but must be situated in this longer trajectory of liberal depoliticization. My approach is to reframe the existing set of facts to explain why, in the middle of the 2008 financial crisis, the American federal government found itself in roughly the same position as the Stockton city council and the CalPERS board: with no alternative to capitulating to the demands of finance.

The epilogue draws lessons for the political struggle against neoliberalism. Formulating an "alternative to neoliberalism" requires breaking with not only neoliberal ideology and policy but also the deep depoliticizing imperatives of liberal government that circumscribe the possibilities for democratic self-rule. Such a process would require the epistemic project of comprehending how political institutions are currently governed *financially* in order to imagine how they might be reclaimed and governed *democratically*. By recasting neoliberalism as a product of liberal distributive politics, opposing neoliberalism becomes a matter of opposing financialization and imagining how distribution might be governed politically. Democracy can change the default course but only if, to borrow Pierre Rosanvallon's phrase, we are able to dismantle the liberalism in our heads.

1

LIBERALISM AND DISTRIBUTIVE CONFLICT

Thus in the beginning all the world was America . . . for no such thing as money was anywhere known.
—John Locke

It was only the prospect of economic growth in which everyone prospered, if not equally or simultaneously, that gave modern democracies their legitimacy and durability.
—Irving Kristol

Long before the word "liberalism" (and its division between "politics" and "economics") entered our political lexicon, Thomas Hobbes theorized the requirements of political order. Conflict and disorder, he argued, originate from the combination of humankind's limitless desire and natural insecurity. The "war of all against all" originates from this natural condition in which unlimited social demands collide with limited social goods.[1] Without an overawing political authority capable of imposing order, Hobbes famously argues, life will be "solitary, poor, nasty, brutish, and short." Reason combined with natural law dictates that we give up the unlimited license of this natural condition in exchange for security and prosperity under an absolute sovereign. Hobbes's sovereign is demanding:

he dictates religion, mandates measurements, stabilizes language, and imposes censorship, conscription, punishments, and taxes. The severity of this solution reflects the severity of the problem: "every little payment appeareth a great grievance but are destitute of those prospective glasses to see a farre off the miseries that hang over them, and cannot without such payments be avoided."[2] Political order cannot be bought at a cheaper price.

Liberals disagree. A few decades later, John Locke inaugurated the more recognizably liberal solution to the problem of political order. Rather than miserable individuals investing what little power they have into one supreme leviathan, Locke's subjects in the state of nature unite into commonwealths "for the mutual preservation of their lives, liberties, and estates, which [he] calls by the general name *property*."[3] Whereas Hobbes imagined mankind's prepolitical condition to be one of sheer anarchic misery, Locke imagined a commodious, prosperous, and peaceful setting (at least prior to the introduction of property and economic surplus) of individuals pursuing their own individual interests without external direction or interference. Locke and future liberals, despite other disagreements, all relocate religion and property from their position under absolutism as a primary state concern to an expanded private sphere rooted in self-ownership and self-responsibility.

John Rawls argues that, historically, the "origin of political liberalism (and of liberalism more generally) is the Reformation and its aftermath. . . . Something like the modern understanding of liberty of conscience and freedom of thought began then."[4] The "aftermath" was nearly two centuries of religious wars between Catholics and Protestants. Liberalism responds to this condition of religious conflict by expelling religion from public life. A precarious truce would replace the constant and bloody struggle for religious dominion among Christians (marginalized and stigmatized religions were another matter). Religion would be freed from the state; the state would be freed from religion. Both state and citizen vow noninterference in private religious matters.⁵ This regime would come to be called "secularism" in which order is maintained through the depoliticization of religious conflict and religious power is forbidden from governing publicly.⁶ Secularism responds to religious pluralism and conflict by formally removing religion from public life.

Private property discursively and institutionally relocates distribution from the state to civil society (literally de-"political"-cizing). Discursively, a settled right to private property explains why the state must not interfere in personal affairs. Institutionally, private property shifts ownership from contingent political grants by the sovereign to inalienable rights that cannot be violated without compensation or consent. Through this shift, liberal subjects become proprietors who are invested with sovereignty over themselves and their possessions and left to their own business without external interference. In both domains, the principle of individual autonomy commands state noninterference.⁷ Consequently, religion and property are privatized and the liberal state is absolved of its responsibility for their particular and particularizing effects. Although histories of political and economic liberalism are typically narrated separately, both depoliticize what cannot legitimately be governed politically.⁸ Both establish a limit to governing, designating what the state cannot touch.

Liberal political equality does not entail an equal distribution of property: liberalism, after all, is not communism. However, the resulting material inequalities require some justification. How can liberal subjects be imagined to consent to liberal distributive regime theoretically (via social contract theory) and in practice (via elections)? At the same time, secularism forbids the state from overtly endorsing or promoting the ends and values of particular religious sects. Liberalism therefore needs a discursive construct that explains how private property optimally provides for each and every individual interest without relying on state direction, valuation, oversight, or planning, enabling decentralized coordination without centralized state coercion. What could combine a universal justification of private property and the inequalities flowing therefrom with an explanation of how order endures with limited state power? Looking backward, the answer is clear: "the market" and its invisible hand discursively guide and divide property in an optimal and unimprovable manner. A new science of "political economy" emerges alongside the birth of political liberalism to explain this secular miracle. It is no coincidence that Locke first formulates what would eventually become the modern "law" of supply and demand that governs "the market." After Locke, liberal political economists began formulating new theories for explaining both the possibility of decentralized economic order and its compatibility with liberal political equality: a "spontaneous order" beyond the state impartially and efficiently mediates humanity's complex interdependence. The liberal state must simply support the operation of this mechanism and restrain itself from self-defeating interventions in an otherwise harmonious process. "The market" is a discursive construct operating within liberalism that reconciles the inherent tension between private property and universal consent.[9]

Discourse alone, however, is insufficient to maintain a condition of general depoliticization. A regime of depoliticized religion (i.e., "secularism"), for instance, requires that the state both rationalize this regime through tolerance discourse *and* cultivate the necessary habits and dispositions for secular civic conduct among its subjects (i.e., accepting the pluralization of religion and the privatization of religious faith). In the immediate aftermath of the Edict of Nantes—granting civil rights to the Protestant minority in Catholic-majority France—neither Catholics nor Protestants abandoned their hegemonic ambitions, so the nascent secular regime ultimately collapsed.[10] Stability requires that subjects themselves desire the liberal peace and that a secular civic culture promotes this desire. We should expect analogous practices that sustain the depoliticization of distributive conflict. What material practices could combine with discourses of "the market" to support a regime of private property and depoliticized distribution? The answers will all converge in *growing* collective wealth rather than making explicit redistributive decisions politically.

It is a commonplace that the role of economic policy in liberal regimes is to maximize growth. As John F. Kennedy explained: "economic growth means strength and vitality; it means we're able to sustain our defenses; it means we're able to meet our commitments abroad." Or, elsewhere and more pithily, "a rising tide lifts all boats." In a debate with Kennedy, Richard Nixon explained "our disagreement is not about the goals for America but only about the means to reach those goals." For Bob Dole, "Economic growth should be the standard by which all economic policies are judged."[11] Clinton advisor Felix Rohatyn argued that "The social and economic problems we face today are varied . . . [and] the single most important requirement to deal with all of them is the wealth and revenues generated by a higher rate of economic growth."[12] Walter Lippmann, in whose honor the famous Colloquium was convened in Paris in 1938, explained that through growth, "The size of the pie can be increased by invention, organization, capital investment, and fiscal policy, and then a whole society, not just one part of it, will grow richer."[13]

In his 1976 book *The Cultural Contradictions of Capitalism*, Daniel Bell observed three related properties of the relationship between economic growth and Western societies. First, he argued that "economic growth" is their "secular religion." By this, he meant that growth is the basis of both motivation and solidarity. Second, growth functions as a "political solvent" for meeting rising material expectations without requiring redistribution or austerity. Finally, growth is linked to inflation that, in 1976, was threatening the undoing of the existing order.[14] Similarly, William Ophuls argued that "growth is the secular religion of American society, providing a social goal, a basis for political solidarity, and a source of individual motivation. . . . The entire society—individuals, enterprises, the government itself—has an enormous vested interest in the continuation of growth."[15] Liberal politics primarily concerns the policies most conducive to growth: the objective is beyond dispute. Policy issues from immigration to education to the environment are presented and evaluated in terms of their contribution to this end. Growth meets material demands without requiring that the liberal state assert a collective interest in equality over the private right of appropriation. Growth ensures that the prerogatives of wealth are not impaired by popular demand. Growth ensures that the liberal state never must explain why some have so much and others have so little despite their nominal political equality.

As with religion and religious conflict, the liberal solution to property and distributive conflict is depoliticization rather than resolution. Latent tension and contradiction remain, constantly lurking and menacing beneath the placid surface of universalistic liberal discourse. Adam Smith himself notes that "it is only under the shelter of the civil magistrate that the owner of that valuable property . . . can sleep a single night in security. . . . Civil government, so far as it is instituted for the security of property, is in reality instituted for the defense of the rich against the poor, or of those who have some property against those who have none at all."[16] Accordingly, direct statements by liberal theorists and politicians on this tension between political equality and economic inequality are rare. These tensions, like so many others within liberal orders, can be kept from erupting into conflict only so long as they remain depoliticized. The liberal solution to the basic Hobbesian problem of order is to remove major conflicts from the political realm. In liberal orders, hegemony endures with less open violence. Therefore, we should not expect liberalism's theoretical proponents to fully explain this problem even as they grapple with it themselves: the problem of liberalism and distributive conflict appears as an implicit problematic rather than explicit concern. From the beginning, the tradition of political liberalism has held this tension close to its heart.

This chapter visits three liberal theorists in three distinct historical eras to surface and examine the problem of liberalism and distributive conflict. We will see how growth and "the market" (or its discursive progenitor) operate at a conceptual level in these different iterations of liberal theory to secure popular investment in this regime. Religion is our model: these thinkers' systematic arguments for secularism (as the depoliticization of religion) scaffold their scattered discussions of property (as the depoliticization of distribution), grounding this account of liberal distribution on features of liberal religion we already know and accept. This chapter argues that just as secularism and tolerance abolish the formal political standing of religion by privatizing and individualizing it, removing it from the purview or prejudice of the state, growth and "the market" abolish the formal political standing of property by transmuting collective social power into autonomous mechanism. Just as religion is shifted from public to private, state to individual, so too is distribution: both expel intractable and destabilizing conflict from the domain of legitimate political contestation; both have their respective political discourses for policing the universal desirability and neutrality of this regime; both have their respective indices of success and targets of state policy; both occlude the powers constructing particular subjects while preserving existing social hierarchies.

I am not tracing a historical development but demonstrating how the same problem, distributive conflict, with a similar solution, referral to markets and economic growth, recurs in these three thinkers despite their different times and places and many other differences in their thought. They grapple with, but do not straightforwardly theorize, this problem. My purpose is not to make a diachronic argument that traces the development of "the market" and economic growth nor to suggest that the thinkers discussed would endorse what I believe to be the entailments of their arguments. Rather, this chapter identifies distributive conflict as a sometimes implicit, sometimes explicit concern for these three liberal theorists and explains how their solution mirrors their own solution to religious conflict as a well-known story. My purpose is to recover distribution as a central concern of liberal theory and highlight its corresponding methods of depoliticization.

Across Locke, Mill, and Rawls, we find three common threads on these matters: (1) distribution cannot be managed politically; (2) "the market" is a discursive device for managing the tension between private property and liberal political equality; and (3) growth is required to maintain popular investment in this regime of material inequality. "The market" and growth together prevent the open disclosure of liberalism's protection of economic inequalities. The lines between "the political" and "the economic" are drawn to depoliticize conflict rather than manifesting some natural autonomous reality.[17]

JOHN LOCKE: LIBERALISM BEFORE THE MARKET

When a nation bogged down in colonial wars with rival powers riven by a feverishly divided body politic faced an unprecedented monetary crisis, political leaders turned to a man crying out alone in a wilderness of intellectual statism with a plan for restoring order. He installed a revolution in monetary policy that proved disastrous for the average person and ground the nation's economy to a halt, paradoxically producing an explosion in credit that led to a cataclysmic financial crisis several decades later. "The business of our money was everybody's talk, everybody's uneasiness," he wrote. Monetary dysfunction threatened a wholesale breakdown in the social order.[18] His task was to lead a political charge against too much political discretion, deploying only the coercive power of the state in accordance with an imagined order of things rather than unbounded power of an arbitrary, capricious, and unaccountable state trying to shape order. His name was John Locke.

Locke is widely hailed as the founder of modern liberalism. But this is so not only in an intellectual sense. After living in exile in Holland, Locke returned to England in Mary's royal flotilla after the Glorious Revolution.[19] Subsequently, Parliament enacted what would become the paradigmatic set of liberal reforms: the Bill of Rights of 1689 greatly expanded the prerogatives of Parliament and furnished British subjects a basic set of liberal rights, and the Toleration Act of 1689 granted religious freedom to religious dissenters. The innocently named Tonnage Act of 1694 established the Bank of England.[20] Locke is unique in the history of political thought in that he actually participated in the founding of the government he advocated.[21]

Locke's distinctive "liberal" break rests in the revolutionary view that the state exists to secure the private interests of its subjects, not the public or private interests of a ruler.[22] What are the interests of subjects? Locke argues there are two principal kinds: religious salvation and property. As a Protestant Christian, Locke's concept of salvation is redemption from sin and eternal life in the kingdom of heaven. Locke's concept of property is "life, liberty, and estates." Both are *individual* rather than *collective* interests: the liberal state protects individuals from encroachments on their ability to pursue these interests privately. The public ordering of property and religion under absolutism, nominally justified in terms of collective interests, is the enemy against which Locke (and his patron Shaftesbury) fights.

In this section, I demonstrate how Locke's account of property in the *Second Treatise* extends the same basic principles of noninterference as those articulated in the *Letter on Toleration*. Secularism and private property are both established when the absolutist state formally withdraws from matters of religion and property. However, a crucial problem emerges: Why would equal subjects in the state of nature consent to a regime of unequal property? I show that Locke's theoretical efforts to resolve this problem are ultimately incomplete but outline the role of "the market" in future liberal theories. Such a concept of "the market" was not yet available to Locke despite his contributions to its formation, yet, as we shall see, Locke implicitly theorizes the problem to which "the market" will emerge as the answer. My purpose is not to say anything new about Locke on the subject of tolerance or property, but to identify this parallelism in Locke's account that establishes the problematic of liberal distributive depoliticization.[23]

Religion

In the *Letter Concerning Toleration*, whose enduring theoretical contribution is to provide the basic rationale for modern Western secularism, Locke argues that England should tolerate all Protestant sects. To this end, the *Letter* posits a sharp division between public and private interests that will be carried over to Locke's account of property. Here Locke defines civil interests as a person's individual liberty, bodily integrity, and property. The purpose of government, through the "impartial execution of equal laws," is to "secure unto all the people in general . . . the just possession of these things."[24] Therefore, "the power of civil government relates only to men's civil interests."[25] The limits of the Lockean state are defined by the limits of state knowledge: whereof it cannot know, thereof it cannot act. Religious belief is one such domain. For Locke, religion and the possibility of salvation are inalienably private matters that cannot be "vested in the magistrate." Instead, Locke argues, each individual is charged with discovering and practicing the form of faith that is both true and "pleasing unto God." The magistrate's power of "outward force" such as "confiscation of estate, imprisonment, [and] torments" cannot generate the "inward persuasion of the mind" necessary for salvation. Accordingly, "the care of souls is not committed to the civil magistrate any more than to other men."[26] Locke postulates a sharp epistemological and ontological divide between what will become "public" and "private."

Locke explains the logic of secularism with an analogy to wealth. Suppose an absolutist sovereign sought to mandate their subjects' wealth as they would religion. How could this be accomplished? Locke considers if professions could be mandated like sacraments.

Several difficulties arise. The first difficulty is epistemic: the sovereign is in no better position than the subject to know the true path to heaven (or to wealth) and cannot remedy the error should they lead their subjects down a wrong path.[27] Locke reminds the reader again and again that the individual judgment of the prince is no better than that of each subject. Accordingly, the sovereign cannot dictate such things to each individual. Even if the sovereign did so, individuals would be unwise to accept: "the one only narrow way which leads to heaven is not better known to the magistrate than to private persons, and therefore I cannot safely take him for my guide, who may probably be ignorant of the way as myself, and who certainly is less concerned for my salvation than I myself am." Therefore, state direction and state persecution cannot achieve its desired ends: the "outward force" of the magistrate cannot generate the "inward persuasion" required for proper religious belief.[28] As the primary instrument of state action, coercion is ontologically incompatible with the domain it seeks to regulate. Noninterference is the only legitimate path. Locke's position, in short, is that each person is the best judge of their own affairs because they alone will bear the consequences of their actions. The state is to leave people to the care of their own soul just as the state leaves people to the care of their own wealth. This analogy suggests an essential relation linking the two domains: "the business of laws is not to provide for the truth of opinions, but for the safety and security of the commonwealth, and of every particular man's goods and person."[29]

Locke immediately extends this argument to all matters of the "public good" by deriving a general principle: "the private judgment . . . of the magistrate does not give him any new right of imposing laws upon his subjects." Because the magistrate's judgment is no better than the individual's, it cannot justifiably be imposed on individuals. As a corollary, individuals bear ultimate responsibility for their actions: "laws provide, as much as possible, that the good and health of subjects be not injured by the fraud or violence of others;

they do not guard them from the negligence or ill-husbandry of the possessors themselves."[30] Locke first applies this principle to limit the magistrate from arbitrarily seizing property:

> The safeguard of men's lives, and of the things that belong unto this life, is the business of the commonwealth; and the preserving of those things unto their owners is the duty of the magistrate. And, therefore, the magistrate cannot take away these worldly things from this man, or party, and give them to that; nor change property amongst fellow-subjects (no, not even by a law) for a cause that has no relation to the end of civil government—I mean, for their religion, which, whether it be true or false, does no prejudice to the worldly concerns of their fellow-subjects.[31]

Locke argues that the sovereign also has a significant interest in tolerance: "the interest of the king of England as head of the Protestants will be much improved by the discountenancing of popery amongst us." Tolerance for all Protestant sects keeps them united in opposition to Catholicism and "knits the Protestant party firmer." Furthermore, tolerance also promotes "the number and industry of [the sovereign's] subjects" and thus "the welfare of the kingdom" by keeping subjects occupied with their own commercial activity rather than the religious propriety of their neighbors.

In sum, the state has no authority to intervene in religious matters; and even if it had the authority, it would have no reason; and even if it had the reason, it would have better reasons not to intervene. The sole objective of the state is to impartially execute equal laws in furtherance of subjects' civil interests. Accordingly, the state must not interfere with private religious belief: religion must be made a private, individual matter—in short, depoliticized. The believer, like the free economic actor, cannot be created by the state. Just as political power wrecks true belief, so too does it wreck the industry and rationality that make the wealth of the nation grow.

Property

In the *Second Treatise of Government*, Locke presents the protection of private property as the principal objective of the state.[32] As the *Letter* established that the state has no legitimate authority over religion, the fifth chapter "Of Property" in the *Second Treatise* argues that the state is established to protect private property but has no legitimate authority over the distribution of property itself. The crucial hinge of the argument is explaining how "men might come to have a property in several parts of that which God gave to mankind in common, and that without any express compact of all the commoners."[33] If God gave the world to mankind in common, how might mankind consent to unequal possession? Locke's answer to this is entwined with his arguments for the privatization of religion producing the conditions for tolerance.

For Locke, tolerance demands that religion be separated from politics, and his critique of Filmer in the *First Treatise of Government* requires that distributive shares are humanly determined rather than divinely ordained. In that work, Locke denies that Adam was the original owner of the world, thereby invalidating monarchical claims to absolute ownership based on their supposed relation to Adam. Locke argues that "no body has originally a private dominion, exclusive of the rest of mankind" because God gave the "world to men in common." Locke's critique of divine right theory therefore requires beginning from a state of equality. However, Locke insists repeatedly, this division cannot occur by "compact." How can property be so divided?

Locke's solution is individual appropriation from the common bounty of the Creator, initially bound by several "natural" restrictions. Locke's argument begins from the "state of perfect equality" in which humanity supposedly originates. The "spontaneous hand of nature" produces resources that initially do not belong to anyone. This initial state of equality, however, does not imply collective ownership of the bounty of nature. The common endowment only becomes useful once it has been appropriated by individuals. Accordingly, "there must of necessity be a means to appropriate them in some way or other before they can be of any use, or at all beneficial to any particular man." How can such appropriation legitimately occur outside of the bounds of a political community? Though nature is initially "common to all men, [every] man has a property in his own person." Labor is the "unquestionable property of the laborer," and whatever it touches "makes it his property." Individuals appropriate that with which they mix their labor. Appropriation through individual labor is justified so long as each person leaves "enough, and as good . . . in common for others."[34] Self-possession (i.e., "possessive individualism") explains how a common endowment by God can be appropriated privately and exclusively.

He considers a simple example: "he that is nourished by the acorns he picked up under an oak, or the apples he gathered from the trees in the wood, has certainly appropriated them to himself." They became property once "labor put a distinction between them and common." Crucially, appropriating "this or that part does not depend on the express consent of the commoners." Instead, "the grass my horse has bit, the turfs my servant has cut, and the ore I have digged in any place where I have a right to them in common with others become my property, without the assignation or consent of anybody. The labour that was mine, removing them out of that common state they were in, hath fixed my property in them."[35] If such explicit consent were necessary, people would starve "notwithstanding the plenty God had given them" because without private appropriation the "common is of no use." Private property arises—one might say naturally and legitimately—from individual appropriation from the common.

Locke extends his argument from "the fruits of the earth" to "the earth itself." Land is appropriated in the exact same way. Enclosures and improvements are similarly justified because they do not diminish the total stock of unappropriated land. Locke explains, "For he that leaves as much as another can make use of, does as good as take nothing at all. Nobody could think himself injured by the drinking of another man, though he took a good draught, who had a whole river of the same water left him to quench his thirst. And the case of land and water, where there is enough of both, is perfectly the same."[36] Appropriation, however, is limited to what an individual can use before it spoils: "Whatever is beyond this, is more than his share, and belongs to others. Nothing was made by God for man to spoil or destroy." Different "degrees of industry . . . give men possessions in different proportions, so this invention of money gave them the opportunity to continue and enlarge them." Consequently, "there could be then little room for quarrels or contentions about property so established."[37] Locke adds that in addition to the existence of an infinite commons to be appropriated, the appropriation of land is inherently limited to small properties. Because an individual's consumption is inherently limited, "it would be impossible for any man, this way, to entrench upon the right of another." Any individual appropriation "would still have room for as good and as large a possession (after the other had taken out his) as before it was appropriated." Even "as full as the world seems," this mode of appropriation is still allowed because in the "vacant places of America" individual possession "would not be very large, nor, even to this day, prejudice the rest of mankind."[38]

Locke confirms his justification for individual appropriation with a seemingly sensible analogy: "By making an explicit consent of every commoner necessary to anyone's appropriating to himself any part of what is given in common, children or servants could not cut the meat which their father or master had provided for them in common, without assigning to everyone his peculiar part."[39] This analogy is meant to confirm the intuition that private appropriation of a common resource is justified as long as enough remains for others.

This argument is a form of *modus tollens*: $P \rightarrow Q, \neg Q$. Thus, $\neg P$. To schematize:

> *P*: Explicit consent of every commoner necessary for appropriation.
>
> *Q*: Servants would need to be assigned their peculiar part to cut meat given in common by their master.
>
> ¬*Q*: Obviously absurd result.
>
> ¬*P*: Explicit consent of every commoner is not required for appropriation/distribution.

But let us examine the logic of this example more closely. To cut meat is to divide it. On what basis will this division be made? Who is entitled to which part? This seemingly trivial example brims with historical significance.

The division of meat was central to the social cosmology of the ancient Greek world. In Greek literary sources, ritualistic slaughter was the source of all meat consumption.[40] These rituals involved specific divisions of various animals for sacrificial and alimentary purposes. The Greek word *moira*, roughly translated as "part" or "portion," has both a social and a distributive dimension: one's portion (*moira*) of meat corresponds to one's social standing (*moira*). The division of meat was thus the definitive marker of social status in the ancient world.[41] This logic is expressed clearly in Plato's *Laws*:

> It is the judgment of Zeus . . . it produces all things good; for it dispenses more to the greater and less to the smaller, giving due measure to each according to nature; and with regard to honors also, by granting the greater to those that are greater in goodness, and the less to those of the opposite character in respect of goodness and education, it assigns in proportion what is fitting to each. Indeed, it is precisely this which constitutes for us "political justice," which is the object we must strive for.[42]

For instance, when Odysseus lands in Phaeacia, his hosts initially cannot determine his social position and thus what he is owed. Eventually, they recognize him as Odysseus, king of Ithaka and hero of the Trojan War, and treat him accordingly, offering meat, wine, and Nausicaa's hand in marriage. The division of meat is a microcosm for the entire rigid hierarchy of the Greek social order, where a theological order is the core distributive principle. Liberalism needs something like this theological order to justify inequalities but itself cannot be overtly theological given the secular settlement requiring a formally unreligious state and public order.

In this example, the master endows a common resource to be divided. Like the state of nature, appropriation from this common does not require explicit consent. Natural law likewise dictates that the servants divide the meat such that "enough and as good" remains for others and that no meat spoils. Explicit consent is avoided because the servants presumably obey these restrictions on their individual appropriation, producing a kind of communism that mirrors the Native Americans Locke uses as his foil. In Locke's other examples, unlimited appropriation is justified on the presumed infinitude of the commons. Appropriation finds its natural limit once the proprietor has stored up the "conveniences of life . . . for him and his family."

Everything changes, however, when the "tacit agreement of men to put a value on . . . little piece[s] of yellow metal" overturns the two limitations on appropriation.[43] Once introduced, money abolishes the spoilage limitation. Individuals are no longer limited to producing only what they consume: perishable goods could now be exchanged for gold, silver, diamonds, shells, or other durable stores of value. As a result, "he might heap up as much of these durable things as he pleased; the exceeding of the bounds of his just property not lying in the largeness of his possession, but the perishing of anything uselessly in it." The introduction of money permits potentially unlimited appropriation.

The requirement of leaving "enough and as good" for others remains even after the spoilage restriction is overcome. Happily for Locke, money has another crucial quality: it permits circulation, exchange, and the production of a surplus. Even in cases of scarcity, significant material inequalities can be justified. Because cultivated land is ten times more productive than land "lying waste in common," the proprietor of a ten-acre estate "may be truly said to give ninety acres to mankind." Thus, ten acres of land in Devonshire are to be preferred to a thousand in the "wild woods and uncultivated waste of America." Money enables growth—the increased productivity of enclosed land—which in turn creates and justifies "a disproportionate and unequal possession of the earth." Money creates orderly relations of exchange among proprietors, permitting the accumulation of wealth.

Locke must introduce money—incipient financialization—into the state of nature to found the legitimacy of private property and permanently insulate it from state authority. With the introduction of money, mankind has "by a tacit and voluntary consent found out a way how a man may fairly possess more land than he himself can use of the product, by receiving in exchange for the overplus gold and silver, which may be hoarded up without injury to anyone."[44] The resulting commercial society precedes the establishment of the liberal state.[45] In Locke's account, however, money is a crucial device for making liberalism work: money establishes the circulation of goods, the accumulation of surplus, and the durable inequalities that characterize "the market." The enlarged possessions of the rich mark their greater contribution to the total social product. For Locke, there can be no reasonable objection to the inequalities of property since "he who appropriates land to himself by his labour, does not lessen but increase the common stock of mankind."[46] This "increase"—what will later be called "growth"—legitimates private property and the inequalities arising therefrom.

"Tacit consent" to money accomplishes what cannot be done via "explicit consent." The resulting "inequality of private possessions" has been "made practicable out of the bounds of society, and without compact, only by putting a value on gold and silver, and tacitly agreeing in the use of money." The division of property is thus left out of the compact that founds liberal government: the distribution of property has no political standing because it is explained as the manifestation of a natural order rather than the subject of explicit consent. Any political interference in it would violate an "original law of nature" that dictates the private appropriation of the commons through individual labor and a market that distributes the surplus from this appropriation, just as earlier natural law dictated absolutist monarchical rule. Just like religion, distribution cannot be the subject of legitimate political contestation. In Lockean liberalism, distribution is depoliticized in just the same way as religion: both are placed beyond the legitimate purview of the civil magistrate. "The market" later formalizes and encapsulates the operation of this order, explaining how it optimally rewards contributions to the total social product.[47] Indeed, Locke was a crucial forerunner of such a concept.

In 1691, Locke wrote a long letter to Parliament entitled "Some Considerations of the Consequences of the Lowering of Interest and the Raising the Value of Money." In the letter, Locke argues against proposed restrictions on the market rate of interest. In making his argument, Locke first articulates several notions that will become cornerstones of liberal political economy. Locke denies that the price of money can be "regulated by Law." Interest, like the price of other commodities, has a "true and natural value" that no law can alter. Prices are solely determined by the "quantity" of an article "in proportion to its vent." The *Oxford English Dictionary* defines "vent" as an obsolete word meaning "the fact, on the part of commodities, of being disposed of by sale." Or, in modern English, "demand." In this letter, Locke establishes the foundations for what will become the economic "law" of "supply and demand." Locke discusses how commodities are circulated through the market by the "Hands of Commerce." When they are removed from circulation through consumption, export, or hoarding, they are "shut out of the Market, and no longer moveable by the Hand of Commerce."[48]

Locke cites several "unavoidable Consequences" of interfering with the natural market price. First, it will obstruct trade as the "Foundation of Riches." Second, the burdens will fall heaviest on those "who most need Assistance and Help, I mean Widows and Orphans." Third, the law would "mightily increase the Advantage of Bankers and Scriveners" who "infallibly get what the true value of interest shall be." Fourth, it will lead to an outbreak of perjury, "a crime than which nothing is more carefully to be prevented by Lawmakers." Locke neatly anticipates several rhetorical staples of contemporary economic discourse.[49]

Locke demonstrates how private property and private religion both follow from the same principle, the role of "the market" in later liberal discourse, and the role of growth in stabilizing a regime of private property. Both property and religion are rendered as individual interests. The state is prohibited from interfering in these matters on an epistemic, ethical, and practical basis. In the case of property, however, the resulting inequalities must be reconciled with individual consent to the social contract that secures it. This reconciliation has two aspects: discourses articulating why these inequalities represent a universal interest and material practices of growth that raise the living standards of the average person.

Locke explains how, when the commons is infinite, differences in wealth are produced by differences in industry and capacity. These inequalities are not politically salient because private appropriation does not impede the ability of others to do the same. Locke thus steers between "the Scylla of compact theory and the Charybdis of robbery."[50] When the argument is transposed into a case of finite common resources, Locke has already explained how everyone is better off when the "industrious and rational," rather than the "quarrelsome and contentious," possess more resources.[51] In an age of mass democracy, however, liberalism will require a thicker mechanism for explaining how these unequal shares are determined and how they comport with the universal interest.

JOHN STUART MILL: THE LIBERALISM OF GROWTH

Today it is widely assumed that liberalism and democracy are necessarily twinned: individual rights and limits on sovereignty are readily explained as being in the interests of the many and more subtly accounted as a formula for dispersing power.[52] This marks a decisive ideological victory by the forces of liberalism. When liberal democracy arose in the nineteenth century, this connection was very much in question. The socialism of Saint-Simon, Sismondi, Marx, and Engels was a live political alternative to the liberalism of Locke, Ricardo, and Mill. Why would the rights of private property be upheld by those who have none? How can a state committed to its own limitation avoid becoming overrun by the demands of mass society? No thinker expresses these tensions better than John Stuart Mill.[53]

Principles of Political Economy

In 1848 as the "springtime of peoples" shook Europe, Mill published his *Principles of Political Economy*, and it became an instant classic. The primary purpose of the work, by Mill's own account, was to update Smith in light of Malthus and Ricardo.[54] In particular, Mill worries about Malthus's claim that population growth will consume improvements in productivity, resulting in an endless treadmill of stagnation and an ever-proliferating working class. Beginning with a paean to Smith's fundamental insight that the principles of political economy are inseparable from the elements of "social philosophy," the massive work is divided into five books.[55] The first three books are staples of treatises on political economy: "Production," "Distribution," and "Exchange." The last two are distinctively Mill: "Influence of the Progress of Society on Production and Distribution" and "Influence of Government." As the book progresses, it becomes increasingly clear to Mill that the laws of political economy will not generate support for the institution of private property among the working class. What then?

Unlike production, which "partake[s] of the character of physical truths," distribution is a "matter of human institution solely."[56] The division of the social product between land, labor, and capital was a central topic in political economic inquiry. Mill observes that appropriation occurs in "almost an inverse ratio to the labour—the largest portions to those who have never worked at all, the next largest to those whose work is almost nominal, and so in descending scale, the remuneration dwindling as the work grows harder and more disagreeable, until the most fatiguing and exhausting bodily labour cannot count with certainty on being able to earn even the necessities of life—if this or Communism were the alternative, all the difficulties, great or small, of Communism would be but as dust in the balance."[57] The profit of capital and land arises from "the productive power of labor and the general profit of the country is always what the productive power of labour makes it."[58] However, a general condition of working-class precarity is essential for the proper functioning of the laissez-faire system. Echoing Locke's proposals for poor law reform, Mill writes that "to extract real work from day labourers, without the power of dismissal, is only practicable by the power of the lash."[59] Unlike Locke, however, Mill acknowledges the tension between liberal principles and corporal punishment and that private property so instituted would hold little appeal for the working class. However, rather than dismiss the system entirely, Mill argues for reform: private property has not been given a fair chance.

Mill defines property as the right of each person "to the exclusive disposal of what he or she have produced by their own exertions, or received either by gift or by fair agreement, without force or fraud, from those who produced it. The foundation of the whole is the right of producers to what they themselves have produced."[60] Mill clarifies that "nothing is implied in property but the right of each to his (or her) own faculties, to what he can produce by them, and to whatever he can get for them in a fair market."[61] Because "private property has never yet had a fair trial in any country," its critics mistake its present shortcomings for innate deficiencies. Thus, Mill observes unironically, the "laws of property have never conformed to the principles on which the justification of private property rests."[62]

To rectify this deficiency, Mill believes that legislation to "favour the diffusion, instead of the concentration of wealth" would cure "the physical and social evils which almost all Socialist writers assume to be inseparable [from the] principle of individual property."[63] Such an arrangement would permit a comparison of "Communism, at its best, with the regime of individual property, not as it is, but as it might be made." A decision on which is better will depend on "which of the two systems is consistent with the greatest amount of human liberty and spontaneity."[64] Rendering a judgment on the "institution of property" would require ensuring that it work in accordance with "that equitable principle of proportion between remuneration and exertion" that grounds all its defenses.[65] Two other additional conditions must prevail: "universal education" and a "due limitation on the numbers of the community."

After his ambivalent defense of property, Mill considers competition and custom as the two forces governing the distribution of property. Mill considers the various regimes of property beginning with slavery; progressing through peasantry, métayer, and cottier; and culminating with wage labor. Though competition's role in determining the resulting distribution increases through this progression, custom still holds sway over aspects of wage labor. Mill argues that "only through the principle of competition has political economy any pretension to the character of a science."[66] Accordingly, if we assume competition to be the "exclusive regulator" of wages, then "principles of broad generality and scientific precision can be laid down, according to which they will be regulated." If these principles prove to be in the interests of the many, then the institution of private property may yet be saved. The purpose of the "science" of political economy is therefore to explain the dynamics of competition such that its results can be theorized as being in the collective interest.

Twenty years before Marx takes us into the "hidden abode of production" in order to discover the secret of capitalist accumulation therein, Mill openly professes Marx's infamous findings. "In no case," Mill writes, "is the mere money which passes from one person to another the fundamental matter in any economic phenomenon."[67] Rather, "the cause of profit is that labour produces more than is required for its support." Or, "to vary the form of the theorem: the reason why capital yields a profit is because food, clothing, materials, and tools last longer than the time which was required to produce them. . . . All they produce in addition to reproducing their own necessaries and instruments have a portion of their time remaining to work for the capitalist." Most of the conceptual coordinates of Karl Marx's *Capital* are contained in this short paragraph: class conflict, surplus value, socially necessary labor time, the working day, and a general theory of capitalist accumulation.[68] Unlike Marx, however, Mill concludes that "every restriction of [competition] is an evil, and every extension of it, even if for the time injuriously affecting some class of labourers, is always an ultimate good."[69]

Mill considers worker associations as a potential resolution to the contradiction between the desirability of private property on the one hand and the rude state of the working classes who will not acknowledge its supremacy on the other. Mill places his hopes in the English cooperative movement as creating neo-Tocquevillian "schools of democracy" that educate the working masses in the habits and virtues required for economic citizenship. Eventually, Mill hopes, capitalists will find it advantageous to furnish cooperatives with resources, thereby replacing the adversarial wage relation that generates so many unfortunate misconceptions. "By a kind of spontaneous process," capital would become "the joint property of all who participate in their productive employment: a transformation which, thus effected, (and assuming of course that both sexes participate equally in the rights and in the government of the association) would be the nearest approach to social justice, and the most beneficial ordering of industrial affairs for the universal good, which it is possible at present to foresee."[70]

The final chapter of *Principles of Political Economy* is entitled "Of the Grounds and Limits of the *Laisser-Faire* or Non-Interference Principle" and considers the "limits of the province of government: the question, to what objects government intervention in the affairs of society may or should extend, over and above those which necessarily appertain to it."[71] Mill's aim in this final chapter is to work out a *principled* basis for the legitimate exercise of governmental power. Mill argues that "there is a circle around every individual human being which no government, be it that of one, of a few, or of the many, ought to be permitted to overstep" and that this circle extends to "include all that part which concerns only the life, whether inward or outward, of the individual, and does not affect the interests of others, or affects them only through the moral influence of example."[72] Across all spheres of social life, Mill argues, "Laisser faire . . . should be the general practice: every departure from it, unless required by some great good, is a certain evil."[73] Eleven years later, Mill published the quintessential defense of liberalism that revisits many of the arguments raised in the concluding chapter to his political economy but has effaced the problem leading him to this solution.

On Liberty

In *On Liberty*, Mill inverts the "laissez-faire" principle that concludes *Principles of Political Economy* into his famous "harm principle." Mill proclaims: "the only purpose for which power can be rightfully exercised over any member of a civilized community, against his will, is to prevent harm to others."[74] Mill shifts to arguing *against* government rather than *for* property. The laissez-faire principle demarcates the *limits* of government action. The "harm principle" identifies what government action is *permitted*. The difference is crucial: the default assumption shifts to state action being unjustified unless it can be shown to meet the requirements of the harm principle, rather than positing specific domains where it ought not interfere. This shift from a justification of private property, markets, and competition to a much more general defense of the individual against the state enables Mill to sidestep the problems raised in the chapters on distribution that he could not resolve. Mill's own political economy revealed the glaring tension between private property and mass democracy.

Mill sidesteps the political tensions raised in *Principles of Political Economy* by explicitly differentiating individual liberty and the "so-called doctrine of Free Trade." This latter concept, Mill argues, rests "on grounds different from, though equally solid with, the principle of individual liberty asserted in this Essay."[75] Accordingly, the principle of individual liberty is "not involved" in questions pertaining to the limits to the doctrine of free trade, such as consumer and worker protections.[76] There is no question that such regulations fall under the rubric of the harm principle: "leaving people to themselves is always better, *ceteris paribus*, than controlling them: but that they may be legitimately controlled for these ends is in principle undeniable."[77] Although Mill claims to support both economic and individual liberty, he only furnishes a justification for the latter. In *On Liberty*, Mill explains this distinction with reference to prohibitions on the sale of alcohol and opium. While the state is permitted to regulate the alcohol or opium trade, a policy outlawing both commodities is an impermissible invasion of the personal liberty of the *buyer* rather than the economic liberty of the seller. Although alcohol and opium are injurious (Mill often worries if the masses' love of alcohol is a permanent impediment to their personal development and the social progress the otherwise debauched masses would impede), if the injury only applies to "the agents themselves," then these activities "ought not to be legally interdicted."[78]

But should one "be free to be a pimp or to keep a gambling house? This case is one of those which lie on the exact boundary line between the two principles [of harm and individual liberty]." On the one hand, if fornication and gambling are allowed, then on what basis would profiting off of the practice "make that criminal which would otherwise be admissible?" On the other, the state has an interest in suppressing "instigators who cannot possible be impartial"—that is to say, those who have a "pecuniary interest in encouraging that excess." Mill eventually settles on vice taxes as an appropriate combination of dissuasion that leaves the individual free to procure their preferred "strong drinks." Limiting the number of "beer or spirit houses for the express purpose of rendering them more difficult of access" is only suited to "a state of society in which the labouring classes are avowedly treated as children or savages, and placed under an education of restraint, to fit them for future admission to the privileges of freedom."[79] Mill argues that no person who "sets due value on freedom will give his adhesion to their being so governed, unless after all efforts have been exhausted to educate them for freedom and govern them as freemen, and it has been definitively proved that they can only be governed as children."[80]

Chapters on Socialism

The implicit tension between political equality and economic inequality becomes Mill's explicit subject in his posthumously published *Chapters on Socialism*. In this work, Mill's primary concern is the tension between private property and mass democracy. Universal male suffrage will soon be the norm in the Euro-Atlantic world, and

Mill sees a movement toward socialism and away from property as the inevitable result: "nothing is more natural than that a working man who has begun to speculate on politics should regard [property] in a very different light" from those who enjoy it as the "double prestige of immemorial custom and of personal interest."[81] The working classes have little reason to support "inequalities of property" electorally.[82] As political power of the working class extends, "the laws of property [will] have to depend for support upon considerations of a public nature" and "upon the estimate made of their conduciveness to the general welfare."[83] Mill examines the arguments for and against both socialism and private property in order to render a judgment on which system is likeliest to bring the greatest happiness to the greatest number.

Mill defines socialism as the "joint ownership by all the members of the community of the instruments and means of production," which in turn entails "that the division of the produce among the body of owners must be a public act, performed according to rules laid down by the community."[84] Socialism for Mill is the exact form of "distribution by compact" that Locke explicitly argued against. Mill agrees with the socialist diagnosis but disagrees with the prescription. Under the current regime, "the very idea of distributive justice, or of any proportionality between success and merit, or between success and exertion, is in the present state of society so manifestly chimerical as to be relegated to the regions of romance."[85] The status quo is manifestly indefensible. However, echoing his position in *Principles of Political Economy*, property can be reformed. Property is not "hurrying us into a state of general indigence and slavery from which only Socialism can save us. The evils and injustices suffered under the present system are great, but they are not increasing; on the contrary, the general tendency is towards their slow diminution."[86] Growth and progress are the crucial salves for mollifying working-class militancy. A keen reader of Tocqueville, Mill exhorts his fellow elites to give shape to this unstoppable movement toward democracy, indeed, of democracy.

Whereas the challenge facing Locke was absolutism, the challenge facing Mill was democracy. How can private property be justified in terms of the latter? Mill's answer is to recast liberal freedoms as instruments for the achievement of human happiness and civilizational progress rather than as codifications of innate natural rights.[87] Ultimately, Mill's defense of property rests on its progressive and instrumental qualities, in short, its benefits rather than its natural or ontological rightness. Property is not innate, but dependent on societal consent.[88] For Mill, growth is an essential index of progress and objective of liberal government. The focus on progress enables Mill to sidestep the contradiction between political equality and economic inequality at the heart of liberal social contract theory. For Mill, liberalism is inseparable from progressivism.[89] Political economy is a crucial body of knowledge for reconciling liberal rights with progressive reform. Unlike Locke, however, laissez-faire aims at bringing about a social revolution rather than installing a durable hegemony of the commercial classes.[90]

Mill observes that "one of the mistakes oftenest committed, and which are the sources of the greatest practical errors in human affairs, is that of supposing that the same name always stands for the same aggregation of ideas. No word has been the subject of more of this kind of misunderstanding than the word property."[91] Consequently, the "idea of property is not one thing, identical throughout history and incapable of alteration, but is variable like all other creatures of the human mind."[92] Recognizing its historical contingency, Mill argues that "society is fully entitled to abrogate or alter any particular right of property which on sufficient consideration it judges to stand in the way of the public good."[93] Taking the socialist critique seriously, Mill concludes, "the assuredly terrible case which . . . Socialists are able to make out against the present economic order of society, demands full consideration of all means by which the institution may have a chance of being made to work in a manner more beneficial to that large portion of society which at present enjoys the least share of its direct benefits."[94] If private property is not reformed, it will be abolished and the wealthy will suffer the consequences of their intransigence.

For Mill, property is a very tenuous institution: it is the product of societal consent, but the vast majority of people are unlikely to view property as being in their interest. Mill recognizes that the labor theory of value, let alone its effects in practice, will not keep mass democracy and private property sutured together. Like Locke, Mill requires a theory justifying the circumvention of the consent requirement in order to implement social arrangements that are ultimately to everyone's benefit. Paradoxically, Mill supports paternalism for the masses in defense of a liberalism that abhors paternalism. Marx explained in the afterword to the second German edition of *Capital*:

> The continental revolution of 1848–9 also had its reaction in England. Men who still claimed some scientific standing and aspired to be something more than mere sophists and sycophants of the ruling classes tried to harmonize the Political Economy of capital with the claims, no longer to be ignored, of the proletariat. Hence the shallow syncretism of which John Stuart Mill is the best representative.[95]

Yet, where Marx saw bourgeois ideology, Mill saw scientific paternalism. Mill acknowledges that economic liberalism is unlikely to survive mass democracy without a constant rise in living standards to soften the tension between political equality and economic inequality. In this way, Mill casts growth as a legitimating power for maintaining popular investment in liberalism.

JOHN RAWLS: THE LAST LIBERAL

John Rawls builds a vast institutional and theoretical apparatus to correct the deficiencies of classical liberalism. Rawls is motivated by the question of: "How is it possible for there to exist over time a just and stable society of free and equal citizens who still remain profoundly divided by reasonable religious, philosophical, and moral doctrines?"[96] Rawlsian liberalism begins from the assumed "fact of reasonable pluralism" and attempts to "apply the principle of toleration" to political philosophy itself to discover this shared basis for political cooperation. In this way, both the normative principles and major institutions of liberal democratic orders can be established without facing either diversity or disagreement. Destabilizing conflicts are thereby avoided and liberal order is preserved. Matters that cannot be decided through these common principles are expelled from liberal politics. A set of fundamental principles derived from the shared public political culture of liberal democracies serves to regulate their common affairs.

Rawls responds to this "fact of reasonable pluralism" by limiting the subject of political agreement (and liberal politics more generally) to "the domain of the political."[97] Limiting the subject of political agreement, in turn, bounds and limits that domain. For Rawls, "deep and unresolvable differences on matters of fundamental significance" are a "permanent condition of human life."[98] The challenge for political liberalism is to specify a basis for social cooperation among citizens who affirm diverse moral, religious, and philosophical doctrines. Rawls's solution is to generate a "public conception of justice" that is "freestanding" of various comprehensive doctrines (i.e., religion, moral, philosophical commitments) that citizens affirm. The gambit of Rawlsian liberalism is that these comprehensive doctrines share enough of an "overlapping consensus" to make liberal government possible. The domain of the political is limited to principles that "widely different and even irreconcilable comprehensive doctrines can endorse."[99]

Coercive state power may only be deployed in accordance with principles derived from the "overlapping consensus" among these contending doctrines. Rawls writes, "in a constitutional democracy the public conception of justice should be, so far as possible, independent of controversial philosophical and religious doctrines."[100] Rawls explains: "The hope is that, by this method of avoidance, as we might call it, existing differences between contending political views can at least be moderated, even if not entirely removed, so that social cooperation on the basis of mutual respect can be maintained."[101] From these brief remarks, we can understand why liberalism requires that economic distribution be depoliticized. Doing otherwise would entail drawing on particular comprehensive doctrines and thus violating the pluralistic heart of the theory. Distribution cannot be managed politically and at the same time in a morally neutral manner, so it therefore must be managed apart from the state. However, such a mechanism must also be something that representative agents in the original position would select for themselves. Rawls therefore needs a distributive mechanism that is both depoliticized and respects liberal freedom.

From the outset of *A Theory of Justice*, Rawls includes "competitive markets" as a constitutive institution of the "basic structure" or "the way in which the major social institutions fit together as one system."[102] The basic structure also includes the monogamous family and the legal protection of freedom of speech, thought, and conscience. While these other institutions and principles are justified on the basis of a corresponding "basic liberty" that is "taken for granted," competitive markets are not.[103] Instead, Rawls includes competitive markets in the basic structure because "it is *only* in this way, I believe, that the problem of distribution can be handled as a case of pure procedural justice."[104] Rawls's illustrative example of pure procedural justice is a game in which parties bet on the outcome of a fair coin toss. The parties involved may have any number of different reasons for taking part in the game in the first place, but these are irrelevant from the standpoint of the procedure itself. If the agreed-upon rules are actually followed, then the outcome is considered just. This is an attractive device for Rawlsian liberalism because it enables citizens who are otherwise divided by conflicting "comprehensive doctrines" to agree to common governing procedures.

Rawls argues that a pure procedural approach to distribution (and thus the neoclassical market) uniquely avoids the need for explicit agreement on distributive shares.[105] "The market" thus enables distribution to "take care of itself." When market efficiency can be presumed, it is "no longer necessary to keep track of the endless variety of circumstances and the changing relative positions of particular persons. One avoids the problem of defining principles to cope with the enormous complexities which would arise if such details were relevant."[106] As a result, the problem of distribution shifts from distributing a given stock of resources to assessing whether or not the distributive system as a whole honors "legitimate claims" of citizens in accordance with "the public system of rules" that determines "what is produced, how much is produced, and by what means." Through an elaborate set of institutions, Rawls transmutes the putative distributive efficiency of the free market into distributive justice.

The Neoclassical Model

Rawls turns to neoclassical economics to establish decentralized markets as a fair process. He explicitly imports the economic theory of, among others, Arrow, Pigou, Samuelson, Viner, Wicksell, and Walras. On this basis, Rawls assumes that "the theory of general equilibrium explains how, given the appropriate conditions, the information supplied by prices leads economic agents to act in ways that sum up to achieve this [Pareto-efficient] outcome. Perfect competition is a perfect procedure with respect to efficiency."[107] More specifically, the first fundamental theorem of welfare economics guarantees the efficiency of competitive markets, and the second theorem guarantees the ability to use lump-sum transfers to move between efficient distributions as the principles of justice require. The mathematical proofs of these theorems encapsulate their procedural logic.[108] These two theorems are deduced from the central assumptions of neoclassical economics.[109] Although there are stronger and weaker versions of the two theorems, economists have not proven the efficiency of competitive markets with less restrictive assumptions.[110] Therefore, the combination of procedural fairness and procedural intelligibility of the general welfare theorems, as a subset of the broader neoclassical tradition, uniquely enables Rawls to assume decentralized markets meet the requirements of pure procedural justice.[111] A Hayekian theory of the market, by contrast, categorically denies that the procedural logic of the market can be encapsulated ex ante and therefore would not be compatible with pure procedural justice despite its other liberal virtues. Neoclassical economics therefore uniquely anchors Rawls's approach of transmuting distributive *efficiency* into distributive *justice*.

General equilibrium theory and the two theorems of welfare economics provide the basic foundation for conceptualizing decentralized markets as perfectly fair and efficient.[112] The first theorem of welfare economics mathematically deduces that market equilibria will be Pareto efficient from the assumptions of perfect information, no transaction costs, and price-taking behavior. The assumptions underlying the neoclassical model are individually necessary and jointly sufficient: all are required in order to mathematically deduce a weakly Pareto-optimal distribution. Given an initial resource endowment, decentralized transactions mediated through the price mechanism will produce a distribution of goods such that there are no incremental trades that can make any individual better off without also making someone else worse off. At this equilibrium point, there are no more welfare-improving transactions left. This result is understood to be a mathematical proof of Adam Smith's Invisible Hand: private agents pursuing their own interests will produce efficient outcomes without any centralized oversight or interference. Through transactions in a system of decentralized markets, each party's position is improved without any coercion or direction. The second welfare theorem holds that any Pareto-efficient distribution can be transmuted into any other through lump-sum transfers. For the purposes of the basic structure, the welfare theorems jointly ensure that decentralized markets produce efficient equilibria that can then be transformed as the principles of the justice require. The neoclassical model both uniquely guarantees the distributive efficiency of decentralized markets (first theorem) and sidesteps trade-offs between efficiency and equality (second theorem). Without these theoretical guarantees, citizens could reasonably disagree both about whether market distributions are actually efficient and the range of acceptable trade-offs between efficiency and justice in the design of economic institutions. Consequently, citizens would face intractable conflict among economic doctrines that, given these trade-offs, articulate incompatible visions of the role of the market in a just basic structure. The fact of "reasonable pluralism" animating Rawlsian liberalism would thus extend to economic doctrines. In this situation, however, the same strategies for finding an "overlapping consensus" among the conflicting doctrines would not suffice. Economic doctrines establish incompatible visions for the proper role of decentralized markets and centralized governments from the standpoint of the basic structure. Without the neoclassical model and the pure procedural approach to distribution the model enables, Rawlsian liberalism would recreate the very problem it aims to resolve.[113]

The resulting situation of conflicting economic doctrines would recapitulate the "fact of reasonable pluralism" that motivates Rawlsian political liberalism in the first place. Just as citizens have different views of the ultimate good, they would also have different views on the acceptable trade-off between efficiency and equality. However, the same solution of limiting the content of the institutional agreement to the "overlapping" elements of reasonable economic doctrines would not resolve the problem. Unlike the conception of the person as a free and equal citizen capable of being a "fully cooperating member of society," the "principles of economic theory" are not "intuitive ideas which we take to be implicit in the public culture of a democratic society."[114] Rawls assumes that the neoclassical model, which theorizes the unimprovable efficiency of free markets, would be accepted by all reasonable citizens as a governing economic model. Yet conflicts among economic doctrines are common in everyday politics. As the world of comprehensive doctrines is populated by "Christians," "Muslims," "Jews," "Atheists," and so on, the world of economic doctrines is populated by "social democrats," "libertarians," "communists," and others. As the former groups affirm conflicting reasonable comprehensive doctrines, the latter represent conflicting reasonable economic doctrines.[115] Rawlsian liberalism cannot mandate a particular reasonable economic doctrine without violating its foundational commitment to what Joseph Raz terms its "epistemic abstinence."

The first and second theorems of welfare economics enable Rawls's assumption that the inclusion of market distribution in the basic structure requires no trade-off to be made between efficiency and justice: efficient distributions can be unproblematically and uncontroversially reshaped in accordance with the chosen principles of justice. Without the neoclassical model, however, Rawlsian liberalism would need to determine when interventions in the name of efficiency are warranted. Such interventions might require violating other liberal reasons for preferring market distribution such as the free choice of occupation, fair equality of opportunity, and decentralization of economic power. Representative agents would therefore reasonably disagree about how these determinations should be made and how far they should go. Rawlsian liberalism is thus opened up to an array of reasonable economic doctrines that orient citizens' beliefs about the design of economic institutions given these trade-offs. Even if we assume the neoclassical model is descriptively accurate, it may still not be universally acceptable. This lack of acceptance causes a problem even if the theory is itself true (the exact problem motivating Hayek and the ordoliberals). The plurality of reasonable economic doctrines is effectively like religious views that a liberal order ought to protect. Raz argues that "asserting the truth of the doctrine of justice ... would negate the very spirit of Rawls's enterprise."[116] Rawls gives no reason why that same logic would not also apply to economic doctrines.

Distribution must be depoliticized for the *exact same* reasons as religion. Pure procedural justice is also Rawls's solution to the problem of distribution because it invites a similar set of difficulties as religious conflict. Rather than allocating a "stock of benefits" given the "needs of known individuals," distribution proceeds in accordance with "the public system of rules and this system determines what is produced, how much is produced, and by what means."[117] Like Locke, Rawls forbids "distribution by compact" because distribution cannot be the result of "desert." A procedural solution avoids imposing public values on private life. However, such a mechanism must also be something that representative agents would select for themselves in the original position.

Rawls explicitly theorizes the neoclassical market as uniquely meeting all these requirements. Rawls argues that "in a free society that all correctly recognize as just there is no need for the illusions and delusions of ideology for society to work properly and for citizens to accept it willingly."[118] Consequently, the neoclassical model of the market must be recognized as true by representative agents in the original position. Rawls uses "fairness" to resolve tension between political equality and economic inequality. Rawls's goal is not to achieve a prespecified distribution of the social product, but to ensure that the basis of this division is itself fair.

Unlike religious liberty, however, the right to own certain kinds of property is not "basic."[119] The problem, seized on by libertarians, is that if property were to be considered basic, then the Rawlsian state could not interfere in the name of equality and justice. Unlike the other suite of liberal freedoms, Rawls does not consider property rights to be inviolable. Yet at the same time, the ownership of property is taken to be an important safeguard against governmental excess.[120] In short, there is a tension here that is always at risk of breaking the social contract Rawls is trying to build: negotiating the boundaries of property rights and governmental intervention invites exactly the kind of conflict among reasonable doctrines that Rawls seeks to avoid. Liberals, social democrats, communists, and libertarians all draw these lines in different and mutually incompatible ways.

LIBERAL DEPOLITICIZATION

Growth and "the market" together depoliticize distribution in the three canonical liberal theories we have been considering. This depoliticizing response to distributive conflict parallels secularism and tolerance as the widely appreciated solutions to religious conflict within liberal theory and actually existing liberal orders. In both cases, depoliticization is achieved through a combination of political discourses and institutional practices. This parallel between religious and distributive conflict is formalized in table 1.1.

Religion and distribution both invite destabilizing social conflicts. In both cases, the liberal solution is to reconstitute the absolutist state as a limited and rule-bound enforcer of public neutrality rather than as an active participant in sectarian conflict. Furthermore, arguments for religious and economic nonintervention are nearly identical. Just as liberal orders preach tolerance and noninterference in matters of

TABLE 1.1 SUMMARY OF PARALLEL BETWEEN THE LIBERAL DEPOLITICIZATION OF RELIGION AND DISTRIBUTION

	Religious conflict	Distributive conflict
Private regime	Religion	Property
Public regime	Secularism	Laissez-faire
Prohibition	Persecution	Intervention
Depoliticizing discourse	Tolerance	"The market"
Depoliticizing practice	Toleration	Growth

religion, so too must they preach laissez-faire and noninterference in matters of distribution. Just as, according to Adam Smith, the mercantilist state mistakenly believes wealth to consist in gold and silver, the absolutist state mistakenly believes that religious belief can be imposed. Just as the liberal state has no business promoting or impeding particular religions, neither does it have any business promoting particular industries or distributive schemas. Such interventions, no matter how well-intentioned, cannot produce their desired ends. By reducing the scope of politics and public action, liberalism aims to reduce sites of conflict.

"The Market": A Discourse of Depoliticization

The theoretical constitution of "the economy" as an independent and autonomous domain governed by natural laws arises from the foundational requirement of distributive depoliticization: if "economic" outcomes are widely grasped as politically constructed or if economic inequalities are not expected to be ameliorated through growth, popular investment in this regime of unfreedom and inequality would not last long. Locke, Mill, and Rawls all deploy some version of "the market" as encoded by economic theory to reconcile liberal political equality with economic inequality. By naturalizing distribution as the result of autonomous scientific processes, the liberal state avoids confronting how distribution is socially determined and its investments in particular distributive constituencies.

For example, these discourses depoliticize economic difference—inequalities of property—by explaining these distributive outcomes as the result of essentialized difference. Wages are thus equal to marginal productivity: differences in income and wealth reflect the market's perfect and impartial evaluation of an individual's contribution to the total social product. The poor are not poor because of any inherent properties of the capitalist wage relation but because they are lazy and unproductive. Class conflict or struggles over distribution—strikes or bread riots—do not symptomatize deep structural injustice but rather naturalized individual difference. If poverty has a cause greater than lack of initiative or industry, it is lack of education, proper family structure, opportunity, or discrimination—never an inherently unequal and unjust regime of property.

Locke, Mill, and Rawls all argue that what generates material inequalities are varying propensities for industry and effort. Inequalities are explained as matters of individual agency or, occasionally, luck. The poor are not poor because their labor is exploited *as a class*, or because capitalism generates classes of poor, but because of their *individual* preferences.[121] Agitating groups thereby "politicize" what is otherwise a spontaneous and efficient harmonization of competing social interests. The neutralization of these conflicts ensures the deeper social structures giving rise to them remain out of public view. "The market" seeks to disappear social powers beneath the placid surface of liberal universalism where, as Marx describes, "equivalents are exchanged for equivalents. . . . There alone rule Equality, Freedom and Bentham."[122]

When material inequalities intrude, potentially destabilizing claims of structural injustice are reconstituted as competing claims of interest group politics that can be duly adjudicated in the neutral arena of liberal politics. Power and its subject-producing effects are thereby washed through the liberal discourse of autonomy, productivity, and "exogenous preferences" to recast institutional domination as the product of individual choice.[123] "The market" as a discursive construct occludes the historical construction of economic identities, positions, and hierarchies.[124] Jürgen Habermas pinpoints the central liberal fiction of identifying the "property owner" with the "human being as such," explaining how the "interest of the owners of private property could converge with that of the freedom of the individual in general."[125] Specific conflicts among proprietors may occur, but there is no general social interest apart from private property itself.

If the poor are poor for any reason besides their lack of *individual* capacity or *individual* industry, then the prevailing system is stripped of its bare pretense of universality: free and equal citizens could not be construed as consenting to such arrangements. Liberalism offers no account of how the groups are constructed. Liberalism must extend opportunity, never redistribute property. Inequalities can then be recast as the result of individual prejudice rather than systemic inequality or unfairness. The political claims arising from these identities and these conflicts can then be safely metabolized by liberalism as claims of private interest, competing in an order of interest group pluralism. Teachers organizing for higher wages are thus made equivalent to corporations lobbying for tax breaks.

Growth: A Practice of Depoliticization

Locke, Mill, and Rawls all argue that growth and improving material conditions justify private property. However, nowhere do they theorize growth directly as an *imperative* arising from the tension between property and democracy. In Mill, for example, growth and progress are the ultimate benefits of private property. Though Mill identifies countless reasons to be dissatisfied with the present condition of mankind, he sees the progressive tendencies of individualism and private property as eventually producing a much more humane social condition. Growth furnishes the material dimension of the popular consent necessary to maintain political order with limited government. Accordingly, liberal mass politics concerns the policies and programs most conducive to growth. However, the liberal state cannot produce growth directly. Such active manipulation would contradict the central motivation of these arrangements. Instead, the liberal state manipulates the system of rules through which growth and progress are generated and sustained.[126]

Mill claims that "all nations which we are accustomed to call civilized increase gradually in production and in population."[127] However, Mill imagines that this "progressive state" characterized by increases in wealth, population, and production will ultimately be replaced by the "stationary state" in which the accumulation of these objects ceases.[128] Although human improvement will continue, economic growth will not.[129] Rawls disclaims growth as an explicit objective of his theory. In *Political Liberalism*, Rawls states that the difference principle "does not require continual economic growth over generations to maximize upward indefinitely the expectations of the least advantaged. It is compatible with Mill's idea of a society in a just stationary state where (real) capital accumulation is zero." Instead, the difference principle requires that "existing inequalities are to be adjusted to contribute in the most effective way to the benefit of the least advanced."[130] Rawls acknowledges that "these brief remarks are hardly clear; they simply indicate the complexities that are not our concern in these lectures." Instead, the primary concern is demonstrating the stability of the principles of justice stability from standpoint of original position. Both Mill and Rawls imagine a state of society in which the growth imperative ceases. However, this is only possible once this underlying paradox has been resolved and subjects are satisfied with both their absolute and relative distributive shares.

Mill and Rawls offer nearly identical lists of protected liberties. However, both carve out property rights from other liberal rights such as religion, speech, and assembly because they recognize the tension with mass democracy and its inherent instability as a political form. At the end of *Principles of Political Economy*, Mill explains why property rights must be subordinate to social purposes. Similarly, Rawls begins *A Theory of Justice* by denying that property rights are "basic." Both Mill and Rawls want to yoke property to progressive ends but do not want distribution itself to be the result of a political process (hence the importance of the price mechanism to both accounts). Samuel Freeman summarizes this "high liberal" view of Mill and

Rawls: "Rights of property, as legally specified, must be revisable by law to meet changing conditions for the sake of efficiency, public safety or convenience, or some other social value. Rights of property are not in these regards fundamental: They can be regulated and revised for reasons other than protecting and maintaining basic rights and liberties."[131] Neoliberals disagree.

* * *

Milton Friedman initially described himself as a "neo-liberal," fashioning himself as a latter-day crusader for classical liberalism against a new age of state overreach. Neo-liberalism, Friedman argued, was an emerging "strong cross-current of opinion" that aimed at establishing a "competitive order" in place of the "collectivism" of the time. Though "neo-liberalism" drew inspiration from nineteenth-century classical liberalism, the neo-liberal state would go beyond the classical maintenance of law and order to "[provide] a framework within which free competition could flourish and the price system operate effectively." This goal would require new functions of the state that would need to ensure the "freedom to establish enterprises in any field" and "the provision of monetary stability." Friedman lamented that such monetary mismanagement forms "so large a part of the alleged case against private enterprise."[132]

To this end, Friedman's monetarism resurrected David Hume's quantity theory of money that trades on some of the oldest liberal tropes against the abuses of sovereign power.[133] In its opposition to the discretionary management of interest rates, monetarism transmutes the philosophical core of classical liberalism into a pervasive social scientific common sense: state intervention in monetary policy necessarily disturbs the otherwise spontaneous efficiency of decentralized market conduct. However, none today would read John Stuart Mill's *Principles of Political Economy* as offering a scientific account of "actually existing" liberal practice in the mid-nineteenth century:

he never enters the Manchester factory, the North Kensington slum, the port of Surat, or the Tidewater plantation.[134] The brutality of liberalism remains safely obscured beneath the placid surface of freedom, rationality, and universalism. Instead, Mill provides a theoretical schematic through which the unfreedom and inequality within actually existing liberal orders can be rendered discursively compatible with the freedom and equality of an idealized liberal subject.

Likewise, Friedman's "neoliberalism" is less an empirical account than another chapter in the long history of liberal depoliticization. Friedman says as much himself, arguing in a famous methodological essay that realism and descriptive accuracy are "irrelevant" to economic theory because "complete 'realism' is clearly unattainable" and "to be important, therefore, a hypothesis must be descriptively false in its assumptions."[135] We must take Friedman at his word: he furnishes not empirical description but discursive rationalization for containing the "discretionary" element in economic policymaking and featuring market forces working apart from social and political demands. Friedman, in contrast to our three liberals, explicitly articulates the role of the market in depoliticizing distributive conflict:

> The use of political channels, while inevitable, tends to strain the social cohesion essential for a stable society. The strain is least if agreement for joint action need be reached only on a limited range of issues on which people in any event have common views. Every extension of the range of issues for which explicit agreement is sought strains further the delicate threads that hold society together. If it goes so far as to touch an issue on which men feel deeply yet differently, it may well disrupt the society. Fundamental differences in basic values can seldom if ever be resolved at the ballot box; ultimately they can be decided, though not resolved, by conflict. The religious and civil wars of history are a bloody testament to this judgment.
>
> The widespread use of the market reduces the strain on the social fabric by rendering conformity unnecessary with respect to any activities

it encompasses. The wider the range of activities covered by the market, the fewer are the issues on which explicitly political decisions are required and hence on which it is necessary to achieve agreement.[136]

Daniel Bell made a similar point two decades later, observing "the virtue of the market is that it disperses responsibility for decisions and effects."[137] An expanded role of the market would replace what can no longer be governed politically.

Equipped with a theorization of liberalism and distributive conflict, we are now ready to move into the neoliberal turn. Here we will see continuities in the story of how growth depoliticizes distributive conflict, but we will also see the consequences of relying on finance to "re-depoliticize" distributive conflict.

2

THE CRISIS OF INFLATION

Upon every account, therefore, the attention of government never was so unnecessarily employed as when directed to watch over the preservation of the quantity of money in any country.
—Adam Smith, *The Wealth of Nations*

They're not sure just what we have in store.
—Billy Corgan, "1979"

In 1982, John Ruggie coined the term "embedded liberalism" to describe the institutional configuration of the postwar liberal order.[1] In contrast to the ruthless laissez-faire of nineteenth-century liberalism, this regime was premised on "embedding" the market in political institutions, yoking it to a modest standard of collective benefit rather than unlimited private interest.[2] The license of capital was circumscribed by an American state newly invigorated from its triumph in World War II. Anchored by the Bretton Woods system internationally and a robust mixed economy domestically, embedded liberalism aimed to reap the benefits of free trade while insulating citizens from the excesses of the market. In this way, embedded liberalism marked another way of drawing the "map" of the liberal world discussed in the previous chapter. Embedded liberal policymaking was guided by the economic ideas of John Maynard Keynes, who articulated an essential role for the state in the maintenance of full employment and economic order.[3] This regime presided over three decades of unprecedented economic growth, investment in public goods, and economic equality. However, Ruggie simultaneously predicted that creeping inflation was "likely to lead to a direct renegotiation of the *modus vivendi* that has characterized embedded liberalism."[4] In the early 1980s, this second great transformation in American liberalism was already well underway.[5]

Inflation began to creep above its postwar baseline in the waning years of the 1960s. Paul Samuelson coined the term "stagflation" in 1974 to refer to this coincidence of high inflation and high unemployment, a phenomenon that the reigning Keynesian orthodoxy seemed unable to explain or contain.[6] A constellation of new economic theories sought to construct inflation as an "all-encompassing social crisis" of embedded liberalism.[7] The ultimate target of these political theories of inflation—the "worms liv[ing] in the bowels of a hegemonic Keynesianism"—was not the Phillips curve, sticky wages, or other elements of the technical apparatus, but the authority of a modestly egalitarian state over private interests.[8] Accordingly, the political opponents of embedded liberalism denied the prevailing view of inflation as a multifaceted crisis of the postwar mixed economy, whose resolution would require delicately managing the structural tensions and distributive conflicts that the embedded liberal state could no longer sustain. Instead, inflation was interpreted as the product of the general Keynesian "zeitgeist" and its corrosion of the prerequisites of economic, social, and moral order.[9] Arresting inflation simply required restoring the supremacy of "free enterprise" over "big government."[10]

In 1980, Ronald Reagan defeated Jimmy Carter with the promise to do just that. Reagan memorably summarized this new governing philosophy in his inaugural address: "In the present crisis, government is not the solution to our problem; government is the problem."

The Reagan administration embarked on a political project of freeing the market from its embedded liberal strictures by cutting taxes, reversing decades of federal regulation, busting unions, slashing social spending, and redeploying the American state in the service of global capital.[11] Inflation and unemployment peaked in 1982 before steadily declining and heralding the coming of "morning in America." The Reagan Revolution, inspired by a hodgepodge of monetarism, supply-side economics, public choice theory, and antigovernment cranks of all stripes, marked a decisive shift in the ideological and political balance of power. After forty years in the wilderness, a transnational "thought collective" warning of creeping statism was seemingly vindicated, much to the distress of political liberals and social democrats.[12]

There can be no doubt the political ascendance of neoliberalism originated in the crisis of inflation. However, the prevailing account of inflation originated in a set of political ideas that attached themselves to the crisis and never let go. What began as a partisan battle cry became a social scientific premise: the academic history of inflation is told by the political victors. In contrast with the conventional wisdom that the inflation of the 1970s was a wage-price spiral unleashed by the contradictions inherent in embedded liberalism and the postwar order, this chapter demonstrates inflation was the monetary manifestation of distributive conflict arising from the breakdown of the postwar growth regime.[13] Its crucial pillars of cheap housing, cheap energy, and state-led investment could not be maintained in the face of the oil shocks, Baby Boom, and backlash against the institutionalization of the social changes of the 1960s.[14] The state response to this multifaceted crisis, begun under Carter, was removing visible regulations on the distribution of these goods. But the removal of state regulations did not simply unleash the efficiency and productivity of the "free market" as neoliberals theorized. Rather, it replaced openly political processes with the depoliticized rule of market forces, while disavowing the role of politics in organizing, abetting, and even supplementing these forces.[15]

Rising prices, especially energy and housing prices, marked a contest for newly scarce resources.[16] These conflicts, in turn, were alleviated through financialization. Crucially, these changes were first and foremost a distinctly liberal political response to crisis rather than a cunning of late Fordist capitalism. I first show how the prevailing view was sedimented on top of what was obvious at the time: inflation was the product of several intersecting distributive crises.[17] Then, I decompose the aggregate measure of "inflation" into its component elements, revealing how price increases symptomatized the breakdown of the postwar growth regime (and not the embedded liberal state violating the timeless and universal laws of economics). Piercing the veil of aggregate statistics reveals the distributive conflicts behind them. Novel financial practices such as commodity futures, repurchase agreements, derivatives, agency bonds, and shadow banking emerged to ease distributive conflicts over scarce social resources such as oil and housing. The cumulative effect of these changes was to reorganize social life in terms of markets, money, and profit maximization and the creation of a global financial system that conducts and organizes the activities of states, firms, and households.[18] This process, repeated across scales and geographies, cumulatively produces the world Alan Greenspan describes bluntly as being "governed by market forces."[19] This chapter revisits the crisis of inflation and the political rise of neoliberalism in this light.

THE NEW COMMON SENSE

Throughout the 1970s, the political opponents of embedded liberalism sought to transform the prevailing understanding of inflation as a series of interlinked crises into a direct consequence of misguided government policy. This conceptual reduction was required to plausibly link inflation to government policy variables such as monetary aggregates, tax rates, and deficits.[20] A flurry of work mixing academic methods with political invective sought to blame inflation on various aspects of the Keynesian policymaking apparatus. As Jonathan Kirshner explains, "ideas about money matter profoundly because they can mask sharp distributional conflicts."[21]

Former Treasury secretary William Simon's *A Time for Truth*, boasting prefaces by both Milton Friedman and F. A. Hayek, argued that "deficit spending, inflation of the money supply, regulatory policy, and wage and price controls" culminated in the "inflationary crisis and recession" of the 1970s.[22] Public choice pioneers James Buchanan and Richard Wagner diagnosed inflation with a similar partisan bluntness: "the legacy or heritage of Lord Keynes is the putative intellectual legitimacy provided to the natural and predictable political biases toward deficit spending, inflation, and the growth of government."[23] While Keynes wasn't exclusively to blame for their exhaustive litany of social ills, Keynesianism was at least responsible for the "zeitgeist" of inflation and the corresponding moral decay.[24]

Another suite of theories explained inflation as the result of policymakers' intentional choices rather than the unintentional consequence of Keynesian policymaking. William Nordhaus's theory of the "political business cycle" concluded that "politically determined policy choice will have lower unemployment and higher inflation than is optimal."[25] Samuel Huntington likewise blamed the "democratic distemper" for producing a "substantial increase in governmental activity" and contributing to the "inflationary tendencies in the economy."[26] Milton Friedman himself explained that "the Federal government is the engine of inflation—the only one there is."[27] In *The Cultural Contradictions of Capitalism*, Daniel Bell argued:

> The inflation which has been plaguing the industrial economies for the past several years seems to be a compound of several convergent factors: a simultaneous increase in demand on a worldwide scale; shortages in primary commodities and raw materials (e.g., food); shortages in primary processing capacity (e.g., steel, paper); wage-cost inflation as

a function of shifts in employment from the industrial to service sectors and the reduced productivity in services; and the inability of governments to reduce expenditures. . . . But underneath all this is a basic change in the character of society which makes it difficult for any polity to use the traditional modes of restraint or "discipline" (in the archaic use of the term) to hold down demand, to increase unemployment, or to reduce governmental expenditures. . . . In sum, the Keynesian revolution—for this is the simplest, symbolic shorthand for the change—has meant a powerful and irreversible revolution in social expectations as well. Put simply, where workers once feared losing a job, which was the common experience of the Depression, they now expect a job and a rising standard of living. And no government can deny that expectation.[28]

For Bell, monetary and fiscal restraint was the obvious but "politically unacceptable" antidote. However, the stew of theories inspiring the Reagan Revolution did not easily cohere. As John Kenneth Galbraith observed at the time, "One cuts taxes to stimulate investment; the other uses murderous levels of interest rates to squelch investment. That you cannot combine economic expansion with economic contraction deserves a place in the small archive of impeccable economic truth."[29]

On September 30, 1979, six weeks after the appointment of Paul Volcker, former Federal Reserve chairman Arthur Burns delivered a lecture in Belgrade entitled "The Anguish of Central Banking." The "anguish" refers to the apparent "paradox" between central banks' "abhorrence of inflation," "the powerful weapons they could wield against it," and their utter failure to contain inflation. Burns begins by acknowledging the role of the "devaluations of the dollar in 1971 and 1973, the worldwide economic boom of 1972–1973, the crop failures and resulting surge in world food prices in 1973–1974, the extraordinary increases in oil prices that became effective in 1974, and the sharp deceleration of productivity growth from the late 1960s onward" in producing inflation. However, despite these concrete, specific, and measurable sources of price increases, the "more fundamental factor" in explaining this "persistent inflationary bias" in Burns's view was the "philosophic and political currents that have been transforming economic life in the United States and elsewhere since the 1930s." The "cumulative effect" of the "interaction of government and citizen activism"—originating with Keynesian philosophy, politics, and economics—was to "impart a strong inflationary bias to the American economy."[30] In 1971, Richard Nixon famously declared, "I am now a Keynesian in economics."[31] In 1979, despite the specific disruptions that Burns catalogs, Keynesianism was squarely to blame for the crisis of inflation.

A similar transformation of inflation from a complex political issue to an error of economic policymaking is evident in the *Economic Report(s) of the President* from this period. Published annually, the *Report* is, definitionally, a statement of the ruling economic orthodoxy. Each report begins with a synthesis of the president's outlook on the economy before presenting reams of macroeconomic statistics. Between 1965 and 1985, Lyndon Johnson's pragmatic uncertainty yields to Reagan's dogmatic optimism. Johnson acknowledges the complexity of the political economic situation: "Seldom can any single choice make or break an economy as strong and healthy as ours. But the series of interrelated decisions we face will affect our economy and that of the whole free world for years to come." The American people must choose "to run our economic affairs responsibly." Johnson warns that "dealing with inflation by creating recession or persistent slack is succumbing to the disease—not curing it."[32]

Nixon's outlook is similarly dour but is more certain as to the root cause: "Government itself is often the cause of wide swings in the economy. . . . We shall have to think carefully about how to choose claims upon the national output that will be met, since we cannot meet them all."[33] This language prefigures Carter's infamous "malaise speech" in which he makes nearly an identical point: "It's clear that the true problems of our Nation are much deeper—deeper than gasoline or energy shortages, deeper than inflation or recession. . . . There is simply no way to avoid sacrifice."[34] Despite their differences, Nixon and Carter both viewed inflation as a complex political problem requiring a vast reimagination of American life.

Reagan, however, argues that "we simply cannot blame crop failures and oil price increases for our basic inflation problem. The continuous, underlying cause was poor government policy. The combination of these two factors—ever higher rates of inflation and ever greater intrusion by the Federal Government into the Nation's economic life—have played a major part in the fundamental deterioration in the performance of our economy."[35] Reagan's diagnosis is straightforward: "The Federal Government has greatly contributed to the persistence of high inflation. Overly stimulative fiscal and monetary policies, on average, have financed excessive spending and thus pushed prices upward." As a result, "inflation has become embedded in the economy" and must be disembedded.[36] In 1985, Reagan writes: "Now is the time to recommit ourselves to the policies that broke that awful pattern [of stagflation]: policies of reduced Federal spending, lower tax rates, and less regulation to free the creative energy of our people and lead us to an even better economic future through strong and sustained economic growth."[37] However, Reagan's own comprehension of the monetary dynamics involved was limited.[38]

The essence of Reagan's position can be found in his coup de grace against Carter during the 1980 presidential debate: "[Carter] has blamed the people for inflation, OPEC, he's blamed the Federal Reserve System, he has blamed the lack of productivity of the American people, he has then accused the people of living too well and that we must share in scarcity, we must sacrifice and get used to doing with less. We don't have inflation because the people are living too well. We have inflation because the government is living too well."[39] In 1965, Johnson identified a number of distinct causes requiring a complex response. By 1985, common sense dictated that government itself was to blame for inflation, now understood as a unified phenomenon. As Reagan budget director David Stockman told William Greider in 1980, "the whole thing is premised on faith . . . on a belief about how the world works." Stockman continued, "whenever there are great strains or changes in the economic system it tends to generate crackpot theories, which then find their way into the legislative channels."[40] Although "Reaganomics" encompassed more than just monetarism, monetarism would prove to be its most durable theoretic plank.[41]

Led by Milton Friedman, monetarists blamed inflation on excessive expansions in the money supply, primarily driven by central bank support for government social programs.[42] Friedman canonically diagnosed inflation as "always and everywhere a monetary phenomenon in the sense that it is and can be produced only by a more rapid increase in the quantity of money than in output."[43] If inflation was indeed an affirmative policy choice, then so too could be disinflation. Monetarism's foundational claim is intuitive: more money in circulation means higher prices. Paul Volcker once wrote that "people don't need an advanced course in economics to understand that inflation has something to do with too much money."[44] Today, if they were to take an advanced course in economics, they would find the same basic story. Greg Mankiw writes in the opening pages of his widely used introductory economics textbook that "the high inflation of the 1970s was associated with rapid growth in the quantity of money, and the low inflation of more recent experience was associated with slow growth in the quantity of money."[45] Reducing inflation, monetarists argued, simply required reducing the rate of growth of the money supply. Consequently, Volcker's course of "practical monetarism" and crushing interest rate hikes are widely credited for finally containing inflation where previous Federal Reserve chairmen and policymaking orthodoxies had failed.[46]

However, the Federal Reserve abandoned monetarism as an explicit policy paradigm almost immediately.[47] By 1982, monetary aggregates and inflation were moving in opposite directions, contradicting monetarism's core causal claim.[48] Despite its remarkable policymaking failure, monetarism's colloquial diagnosis of inflation as "too much money chasing too few goods" remains ubiquitous. Under a section heading entitled "Facts," monetarist economist Thomas Sargent asks, "Inflation was low during the late 1950's and early 1960's, swept upward into the 1970's, then fell abruptly with Volcker's stabilization in the early 1980's. If we take it for granted that inflation is under the control of the Federal Reserve, how can we explain these observations?"[49] Despite the widespread insistence that Volcker's tenure marked an immediate shift in the conduct of monetary policy, Volcker continued the path of interest rate increases that began under Arthur Burns and G. William Miller. The effective federal funds rate increased from 5 percent at the beginning of 1977 to 15 percent at the beginning of 1980, spanning the tenures of three different Fed chairmen. For this reason, the Volcker shock cannot be characterized as a "coup" because he continued the trajectory of interest rate increases spanning three previous Fed chairmen in accordance with the reigning policy orthodoxy.[50]

Monetarism posits a direct causal relation between changes in the money supply and changes in inflation. However, this causal link requires reifying "money" and "inflation" as things that are measured by statistical indices constructed by government bureaus. Social scientists have long considered the many ways in which such statistics do not transparently and impartially represent an underlying reality.[51] Measures of monetary aggregates, for example, require constant revision in light of new financial innovations.[52] Measures of inflation, as we will see, can be altered when politically expedient. In both cases, monetarism naturalizes a composite index as an economic primitive, obscuring the underlying elements that actually compose these statistical measures and to which the hypothesized causal mechanism may not apply. Nevertheless, monetarism argues, "the 'basis of the world inflation is the expansion of the world money supply,' and any attempt to bring in other factors, particularly those of the cost-push variety, represents a distressing resort to 'amateur sociology and politics' which can play 'no part whatsoever in the problem.'"[53]

Critics of neoliberalism have largely abided this territorial marking. The leading sociopolitical theorists at the time also argued that inflation augured a crisis of the Keynesian state, albeit of a very different kind.[54] These theories understood inflation as an intentional state strategy for masking terminal contradictions in the postwar capitalist order.[55] This interpretation buttressed the emerging common sense that inflation, whether intentional or unintentional, was a necessary product of embedded liberalism. In the *Annual Review of Sociology* in 1981, Fred Block wrote:

> Since the late 1960s, the pressures for a continuing expansion of the state budget have intensified at a time when the overall rate of economic growth has slowed. The result has been a fiscal crisis as governments are unable to support their expenditures with revenues and are forced to resort to inflationary tax increases or deficit financing. The inflationary consequences of state growth have, in turn, generated profound pressures for cutting back or slowing the growth of state expenditures.[56]

Inflation was seen by sociopolitical theory more broadly as symptomatizing "fundamental strains in advanced capitalism."[57]

James O'Connor's *The Fiscal Crisis of the State* shared this interpretation. O'Connor argued that traditional economics ignores the role of growth and the determinants of public expenditures. When these factors are included in economic analysis, it becomes clear that the state must *accumulate* and *legitimate* by creating "conditions in which profitable capital accumulation is possible" and "the conditions for social harmony."[58] O'Connor, whose formulations would influence those of Habermas in *Legitimation Crisis*, argued that inflation symptomatizes the state's inability to fulfill these twinned functions.[59] Albert Hirschman likewise saw inflation as a deliberate state strategy, arguing that "to the extent that the process is understood one might say that the state hands over to inflation the disagreeable job of saying no."[60] Inflation is thus interpreted as a method for the state to revalue claims without requiring explicit agreement or contestation. Inflation is set off when "a social group holds enough power or influence to command additional wealth and income for itself, *but not enough* to do so in a permanent way through a definitive transfer."[61] Albert Wojnilower at First Boston similarly argued that "inflation is a standard historical response for societies forced to reduce their economic aspirations—and is useful up to a point in averting divisive internal strife about how the new burdens are to be distributed."[62]

In his classic text *The Limits to Capital*, David Harvey also diagnosed inflation through the lens of Marxian analysis. For Harvey, the inflation of the 1970s marked the conversion of the "devaluation of commodities" into the "devaluation of money."[63] With the prevailing "technological mix" of production no longer able to ensure "further balanced accumulation," state money printing enabled profits to be realized in realm of exchange despite the "fall-off in real surplus value production." Rationally, according to the laws of capital, this fall-off can only be corrected by devaluing commodities in money terms to reflect this decline in surplus value. A general devaluation is required in order to restore balanced capitalist accumulation. Like monetarists, Harvey argued that the state creates new money to forestall a painful reckoning with the laws of capital: "inflation defuses conflict by broadening it and refocusing it on the state."[64]

The state, and by extension the capitalist ruling class, face a tension "between the need to sustain accumulation through credit creation and the need to preserve the quality of money. If the former is inhibited, we end up with an overaccumulation of commodities and specific devaluation. If the quality of money is allowed to go to the dogs, we have generalized devaluation through chronic inflation."[65] Either money or commodities can be devalued. The choice is either inflation or depression. But, Harvey observed, "in the event that monetary policy is dedicated to avoiding both, it will merely end up incurring both (as the current state of capitalism illustrates)."[66] On the subject of price controls as a potential response to inflation, Harvey noted: "Monetarists argue that [wage and price controls] merely distort price signals and thereby destroy any proper basis for the resumption of accumulation. Marxian theory accords with that judgment."[67] The "attribution" of inflation to "inefficient and ineffective government, in erroneous fiscal and monetary policies" is "correct as regards the immediate cause. What it ignores is the underlying structure of class relations which generates crises of overaccumulation-devaluation in the first place."[68] Harvey also characterized the Volcker shock as abandoning "Keynesian fiscal and monetary policies with full employment as the key objective . . . in favor of a policy designed to quell inflation no matter what the consequences might be for employment."[69] There is surprisingly little distance between Marxian and bourgeois political economy as to the diagnosis of inflation in the late 1970s.

We must look behind the monetary veil to see the distributive conflicts underneath.

DECOMPOSING "INFLATION"

The term *inflation* is generally used metonymically to refer to the annualized rate of increase in the Consumer Price Index for Urban Consumers (CPI-U) published monthly by the Bureau of Labor Statistics (BLS). The CPI is constructed through a survey of thousands of items comprising what the BLS terms the *consumption basket* of a representative American household. These individual prices are aggregated into various subcomponents that are then rolled up into the top-level components such as housing or transportation. Each category and subcategory are assigned a weighting

TABLE 2.1 1980 CPI-U INDEX WEIGHT

Component	Weight
Housing	46%
Transportation	19%
Food and beverages	18%
Apparel	5%
Medical care	5%
Entertainment	4%
Other	4%

Source: Bureau of Labor Statistics.

in the index designed to represent the "relative importance" of a particular group of items to a household's overall expenditures.[70] The index weights for major categories of the CPI-U in 1980 are listed in table 2.1.

Each of these categories, in turn, comprises an array of subcategories. For example, the "transportation" category includes subcategories such as "motor fuel," "maintenance and repair," "new and used motor vehicles," and "intercity bus fare"; each in turn reflects an array of individual products tracked by BLS workers and private households in nearly one hundred American cities. The aggregate measure of "inflation" is therefore a composite of changes in the price of thousands of individual products. Changes in macroeconomic variables such as the federal funds rate, marginal tax rates, unemployment, or monetary aggregates affect the CPI only to the extent that they produce price changes in the specific markets that compose it (see Figure 2.1). Looking at these specific components allows us to see what's driving price increases in each case. What we find is not a violation of the timeless laws of economics but cornerstones of the postwar order coming undone. Inflation itself was the manifestation of the crisis, not the crisis itself.

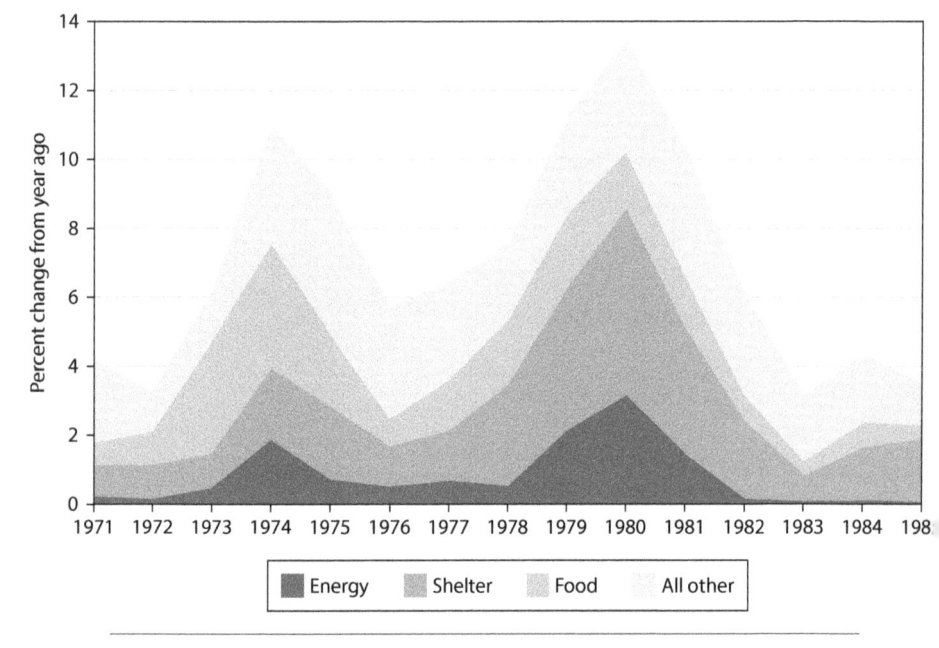

FIGURE 2.1 Consumer Price Index (CPI) decomposition.
Source: Bureau of Labor Statistics.

Housing

The postwar growth regime in the United States was built on the transformation of an industrial war economy to a postindustrial Cold War economy. Deep inside the state apparatus, a top-secret group within the National Security Council drafted a report entitled *United States Objectives and Programs for National Security* (NSC-68).[71] The report called for a massive buildup in military spending and technological capacity to contain the Soviet Union. The authors of the report write, "The necessary build-up could be accomplished without a decrease in the national standard of living because the required resources could be obtained by siphoning a part of the annual increment in the gross national product." Growth, in other words, would be the cornerstone of the American Cold War strategy: the American system of free enterprise would achieve both egalitarian ends and military dominance without resorting to confiscatory taxation and overt redistribution.

After V-J Day, the most pressing social priority was reintegrating the sixteen million returning veterans into civilian life. The Servicemen's Readjustment Act of 1944—known as the GI Bill—helped ease redeployment into the postwar postindustrial economy by providing no-money-down mortgages, funding for postsecondary education, unemployment pay, and other benefits. The most immediate problem was a massive undersupply of housing. Residential construction had largely ceased during the war, and demand from returning soldiers and their newly formed families had never been higher. As part of Truman's Fair Deal, Congress passed the Housing Act of 1949, which expanded mortgage insurance, funding for public housing, and urban redevelopment projects. These new redevelopment authorities were the favored tool of Robert Moses in his remaking of New York City.[72] Funds from the act built the infamous Pruitt-Igoe complex in St. Louis and the Cabrini-Green complex in Chicago. The act helped solidify a racialized housing order in which subsidized credit flowed to white suburbs while Blacks were concentrated in urban ghettoes.[73]

Suburbanization required major federal policy support. From massive investment in the Interstate Highway System to the mortgage interest deduction and accelerated depreciation schedules, nearly every major postwar domestic policy, John Mollenkopf argues, had the effect of encouraging "the suburbanization of employment and residential population."[74] In California, Nevada, and Arizona, suburbanization also required the massive water infrastructure projects that irrigated the deserts of the southland.[75] Kenneth Jackson agrees, arguing that public policy rendered suburban homeownership the only "economically feasible" option.[76]

Suburbanization, the cumulative product of the postwar growth regime, radically transformed the economic and political geography of the postindustrializing economy. The Lehigh Valley machinist was replaced by the San Fernando Valley aerospace engineer as the prototypical American worker. The postwar surge of defense spending was funneled to the nonunionized Sun Belt, far from the grip of Democratic machine politics and the racial complexities of eastern cities. The personal automobile enabled these new white-picket utopias, with the number of motor vehicles increasing from 30 million in 1945 to nearly 110 million in 1970.[77]

The suburbs were built by a newly ascendant political class of commercial homebuilders such as KB Home, Levitt & Sons, and AG Spanos. These firms pioneered the application of Fordist production techniques to homebuilding. Like the Model T, the tract home brought homeownership to the masses. As a result, the homeownership rate rose by nearly twenty percentage points between 1945 and 1965. For the first time in American history, the mythic "median voter" was now a homeowner. The suburban home was also the "bedrock of the postwar mass consumption economy."[78] Home ownership required at least one automobile, kitchen appliances, television sets, furniture, and other trappings of the ascendant middle class. Magazines such as *Life* and *Good Housekeeping* reassured these newly formed consumer units that consumption was their patriotic duty: spending, not thrift, was the key to continuing national prosperity. The gray days of the Depression were now only a distant memory.

Orange County was the apotheosis of the postwar model of suburban-based growth and growing suburbs. In the years after the war, dozens of major defense contractors established or expanded operations in southern California. Developers bulldozed the eponymous citrus orchards to make way for suburban civilization. The result of this *ex nihilo* suburbanization was a landscape devoid of public space and wholly dependent on the private automobile. The influx of veterans into the University of California system necessitated expansion. The Irvine Company, one of California's largest landowners, planned a city around a new university that would be named in the company's honor. Orange County served as the prototype for the now familiar American landscape: an endless tessellation of subdivisions, corporate office parks, highways, shopping malls, and gas stations.[79]

Many scholars have charted the political correlates of suburbanization. White-collar workers in southern California, literally enlisted in the national fight against communism, were ideal subjects for right-wing politics.[80] Homeownership further nudged the suburban working class toward conservative politics.[81] The suburbs were also the site of other new cultural pathologies. M. P. Baumgartner argued that suburban life was characterized by "moral minimalism" and the avoidance of almost all forms of social conflict.[82] Likewise, Lewis Mumford argued that the suburban citizen tends to "retreat from unpleasant realities, to shirk public duties, and to find the whole meaning of life in the most elemental social group, the family, or even in the still more isolated and self-centered individual."[83] C. Wright Mills identified the pervasive "marketing mentality" of the American middle class.[84] An increasing number of jobs revolved around "handling" people, whether in sales, human resources, public relations, or advertising, producing a pervasive "other-directed" cultural type.[85] Indeed, the unprecedented prosperity in the postwar era, Herbert Marcuse lamented, generated blind conformity to the system that "delivers the goods"—or at least while it lasted.[86]

In the late 1960s, the Baby Boomers began to settle down.[87] Annual "household formations" topped one million, marking a 50 percent increase over the first half of the decade. This created yet another surge in demand for housing and credit that the federal government and the private sector were unprepared to address. In 1966, America encountered its first postwar financial crisis. This "credit crunch" resulted from market interest rates rising above their regulatory limits. The result was an abrupt cessation of credit creation and a sharp reduction in new residential construction. A widespread banking panic was narrowly avoided. The Federal Reserve wrote in a letter to all member banks that "the aggregate total of credit-financed business spending has tended towards unsustainable levels and has added appreciably to current inflationary pressures"[88] and urged "a moderation in the rate of bank loan expansion."[89]

The demand surge coupled with the credit crunch–induced collapse in homebuilding led Congress to pass the Housing and Urban Development Act of 1968 that transformed the American housing market.[90] The overall goal was to create government programs to counteract the procyclicality of mortgage lending wherein financing would evaporate during credit crunches or recessions. As evidence of the scale of the problem, the act set a goal of building 25.5 million new housing units between 1969 and 1978, compared to 14.5 million built in the preceding decade. Housing starts reached an all-time high of 2.4 million new units in 1972. Over 400,000 of these housing starts were for subsidized units for newly created programs. To meet this demand, residential mortgage credit ballooned from $19 billion in 1965 to $48 billion in 1972, or a nearly 15 percent compounded annual growth rate.[91]

A flurry of legislation during this period created and expanded the role of government-sponsored enterprises (GSEs) including Ginnie Mae (Government National Mortgage Association), Fannie Mae (Federal National Mortgage Association), and Freddie Mac (Federal Home Loan Mortgage Corporation). The goal of these GSEs is "improving the availability of housing to all Americans" by increasing "the secondary market volume of sales and purchases of residential mortgages and, thus, to increase the effective supply of mortgage financing."[92] Generally speaking, these entities provide a large and stable source of demand in the secondary mortgage market (i.e., mortgages that have been originated elsewhere, likely a thrift, then sold to a GSE) that counteracts the cyclicality of the mortgage lending and homebuilding markets with a large and stable source of demand for mortgages. The net effect of these changes was to massively increase the federal government's role in supporting the housing market through "submerged" financial channels.[93]

Alongside this new demand, Congress came under pressure to shrink the size of the federal deficit. The primary rationale for transforming Fannie Mae into a quasi-private entity was to keep its debt off of the government's balance sheet, though it retained its access to privileged lines of credit from the Treasury and preferential tax treatment. During the Johnson administration, policymakers worried about ensuring the availability of mortgages amid a credit crunch and baby boom. The GSEs allowed the budget deficits to be outsourced with implicit state guarantees and insulation from the usual budget politics.[94]

On May 21, 1970, George Romney, secretary of the Department of Housing and Urban Development (HUD), declared Fannie Mae a private corporation and its stock began trading on the New York Stock Exchange (NYSE) on August 31. The same year, the Emergency Home Finance Act created Freddie Mac to buy mortgages originated by thrifts and permitted Fannie Mae to buy conventional (i.e., not federally insured) mortgages in an attempt to address what Nixon described as the "nation's critical housing shortage."[95] Throughout the 1970s, there was a monotonic increase in the financial risk taken on by the federal government via the GSEs in the form of increases on statutory leverage limits and price caps alongside relaxed loan-to-value requirements for eligible mortgages.[96] Working through financial markets enabled the federal government to stabilize the provision of housing without overtly meddling in the "free market" or, in what amounts to the same thing, obviously favoring certain groups.[97]

From 1972 to 1982, the average sale price of a new single-family home increased from $30,100 to $80,500. In 1983, the cost of a new single-family house broke down as follows: labor—16 percent, materials—30 percent, land—23 percent, financing—11 percent, overhead—14 percent, and marketing and other—6 percent.[98] A report to Congress in 1983 discusses the sources of housing price increases: "Over the past decade, onsite labor and materials—the hard costs—have declined as a proportion of total development costs; financing charges and land costs have risen."[99] Although wages were rising in the construction industry, they constituted a relatively small and decreasing share of the overall price of new housing units. Instead, rising prices for new construction were largely driven by increases in land prices, builder financing costs resulting from rising interest rates, and increasingly stringent and expensive local permitting and planning costs.

Isaac William Martin traces how a seemingly innocuous and technocratic program for modernizing in the administration of the California state property tax launched the "tax revolt" that would transform American politics.[100] Under the old system, an elaborate system of patronage governed property tax assessment. Now, assessments would be set at 25 percent of market value.[101] An overheating housing market in the 1970s meant that homeowners faced skyrocketing property tax bills. Home prices in west Los Angeles, for instance, rose by a factor of six between 1970 and 1980.[102] Unsurprisingly, suburban Los Angeles became the nexus of a bourgeoning "tax revolt" where homeowners demanded protection from rising tax bills. The result was Proposition 13. In June 1978, California voters approved a constitutional amendment that set strict limits on taxes in the state. Among other changes, Proposition 13 required a two-thirds vote of the California legislature for most tax increases and capped annual property tax increases at 2 percent. Reassessments are only triggered upon sale or transfer. By a 2-to-1 margin, voters in the largest and most liberal state approved dramatic tax cuts. The implementation would be left to Governor Jerry Brown.

No politician benefited more from Proposition 13 than former governor Ronald Reagan. After narrowly losing the 1976 Republican presidential primary to Gerald Ford, Reagan spent the duration of the Carter presidency criticizing him from his bully pulpits of talk shows, newspaper editorials, and rallies. As Thomas and Mary Edsall describe, tax cuts like Proposition 13 provided "conservatism with a powerful internal coherence, shaping an anti-government ethic, and firmly establishing new grounds for the disaffection of white working- and middle-class voters from their traditional Democratic roots." More generally, they argued:

> The twin issues of race and taxes have created a new, ideologically coherent coalition by pitting taxpayers against tax recipients, by pitting the advocates of meritocracy against proponents of special preference, by putting the private sector against the public sector, by putting those in the labor force against the jobless, and by pitting those who bear many of the costs of federal intervention against those whose struggle for equality has been advanced by interventionist government policies.... Opposition to busing, affirmative action, quotas, housing integration have given a segment of the traditionally Democratic white electorate ideological common ground with business and the affluent in shared opposition to the federal regulatory apparatus.[103]

Tax cuts united big business opposition to the New Deal and white working-class opposition to the Civil Rights Act and the Great Society. As a result, Martin argues, the most enduring legacy of Proposition 13 was that "Republican politicians began to distinguish themselves from their Democratic counterparts by their opposition to high taxes and big government."[104] Reagan was the perfect vessel to deliver this message.[105]

Food

American consumers experienced a drastic increase in the price of food products in the early 1970s. From August 1972 to August 1973, the price of wheat tripled and the price of corn and soybeans doubled.[106] The price of feed and fertilizer inputs oscillated wildly with energy prices. The 1973 oil embargo also created widespread fertilizer shortages. This had a number of cascading effects in adjacent commodity markets such as cattle, hogs, and dairy that are key consumers of grain feeds. These price increases were further exacerbated by El Niño and the resulting collapse of the Peruvian wild anchovy catch that serves as a crucial protein source for animal feeds.[107] Meat prices increased 30 percent on a year-over-year basis, which, given the weighting of this category in the CPI, contributed nearly two percentage points to the CPI from this category alone in 1974.

This drastic price jump resulted from the confluence of meteorological, geopolitical, and bureaucratic factors. A global drought in 1972 reduced worldwide grain production by 36 million metric tons, concentrated especially in the Soviet Union. On July 8, 1972, President Nixon signed an agreement creating a $750 million line of credit for the Soviets to purchase wheat from U.S. growers. The Soviets bought 440 million bushels of the record 1.1-billion-bushel export crop.[108] Total grain exports totaled nearly 80 percent of the average annual harvest of the United States over the preceding few years.

Nixon was eager to use the position of the United States as the only major grain exporter during a worldwide drought to his advantage. Nixon hoped that boosting grain exports would alleviate the deficit, curry favor with farmers, and solidify the nascent detente with the Soviets all at once.[109] However, the administration simultaneously enacted a maximum acreage "set-aside" for wheat that restricted supply amid unprecedented global demand. Combined with the devaluation of the dollar in the wake of a decision the previous year to suspend dollar convertibility (since commodities are largely denominated in dollars), this made foreign purchases of U.S. agricultural commodities comparatively more attractive.

The food price spike resulted from declines in global production, rapid growth of meat demand in developing countries, U.S. farm policies, errors in the administration of subsidy policy, and dollar devaluation.[110] Cattle prices doubled between 1976 and 1978 as the national herd shrunk from 132 million in 1975 to 116 million in 1978.[111] The year

1977 was the driest on record to date in California and much of the western United States.[112] The exceptionally harsh winters of 1977 and 1978 further strained meat producers. The 1980 heat wave and drought still ranks as one of the costliest ever. Once again, rising meat prices contributed one percentage point to the rate of increase in the CPI.

Transportation

During March 1956 at the Spring Meeting of the American Petroleum Institute in San Antonio, chief geologist of Shell Oil, M. King Hubbert, presented a paper entitled "Nuclear Energy and the Fossil Fuels." In the paper, Hubbert argued that "no finite resource can sustain for longer than a brief period such [an exponential] rate of growth of production; therefore, although production rates tend initially to increase exponentially, physical limits prevent their continuing to do so."[113] In other words, Hubbert argued that the rapid growth in domestic oil production over the preceding decade would soon slow, bringing the oil-dependent American economy down with it. From 1950 to 1970, the price of oil averaged around $2 per barrel. New domestic capacity could readily be brought online to meet incremental demand, thus keeping prices steady. Just as Hubbert predicted, rapid growth in oil production could not be sustained indefinitely. The reasons, however, were ultimately more political than geological.

On January 28, 1969, Union Oil's Platform A in the Santa Barbara Channel blew out. Millions of gallons of oil gushed through the ocean floor, coating beaches and devastating marine life. Images of Santa Barbarans attempting to clean oil-slicked seabirds were a constant fixture on the evening news. The spill galvanized the emerging environmental movement in the United States, ultimately leading to the creation of the Environmental Protection Agency and the passage of the Clean Air Act, Clean Water Act, and the National Environmental Policy Act. Environmental opposition stalled construction of the trans-Alaska pipeline that would deliver crude from the massive Prudhoe Bay field to Valdez and on to world markets. In September 1969, Colonel Muammar Gaddafi overthrew King Idris and began nationalizing Western oil facilities in Libya, highlighting the vulnerability of monarchs cozy with American oil companies to growing nationalist sentiment.

By 1971, there was no remaining domestic surplus production capacity, forcing a turn to world markets.[114] As a result, oil imports doubled between 1970 and 1973. Between 1970 and 1977, imports from OPEC (Organization of the Petroleum Exporting Countries) rose from 10 percent to 40 percent of total consumption, leaving the United States heavily dependent on the uninterrupted availability of foreign supply and increasingly concerned with Middle Eastern geopolitics.[115] The postwar order required growth. Growth, in turn, required oil. Timothy Mitchell argues that oil generated a "peculiar orientation towards the future: the future was a limitless horizon of growth."[116]

On October 6, 1973, the Egyptian military crossed the Suez Canal and into the Sinai Peninsula, while the Syrian military entered the Golan Heights. Both U.S. and Israeli policymakers assumed that any potential conflict would be short-lived owing to Israeli military superiority. However, Soviet surface-to-air missiles proved unexpectedly effective against Israeli air power. This development led Israeli Prime Minister Golda Meir to authorize the assembly of thirteen 20-kiloton nuclear weapons, each roughly equivalent in yield to the bombs dropped on Hiroshima and Nagasaki, on the night of October 8.

The next day, Nixon authorized Operation Nickel Grass to resupply Israel with a series of strategic airlifts to prevent the possibility of a nuclear escalation. North Atlantic Treaty Organization (NATO) allies, dependent on OPEC for upward of 90 percent of their oil consumption and therefore fearful of provoking an embargo, refused to let Israel-bound cargo planes make refueling stops in their countries. In a private meeting, Exxon chairman Kenneth Jamieson told Henry

Kissinger: "The American public is just not geared up for the kind of crisis we face. . . . What we are talking about is the possible breakdown of the economy."[117] On October 16, OPEC raised its posted oil prices by 70 percent. Three days later, the Arab members of OPEC declared a total embargo against the United States, soon producing gas lines, rationing, and lingering social unrest.[118]

Nixon was particularly interested in the potential political optics of breaking the embargo, in hopes of distracting from the simmering Watergate scandal.[119] Before the embargo, Nixon wanted to increase oil imports "to defuse social tensions and avoid ugly conflicts."[120] Afterward, however, reducing oil imports became a national priority. The embargo was officially lifted on March 18, 1974. The production cutbacks were ultimately more significant than the embargo itself, with much of the lost supply made up from countries not party to the embargo.[121]

The political effort to encourage conservation was not successful. The much-ridiculed National Maximum Speed Limit Law signed by Nixon in January of 1974 was one feeble attempt to curb Americans' oil consumption. Policymakers hoped that a national speed limit of 55 miles per hour would cut gasoline usage by 2 percent. However, the law was sporadically enforced and eventually repealed. Congress also experimented with a year-long daylight savings time from 1974 to 1975 in an effort to reduce consumption. President Ford proposed a $2 per barrel tax on imports in 1975 that was struck down by Congress.[122] None of these policies succeeded in reducing oil consumption. Simultaneously, the Department of Energy began filling the Strategic Petroleum Reserve in 1977, putting further upward pressure on prices.[123]

Oil prices increased modestly from 1975 to 1978, only to skyrocket again in the wake of the Islamic Revolution in Iran and its subsequent halting of oil exports in December 1978. Although this only amounted to a 4–5 percent decline in world production, the price of oil nearly tripled from $13 to $34 in response. The contractual structure between upstream and downstream players in the oil market was susceptible to such a disruption: companies more dependent on Iranian oil flooded the market in an attempt to replace their lost supply. Other producers were eager to wring price increases at every opportunity and could pit these newly desperate buyers against their existing customers, resulting in dramatic price increases. There was also the lurking question of contagion in the market: Which other oil-exporting nation would succumb to domestic political unrest next? Finally, panic buying gripped producers and consumers alike, effectively doubling the shortage by increasing demand by 5 million barrels per day (mbpd) in response to a 2-mbpd cut in supply. However, between 1978 and 1982, consumption fell from 18.8 to 15.2 mbpd and OPEC imports fell from 6 to 2 mbpd.[124] The total oil bill in the United States increased to nearly 8 percent of gross domestic product (GDP) from its postwar baseline of 2 percent. Despite the massive price increases, consumption increased from 11.5 mbpd in 1965 to 18.8 mbpd in 1980.[125]

The turmoil upended the carefully negotiated structure of the global oil market. In an earlier era of integrated production, little crude oil changed hands between the ground and the refinery: both the "upstream" exploration and "downstream" refining processes were contained within the same corporate entity. The rise of the state oil companies like Saudi Aramco with little to no refining capacity necessitated the ability to trade oil between corporate entities. This new phenomenon enabled the rise of the oil trader who could arbitrage the futures market and the spot market to take advantage of these structural dislocations. Now, producers could play anxious buyers off of one another in frantic spot markets for immediate delivery. Prior to 1980, domestic oil production and foreign imports were subject to a complex regulatory structure that had been stitched together in a piecemeal fashion over the previous decades. Oil was sold in a tiered structure depending on whether or not the well was drilled prior to 1973. An undersecretary in the Department of the Interior and future founder of Enron, Kenneth Lay, authored legislation that would remove natural gas price controls in order to create one national market for natural gas. Lay wrote to Nixon that "our problem . . . has resulted from outmoded Government policies—from excessive tinkering with the time-tested mechanisms of the free market."[126]

The dramatic oil price spike was especially disruptive for independent truckers, heirs of the Jeffersonian farmer, and the frontier cowboy as the image of rugged American individualism.[127] The trucking industry was subject to an amalgam of New Deal era policies that created a dual-track system of "regulated" and "exempt" loads. The Interstate Commerce Commission (ICC) was responsible for regulating trucking prices in nonexempt industries. The entrenched alliance between the Teamsters Union—led by James R. Hoffa—and the ICC was the perfect target for a rising tide of antigovernment sentiment.[128]

Agricultural commodities were a crucial exemption from ICC regulation. However, it was not always clear when an "agricultural commodity" transformed into a "manufactured commodity" and thus a regulated one. In a case before the Supreme Court, an attorney for the U.S. Department of Agriculture (USDA) argued that a frozen chicken maintains a "continuing substantial identity" as a chicken and thus should be considered an agricultural commodity.[129] The court agreed, creating an opening for the deregulation of frozen food trucking rates. The resulting price declines in these newly "exempted" markets were touted as clear evidence for the anti-inflationary effects of deregulation more broadly. An interview with Milton Friedman was published in the March 1973 edition of *Overdrive* magazine ("The Voice of the American Trucker").[130] His interviewer, editor Mike Parkhurst, lauded Friedman for being a fellow believer in the virtue "free enterprise." Democrats also spied an opportunity to turn deregulation into a pro-consumer issue. Senator Ted Kennedy, in his bid to win the 1980 presidential nomination from Jimmy Carter, championed the Motor Carrier Act, which would deregulate the trucking industry in order to lower prices for consumers.[131] On July 1, 1980, Jimmy Carter signed the act into law. Historian Shane Hamilton characterizes the deregulation of the trucking industry as a crucial step toward the creation of a "low-wage, low-price capitalism."[132]

Carter enacted a sweeping "decontrol" of domestic oil prices. The previous politically negotiated system of tiered pricing was dismantled and replaced with one globalized market price. Meanwhile, OPEC's internal political structure could not withstand the force of greed and opportunism unleashed by the oil price spike. Members were eager to abandon the preexisting structure in order to accrue short-term profits. Michel Foucault perspicaciously observed in 1978 that the "increase in the cost of energy [was] due not to the formation of a cartel of sellers fixing a price which was too high, but rather to the reduction of the economic and political influence of the cartel of buyers and the formation of a market price for both oil and energy generally."[133]

The resulting windfalls for oil exporters birthed the "petrodollar." Oil exporters newly awash with dollars "recycled" them through American banks and special nonmarketable Treasury issues.[134] A significant portion of these dollars ended up in Latin America, setting the stage for the 1982 debt crisis. Former Ford administration economic advisor William Seidman recalled that the administration "told the large banks that the process of recycling petrodollars to the less developed countries was beneficial, and perhaps a patriotic duty."[135] Oil exporters also began establishing sovereign wealth funds to manage their windfalls and diversify their state revenue streams.[136] In 1983, the first crude oil futures contract began trading on the New York Mercantile Exchange, enabling any exchange member to speculate on oil prices. After their peak in 1980, oil prices steadily declined for the remainder of the decade.[137]

From 1975 to 1976, the price index of the "motor vehicle insurance" subcategory increased by 27 percent nationally. This subcategory is itself misleading because there is no national market for auto insurance. Instead, the auto insurance market is highly regulated at the state level, so the "national" price increase represents a composite of state-level price increases. In New York, for example, the state insurance commission approved a 55 percent year-over-year increase in premiums. The proximate cause was the near collapse of GEICO. The state, whose teachers' pension fund owned the mortgage on the GEICO headquarters building, would be unable to assume GEICO's claim obligations because the bulk of its insurance insolvency fund was tied up in the rescue of the Urban Development Corporation during New York City's fiscal crisis the previous year.[138] As a result, a private bailout had to be engineered. In repayment, the state's insurance commission was willing to grant insurers' requests for drastic premium hikes. The acting federal insurance administrator dubbed these premium increases a result of the "politics of the situation."[139]

Interest

The interest rate is often conceptualized as the "price of money" and is the only price that is *directly* influenced by Federal Reserve policy. Throughout the year, the Fed will set a "target" for the federal funds rate—the annualized interest rate at which member banks lend excess deposits in their Federal Reserve accounts to one another overnight on an unsecured basis. Through purchases and sales of U.S. government securities ("open market operations"), the Fed injects or withdraws money from bank reserve accounts to guide this "effective" rate toward their desired "target" in accordance with their "dual mandate" of maximizing employment while maintaining price stability.

For much of the postwar period, monetary policy was guided by an imagined trade-off between inflation and unemployment. The origin of this approach was a paper by economist A. W. Phillips that observed a negative historical correlation between unemployment and wage rates in the United Kingdom.[140] The general observation makes intuitive sense: when unemployment is low, workers can bargain for higher wages. Conversely, when unemployment is high, employed workers are disciplined by the threat of joblessness.[141] Phillips notes, however, that his statistical evidence supports this hypothesis "except in or immediately after those years in which there is a sufficiently rapid rise in import prices to offset the tendency for increasing productivity to reduce the cost of living."[142]

Two years later, Paul Samuelson and Robert Solow published a paper that drew a "Phillips curve" illustrating the "menu of choice between different degrees of unemployment and price stability."[143] Before the onset of stagflation, postwar macroeconomic policy was guided by this policy paradigm. The boom-bust oscillations of the business cycle could be smoothed with the proper monetary and fiscal policy: raise interest rates to cool economic activity and lower interest rates to stimulate economic activity as circumstances warrant. Monetarists decried this arbitrary and capricious governmental discretion over the free market. Friedman's alternative was to enforce a fixed rate of growth in the money supply, thereby removing discretion from Federal Reserve policymaking. In an address to the American Economic Association, Harry Johnson explained that "the monetarist counter-revolution has ultimately been successful because it has encountered a policy problem—inflation—for which the prevailing Keynesian orthodoxy has been able to prescribe only policies of proven or presumptive incompetence."[144] Despite their technical incommensurability, these theories, as Michel Foucault keenly observed at the time, all shared Keynesianism as their "main doctrinal adversary."[145] Rising inflation and unemployment presented a problem that the Phillips curve paradigm was unable to address. Only monetarists seemed to have an answer.

Volcker's eponymous "shock" came on October 6, 1979, when the Fed announced a new policy regime of targeting the total level of bank reserves rather than interest rates. This was seen as a victory for the monetarist elements within the Federal Reserve that sought to institute a version of Milton Friedman's "constant growth in the money stock" as a cardinal rule for monetary policy. Although there were several Fed governors who were ardent and avowed monetarists, monetarism was not the median position of the board. Volcker believed breaking inflation required inducing a severe recession via interest rate increases. However, as William Greider explains, this policy shift was more about providing political cover for tightening interest rates beyond what the Fed thought was politically palatable than a genuine ideological conversion.[146] The "reluctant monetarism" of Volcker was ultimately a commitment to the basic monetary policy framework of the postwar period.

However, this policy change had almost no effect on the rate of credit growth because market participants could not decipher what the change meant for the future path of interest rates. The Fed's long-sought-after goal of a decline in credit was not achieved until President Carter invoked the Credit Control Act on March 14, 1980. Carter ordered the Fed to "impose new restraints on the growth of credit on a limited and carefully targeted basis." Accordingly, the Fed introduced a series of enhanced deposit requirements on certain kinds of loans. The resulting contraction in credit growth finally tipped the economy into a recession that lasted the first half of 1980.[147] After briefly recovering in the second half of the year as interest rates sharply fell, the economy again entered a severe recession lasting officially from July 1981 to November 1982. Job losses were concentrated in primary goods-producing industries such as manufacturing, mining, and residential construction. Steel production centers in the upper Midwest like Gary, Indiana, Bethlehem, Pennsylvania, and Youngstown, Ohio, were hit especially hard.

Like oil, interest is an input into nearly every aspect of the American economy. Higher interest rates, like higher oil prices, manifest both as direct costs borne by consumers (e.g., retail gasoline purchases and mortgage interest payments) and as indirect costs passed through from producers. A BLS report explains that "the advance [in the CPI] in 1980, was like that in 1979, due primarily to the housing and transportation components, which accounted for almost three-fourths of the increase in the CPI."[148] In particular, the "shelter" subcomponent of the Housing category rose in lockstep with increases in the federal funds rate. The prime rate tripled from 6.25 percent in March 1977 to 20 percent in April 1980, and the thirty-year fixed-rate mortgage average increased from 8.85 percent in 1977 to 13.75 percent in 1980.[149] In 1980, the "Financing, taxes, and insurance" subcomponent comprised roughly 11 percent of the entire CPI, and the price index for this category was rising at roughly a 20 percent annualized rate. Without mortgage interest, the BLS computed that the CPI increase would have only been 7.7 percent in 1981.[150] Exactly like oil and housing, a higher price for credit did not reduce demand. Rather, as Albert Wojnilower argued, "cyclically significant . . . reductions in credit and aggregate demand occur only when there is an interruption in the supply of credit—a 'credit crunch.'"[151] Unlike oil and housing, however, these price increases were the direct result of Fed policy.

In effect, the Fed was chasing its own tail. As a BLS report notes: "Interest rates aggravated inflation in that mortgage interest rates at or near record-high levels served to raise the reported inflation rate for the CPI; in addition, soaring financing costs were sometimes passed through to buyers in increased prices charged by businesses trying to protect their profits or to minimize their losses."[152] In January 1983, the BLS changed the calculation of the "shelter" subcomponent. Previously, it included house prices, mortgage interest rates, property taxes, insurance, and maintenance in the computation of housing costs. The new methodology relied on a "rental equivalence approach" that focused solely on the cost of shelter, removing the investment metrics from the housing component of the index.[153]

The stated rationale for the change was the difficulty in "obtaining reliable data on these components." In particular, new financial products such as floating rate mortgages are "impossible to use [in] computing the CPI which assumes a long-term mortgage at fixed interest rates." The house prices used to compute the CPI were derived solely from sales of Federal Housing Administration–insured mortgages. The authors note that "this data base represents a small and specialized segment of the housing market and presents BLS with increasingly serious estimation problems."[154] This technical change had an immediate impact on the CPI. Whereas the previous methodology incorporated the dramatic increase in both house prices and interest rates, exempting these subcomponents from the calculation immediately "reduced" inflation by two percentage points.[155] The five experimental indices under consideration by the BLS ranged wildly in their representations of "inflation" and thus the popular and political response. However, a BLS report reassures the reader that "decisions about CPI measurement are carefully insulated from politics."[156]

The exploding deficit contradicted Reagan's own confident pronouncement that "we know now that inflation results from all that deficit."[157] Instead, in Dick Cheney's words, "Reagan proved deficits don't matter."[158] Meanwhile, economists David Romer and Christina Romer argued that "the public has only a limited understanding of the links between deficit spending and inflation. The harms of reduced deficits, such as higher taxes, reduced government employment, and higher prices of subsidized goods are readily apparent and thus likely to be well understood. But as Romer and Romer argue, the benefit of reduced deficits—namely, lower inflation—is not as clearly linked to fiscal policy, and thus may be systematically underestimated."[159] Therefore, "in order to reduce monetary policy mistakes," control of monetary policy should be given over to specialists insulated from political concerns.[160]

Combined with Volcker's unprecedented monetary tightening, interest payments on federal debt as a share of GDP increased by two full percentage points. This increase was roughly equivalent to the entire agricultural sector of the American economy. The Volcker shock precipitated a massive wealth transfer to the financial sector and distorted investment incentives toward financial channels.[161] In a world of maximizing return, few real investment opportunities could compete with treasury bills yielding 15 percent.[162]

The Fed recreated the same dynamic in the credit markets as the oil shocks had created in the energy and transportation markets: rising prices (interest rates) collided with government price regulations (statutory ceilings). These regulations likewise became the target for popular dissatisfaction with the government's response to inflation. "Financial deregulation," like oil decontrol, appeared to policymakers as a way out of the impasse. The Depository Institutions Act of 1980 phased out interest rate caps on deposit accounts and subjected all deposit-accepting financial institutions to Federal Reserve oversight and reserve requirements. Once again, the political response was to remove the visible state structure from financial markets.

The Garn-St. Germain Act of 1982 deregulated savings and loan associations and permitted the issuance of "alternative" mortgages, such as adjustable-rate and interest-only mortgages. As the law described it, "alternative mortgage transactions are essential to the provision of an adequate supply of credit secured by residential property necessary to meet the demand expected during the 1980's."[163] This burst of deregulation was immediately followed by the savings and loan crisis that would smolder for the remainder of the decade and cost taxpayers nearly $200 billion to bail out and wind down failing thrifts. The sleepy world of "3-6-3" banking (borrow money at 3 percent, lend money at 6 percent, and tee off at 3:00 P.M.) was transformed into the frenetic world of slick dealmaking as chronicled in works such as *The Bonfire of the Vanities*, *Wall Street*, *The Art of the Deal*, *American Psycho*, *Barbarians at the Gate*, and *Liar's Poker*.[164] Banking was no longer a safe utility but a high-flying profit center with the potential for astronomical rewards and devastating crashes.

Financial deregulation produced a parallel financial system beyond the existing regulated banking system. This "shadow banking system" provides bank-like functions such as maturity, liquidity, and credit transformation without access to either regulated deposits or central bank guarantees.¹⁶⁵ Repurchase agreements were one such financial innovation that evolved into a cornerstone of the shadow banking system. A repurchase agreement (or "repo") is akin to a short-term secured loan in which one party lends another money for some period of time with a promise to repay with interest. The security used to collateralize this loan is "repurchased" after some period of time. Collateral for these transactions are typically Treasury or agency securities that the lender holds for the duration of the loan in case of borrower default. From 1971 onward, they grew rapidly as a result of higher interest rates, an expanded pool of available collateral, and technological innovations facilitating clearing and settlement.

Repurchase agreements also became a popular way for independent broker-dealers to fund their assets. In 1982, Drysdale Securities and Lombard-Wall, both such entities, collapsed. Although they had a small amount of capital, they were able to amass huge positions through the practice of "rehypothecation" in which the same collateral can be used to secure multiple different repo transactions. This structure lends itself toward cascading failures in case of strain somewhere along these collateral chains.¹⁶⁶ The uncertainty paralyzed repo markets until a larger firm could be found to guarantee their liabilities. This prompted the development of a "tri-party" repo market structure—foreshadowing the birth of "too big to fail"—in which a third party, typically a large investment bank, oversees and guarantees the transaction akin to a futures exchange.¹⁶⁷

By removing price caps and subsidizing finance, the state avoided intentionally and overtly revaluing claims that could no longer be redeemed in accordance with citizens' expectations, owing to events such as commodity embargoes or abrupt demographic shifts. Replacing public provision with a "democracy of credit" simultaneously neutralized political conflict and radically reshaped the Keynesian welfare state around conservative morality.¹⁶⁸ The resulting explosion in financial assets marks the resulting reach and intensity of financial relationships. Novel financial practices like interest rate swaps, credit default swaps, FX futures, bond futures, and other examples of "financial innovation" arose in response to these dislocations and resulting demands. By 1982, many of the major ingredients for the 2008 financial crisis—dealer books funded on repo, mortgage-backed securities, mark-to-market accounting, money market mutual funds, GSEs, credit default swaps, and cross-jurisdictional regulatory arbitrage—were in place.[169] Each of these financial innovations was a component of the overall political response to the crisis of inflation.

In the oil market, the response was to remove visible state regulations on price and to massively increase dependence on oil imports. Now all households and businesses were exposed to a global price of oil that the state can no longer regulate. The state must ensure the constant availability of oil imports to bridge the gap between demand and domestic production. Likewise, the response to an unprecedented demand for housing was to expand state support for the housing finance market and allow the creation of new mortgage products to encourage lending to marginal borrowers. In the money market, the response was to remove interest rate caps and other regulations on credit, enabling the development of the shadow banking system.[170] As a result, households, corporations, and governments were exposed to new risks in need of new financial solutions. This means that individual households, firms, and states themselves are increasingly subject to global market forces. "Freeing" the oil, housing, and financial markets from state regulation does not create the happy world of market equilibrium described in economics textbooks. Rather, it generates the depoliticized rule of *finance*. Financialization, therefore, is not simply a matter of "more" money but a fundamental change in the structure of social provision, inserting money and financial relationships into domains that were previously managed politically.

The political response to price increases was to depoliticize the state's visible role in shaping distribution by removing overt price regulations. Rather than forging a new distributive compromise reflecting prevailing conditions (e.g., Carter's various exhortations for conservation and austerity), the state increasingly relied on "the market" to make the necessary trade-offs under the cover of an impartial and automatic mechanism. The state response in each case was to replace a negotiated political settlement encoding some modest standard of collective interest with the depoliticized rule of market forces. The state structured financial markets with certain goals in mind, but these choices generated a number of unintended consequences. The result was not the market utopia neoliberals theorized, but subjection to financial motives, financial interests, and financial imperatives. The cumulative effect was the replacement of the state as the primary conductor of investment—as it had been under embedded liberalism—with financial markets. Under embedded liberalism, the provision of certain goods was "decommodified." This did not mean that they were produced outside of capitalist production but that, to some minimal degree, they were distributed on a basis beyond profit maximization. "Decontrol," "deregulation," and "liberalization" replaced this modest political buffer with the depoliticized rule of finance.

DISTRIBUTIVE CONFLICT AND FINANCIALIZATION

The arc of inflation during the critical period from 1970 to 1985 bears little resemblance to neoliberalism's theoretical predictions: money, credit, and deficits ballooned, while inflation finally eased. Far from symptomatizing a congenital pathology of embedded liberalism, inflation exposed compounding crises propagating through politically constructed markets. The political response to these disruptions was to replace a preexisting political structure with the depoliticized rule of finance, which is nowhere theorized in the neoliberal canon. The combined forces of capital and conservatism were able to exploit this conjuncture, but their political arguments fail as empirical explanations of this transformation despite their use as justifications for tax cuts, privatization, deregulation, and austerity. Neoliberals achieved their goal of dismantling embedded liberalism and replacing democracy with markets and morality, but the intellectual apparatus abetting this transformation does not explain either the antecedent crisis or the totality of the state response. Although there can be no doubt about the existence of an organized political project to restore class power that capitalized on the opportunity, this project did not succeed on its own terms.[171]

As the principal antecedent to the neoliberal turn, the inflation of the 1970s symptomatized neither a terminally declining rate of profit nor fatal violations of recently discovered laws of economics.[172] Rather, "inflation" was a composite phenomenon defined by intersecting and compounding disruptions to the embedded liberal growth regime. The crisis of inflation was thus not an economic crisis of "late capitalism" or "big government" but a political crisis of postwar liberalism. The growth regime secured by cheap oil, cheap suburban housing, and a tightly regulated financial system, which kept a tenuous lid on a range of social conflicts, could not be sustained indefinitely.[173] Inflation marked the limits of this regime. The nearly spontaneous political response to inflation was to deregulate finance and increase public subsidies for financial risk-taking in an effort to contain the resulting conflicts over newly scarce social resources. Financialization was not enacted out of an ideological commitment to "free markets" but as a desperate and pragmatic response to a deteriorating political condition.

Linking inflation to financialization requires abandoning the monetarist frame that dominates existing accounts. Inflation was not caused by "too much money," and financialization did not resolve inflation by opening the floodgates of newly mobile international capital. Instead, inflation was the monetary manifestation of the breakdown of the postwar growth regime. With fewer resources to allocate, not everyone could receive their accustomed share at prevailing prices. As a result, the political construction and mediation of distribution become newly salient and politicized: the mild regulatory and redistributive regime is blamed for the disruptions themselves. Carter's pleas to make do with less are exactly what liberalism cannot tolerate: growth and improving material conditions are required to forestall such a political determination of distributive shares. What principle of solidarity could anchor such a project?

Restaging inflation and financialization through the lens of *liberalism* and the depoliticization of distributive conflict allows us to see the specific political conflicts and their financial resolutions hidden behind the monetary veil.[174] The oil, trucking, airline, and credit markets were all deregulated under Carter not as a conscious implementation of a definite theoretical program, but as a desperate attempt to respond to inflation and stave off political challenges from both the right and the left.[175] Reagan, through his rhetorical skill, was able to parlay these specific changes into a larger economic philosophy and governing rationality despite its many internal incoherencies. These reforms did not create the perfect competitive market order (of efficiency and equilibrium) but the depoliticized rule of *finance* (logic of generating a positive monetary return).

Financialization and a set of new liberal discourses successfully "re-depoliticized" distribution by provisioning new sources of financial supply under the guise of free markets and small government. Financialization relieved a serious political impasse over the newly scarce preconditions of Fordism by opening new avenues for supplementing stagnating real wages. Rising asset prices (e.g., 401[k]s, home prices) and falling consumer prices offset stagnating incomes.[176] Eventually, this phenomenon would be termed as the "wealth effect" of rising financial asset prices and an integral component to Federal Reserve policymaking.[177] New financial products like home equity loans enabled households to transmute these rising asset prices into income and wealth.[178] This set of practices hews to a logic similar to that of growth: a rising tide of financial asset prices lifts some boats without relying on political policies of redistribution, especially through taxation and spending.

Financialization was not the result of an ideological imposition but a nearly spontaneous political reaction to distributive crisis. Accordingly, financialization is not originally an "economic" phenomenon that later infiltrates "politics," but a new chapter in the old story of liberal depoliticization. However, the consequences of financialization for liberalism will be invisible from inherited schemas focusing on the consequences of financialization for "the economy" or "capitalism." From this perspective, inflation marks less of a crisis of accumulation within capitalism than a crisis of distribution within liberalism. The growth imperative arises not only from demands of capital but also from requirements for maintaining a liberal political order.

When embedded liberalism was threatened by intersecting and compounding crises in the 1970s, the state was blamed for its purported disrespect of these laws. By casting the problem in terms of implementing the "correct" policymaking orthodoxy, the problem of distributive conflict is never disclosed despite the manifest failures of monetarism as both explanation and policymaking paradigm. The alternative would have been to address the necessary conditions for the sustainability of the prevailing liberal order and to openly manage the crises politically. Recast in terms of liberalism, inflation marked the breakdown of the incumbent regime of distributive depoliticization ("Fordism") and the reemergence of distributive conflict ("inflation"). Explanations of neoliberalism as the implementation of a theoretical orthodoxy that successfully tamed inflation remain blinkered by discourses of liberal depoliticization. Rather than acquiescing, explanation of neoliberalism must center distributive conflict and new techniques of depoliticization that arise in response to the crisis of inflation.

* * *

In 1978, a young professor of history at West Georgia College was elected to Congress. Dr. Newton Gingrich had campaigned primarily on a platform of lower taxes, capitalizing on the nationwide momentum toward tax cuts following the passage of Proposition 13 in California in June.[179] Gingrich, one of the first Republicans elected in the South since Reconstruction, combined neoliberal policy with a fervor for naked power politics. For Gingrich, politics is not about ideology, compromise, or the common good. Rather, politics is a pitched battle for one's private interest waged against the forces of equality, inclusion, and redistribution.[180] Political ideology is a weapon to be wielded like a mace on a battlefield. Combatants must be strategic, flexible, opportunistic, ruthless, and, above all, partisan. Whereas Reagan rose above the fray with an expansive and uplifting vision of American renewal, Gingrich descended into the trenches. For politicians like Gingrich, there is no contradiction, much less bad conscience, in railing against the inflationary consequences of public deficits on the campaign trail and then defending public deficits while in office. Politics is about power and survival, not principle.

In a speech to a group of College Republicans at a Holiday Inn in Atlanta, Gingrich defined politics as "a war for power." Two years earlier in a lecture to a group of college students at the Collège de France in Paris, Michel Foucault considered whether politics could be defined as "the continuation of war by other means."[181]

3

THE FINANCIALIZATION OF LIBERALISM

Politics is in principle superior to the power of money, but in practice it has become its bondsman.

—Karl Marx

My true adversary has no name, no face, no party. He will never stand for election and will never be elected. Despite all this, he is in charge. My enemy is the world of finance.

—Francois Hollande

As an intentional political program, neoliberalism presents itself as handing political processes over to "the market" as an impartial, efficient, and freedom-maximizing mechanism. However, as the previous chapter demonstrated, neither the theories of Milton Friedman nor the policies of Ronald Reagan straightforwardly explain the world they helped bring into being. The political response to inflation was to depoliticize the state's role in structuring distribution in key markets by abdicating to finance. For this reason, grounding an account of neoliberalism on the political ideology of avowed neoliberals can only go so far.[1]

Nor, too, can we simply revisit and revise our canonical liberals from chapter 1 in light of financialization. Attempting to understand the problem of distributive conflict and the powers unleashed by liberal depoliticization from the standpoint of orthodox liberal theory would look in the wrong way in the wrong places for the wrong things—liberalism has no organ for perceiving, much less comprehending, the depoliticized social powers on which it is premised.[2] Michael Walzer, as our representative contemporary liberal, freely admits that "liberal theorists literally [do] not 'see' individual wealth and corporate power as social forces."[3] Liberal theory, by extension, cannot "see" the powers governing distributive conflict in liberal orders. Instead, this domain is shielded by a quasi-scientific discourse, ensuring no reasonable objection to "the free market" can be levied.

Where finance appears at all in orthodox economics, it is explained as a neutral veil between production and consumption and savings and investment. Monetary variables are presumed not to influence "real" variables over the long run and thus are not relevant factors in economic modeling.[4] Given the centrality of finance to actual economic life, this is a surprising omission. Michel Aglietta and André Orléan argue that this peculiar move belies money as the locus where a number of central liberal fictions converge. Orthodox economics wants to purify their models of what money would otherwise bring into social analysis: society, conflict, violence, value, and other inconvenient aspects of actual social experience.[5] Consequently, most liberal political and economic thought works in the domain of "ideal theory," where inconvenient truths about actual political and economic life are dismissed as irrelevant detail.[6] Such theories presume away the unfreedom and coercion inherent in money as a depoliticized social power. But monetary relations, as power relations, are ubiquitous.

Although critical theorists have explored how social powers like race, gender, and sexuality operate through a complex network of discursive and other practices, rationalities, and institutional structures, "capital" is still commonly theorized as belonging to an autonomous domain of "the economy," obeying timeless and universal laws. David Harvey's use of the hydrological cycle as a "template for depicting how capital works" exemplifies this tendency.⁷ At the same time, orthodox economics casts finance as a process of channeling "savings" into "investment." Seeing the significance of finance in organizing society requires a critical perspective attuned to the social powers liberalism disavows yet presupposes. A theory of finance cannot be passively imported from elsewhere. The objective is to explain how finance infiltrates and redirects liberal orders without presuming the veracity of various depoliticizing discourses, themselves inseparable from the transformation being studied.

* * *

In the late 1970s, while Jimmy Carter struggled against inflation in the United States, Michel Foucault delivered a series of lectures at the Collège de France. In these lectures, Foucault offered the provisional hypothesis that the ongoing crisis in the Euro-Atlantic world marked not a crisis of *capitalism*, but a crisis of *liberalism*. Looming on the horizon, Foucault saw a "new programming of liberal governmentality" led by the "American neo-liberals" who seek to project the "formal principles of a market economy" into a "general art of government."⁸ Foucault's lectures provide an important early window into the emerging political rationality of neoliberalism.⁹ Foucault emphasizes that his subject is "the art of governing" and not "real governmental practice." The latter kind of study, he notes, would include "determining the particular situations [government] deals with, the problems raised, the tactics chosen, the instruments employed, forged, or remodeled."¹⁰

I turn to the work of Michel Foucault for an approach to theorizing liberalism and finance outside of inherited schemas. Foucault centers the creative discontinuity between discourses and practices, forms of power beyond the state, and a critical method for analyzing reified social artifacts. Foucault's account of modern power—decentralized and operating through networks, practices, and rationalities—is enormously helpful in understanding the political force of finance. Notwithstanding Foucault's circumscription of his own purposes, a Foucauldian-inflected theory of liberalism and finance can be developed. Foucault's analytic grid helps identify the channels through which finance grabs hold of liberal subjects and polities in a way that exceeds commodification or monetization.[11]

Foucault interrogates seemingly natural fixtures of the social landscape to reveal their contingency and historical specificity and, thus, to disrupt the givenness of the present. He reveals formations such as madness, sexuality, and psychiatry as forming from and governing through a "knowledge-power" apparatus that takes shape within the histories he traces. These new formations cannot be reduced to concern with economic profitability yet generate a certain "political profit" or "economic utility" that explains their ascendance or prominence at a specific time.[12] If we can explain this profit and utility, then, Foucault argues, "we can understand how these mechanisms actually and eventually became part of the whole."[13]

My approach is to develop a similar analysis of finance, building on the work of Daniel Defert, Francois Ewald, and Thomas Biebricher.[14] From this Foucauldian perspective, finance is neither "fictitious capital" nor "the group of institutions in the economy that help to match one person's saving with another person's investment," but an interlocking network of techniques for generating monetary return.[15] From this perspective, financialization is not simply an injection of more money or financial institutions into an autonomous domain of "the economy" or "capitalism," but a fundamental transformation in the powers governing liberal orders.

Although neoliberalism was one of Foucault's primary subjects in *The Birth of Biopolitics* lecture series, his project was not explaining how neoliberalism comes to dominate—such a thing would have been impossible in 1979. Thus, what follows connects the dots with the benefit of hindsight, taking the crisis of liberalism in the 1970s and the subsequent deployment of neoliberalism as fixed points. Foucault provides an approach rather than a scripture, grounding a denaturalizing critique of finance in a theorization of liberalism that far exceeds the state. The theoretical account of the financialization of liberalism serves as a schema and vocabulary for the subsequent case studies.[16] The objective is not to "complete" a Foucauldian genealogy of neoliberalism but, rather, to develop and mobilize his analytic framework for appreciating the specific transformations that financialization brings about in liberal orders.

By combining the problematic of distributive conflict developed in chapter 1 with a Foucauldian-inflected retheorization of finance and liberalism, this chapter explains neoliberalism as the compounding and cumulative consequence of depoliticizing distributive conflict through finance. I demonstrate how finance operates as a form of social power that induces neoliberalism without straightforwardly instantiating or implementing neoliberal ideology. As a depoliticizing response to distributive conflict, finance infiltrates and redirects the existing forms of power at work in liberal orders. Finance enters almost invisibly by promising to supplement growth, distract from distributive conflict, and restore the status quo. Once inside, however, finance reorients everything it touches around financial market imperatives and the imperative of generating monetary return. Finance transforms not only "politics" or "the economy" but the entire ensemble of powers at work in modernity.

THEORIZING LIBERALISM AND FINANCE

For Foucault, liberalism and neoliberalism are neither utopian philosophies nor ideological correlates of the capitalist mode of production. Rather, they are eras in the "history of governmentality."[17] As a form of governmentality, which we will define in more detail, liberalism is not the walled world of Walzer, featuring relatively autonomous domains of "politics" and "the economy." Rather, liberalism encompasses these divisions, formulates their relation to each other (the economy "limits" the state), and is structured by a complex array of powers beyond the sovereign power of the state. The concept of "governmentality" is oriented toward the totality of governmental forces at work in a specific historical conjuncture.

Theorizing liberalism as a form of governmentality provides a framework for relating discourses and forms of social power without presuming that the former straightforwardly explains the latter. Unlike a positivist or Marxist interpretation, official discourses are neither transparent descriptions of governmental practice nor ideological mystifications. Rather, they are the system of rules and norms for justifying, ordering, and rationalizing the operation of power within a particular governmental regime. From this perspective, liberal discourses rationalize and legitimize liberal government but do not straightforwardly describe it. Even when a state acts in accordance with a stated orthodoxy, this is never a comprehensive statement of governmental practice or operative forms of power.

For Foucault, there is neither base nor superstructure nor autonomous spheres. Rather, Foucault argues, "Politics and the economy are not things that exist, or errors, or illusions, or ideologies. They are things that do not exist and yet which are inscribed in reality and fall under a regime of truth dividing the true and the false."[18] Our customary liberal divisions, both in theory and in practice, are contingent solutions to historical circumstance rather than manifestations of some deeper transcendental reality. Foucault's theorization of liberalism as governmentality is thus uniquely attuned to both the discontinuity between official liberal discourses and the operation of liberal government, drawing attention to the many forms of social power irrigating liberal orders and the many ways in which these social powers do not accord with the contentions of orthodox theory.[19]

Foucault's challenge to the established theoretical order is perhaps most memorably summarized by his provocation that "what we need, however, is a political philosophy that isn't erected around the problem of sovereignty. . . . We need to cut off the King's head: in political theory that has still to be done."[20] Foucault's lectures at the Collège de France in the late 1970s can be read as a response to his own provocation. The vision of power as the Hobbesian leviathan repressing and constraining its subjects is inapt to modernity, especially late modernity, where power vastly exceeds the coercive power of the state. Liberal theory, however, remains oriented around the juridical edifice of sovereignty and the corresponding problematics of law, rights, and legitimacy. Foucault demonstrates that this picture is radically incomplete. The social regulation of madness, sexuality, and criminality, to take Foucault's own examples, is achieved largely without sovereign dictate. Focus on sovereign power alone (i.e., "the king") will miss the other forms of power at work. Foucault's inescapable insight is that power in modern societies is not only the hierarchical, repressive, and rule-bound application of coercive state power but also dispersed, creative, and capillary.

Through his lecture series, Foucault demarcates three forms in the history of governmentality—*raison d'etat*, liberalism, and neoliberalism—identified by new discourses and forms of power that arise within a preexisting regime. Governmentality is not a unified totality or the instantiation of a theoretical orthodoxy, but a multitude of intersecting, complimentary, but potentially also conflicting practices, tactics, knowledges, and forms of social power.[21] Foucault's argument is not that these novel formations simply replace earlier forms but rather "what above all changes is the dominant characteristic, or more exactly, the system of correlation" among the various mechanisms.[22] New technologies and rationalities arise in response to the limitations of the previous ensemble but do not replace, succeed, or abolish them. Instead, they infiltrate, redirect, and reprogram. We are not looking for a Hegelian sublation of contradictions or superstructural collapse but initially subtle alterations that compound into entirely novel forms.

Accordingly, Foucault focuses on critical junctures in this history of governmentality where new forms of power emerge to "release" governmentality from a "blocked situation."[23] These situations are not "contradictions" but conjunctures in which existing power relations de-cohere. In one such instance, the new ensemble of "liberalism" is born from the solution to the problem of scarcity within the earlier regime of *raison d'Etat*, corresponding to the era of European absolutism. While seventeenth-century political economy was dominated by the juridical and disciplinary system of price controls, *police des graines*, export limitations, and other similar regulations, eighteenth-century political economy marked an effort to "unblock this system" through the self-regulating market.[24] This new formation was built around the "free circulation of grain" because it "was not only a better source of profit, but also a much better mechanism of security against the scourge of scarcity." By "letting things happen"—laissez-faire—and tolerating localized cases of shortage and starvation, the overall phenomenon of "famine" could be made to disappear. Political economy and several new technologies of power emerge as conjoined devices for "unblocking" or "releasing" the governmentality of *raison d'Etat* from this impasse, producing the new configuration known as liberalism.[25]

Accompanying and enabling the transformation of unlimited despotism to "frugal government" are new techniques of power. In *Discipline & Punish*, Foucault presents one such technique, "disciplinary" power, through an examination of a curious dream of Jeremy Bentham. Bentham's panopticon is the perfect diagram of this new form of power that "[induces] in the inmate a state of conscious and permanent visibility that assures the automatic functioning of power."[26] Unlike sovereignty, discipline is "indefinitely generalizable" in that it can "bring the effects of power to the most minute and distant elements."[27] Foucault writes, "discipline had to solve a number of problems for which the old economy of power was not sufficiently equipped."[28] Against the backdrop of the juridical system of formal rights arose new "tiny, everyday, physical mechanisms" of power capable of extending and multiplying its operation into new domains and with a greater economy. The desired behavior is induced without requiring overt or costly coercive measures. These technologies include "hierarchical surveillance, continuous registration, perpetual assessment and classification" that all serve to shape behavior of people around a given norm and are captured under the heading of "disciplinary power" that defies the sovereign model of the state enforcing its dictates under pain of death.[29] Sovereign power was unsuited to this task: the complex political economy emerging in the eighteenth century was incompatible with absolutism or a police state.[30] The construction of an urban proletariat required fundamentally new technologies of power.

The logic of disciplinary power is to bring its effects to maximum intensity and be felt as widely as possible, and to increase docility of the population being managed, all without directly touching or threatening subjects in the way of sovereign power.[31] These tactics enable larger agglomerations of people to be managed at relatively low costs and also incorporate the subject itself into the task of enforcement. A well-disciplined subject is one who acts in accord with norms that have been deeply internalized, thus without need of external policing. The Industrial Revolution would have been impossible without the development of these disciplinary techniques capable of transforming the peasant into factory worker. These mechanisms of continuous and permanent surveillance, again internalized, enable the extraction of "time and labor, rather than commodities and wealth, from bodies."[32] Disciplinary power therefore takes the form of a "tightly meshed grid of material coercions rather than the physical existence of a sovereign, and it therefore defined a new economy of power based upon the principle that there had to be an increase both in the subjugated forces and in the force and efficacy of that which subjugated them."[33] The rise of disciplinary power was an essential development enabling the transition to an industrial economy.

At the end of the eighteenth century, there is a "second adjustment; the mechanisms [of power] are adjusted to the phenomena of population, to the biological . . . processes of human masses."[34] This form of power—"biopower"—targets "population" as a novel field of governmental action. Population is not an assemblage of juridical subjects of right or of equal citizens, but a particular way of constituting individuals as groups defined by statistical regularities, such as in public health statistics or actuarial tables. Initially, biopower refers to the tactics and methods through which the attributes of populations, such as birth rate, incidence of disease, or life expectancy, can be altered. The state acts on the population rather than on juridical subjects through avenues like public health and sanitation. Unlike discipline, biopower manages particular phenomena, such as famine or disease outbreaks, within a field of "probable events" by acting on the milieu rather than on the individual.[35] Biopower takes hold of a population that has already been disciplined at the individual level, enabling a more precise and comprehensive regulation. Discipline conducts subjects in their specificity; biopower conducts subjects in their generality. Whereas discipline makes sure that nothing escapes, biopower lets things happen.

Foucault sees an essential similarity between the establishment of the market as a site of veridiction of governmental practice and the analogous transformations of psychiatry, punishment, and sexuality from "jurisdiction" to "veridiction." These "regimes of veridiction" are not truths, errors, or ideologies but "the set of rules enabling one to establish which statements in a given discourse can be described as true and false" in a domain that is neither true nor false.[36] These regimes of veridiction are "level[s] of reality and field[s] of intervention for government" against which it can evaluate the efficiency and efficacy of its actions.[37] Government must respect and govern in accordance with the nature posited in and through these regimes. Thus, Foucault argues, these regimes are "lateral" to the art of governing: they are not vehicles through which governmental aims are achieved directly, but a reality principle that evaluates whether a given action is correct or incorrect. The practices of government, therefore, require and are intimately bound to the particular knowledges and rationalities that demarcate the field of necessary and appropriate intervention.

Government "is only to intervene when it sees that something is not happening according to the general mechanics of behavior, exchange, and economic life."[38] This "self limitation of governmental reason," Foucault argues, "is broadly what is called 'liberalism.'"[39]

Although the 1978–1979 lecture series is titled *The Birth of Biopolitics*, the majority of the lectures are devoted to "the present crisis of liberalism," referring to the interlinked crises of inflation and the welfare state and the response of the German ordoliberals and the American neoliberals to this crisis.[40] From these perspectives, Keynesian interventionism generated a "crisis of liberalism" manifest as these "re-evaluations, re-appraisals, and new projects in the art of government."[41] This crisis of liberalism is not "just the pure and simple or direct projection of these crises of capitalism into the political sphere." Rather, it is a "crisis of the general apparatus (*dispositif*) of governmentality."[42] Foucault frames his subsequent project as clarifying "the way in which the crisis of the apparatus of governmentality is currently experienced, lived, practiced, and formulated."[43] Foucault does not give us an *explanation* of neoliberalism (in the same way he disavows that his project in the earlier lectures is presenting a comprehensive history of liberalism from the eighteenth century to the present), but rather charts the political rationality of an emerging variant of liberal governmentality. With the benefit of hindsight, we can push the analytic further.

Foucault argues that "American neo-liberalism [involves] the generalization of the economic form of the market. It involves generalizing it throughout the social body and including the whole of the social system not usually conducted or sanctioned by monetary exchanges."[44] The theory of human capital, and particularly the work of Chicago economist Gary Becker, is a particularly significant and interesting development.[45] All human conduct can now be properly understood in terms of market conduct. Intimate questions of marriage and reproduction can be analyzed and explained in terms of human capital maximization. "The market" is no longer that of traditional liberal economic models, but now of entrepreneurial enterprise-units engaged in a competitive struggle for maximization.[46] The emphasis shifts from exchange to production. Neoliberal discourses of the market are extended as a "grid of decipherment" into new domains and anchor "a permanent political criticism of political and governmental action." Unlike liberal political economy that sought to construct the market as a domain free from governmental influence, the neoliberal market is constructed as "a sort of permanent economic tribunal confronting government."[47] Rather than the state achieving its aims through the market, all state actions are now evaluated in market terms.

Neoliberalism, like other regimes Foucault studies, is not "only" discursive construct. Rather, these regimes are correlated with a definite set of practices including "discourses, institutions, architectural forms, regulatory decisions, laws, administrative measures, scientific statements, philosophical, moral and philanthropic propositions—in short, the said as much as the unsaid."[48] Apparatuses develop and respond to some "urgent need" and can produce "entirely unforeseen [effects] which had nothing to do with any kind of strategic ruse on the part of some meta- or trans-historical subject conceiving and willing it."[49] These forms "coupl[e] a set of practices and a regime of truth [forms] an apparatus (*dispositif*) of knowledge-power that effectively marks out in reality that which does not exist and legitimately submits it to the division between true and false."[50] What practices accompany this new regime of truth?

Foucault's partner and executor of his estate, Daniel Defert, as well as his assistant at the Collège de France, Francois Ewald, analyze insurance as such a practice. Ewald defines insurance as a "technology of risk" that "is the practice of a certain type of rationality. It has no special field of operations; rather than being defined in terms of its objects, it is a kind of ubiquitous form. It provides a general principle for the objectification of things, people and their relations."[51] The insurance apparatus is "a schema of social rationality and social management" oriented around the protection of wealth.[52] The apparatus of insurance inflects pieces of the social world with a particular set of properties and orders them in a particular manner. Likewise, Defert defines insurance as a "generalizable technology for rationalizing societies."[53] Insurance, understood as both a technology and a rationality, produces the entirely new social ensemble of the "risk society" wherein "societies envisage themselves as a vast system of insurance, and by overtly adopting insurance's forms they suppose that they are thus conforming to their own nature."[54] Insurance, as a particular technology for ordering and arranging the social world, deploys a number of significant political and social transformations. We must understand finance in the same way: what Foucault identifies in a different context as "the techniques, the practices, which give a concrete form to this new political rationality and to this new kind of relationship between the social entity and the individual."[55]

To paraphrase Ewald, "we want to understand the ways in which in a given social context, profitable, useful and necessary uses can be found for [financial] technology." To do this, we must return to the original imperative for distributive depoliticization to explain how finance attaches itself to distributive crisis.

FINANCIAL DEPOLITICIZATION

Distributive crisis marks the breakdown of distributive order. Stalled growth, resource shortages, geopolitical turmoil, natural disasters, and other disruptions threaten the stability and sustainability of the liberal status quo. With the scent of Hobbesian civil war in the air, liberal governments must find a way to soothe the unrest. An absolutist state can direct adjustment costs as it sees fit because there is no pretense of neutrality or consent. The liberal state, however, can neither manage this process of adjustment publicly nor buck its external commitments on which the existing distributive order depends. How does finance resolve such impasses? First, we need to consider the basic structure of finance.

In many financial transactions, a borrower agrees to repay some principal amount with interest according to a predefined payment schedule in which the money owed exceeds the money borrowed, thus yielding a financial gain for the creditor. Finance generally takes the form of a contract that specifies the obligations of the borrower and the recourses of the lender. These financial contracts typically have three components: principal amount, interest rate, and covenants. The principal is the amount of money delivered from the lender to the borrower. The interest rate (percentage of principal) determines the amount that must be paid to the lender in regular installments (usually monthly, quarterly, or semiannually). The interest rate, in turn, is composed of the "risk-free rate" and a credit spread. The risk-free rate is the interest rate paid by borrowers with no risk of default (e.g., the U.S. federal government). A credit spread is the additional amount that risky borrowers pay, determined by their estimated likelihood of default.

Financial contracts are generally collateralized, meaning that the borrower pledges an asset to the lender that can be legally seized by the lender in the event of default or nonpayment.[56] Covenants are a set of required actions and restrictions placed on the borrower by the financial contract. These range from maintaining certain financial ratios (e.g., debt to income) to limits on other financial activity. Violating a covenant might raise the interest rate or the amount of required collateral or precipitate a demand for immediate repayment. In sum, finance contractually obligates the borrower to generate a positive return for the lender under pain of various contractually enumerated penalties. Finance is indifferent to *how* this return is produced. Covenants and collateralization mean the borrower risks expropriation if these obligations are not met. Financial claims therefore take precedence over all other claims in a material, immediate, and tangible way.[57] A financialized entity *must* meet its financial obligations; it *must* think in terms of return on investment; it *must* privilege financial claims over political claims; it *must* account for and conduct itself in terms of a monetary bottom line.[58]

For political entities, financialization imposes a teleology: to become financialized is to become conducted in terms of money and monetary maximization. For a business used to thinking in terms of cash flow, profit, and revenue, these impositions may require increased clerical hygiene, an increased sensitivity to profit and loss, or a privileging of investor demands, but does not require any substantial reorientation in purpose, priorities, or outlook. The extension of finance into new domains, however, transforms goals and internal processes that were not primarily expressed or articulated in monetary terms. Financialization is a form of social power that ensures that the only possible actions are those that increase profits and portfolio values and ensnares an increasing swath of social life.

Moreover, financialization insulates the demands of creditors—and the effects of these demands—from political contestation. Financialization renders political life less and less capable of responding to political demands while it remains cloaked in the husk of the liberal democratic political form it has eviscerated. The ultimate result of this process of financialization is the reprogramming of liberal democratic politics by financial market imperatives: covenants must be upheld, interest payments must be made, the tax base must be grown—not to redistribute wealth or achieve collective goals but to pay off creditors. There is no longer room for non–profit-generating activity. The market logic of maximizing cash flows and portfolio values replaces negotiated political settlements, firmly confining liberal democracies within the bounds of market conduct.

Financial depoliticization can take on several forms: deregulation, subsidies, and direct financial risk-taking. Deregulation is one familiar form of financial depoliticization. A regulation can be understood as a prohibition on some otherwise profitable action or a requirement for some otherwise unprofitable action. Deregulation is the removal of that restriction. However, "freeing" private economic activity from such mandates does not "increase efficiency" or recapture the "deadweight loss" created by the state. Rather, deregulation removes the political bulwark against market forces. By removing its overt role in structuring distribution, the state leaves citizens to the default path of finance and private interest. The repeal of usury laws and interest rate caps discussed in chapter 2 also embodies this logic of depoliticization. These regulations prohibited interest rates above certain thresholds in the name of consumer protection and financial stability.[59] When market interest rates reached these statutory limits, the state was placed itself between borrowers and loans. By removing these financial regulations, the state freed itself from its role in managing and mediating these conflicts. State subsidies are another form of financial depoliticization. In these cases, the state provides a public subsidy for private financial risk-taking. A private lender provides credit to a borrower with some form of state guarantee. Through this state support, demand is met privately without direct state involvement. However, private credit would not be forthcoming without these state guarantees and subsidies.[60]

The state can also assume financial risk directly on its own behalf. From borrowing for public investment to outright financial speculation, the state can directly provision resources through financial risk-taking. In these cases, the state is locked into a financial contract for a period of time. Although politicians come and go, these obligations remain. Again, the logic of financial provision dictates that whatever is borrowed is returned with interest. These deals are only validated if the resulting growth in tax revenue is greater than the interest payments. Both the interest and principal must be diverted from income streams (i.e., taxes). If these deals do not work out as planned, tax revenue earmarked for other public uses must be redirected to meet these financial obligations. The ransom effect of finance ensures that its claims are always prioritized over political claims. The result is transfer from households to the financial system through public distributive bargains.

Through this process of financialization, public provision is replaced with financial imperatives. The logics are importantly distinct. Financial investment is only undertaken on the basis of clearing a certain hurdle rate. Occasionally the demands of finance will align with the logics of public investment, but often they do not. Financial logic dictates that investments generate a positive net present value and/or discounted cash flow. Provision is now a matter of a subject's ability to pay the global market price. Rather than the state provisioning citizens as a matter of right, creditors invest in human capital at the right price. For example, the government did not directly benefit in monetary terms from programs like the Interstate Highway System, Central Valley Project, and Defense Advanced Research Projects Agency (DARPA). The social surplus generated through these massive public projects was shared, however imperfectly, among a wide array of constituents rather than appropriated by private investors.

The saturation of society with the norms and metrics of financializations also recasts citizens as financial subjects beholden to attracting investment in the open market.[61] Competition replaces solidarity: benefits are no longer distributed on the basis of some modicum of public value solidarity but on the basis of financial value maximization. Risks that were previously managed publicly are now privatized: individual retirement accounts replace pensions, school vouchers replace public education, even a national healthcare program requires that individuals purchase insurance on the "exchanges."[62] Consequently, the costs of developing human capital are increasingly devolved to the normative family unit.[63] T. H. Marshall's "social citizenship" entailing state responsibility for promoting the well-being of its citizens is replaced with Friedman's "the social responsibility of business is to increase its profits."[64] However much neoliberals might cheer these developments, financialization is the actual driving mechanism.

NEOLIBERALISM

In response to distributive crisis, the embedded liberal state "re-depoliticizes" conflict through financialization. Social functions previously insulated from "the market" are conscripted in the service of generating monetary surplus under constant threat of expropriation. The neoliberal profit imperative thus replaces the liberal profit motive. Once financialized, the generation of monetary return is no longer a choice. The preexisting liberal regime is reoriented around this financial axis: sovereign power, disciplinary power, and biopower are all redeployed toward this end. Previously they were indexed on the maximization of economic growth. Now they are indexed on the maximization of monetary return. Through this process, political solidarity is replaced with economic competition, and market logics are disseminated to previously insulated corners of human life. To repeat our formula: *finance deploys neoliberalism*. Working through Foucault's analytic grid, this section sketches some of the consequences of the financialization of liberalism.

Sovereignty

A financialized sovereign, like any other entity, must generate money to meet its financial obligations. The financial infiltration of the state and the consequent erosion of sovereignty are familiar themes in international political economy, economic sociology, and critical theory.[65] Finance does not simply eclipse or replace sovereign power, but instead redirects sovereign power for its own purposes.[66] Where tax increases are politically challenging or impossible, expenditures must be reduced. This imperative often manifests as privatizing various state functions such as pensions, prisons, infrastructure, and the military while enacting sweeping cuts to various forms of social provision.[67] A cash-strapped state economizing its core functions will produce novel arrangements and imbrications of sovereign and financial power that are not reducible to either factor alone. The privatization of these core state functions produces a peculiar ensemble of coercive power animated by the impetus to maximize portfolio value.[68] Where the state once regulated usury, it now pays private creditors usurious rates of interest.

The domain of sovereign action thereby becomes firmly constrained by globalized capital. The paradigmatic articulation of these policies is the Washington Consensus program of privatization of public enterprises and functions, liberalization of product and financial markets, and extension of property rights to foreign owners. Thomas Friedman's "electronic herd" of bond and currency traders enforces the strictures of this "golden straitjacket" by buying or selling a country's financial assets in accordance with the country's financial propriety.[69] For countries heavily dependent on foreign creditors, the electronic herd's abrupt withdrawal of funds can precipitate a financial crisis, as experienced in Latin America in 1982 or Southeast Asia in 1998. States have every incentive to restrict their sovereign action to what mobile foreign capital deems acceptable.

Credit rating agencies (CRAs) are a unique product of financialized sovereignty: they are at once sovereign creations and limitations on sovereign authority. CRAs are constituted via state action and are then used to rate sovereign credit, and their rating scales serve as a category in transnational regulation.[70] The need to placate the concerns of CRAs is a key concern in sovereign debt management. Under these conditions, the state must "actively supporting the infrastructure of market finance."[71] To paraphrase Henry Ford, the financialized sovereign can do whatever it wants, so long as it makes money. Financialization does not formally usurp state sovereignty, but bores deeply into its operation to ensure it produces monetary return.

Discipline

In English, the word "finance" arises from "fine" or "paying a penalty."[72] From the Latin *finis* or "end," the etymology of the term suggests a disciplinary origin. Finance similarly infiltrates and reorients nonsovereign or "disciplinary" apparatuses toward portfolio value maximization. Financialized discipline comprises the knowledge, techniques, and mechanisms applied to individual portfolios such as classification, hierarchicalization, inspections, reports, examinations, and audits that combine to ensure financial value appreciation. At the level of the individual, financial discipline manifests as the diverse forms of self-tracking, self-management, and algorithmic governance all aimed at maximizing portfolio value or human capital.[73] As "a good discipline tells you what you must do at every moment," financialized discipline tells you what to do at every moment to increase your portfolio value.[74]

Financial discipline operates as a perpetual and boundless financial Taylorism of the self. These disciplines tell financial subjects when to exercise, when to sleep, what to eat, when to buy a house, who to date, when to have children, and how to spend money. A contributor to *Inc. Magazine* and founder of 1-800-GOT-JUNK? recounts his experience with "running [his] life like a business": "I schedule my working days down to the minute—from the moment I wake up to the moment I go to sleep. This allows me to maximize my time so there's never a second wasted. . . . I wear the same thing everyday. . . . I run my life the same way I run my company: with streamlined systems and processes to guarantee success."[75]

Many personal finance discourses explicitly employ the term "discipline" to refer to the set of practices composing proper financial hygiene. For instance, accounting and tax-preparation software company Quicken defines financial discipline: "Though most people associate discipline with social behaviors, it also applies to how you manage your money. Financial discipline refers to how well you are able to conform your spending and saving to the plans that you have set to achieve your monetary goals."[76] Similarly, *Money Magazine* lists fifty "Personal Finance Habits": "2. Tracking your income and expenses . . . 11. Keeping the money in your wallet to a minimum . . . 22. Properly maintaining your car . . . 36. Avoiding cigarettes . . . 37. Avoiding wasted time clipping coupons you'll never use . . . 43. Negotiating whenever the opportunity presents itself . . . 50. Treating your household like a business."[77] Notably, *Money* encourages readers to avoid cigarettes not because they are unhealthy, but because they are expensive. For every choice facing the financial subject, financial discipline prescribes the proper course of action. In some cases, this requires a particular orientation toward decision-making; in others, it prescribes engaging in speculative financial conduct to maximize their portfolio value.

The financial market perfectly instantiates the diagram and program contained in Bentham's famous panopticon: at every moment, every entity is observing every other, watching healthy entities for signs of deviance and deviant entities for signs of health that will be responded to with financial asset sales or purchases as a nearly instantaneous response. Most large investment banks have equity research departments that are responsible for publishing quarterly reports that scrutinize companies' current activities and estimate their future performance. There are no overt forces or dictates, but "midpoint estimates" and "targets" originating from a stable of analysts.[78] This panoptic power is applied at a distance and with every market participant simultaneously acting as prisoner and prison guard in turn. No matter who operates the panopticon, as Foucault predicts, it produces "homogenous effects of power."[79] It is irrelevant whether the operator is a Middle Eastern sovereign wealth fund, a Dutch pension fund, "Mrs. Watanabe"— the stereotyped Japanese housewife and currency speculator, a Brazilian multinational corporation, or a day trader in Missouri.

All impose the same set of imperatives on themselves and on another in their endless pursuit of portfolio value.

Many corporate managers, and increasingly lower-level employees, are compensated with stock options that incentivize them to attend carefully to their company's share price and lash them to this disciplinary apparatus. Ensuring constant and predictable stock price growth requires proper management of both the company and the market's expectations. A financial journalist writes, "executives of public companies have always strived to live up to investors' expectations, and keeping earnings rising smoothly and predictably has long been seen as the surest way to do that. . . . This is what chief executives and chief financial officers dream of: quarter after quarter after blessed quarter of not disappointing Wall Street."[80] As long as Wall Street is not disappointed, the manager will in turn be rewarded with the ability to exercise their options.

The disciplinary effects of financialization can be seen in a recent offering memorandum for a securitized portfolio of loans issued by Ford Motor's credit arm to Ford dealerships for inventory financing: "Ford Credit electronically monitors dealer performance. . . . If a dealer exhibits adverse payment patterns or trends, appropriate actions are taken such as contacting the dealer, placing the dealer on higher levels of monitoring and review, conducting an on-site vehicle inventory audit, performing a credit review, suspending the dealer's credit line or classifying the dealer as status." Through constant financial surveillance, Ford Credit ensures that dealerships are managing themselves properly. If they are not, they are classified as "status." When a dealer is so classified, Ford Credit will: "demand payment of all or a portion of the related receivables, suspend the dealer's credit lines, place Ford Credit employees or security personnel at the dealership, secure the dealer inventory by holding vehicle keys and documents evidencing ownership, require certified funds for all sold vehicles, initiate legal actions . . . or increase the dealer's floorplan interest rate."[81]

Security

While financialized discipline refers to the techniques applied to the individual subject to maximize their portfolio value, financialized security refers to the set of techniques and knowledge applied at the level of the *population*. By working with probabilities, regularities, and prediction, security works on groupings of subjects already subject to financial discipline.[82] The key innovation of security is the ability to anticipate, tolerate, and accommodate deviance rather than requiring unlimited discipline to avoid or curtail it. Security at once pushes populations toward the desired norm while expecting and accommodating a certain degree of deviation from that norm. Like actuaries determining insurance premiums, financial creditors estimate the likelihood of default and adjust their terms accordingly. The key is aligning (and enforcing) the future in terms of these expectations. As perceived risk increases, so too does the required compensation. Borrowers, therefore, are incentivized to manage and present themselves as a *safe* investment. Security classifies individuals into populations in order to anticipate their financial behavior. Such classifications might include "AAA," "DINK," "Starbucks Customer," "PIIGS," or "high net worth individuals." These techniques are forms of tracking and classification that do not directly arise from law or the state yet are extraordinarily significant in determining a subject's life chances.[83]

The apparatuses of security work on and within the reality of the financialized economy where everything can be represented in terms of risk, return, and correlation. The objective is to accurately estimate the risk that financial subjects will not produce money as they are contractually obligated. Riskier borrowers must prove themselves to be well-behaved financial subjects in order to be rewarded with lower interest rates. The lender is generally ambivalent about the particular grouping so long as it is accurate: whether or not an individual falls into a low- or high-risk category is of no concern so long as the risk of deviance has been accounted for. Every individual composing a mortgage pool, for instance, is expected to behave in a similar enough way such that the financial performance of the overall pool can be precisely quantified ex ante. Measures such as FICO scores, loan-to-value ratios, and debt-to-income ratios enable individual subjects to be placed in actuarial groupings like "prime" or "subprime."

Although not usually framed in these terms, an extensive scholarly literature has charted the effects of actuarial techniques.[84] Credit ratings, as one notable example, both enforce financial discipline on the rated entity *and* enable population-level management and prediction. Here again, Foucault would remind us that "discipline" and "security" do not represent successive or exclusive stages in a grand history of power, but instead are historically specific, and often historically reshaped, tactics and strategies.[85] Credit rating agency Moody's utilizes an exhaustive "scorecard" for classifying debt instruments on the basis of a series of tightly defined metrics with precisely specified parameters indicating health or abnormality.[86] Notably, credit rating agencies are themselves creatures of the state and rely on government statistics to formulate their rankings, ratings, and reports. Other data are generated through inspections and evaluations of the entity's financial statements and organizational practices. These data collected on individual behavior are used to then classify the entity into the appropriate population of financial securities.

The Financialized Subject and Polity

The figure of *Homo economicus* is formed and governed by these modes of social power. The neoliberal iteration of *Homo economicus* is not Adam Smith's economic man with his natural propensity to truck, barter, and exchange.[87] Rather, "he is the man of enterprise and production," a rational, self-interested, utility-maximizer.[88] A subject beholden to these intersecting forms of financial power has no alternative. A competitive pool of human capital constantly striving for value, competitive positioning, credit rating, and investment, this subject is, in Foucault's telling, "an entrepreneur of himself" within a larger grid of an "enterprise society" oriented around competition and production.[89] *Homo economicus* always responds to the world in terms of the grid of the economic. The rational economic man responds rationally to "modifications in the variables of the environment."[90] In this respect, he "accepts reality" and "becomes governmentalizable, that power gets a hold on him to the extent, and only to the extent, that he is a *homo oeconomicus*."[91]

Michel Feher shifts the Foucauldian *Homo economicus* into a financialized register: human capital is something we invest. Accordingly, the financialized subject is highly responsive to market signals, refinancing mortgages when interest rates fall, actively managing 401(k)s, and responding rationally to changes in the tax code—a calculating being interested solely in their portfolio value.[92] The individual surveying their bank balances and monthly expenses, the bond rating agency surveying the state of municipal finances, or financial market actors surveying the market for abnormal pricing all take on a similar form and punish deviant behavior like a clinic, asylum, school, or prison. Indeed, a subject who does not produce portfolio values is likely to be remanded to one or more of these institutions.

The "financial system" operates as an all-encompassing apparatus of social surveillance, normalization, and control for ensuring that the neoliberal *Homo economicus* is engaged in proper financial conduct. Indicators such as stock price, credit score, or gross income measure the propriety of market conduct operating in what Stephen Gill describes as "disciplinary neoliberalism," or a formation that combines "the structural power of capital with 'capillary power' and 'panopticism.'"[93] Financialized discipline operates as such a form of "continuous surveillance" that intervenes at a distance when the subject acts improperly.[94]

Financial markets constantly evaluate the conduct of every financial subject. Individual market participants augment their own portfolio value by making correct judgments about other entities' financial conduct.[95] For the subject of financial power, market conduct is the only possible conduct. The neoliberal incarnation of *Homo economicus* is a juridical subject of rights, a body to which discipline is applied, a member of a population, and a portfolio of human and nonhuman capital. *Homo economicus* is formed at the confluence of financialized sovereignty, financialized discipline, and financialized security. In sum, these diverse forms of power produce a world that, as Neil Fligstein and Adam Goldstein describe, "increasingly orbits around financial markets and their signals."[96]

Once financialized, a liberal polity will act very similarly to a financialized corporation: they will hire the same consulting firms, rely on the same investment banks, and operate according to the same logic of financial maximization. Once public organizations, and above all governments, financialize, they become beholden to the same logic that structures financialized "economic" life. Financialized organizations, like financialized individuals, must generate cash flows (or new investment) sufficient to meet their financial obligations. When brought together, *Homo economicus* forms a "portfolio society" rather than a democracy.[97] Portfolio value appreciation and cash flow generation thus become the only possible political vocabularies, aims, and purposes. Claims by political constituents are subordinated by claims of financial markets. Financial investment, by its very nature, is based on maximizing portfolio value rather than some notion of the public interest.[98] The aim is not simply to generate profit but *return*: a relationship that persists through time.

This chapter has argued that financialization is more than the tendency toward massive expansion of sovereign debt and financial "deregulation" begun in the early 1980s. Rather, financialization marks the realignment of the whole ensemble of social powers comprising liberal orders along a financial axis. Financial discipline manages us from below; financial governmentality manages us from above. We vote for who will develop and control the financialized state. This ensemble of financialized power (depoliticized and absent from liberal discourse) forms neoliberal subjects and publics. Financialization is not a once and for all transformation but rather a generalizable form and dynamic of liberal government.

The following chapters present three case studies of the recent history of the city of Stockton, California, the California Public Employees Retirement System, and the American financial system. These cases chart neither a victory for neoliberal ideas nor the class power of capital. While big banks and other avatars of high finance are doubtlessly in a privileged position vis-à-vis an overstretched pension fund and a struggling mid-sized postindustrial city, the rise of neoliberalism requires a distributive crisis, a collective inability to negotiate a new political compromise, and a fateful turn to finance.

4

GROWTH MACHINE POLITICS

TO INSPIRE A NOBLER CIVIC LIFE, TO FULFILL JUSTICE, TO SERVE THE PEOPLE
—Inscription on Stockton City Hall

Growth politics, in general, seems to militate against class politics.
—Mike Davis

In the years preceding the 2008 financial crisis, an unremarkable office building located at 400 East Main Street in downtown Stockton, California, served as regional headquarters for Washington Mutual, a leading originator and packager of subprime mortgages.[1] Stockton was an epicenter of the subprime mortgage bubble: in 2000, its median home price was $110,000; by 2006, it had nearly quadrupled to $400,000. The subprime housing boom generated windfall revenues for the city in the form of increased sales and property taxes. But as the housing market began to crest, Washington Mutual's business faltered and many of its employees working at 400 East Main Street were laid off. In late 2007, the Stockton City Council acquired 400 East Main Street, with the intention of making the building its new city hall. On September 25, 2008, the government placed Washington Mutual into receivership, resulting in the second-largest corporate bankruptcy in U.S. history (surpassed only by Lehman Brothers, which just one year before led a $125 million pension obligation bond issuance for Stockton).

As the scale of the Great Recession became apparent in 2009, Stockton was named the "Most Miserable City in America" by *Forbes* for leading the nation in foreclosures per capita (nearly 10 percent of the city's housing units were foreclosed on that year). Instead of becoming a new city hall as planned, 400 East Main sat mostly empty for four years; the city could not afford to move its operations into the new building. After missing several bond payments, Wells Fargo foreclosed on the building in May 2012. The following month, Stockton became the largest city to declare bankruptcy in the history of the United States.[2] As a result, Stockton endured deep cuts to public services and public employment; increased its courtship of private capital; became beholden to benchmarks, metrics, and ratings; and reoriented itself around the discourse of entrepreneurialism and governance. Public employment was cut by 40 percent, and public expenditures were cut by 25 percent. In a word, "neoliberalism" came to Stockton.

This case might seem to follow the usual story. Stockton's public servants were snowed by well-heeled Wall Street bankers into financial arrangements they didn't understand and placidly rubber-stamped the recommendations of lawyers, consultants, and experts. The vicissitudes of global capital flows claimed yet another postindustrial city of the American heartland. At the direction of political leaders, austerity and market-promoting policies took the place of public goods. But closer inspection reveals that existing theories cannot account for this case: conservative activists, financiers, lawyers, accountants, bond raters, bond vigilantes, arbitrators, economists, ideologues, business interests, and other similar figures did not push Stockton toward market rationality, market practices, and market discipline.[3] Indeed, the outcome in Stockton was far more severe than any neoliberal could have dreamed or any critic could have feared.

Such characters were present but were not driving Stockton's political decision-making at critical junctures.

Stockton's transformation does not comport with existing accounts of neoliberalism as an elite project or of urban financialization as a reaction to structural changes in American fiscal federalism.[4] To the former, the extent of public retrenchment in Stockton far exceeded the neoliberal prescription, reconfiguring it as a "minimal city" incapable of providing many essential services, rather than the "nightwatchman" ideal of the neoliberal state.[5] To the latter, the timing and specific aims of the financial deals the city entered into were not responses to the decline of Keynesian fiscal federalism[6] or initiated by financial professionals within the city's fiscal policymaking apparatus.[7] Unlike the more well-known cases of Detroit and Youngstown, Stockton did not suffer from de-industrialization and population decline.[8] What then explains Stockton's neoliberal reconfiguration?

Stockton, like other liberal political entities, operates as a "growth machine" where the dominant politically engaged interest groups all share an overriding investment in the city's economic growth.[9] City budgets, in turn, are "bets on future growth" that codify distributive bargains among these constituencies.[10] Every annual budget depends on revenue projections that determine spending capacity for a given year. More projected revenue enables more spending. Projections, forecasts, and other "images of the future" therefore play a crucial political role in determining what political resources are available for which constituencies. However, these groups care about expanding their distributive share, not growth per se. Financial risk-taking, like economic growth, appears to expand distributive shares without impinging on other groups. The same political logic of growth machine politics therefore extends to financial speculation. Stockton expanded the distributive rewards of economic growth through vehicles such as tax-increment financing, pension obligation bonds, revenue bonds, and its employment contracts. Whereas a budget is a bet on tax revenue for a single year, each of these financial deals requires pledging tax revenue for upward of forty years. If these bets sour, financial claims take priority over other distributive claims.[11] The theoretical framework developed in the preceding chapters helps explain how the introduction of finance into liberal distributive politics explains Stockton's subsequent neoliberal reconfiguration.

The effect of the organization of interests on the structure of politics is a perennial theme in the study of politics.[12] However, pioneering studies on the subject all occurred well before the era of financialization. Financial entities are distinct from other growth machine interest groups: they have no stake in the community apart from their financial investment, are highly concentrated interests, can cooperate strategically with other financial entities, and have claims that have special legal standing. These features endow finance with a unique ransom effect. For a city already dependent on finance, the ability to access future financing is essential. Any action impairing a particular financial obligation would be met with both an enforcement action by the particular creditor (e.g., foreclosure) and a global ratings downgrade. Although contracts between Stockton and its major bargaining units all had no-strike clauses, financial creditors are free to boycott future deals if their demands are not met.

This ransom effect of finance, combined with its legal privileges, endows financial claims with a de facto and de jure priority over others.[13] Meeting these financial obligations, in turn, requires submitting previously nonmarketized domains to the tribunal of profit and loss in a bid to generate cash. Consequently, Stockton's City Council had no choice but to impose crippling austerity without any ideological sugar-coating or the ability to "buy time" through general obligation deficit borrowing.[14] City activities previously insulated from market discipline were reanimated around the imperative to generate positive cash flow. Through this process, Stockton was progressively reorganized around market imperatives, market values, and market rationality.

To explain how this process unfolds, this chapter examines four major examples of Stockton's financial risk-taking—the Stockton

Arena, the 2007 pension obligation bond issuance, the acquisition of the 400 East Main Street building, and employment contracts with its bargaining units—to demonstrate how each resulted from the structure of the city's growth machine politics. I then show how the introduction of finance into the city's distributive politics, both as an actor and as a political logic, enacts Stockton's neoliberal transformation. Though Stockton is an extreme case, its trajectory reveals the mechanism linking growth machine politics to financialization and financialization to neoliberalism.

THE POLITICAL ORIGINS OF FINANCIALIZATION

In the 1980s, Stockton was a favored target of the *Los Angeles Times* for its "Inferiority Complex on a Rampage."[15] One columnist derided Stockton as decidedly not a part of "trendy, laid-back California lotus land," instead describing its citizens as "a multiracial cast for 'The Grapes of Wrath.'" In 2012, *Reuters* dismissed Stockton as San Francisco's "polyester, buy-generic cousin, a dingy commercial hub for Central Valley farms that was just far enough from the San Francisco Bay area to be an irrelevance for the state's coastal elites."[16] City officials were keenly aware of this image. Councilmembers often refer to their desire to shed the city's image as the "armpit of the Central Valley" and to enjoy the unenumerated privileges of being recognized as a big city.

Given the limitations on property taxes installed by Proposition 13, Stockton, like other California cities, became highly dependent on sales and business license taxes for incremental general fund revenues. Although cities can increase their sales tax rates, these rates are subject to a maximum cap. The state of California also sets several important parameters for city finances including property tax and vehicle license fee allocations, pension contributions, and employment contract standards. Changes in state law can therefore have drastic consequences for municipal finances; city revenues are largely out of the control of the city itself.[17] Increasing city expenditures requires increasing economic growth. But there was a financial workaround.

In 1952, California voters approved Proposition 18, permitting tax-increment financing (TIF) to fund redevelopment projects in "blighted" neighborhoods.[18] TIF allowed for "paying for redevelopment activity with anticipated increased property tax revenues from the redevelopment project itself."[19] TIF is a speculation on future property values within a given area targeted for redevelopment: the deal only generates its intended profit if incremental property tax revenues ultimately exceed the cost of the necessary investments.[20] TIF was an attractive vehicle for reinvention. More broadly, financial speculation enabled California cities to circumvent statutory fiscal limits.[21]

Like other cities in California, Stockton aggressively pursued redevelopment projects in the early 2000s. A footnote in Stockton's 2004–2005 annual budget, though, raises a troubling possibility concerning this redevelopment: "As the need arises and as contracts are executed related to specific projects, it may become necessary for the Agency to borrow funds from various City revenue sources including, but not limited to, the General Fund."[22] In other words, if the incremental tax revenues from these projects didn't materialize, the city would be forced to backfill these obligations with its general fund. Since the city's revenues are largely fixed, meeting these financial claims must necessarily supplant other existing appropriations.

Under Mayor Gary Podesto, Stockton pursued projects including downtown housing, renovations of historic theaters, and an events complex along the riverfront. In 2002, Mayor Podesto championed an initiative to privatize Stockton's municipal water utility, claiming "it's time that Stockton enter the 21st century in its delivery of services and think of our citizens as customers." To this end, Podesto spearheaded a proposal to sell the city's water utilities to a consortium including

Thames Water, a London utility founded in the 1600s privatized under the Thatcher government in the late 1980s. Podesto's pitch for the deal was that the utility, as a monopoly, has "no competition so no incentive to improve." Despite the complexity of the deal—the proposal and contract nearing a thousand pages in length—Podesto argued that citizens should feel confident deferring to their representatives to make the necessary "tough choices" for Stockton.

A grassroots citizens' group—the Concerned Citizens Coalition of Stockton—arose in response to the plan. One citizen explained that the potential harms of privatizing the city's water system "wasn't something so abstract because it was happening right here." The group's immediate aim was to force a ballot referendum on the deal so that the voters could have a voice in the proposed deal. Mayor Podesto was vociferously opposed to this initiative. Several councilmembers took up the group's cause. During one council meeting, former councilmember and future mayor, Ann Johnston, was unsparing: "I am ashamed that we've followed this path and have gone down the road of making something happen that was not consensus-building, not citizen-involved, but basically handed down as a dictate. This is not the principle of an All-America City." Likewise, Councilmember Richard Nickerson was adamant that the issue be put to the voters: "Obviously the people who founded the [American] republic didn't think the people were too dumb to run it." The privatization plan passed 4–3 with Councilmembers Nickerson, Bestolarides, and Ruhstaller voting against. The Concerned Citizens group organized to collect signatures to put the issue to referendum through other channels but failed to collect 10,500 valid signatures.

The Concerned Citizens Coalition, in conjunction with the Sierra Club and the League of Women Voters of San Joaquin County, filed suit against the city for claiming an exemption from the California Environmental Quality Act (CEQA) and not conducting the required environmental impact assessment prior to awarding the no-bid contract. The court agreed and ordered the city to cancel the contract and restore control of the utility to the city. The city initially voted to pursue an appeal, but it was abandoned in 2007 after incurring millions of dollars in legal fees and contract termination charges. Ultimately, the failure of the grassroots campaign to collect enough valid signatures was offset by the city's failure to perform the necessary environmental impact assessment.

Stockton Arena

The Stockton Arena was the crown jewel of the city's redevelopment efforts. Then-city manager, Mark Lewis, explained how Stockton could use such projects to revamp its image: "Every other major city in California has undergone a redevelopment of its downtown core: Sacramento, Long Beach, San Diego, San Jose. If we all think back on what San Jose was 15 years ago, they had worse conditions than we had in our downtown 4–5 years ago. . . . It was very controversial at times, but I think today on what occurred in San Jose. . . . It is dramatic and a huge improvement to that city. We also hope that these efforts will forever change for the positive the city of Stockton."[23]

In 2002, the city commissioned a study to address the feasibility of constructing an arena on the Stockton waterfront. That report recommended a 6,000-seat arena. At a February 17, 2004, meeting, the City Council considered a new study recommending a 10,500-seat arena (with 500 luxury seats). The consultant responsible for this new study was in attendance to explain their findings to the council. Mayor Podesto addressed the consultant's presence directly: "Not being experts ourselves, we have to rely on the information given to us like people such as yourself." During the councilmembers' review of the prepared report, they discussed its underlying revenue assumptions: 105 event days per year with 4,800 average attendance, three professional sports teams, $15 million in annual revenue, $8 million in expenditures, and 506,000 annual event attendees. Next comes

GROWTH MACHINE POLITICS • 143

financing: the arena would cost an estimated $110 million, with $40 million being raised from a new revenue bond issue. Councilmember Steve Bestolarides was skeptical. He noted that the report didn't disclose comparable revenue figures for other similar arenas and rested on a number of heroic assumptions:

> The last study projected that we would have 5 circuses in the city of Stockton. The new study projects that we will have 10 circuses in the city of Stockton. I know that Arco [Sacramento's arena] does roughly 1 to 2 a year. The subjective increase in that number without any justification was pretty puzzling. . . . I regret there wasn't more substantive testing. . . . The analysis done was very elementary and they noted that was largely driven by ourselves as the client and . . . the output we wanted. . . . We're going down that slippery slope again. I've looked for reasons and want this thing to happen but I cannot rely on this report to get me there.

A member of the audience cautioned the council from thinking too much in terms of dollars and cents: "It's hard to quantify the impact this type of facility will have. It's more of an investment in our city." The speaker then went on to detail the impact of the Packers on the city of Green Bay, Wisconsin. Mayor Podesto noted, "This is a 50-year decision that we're making," implying that a hard-nosed dollars-and-cents analysis would be inappropriate given the "intangible" impacts the arena would have on the city. After a few more eddies of conversation, Councilmember Nickerson listed the draconian measures the state was already taking to claw back money from cities and argued:

> Now all of these things have to be taken into account. They aren't going to disappear because we would like to build an event center. Sure, we would like to build an event center. There are a lot of things we'd like. The problem is, what can we afford? The people of this city could end up staring at a disaster for a long time. So as much as I would like to

see this thing accomplished, I got to have somebody answer how you're going to overcome all these things [risks]. And I am talking about outside of having some cheering section standing up and playing with pom-poms. I would like to hear a real analysis of how do you get around all of these problems. It would be a wonderful thing if it works, but I am telling you, you've got a lot of problems.

There was no discussion of the problems raised by Nickerson. Stockton's own analysis of its bankruptcy would later vindicate Nickerson's skepticism entirely. The risks were readily apparent, but the rest of the council was unmoved. The motion was promptly moved, seconded, and carried 5 to 2, with Bestolarides and Nickerson voting against.[24]

At the next meeting two weeks later on March 2, the largest developers in Stockton appeared during the public comment session. The first to speak was a prominent local developer. He began by comparing the arena proposal to his company's construction of Brookside, the affluent walled subdivision on the west side of Interstate 5: "If you make this place special enough, they will come, they will invest, and they will make money. I think it's important to set that style. The city needs to be the lead developer to encourage others to invest money." If the city does this, "it's going to cause real estate values to appreciate, it's going to cause gentrification like you haven't seen before and you're also going to see more private capital come in." Representatives from the other two major developers made similar points. Shortly after, Ann Johnston, former councilmember and proprietor of The Balloonery on East Harding Way, approached the podium. Johnston put it simply: "It's all about money . . . of course the developers are excited, they aren't putting in a dime." She continued: "Where are the questions about the financing? What will this impact in city services? It all sounds wonderful, but do the due diligence to make sure that we're going into this with our eyes wide open [and make sure we're] not going to have to lay down a 1/4 cent sales tax to cover unexpected expenses in our general fund."

Incoming mayor Ed Chavez called for a city referendum on the arena issue. Podesto was adamantly opposed. One speaker addressed this issue: "Nothing that's great comes without a risk. There's been talk about a public vote about this issue. Well I happen to believe we set up a representative democratic form of government for ourselves to look at these complex issues and vote on them. The last time you had direct citizen vote on every issue all the time was Athens, Greece, because it doesn't work." A local reverend echoed the same sentiment that "you can only accomplish great things if you take some risk." A parade of members of construction unions, other minor developers, and local business organizations all spoke in favor of the project. All stood to gain financially from construction. Many again cited Green Bay as an example of a city that reinvented itself around a stadium. The meeting then moved into council debate. Again, Dr. Nickerson was the only member who wished to speak:

> If things go wrong, what has to be shorted to make it up? Police? Fire? Parks? Roads? What? It's already projected to be a deficit budget. We think we can fund $200,000 out of the general fund that this project is losing. We thought it would cost maybe a couple hundred thousand on [wastewater] privatization. Where are we today? Millions? And it isn't done yet. It's not like we're incapable of making an error.... We've strained everything we've got to get to a place where we can finance this project. If it doesn't go perfect, if the state is in trouble, if we are in trouble, heaven help us.

Bestolarides replied: "If you look at this investment on a strictly financial basis, it doesn't make sense. To say that it does would be not realistic. However, I think it's important to recognize we don't do a lot of these redevelopment projects to make money but for the greater good of the community. I have been able to embrace that." This reasoning couldn't be farther from that of *Homo economicus*. Dr. Nickerson concluded: "When we finance this, the cupboard is bare.

Every penny from every hidden fund, every anything is going into the financing and you've still borrowed millions of dollars. If something goes wrong, where's your backup? It isn't in the city's finances."[25]

No one responded. Vice Mayor Nomura's motion to approve the project carried 6 to 1. The room promptly emptied. In January 2006, Neil Diamond headlined the opening of the new Stockton Arena. Stockton would never again have it "so good, so good, so good."[26]

Pension Obligation Bonds

Like other public agencies in California, a significant portion of Stockton's employee compensation is accrued through a defined-benefit pension program. Unlike other "pay-as-you-go" benefits like retiree health benefits (where benefits are paid with current revenues), worker pensions are financed by a dedicated fund managed to maximize risk-adjusted return. The city's payments to its pension manager—the California Public Employee Retirement System (CalPERS)—have two components: the normal cost and the unfunded accrued liability (UAL) payment. The normal cost is calculated as a percentage of the employees' salary that they will receive in retirement. The UAL payment covers the gap between promised benefits and the money held by CalPERS to pay these benefits on behalf of the city.

In the 1990s, Stockton's pension administrator, CalPERS, allowed member agencies to suspend contributions due to exceptional investment performance. When the stock market crashed in 2000, CalPERS switched from a "fresh start" to a "rolling" amortization scheme for calculating pension contributions. This new rolling schedule was devised to even out the impact of market returns on contributions. Instead of required payments being calculated "fresh" each year, they now would be calculated based on a "rolling" average of returns. This change suddenly and massively increased Stockton's pension liability.

On August 31, 2006, Lehman Brothers pitched the City Council on a potential pension obligation bond (POB) offering. At the time, Stockton's "miscellaneous" plan was 88 percent funded and its "safety" plan was 80 percent funded. A POB is essentially a general obligation bond whose proceeds are used to reduce the unfunded actuarial liability on the city's pension obligations. Crucially, POBs circumvent the requirement of Proposition 13 that all general obligation debt be voter approved, because the proceeds are for paying "obligations imposed by law," which Proposition 13 explicitly exempts. The Lehman representative laid out the problem facing the city of "rating agencies see[ing] unfunded liabilities as tantamount to debt" and asked if "these obligations crowd out other priorities and dampen financial flexibility."

The bottom line of the pitch was that "POBs can save the City $4.7mm in cashflow and completely eliminate the $216.7MM UAL balance in FY 2037." He explained that this plan would not result in taking on *more* debt, but instead "exchang[e] one liability for another . . . [and] no new debt is being created" because "those liabilities are [already] factored into your credit profile." Financial risk-taking, in the form of a POB, would preserve existing distributive bargains without requiring either cuts to benefits or other programs to preserve existing benefit levels.[27]

The deal was presented in terms of the logic of refinancing: instead of paying 7.75 percent to CalPERS on their unfunded liability, Stockton would instead pay its bondholders somewhere between 5 and 6 percent (Lehman's forecast was that there would be "two more 25bps rate hikes expected by end of 2006," making a swift decision to maximize the potential savings imperative) and save the difference.[28] Furthermore, the Lehman representative explained, "If PERS doesn't earn more than 5.81 percent over 30 years then [this deal] was not a good idea. We would submit to you that if PERS doesn't earn 5.81 percent over 30 years you have much bigger problems."

Though the size of this issue was $125 million, nearly double that of the arena deal, it garnered no public comments and only five minutes of council discussion. The council was assured that the budget committee endorsed the proposal, having "heard the long version." City Chief Financial Officer (CFO) Mark Moses enthusiastically supported the deal and reiterated that it would not increase the city's capacity for providing additional benefits to employees. Instead, if market returns exceeded the cost of borrowing over the lifetime of the deal, the deal would ensure the city's ability to meet its existing obligations at a lower cost.

The POB motion carried 7–0. The day after the meeting, a local paper published an article entitled "City Owes Retirees $152m," advocating for the deal. "There comes a day of reckoning," Moses remarked.[29] Like the arena deal, there was no political opposition to financial risk-taking as a means of maintaining the depoliticized status quo.

400 East Main Street

Prior to 2008, Washington Mutual was the largest employer in downtown Stockton, occupying most of an office building at 400 East Main Street. When the subprime market began to crest in 2006, Washington Mutual fired one hundred employees, then another hundred the following year. On September 26, 2008, Washington Mutual filed for Chapter 11 bankruptcy, and most of its business was taken over by JPMorgan Chase. That December, Washington Mutual's remaining 335 employees working at 400 East Main Street were fired.

Given the age, inaccessibility, and size of the historic city hall at 425 North El Dorado Street, the council wanted to move into a more practical turnkey office space. The building at 400 East Main Street provided such an opportunity. To acquire the building, the city issued $40 million of variable-rate bonds with a forty-year maturity. The amortization schedule was backloaded, meaning that payments would increase substantially as time went on. In the words of the city financial planner, the "consultants and staff [felt] confident that the risk associated with a variable rate structure is more than worth it given the significant cost savings." In particular, they thought that a variable-rate structure could save upward of $450,000 annually over a fixed-rate issue.

Councilmember Bestolarides was convinced: "I think this is going to be one of those monumental deals. . . . There are not many opportunities sitting up in the dais where this project is rightside up from the start. . . . Because the price is so favorable, the terms aren't as important. . . . It is really financially prudent to do it this way." Councilmember Eggman was just as optimistic: "Maybe at some point we'll have a historic card declared at the site of the best deal the city has ever made."[30]

There were no public comments. The motion carried 7–0.[31]

Employee Contracts

Stockton's contracts with its bargaining units committed the city to multiyear benefit and compensation increases. These contracts therefore required the city to assume the risk that revenues would be sufficient to meet these obligations. As with previous examples of financial risk-taking, the "image of the future" implicit in these promises must actually come to pass, or else money must be reallocated from elsewhere. In the 1980s, the city began paying for retired city employees' health insurance, no matter the length of an employee's tenure. This benefit required the city to assume the risks associated with employee longevity and the prevailing cost of health insurance. Unlike the city's pension plans, this benefit was funded entirely by current revenues.

The Stockton City Employees' Association (SCEA) represents most non–public safety workers. During the subprime housing boom, the city agreed to increase the salaries of all applicable employees by 90 percent of the growth of city revenues, with a 2.5 percent minimum.

The firefighter and police unions similarly negotiated an annual cost of living inflator equal to 80 percent of the Consumer Price Index for Urban Wage Earners, but not less than 2.5 percent. In 2007, Stockton hired Public Sector Personnel Consultants to conduct its first comprehensive classification and compensation study since 1988.[32] The goal of the study was to "remain competitive in today's market" by "offer[ing] a level of compensation and benefits that is attractive to the targeted applicant pool," and it found that the "under market variance" of the city's base salary was upward of 16 percent for some positions.[33] The parties agreed to increase compensation to the market average over the next two years.

A similar study was conducted for the firefighters' union, surveying sixteen other fire agencies. The city agreed to increase total compensation (inclusive of pension and other benefits) such that the top step of the city's firefighter pay scale was equivalent to the agency-ranked fifth. Comparison agencies included a combination of comparable cities in size, demographics, and income (Anaheim, Fresno, Modesto, San Bernardino, and Sacramento) and much wealthier cities (Huntington Beach, Livermore, Pasadena, Pleasanton, and Torrance).[34] This process ultimately committed the city to an 8.5 percent salary increase, scheduled to take effect July 1, 2010. Given that salaries for public safety employees were the largest single item in the budget, the city had to assume a corresponding increase in revenues in order to support this increase.

THE POLITICAL CONSEQUENCES OF FINANCIALIZATION

By May 2008, the City Council began suspecting that something was wrong: property and sales tax revenues were falling significantly short of expectations, and it was clear that major cuts were needed to the just-approved city budget. Nearby Vallejo filed for bankruptcy, alarming the council. The city manager assured them that the two situations were not comparable:

> We have been much more diligent in how we provide funding for covering our costs. . . . We have tried very hard to cover our operating costs from our operating revenues. . . . In the case of Vallejo, they ran out of that 'one-time money.' We have been working very hard to avoid finding ourselves in a similar situation. Our challenge is that our revenue sources are flat probably at best for the general fund, which is why we're facing this very difficult year coming up and probably next year as well.[35]

Additionally, Vallejo's flagship redevelopment project cost the city's general fund almost $5 million per year.[36] In July, the city discovered that the San Joaquin county assessor rolled back assessment values for recently sold properties in response to the housing market collapse. Rather than the expected 2 percent increase in assessed values, the city was facing declines in property tax revenues resulting from these lower valuations.

By August, the council needed to find another $16 million in cuts to balance the budget for the next fiscal year. In such a process, the shortfall between expected and actual revenues dictates the size of the necessary cuts. Councilmember Clem Lee was unsparing in his assessment of the situation facing the city:

> Out of desperation is born opportunity. What's occurring is the culmination of decades of marginal practices in budgeting. . . . Shame on anyone who thinks there are any sacred cows left in this budget, because there are not. Everything is on the table. Every. Single. Thing. In the budget is on the table. . . . We need to be steady and deliberative and if we are, as painful as this is going to be, we can get on the right path for the future.[37]

The council's narrative fits with other similar cases of fiscal crisis narrated largely in terms of the city's own failures of fiscal management.[38] City Manager Palmer noted how "financial commitments" such as Memorandums of Understanding (MOUs) with labor units and covenants with creditors drastically reduced the "organizational flexibility" of responding to downturns. Whereas the earlier version of the budget had seen wrangling about what might be added, now the city faced a reality where it had to "[look] at what we cut." Palmer noted that "the local government business model is precarious." This position was echoed later in the meeting by CFO Mark Moses, who explained to the council that "we're working with a very tenuous business model." Mayor Chavez characterized previous budgeting processes as a "dog and pony show" in which the council was expected to "rubber stamp" the budget without any serious involvement or analysis.[39]

Around this time, the city began worrying about the impact of a possible ratings downgrade.[40] Given the city's inadequate fiscal reserves, a continued decline in revenues would almost certainly trigger a downgrade and, therefore, increase Stockton's obligations to creditors. By October, the city's projected deficit had grown to $20 million. Fifty miles north in Sacramento, the state of California was facing a $20 billion deficit. On November 4, Ann Johnston defeated Clem Lee to become Stockton's next mayor. Two days later, the council approved a modification to the previously approved fiscal year (FY) 2008–2009 budget, reflecting the new economic reality. But the deficit continued to grow. By May 2009, it was $30 million. The council discussed ways to maximize revenue from city properties including golf courses, auditoriums, and parks. The library system's goals included "upgrading self-check-out equipment" and "increas[ing] library cardholders by 15 percent." The library director proposed using the bookmobile as a billboard to underwrite program costs and entering a partnership with Barnes and Noble to sponsor "reading rooms" at city libraries.

Stockton's dire and deteriorating situation began attracting the attention of the national media. After *Forbes Magazine* named Stockton the "most miserable city in America," ahead of Cleveland, Memphis, Detroit, and Flint, *CBS News* ran a profile of the city, in which a reporter asked Mayor Johnston if she was "mayor of America's most miserable city." Johnston replied, "No, I'm mayor of the nation's All-America City." Around the same time, former mayor Chavez's condominium was sold in a "short sale" foreclosure.[41] Relationships between the city and its employees continued to deteriorate. Echoing New York's "Fear City" campaign during the 1975 budget crisis, the Stockton Police Officers Association put up blood-spattered billboards around Stockton that read: "Welcome to the 2nd Most Dangerous City in California. Stop Laying Off Cops! City Manager 937–8457."[42] Another billboard displayed the city's "body count" for that year. According to Councilmember Fritchen, after a City Council meeting, the vice president of the Stockton Police Officers Association "put his hand on my shoulder and said, 'Well, game on. Be safe out there.'"[43]

As a result of layoffs and increased service demands, the city became increasingly reliant on outsourced consultants to meet basic staffing requirements. Downsizing city departments had the perverse effect of increasing overall costs. The city attorney raised the specter of malpractice lawsuits resulting from severe understaffing. The increased reliance on outside counsel cost the city double what it would cost internally. Mayor Johnston lamented of the city attorney's office, "It is unfortunate that your department has been decimated because you provide such a valuable function for everybody." Councilmember Martin similarly noted how "the customers, the taxpayers, won't see the effect of the inability to have the necessary resources." Community development staffing was reduced from 88 to 42 in one year. Public works staffing was reduced from 212 to 142. The city stopped irrigating parks and nearly eliminated its tree maintenance program despite the thousands of service requests in its backlog. Police department headcount shrank by a hundred full-time employees over the preceding year. It eliminated its truancy program, park patrols, and auto theft division, and fired half of its counter-narcotics officers.[44]

The scale of cuts required to balance the budget began to dawn on the council. Tax increases were out of the question, as such a solution would be both politically fraught for the council and insufficient (increasing sales taxes to the statutory maximum would only close half of the deficit). The next week, Councilmember Fritchen remarked, "I feel like I have even less power than last year. Our only decision to make is whether to lay employees off or get other concessions. We have to balance the budget. It is now in the hands of the employee groups." City Manager O'Rourke quipped: "We're at the top of the tree." Mayor Johnston solemnly noted that no one knew how many more years of cuts would be required.[45]

In March 2010, the council considered launching a community survey and a series of town hall events to gather public input about the budget crisis. By April, the deficit forecast had increased by another $10 million, as property tax revenues continued declining, due now to the state reducing its allocation to local agencies from vehicle license fees. On May 6, Mayor Johnston held a lightly attended town hall meeting centering on the message that "things are not getting any better for the city of Stockton. . . . There is no good this year. It's all bad."[46] There was no attempt to sugarcoat the austerity. On May 26, 2010, Stockton declared its first state of fiscal emergency. The immediate impact of this declaration was to suspend scheduled pay increases for the police and fire departments.

The city manager presented a menu of proposed cuts to the council. As he characterized it, "major policy decisions and resource allocations . . . that's our newspeak for going over the list of things we have talked to you about and seeking direction from you on what you will accept in terms of budget reductions that have been proposed."[47] The city had to both break promised increases in compensation and benefits and then countenance how current expenditures would then be reduced. By June 9, 2010, only $8.7 million of the $23 million deficit had been closed. Two options remained for closing the remaining deficit: "either successful negotiations or imposition [under fiscal crisis]." On June 22, the council passed a budget for the 2010–2011 fiscal year without any members of the public wishing to comment. Budgets were slashed, services were cut, and the deficit was closed. A month later, on July 27, huge crowds packed the council chambers in the wake of the fatal shooting of unarmed sixteen-year-old James Rivera by two Stockton police officers and a San Joaquin County sheriff's deputy.

In September, new city manager Bob Deis raised the specter of the "bankruptcy option," should the city be unable to reduce its labor costs.[48] In November, Stockton voters narrowly approved Measure H, removing protections for the fire department in the city's bylaws, thereby giving city management increased flexibility in renegotiating employment contracts. The crux of the conflict involved provisions in the fire department's contract that proscribed minimum staffing levels and barred layoffs. The fiscal crisis meant that Stockton could not both meet these obligations and balance its budget as constitutionally required, auguring deeper changes to come. On January 20, 2011, Moody's downgraded Stockton from Aa3 to A1. Moody's cited a "potential decline in city's already narrow finances" as a principal reason for the downgrade. Because of Stockton's large and "economically challenged tax base," there was significant risk of further "negative credit consequences" if the binding arbitration with the fire department resulted in an "adverse ruling."[49] Moody's wrote of Measure H: "the city's ability to use these new powers to achieve a sustainable balanced budget in fiscal 2012 and beyond will be critical to maintaining its rating over the longer term." Like any other city, Stockton's ability to refinance or issue new debt depended on its bond rating.[50]

Vallejo's unfolding bankruptcy made clear to both the city and its bargaining units that collective bargaining agreements could and would be discharged in bankruptcy. At the council's February 15, 2011, meeting, the city identified the increasing cost of retiree medical benefits as an untenable fiscal commitment. The cost of this benefit doubled from $8.5 million in 2007 to $16.8 million in 2010 as revenues sharply declined. By March, the city needed to begin its annual budgeting process but was still waiting for the outcome of arbitration with several of its unions over the contract impairments made under the auspices of fiscal crisis. In Deis's characterization, the city needed to "create permanent and structural change to [its] expenditure." The budget process was like "God asking Abraham which son he wants to give up. There's no 'no' option."[51] Full-time employees fell from 1,360 in 2008 to 800 in 2011. The police department eliminated its gang, vice, and graffiti abatement units and most civilian staffing. While call volume stayed constant, the number of arrests and sworn officers decreased.

In May, the city renewed its declaration of fiscal emergency. On June 21, Mayor Johnston opened a public hearing on the budget at 9:51 P.M. The budget was approved at 9:58 P.M. Simultaneously, Dexia, the parent company of Stockton's bond insurer, was downgraded, changing the payment schedule of the 2007 lease revenue bonds for the 400 East Main Street building. On June 28, Moody's downgraded Stockton once again from A1 to A3 with a negative outlook. They noted that the city now faced a $37 million deficit for the upcoming fiscal year, owing largely to "cost escalations built into the city's existing labor agreements and growing pension requirements."[52] The city's financial obligations, owing largely to the deals discussed above, increased dramatically as revenues fell, doubly squeezing city finances. On November 8, Stockton was downgraded again to Baa1, nearing junk status. By 2011, general fund revenues were $27 million less than they were in 2007. The necessary cuts were almost double the actual revenue declines, as expenditures were budgeted based on projected revenue increases.

On February 1, 2012, all redevelopment agencies in California were dissolved. The state was eager to recoup any and all potential sources of tax revenue as its fiscal crisis dragged on. Stockton, like many other cities, designated itself as the "successor agency," thereby assuming many of the responsibilities—and operating deficits—of the Stockton redevelopment agency. The state government demanded "ransom payments" from cities in order to continue operating their redevelopment agencies. A new measure passed after the Vallejo bankruptcy—AB506—required cities and creditors to negotiate before the state would allow them to file for bankruptcy. On February 28, Stockton became the first city to enter this new mediation process as a mandatory prerequisite for its now inevitable bankruptcy filing. Additionally, the council directed the city manager to take "liquidity-preserving" steps such as suspending debt payments and the ability of employees to "sell back" their accrued time off to the city to conserve cash in the interim. All available balances from solvent city funds, such as the arts endowment, were swept into the general fund as a final desperate step. Stockton was perilously close to missing payroll. Finally, the council voted to accept the finding of Management Consultants that the general fund was insolvent both from a "service delivery" and a "budget" perspective and hired the same firm to manage the AB506 process.

The city amended the budget to reflect both its continued revenue losses and the new expenses associated with the mediation process and the unions' lawsuits against the city.[53] Several million dollars of the "savings" associated with the suspension of debt payments were immediately earmarked for this litigation. As part of the city's comprehensive review of its financial practices, it continued to uncover significant administrative errors that worsened its position. As one representative example, for two and a half years, "two different Police Department employees faithfully recorded the same set of cash receipts"; both were posted to the city's cash ledger, resulting in a $500,000 double counting.[54] Despite the looming inevitability of bankruptcy, Deis's tone was cautiously optimistic: "In the private sector there are numerous examples of financial restructuring that resulted in sustainable and healthy enterprises going forward, such as in the auto industry, airlines, and the hi-tech industry."[55] However, "we can't 'grow our way out' of the problem and no amount of forward looking financial planning will properly fix it."[56] Deis summarized:

> The problems the City face are so severe that neither increasing taxes nor cutting services, even if implemented aggressively, are enough to mitigate the situation and make Stockton a viable city. Focusing only on current revenues and expenditures avoids a large source of the problem—debt and other contractual liabilities—that can only be addressed through the AB506 mediation process and/or chapter 9 bankruptcy proceedings.[57]

After the city failed to make rent payments, Wells Fargo repossessed the new city hall building at 400 East Main Street.[58] The council was faced with a $26 million deficit and nothing left to cut.

The situation in the city had become increasingly dire. Police Chief Eric Jones noted his department was "having difficulty finding qualified [police officer] applicants" and that officers were only able to respond to crimes in progress. This meant the city was paying higher overtime rates for existing officers. Similarly, interim fire chief Dave Rudat noted that the city's emergency rooms "shut down on a daily basis" because of overutilization and understaffing and that Stockton was on pace to match Fresno, Oakland, and Sacramento in number of structure fires, despite having 40 percent fewer residents than those cities. Deis explained that his office would have an interim "Pendency Plan" ready for the twenty-sixth in the event that AB506 negotiations did not produce an adequate solution by their conclusion on the twenty-fifth. Although these negotiations yielded concessions from eight of the nine bargaining groups, they were insufficient to close the deficit.[59]

On June 26, the city adopted the Pendency Plan, making national headlines, and officially filed for bankruptcy two days later.[60]

From Bankruptcy to Populism

The purpose of bankruptcy is to break "existing contractual obligations for the purpose of allowing continued General Fund operations" with court protection from creditors' enforcement actions.[61] The official Plan of Adjustment filed with the court summarizes the causes of the crisis facing Stockton: "When the City was flush with cash, it made financial decisions and commitments based on the assumption that its economic growth would continue indefinitely. These commitments included unsustainable labor costs, retiree health benefits, and public debt.... When the Great Recession hit, the City found its financial obligations quickly outpacing its revenues. Compounding these economic challenges, the City—like all California cities—is limited by law in its ability to generate new revenues."[62]

In total, Stockton's debt burden increased by a factor of six in six years, with the city increasingly relying on the general fund as backup security for repayments. General fund debt service payments increased from $3 million in 2006 to $17.2 million in 2012. This increase was nearly equivalent to the total decline in property and sales tax revenues over the same period. The component deals included $13 million for downtown housing projects, $46 million for the arena, $32 million for three parking garages, $13.5 million for the Essential Services Building, $11 million for the downtown marina, $40 million for the 400 East Main Street building, $125 million for the pension obligation bonds, and $35 million for other city buildings. On the eve of its bankruptcy, Stockton's total debt load amounted to just under $300 million.

In addition to suspending debt payments, the city immediately discontinued its health insurance benefit for retired employees. As the city explained in a letter to employees, "The City simply did not set aside any funds to properly finance the retiree medical benefit. In order to catch up and fund the current program going forward, we would have to set aside 30 percent of our payroll each year for the next

30 years."⁶³ A consortium of retirees filed for a temporary restraining order that would enjoin the city from discontinuing these payments. In support of this motion, dozens of employees submitted affidavits explaining the harm of the city's actions. In his declaration to the court, a retired park worker wrote of the tremendous human cost:

> I take 9 prescriptions daily. I suffer from GERD, bleeding ulcers, irritable bowel syndrome, high blood pressure, high triglycerides, hypothyroid, dislocated collar bone, osteoarthritis, enlarged lymph nodes from chemicals used at work, a herniated disc in lower back after injury at work, enlarged prostate and clinical depression. . . . Paying $1,126.66 a month is obviously not an option. . . . My wife cries all the time. She don't [sic] understand how when you retire and they promise you all this stuff, then they just take it away.⁶⁴

Other similarly affected city retirees highlighted, in filings, years of service to the city, the number and severity of their medical conditions, and the impact of this change on their personal finances. However, the bankruptcy code expressly forbids the court from "interfering with political or governmental powers, property or revenues, and use or enjoyment of income-producing property."⁶⁵ Judge Christopher Klein denied the motion for a temporary restraining order. This enabled the city to discharge a $545 million unfunded liability as a one-time $5.4 million payout to beneficiaries, one of the most significant obligations discharged as part of the bankruptcy proceedings.

On April 1, 2013, Judge Klein ruled that Stockton was eligible for Chapter 9 protection.⁶⁶ Creditors insisted that the city must attempt to restructure its obligations with CalPERS before Chapter 9. Klein rejected this claim on the basis of the more than ninety days of meetings the city took with various creditors. Klein would later find that CalPERS was merely a "pass-through" creditor as its claims were not for itself but rather on behalf of the city employees whose pensions it manages. In an op-ed in the *Wall Street Journal*, Deis explained why the city did not want to cut pensions: "considering the city's cost-cutting actions, citizens, employees, and retirees have endured far more cuts—and created far more savings—than the capital-market creditors."[67] Financial creditors wanted to frame the crisis as resulting from pension obligations so that these claims would be impaired before theirs. Ultimately, payments to CalPERS were unaffected in both Stockton and San Bernardino, a demographically and economically comparable city in southern California that filed for bankruptcy three weeks after Stockton.[68] Employee contracts were drastically restructured under the Pendency Plan. The city cancelled all annual compensation inflators and planned compensation increases, stopped paying the 7 percent required employee contribution to CalPERS, and raised the retirement age for new employees. Paid time off accrual was cut by roughly 10 percent, and the city mandated an escalating number of furlough hours.[69]

Like elsewhere, Stockton experienced a brief frisson of populism in the aftermath of austerity. On June 27, 2012, Ann Johnston and Anthony Silva advanced to the November runoff election for mayor. All major candidates in the primary election had the same basic platform: reducing crime, addressing the fiscal crisis, and bringing prosperity back to Stockton. The election pitted Silva, a brusque political novice with a checkered employment history and several allegations of serious sexual misconduct against him who promised to self-fund his campaign, against Johnston, a technocratic multidecade fixture of Stockton politics.[70] Johnston nearly doubled Silva's vote totals in the primary election, and few in the city expected that Silva represented a serious challenge to Johnston's reelection. However, that summer witnessed an exceptional surge of violence in which Stockton surpassed Chicago's per-capita homicide rate. In the week preceding the election, there were nine homicides in forty-eight hours.[71] Silva managed to successfully tie the summer's crime surge to the city's bankruptcy. On November 6, 2012, Anthony Silva routed Ann Johnston (59 percent to 41 percent) to become the next mayor of Stockton. As a local newspaper columnist put it: "Bankruptcy plus violence equals upset."[72] The column continued, "Silva's populist rhetoric is appealing to many residents who have felt left out of political decisions made for years by more polished politicians."[73]

Silva initially promised to decline the mayor's salary until the budget was balanced but eventually accepted both the salary and back pay. During Silva's first "State of the City" address in 2013, he donned a medieval helmet and mace and posed the question, "Who is willing to fight for Stockton?" Silva awarded a key to the city to God in the wake of a shooting and discussed importing Florida manatees to control the growth of delta hyacinths in Stockton's shipping channel.[74] Silva, on the eve of a council censure vote for one of his many improprieties, posted on Facebook: "If people spent as much time trying to IMPROVE this City rather than trying to attack me; then just imagine the possibilities!!!"[75] Silva's most notable policy initiative was a 3/4 cent sales tax increase to fund 120 police officers (Measure A) approved by voters on November 5, 2013. This initiative dovetailed with the "Marshall Plan on Crime" begun in late 2011 under Johnston in an effort to reduce the city's rapidly escalating crime rate. Silva hired former New York Police Department commissioner William Bratton to stump on behalf of the initiative.

In 2013, bond insurer Assured Guaranty repossessed the new Stockton city hall building at 400 East Main Street. As part of the bankruptcy settlement, Assured Guaranty became entitled to a share of Stockton's "surplus revenues." The agreement states: "The premise of this model is that, had the revenues achieved the Expected Core Revenue curve, the City would have been able to pay all of its debts and would not have had to file for bankruptcy; therefore, the closer the City gets in the future to achieving those Expected Core Revenues, the closer the City should get to making full payment on obligations of the Participating Creditors."[76] Assured Guaranty is thus entitled to a share of incremental city revenues above the expected baseline through 2052. A recent budget document establishes an explicit link between financial obligations and public-sector retrenchment: "[The budget] includes expenditure increases for debt service payments to Assured Guaranty of $3.4 million. . . . These increases are offset by reductions for capital projects, recreation programs, library programs and capital outlay."[77]

Stockton exited bankruptcy in February 2015. Later that year, the National Civic League renewed Stockton's status as an All-America City.[78]

***

Today, Stockton is rated one of the most fiscally stable cities in America. City Manager Kurt Wilson wrote in the 2017–2018 Stockton budget, "We are a city of many unmet needs but, despite a strong current financial position, we must maintain painfully high levels of discipline because of what we know the future holds." In 2017, Silva was arrested and charged with embezzlement and money laundering.[79] In 2018, the city acquired the Waterfront Towers built by Eckhard Schmitz (a developer who worked with the city on several redevelopment projects until he fled the country in the 1980s after being accused of molesting teenage boys) for a new city hall.[80] As of 2021, an estimated $63 million in repairs were required before the city could move into the building.[81]

This chapter has charted how Stockton's neoliberal reconfiguration resulted from the financialization of its growth machine politics: interest groups successfully lobbied the city council to extend their distributive shares through the public assumption of financial risk. Through financialization, developers, construction unions, firefighters, police officers, and city employees could all have their demands met without raising taxes or impairing other groups' allocations. Initially, these deals promised immediate material benefit at seemingly no cost and held the promise of "avoiding" difficult and contentious political questions of relative need and desert by replacing them with formal parameters of technocratic management.[82] In the aftermath of the subprime market collapse, however, the costs of financialization became painfully apparent. Stockton found itself in a structural predicament where its only options were varieties of neoliberalism: meeting these imperatives required closing libraries, slashing public employment, privatizing city assets, and seeking private investment. Finance rather than neoliberal ideologues drove this transformation.

5

DEMOCRACY AND FINANCE IN CALIFORNIA

May we pray to God that our virtues grow with California and be durable, and that our vision for California be liberal and responsible.
—Pat Brown

Growth should mean increased prosperity and thus a lightening of the load each individual must bear. If this isn't true, then you and I should be planning how we can put up a fence along the Colorado River and seal our borders.
—Ronald Reagan

If "socialism" is defined as "ownership of the means of production by the workers" . . . then the United States is the first truly "Socialist" country.
—Peter Drucker

"GOP LANDSLIDE IN CALIFORNIA" blared the headline of the *Los Angeles Times* on the morning of November 5, 1930. Republican James Rolph, Jr., resoundingly defeated both Democrat Milton Young and Socialist Upton Sinclair to become the twenty-seventh governor of California. On November 2, the *Times* had filled most of their front page with a special

"How to Mark Your Ballot Next Tuesday" section indicating their preferred choices for elected offices (all Republican) and the slate of ballot propositions. The editors wrote of Proposition 5: "This proposed constitutional amendment would create a pension system for State employees. . . . The *Times* recommends a vote of 'No,' on No. 5." Although the final result wouldn't be known for several weeks, California voters narrowly approved the proposition.

Today, the entity created by Proposition 5 is the single largest portfolio of financial capital in the United States. As of 2023, the California Public Employees Retirement System (CalPERS) manages $450 billion on behalf of nearly six hundred public employers in California.[1] Public employers like cities, counties, water districts, and public transit agencies contract with CalPERS to administer pension plans for their employees. In these "defined benefit" retirement plans, employees receive a percentage of their compensation as an annual retirement benefit. Both employers and employees contribute a percentage of their salary to fund this benefit. Because these funds are not immediately used, they are invested to earn a return. The more these investments earn, the less tax revenue is required to pay pension benefits. CalPERS manages these investments on behalf of contracting public agencies.

The time lag between the accrual and delivery of benefits requires delicate actuarial management. The constant struggle for pension funds like CalPERS is to maintain a rough balance between the present value of benefits owed to employees and the accumulated financial assets available to pay those benefits. The "discount rate" is the all-important parameter linking present and future, specifying how much the plan's assets are expected to earn over the long term to meet these obligations and thus the current contribution level required to fund future benefits. The "funding ratio" expresses the percentage of benefits that can be paid with current assets. The principal fiduciary goal of pension fund managers is to ensure that investment returns closely approximate the discount rate over the long term.

Initially, this task was straightforward. From 1930 to 1966, the discount rate was set at 4 percent, corresponding to the prevailing nominal interest rate. Accordingly, the CalPERS portfolio was invested in a conservative mix of government, municipal, and corporate bonds. The required rate of return was readily generated through "productive" investments in stalwarts of the postwar economy like Bethlehem Steel, state building certificates, and public utilities. But over time, the portfolio steadily shifted toward equities: the financial returns used to pay pension benefits for public workers were increasingly generated from ownership stakes in American businesses. Unlike bonds, corporate shares generate returns through current profits and the prospect of increasing profitability. The solvency of the fund thus depends on profits generated from globalization, deindustrialization, deregulation, and labor discipline. CalPERS's search for return helped seed a new asset class called "private equity" and led the fund to evangelize the "shareholder value" revolution of the 1980s at home and abroad. How did a public pension system, one of labor's great victories in the postwar era, become an agent of upward redistribution?

This chapter focuses on four episodes in which incremental financial risk-taking soothed contentious distributive politics. Through these episodes, I chart how CalPERS steadily reallocated to asset classes like private equity and real estate in order to increase returns and preempt political intervention from the state. Although CalPERS is a statutory entity under the control of labor unions and elected state officeholders, it nevertheless behaves like any other private investor seeking to maximize risk-adjusted return on a diversified portfolio of financial assets. Concerns for other workers, environmental sustainability, or human rights are trumped by the ceaseless search for financial return. The search for return fueled shareholder value ideology, private equity, and subprime mortgages.[2]

The chapter begins by sketching the political backdrop of the rise of Ronald Reagan in California. Reagan exploited the breakdown in the political consensus that underwrote the projects and programs of

Pat Brown's administration. Next, I show how the passage of Proposition 13 in 1978 pushed CalPERS away from "productive" investments and toward real estate, mortgages, and stocks. A decade later, the recession of the early 1990s similarly led CalPERS to begin investing in private equity and further increase its allocation to stocks. The dotcom and subprime crashes of the 1990s and 2000s repeated this same formula, driving further allocations to real estate and private equity and firmly tethering CalPERS's future to that of global finance.

THE FIRST REAGAN REVOLUTION

On November 7, 1962, Richard Nixon swore off politics. Nixon had just lost a close gubernatorial race to incumbent Pat Brown. Two years earlier, Nixon lost the presidency to John F. Kennedy by an even narrower margin. "You won't have Dick Nixon to kick around anymore," he proclaimed to reporters assembled at the Beverly Hilton. That year, California surpassed New York to become the most populous state in the union.

Pat Brown oversaw the golden age of liberalism in California from 1958 to 1966.[3] In his inaugural address, Brown framed his vision for "responsible liberalism" in managing California's explosive growth: "I pledge a confident, pioneering leadership, ready to welcome growth, pursue its promise, and prepare for tomorrow."[4] In 1960, he signed the Donahoe Higher Education Act into law. This "Master Plan for Higher Education" in California presented a radically democratic vision for public higher education in America's largest state. The following year, work began on the massive California State Water Project. Via a series of dams, canals, and pumps, precipitation in the northern Sierra Nevada would be carried seven hundred miles to greater Los Angeles. For Pat Brown, the state had a positive role to play in job creation, consumer protection, economic development, worker protection, safety, health, and education.

But beneath this bold liberal vision for California lay deep political fractures. Over the previous two decades, nearly half a million African Americans moved to California to work its shipyards and manufacturing plants. In the aftermath of the *Shelley v. Kraemer* Supreme Court decision outlawing racist housing covenants, California's white supermajority responded by creating a de facto regime of racial segregation rivaling and perhaps exceeding that of the Jim Crow South.[5] More than one hundred California cities became "sundown towns" where African Americans remaining in public after dark were subject to arrest.[6] In 1960, all but 4,000 of the 460,000 African Americans living in Los Angeles were confined to majority Black ghettoes. Cities across California adopted restrictive zoning in response to sizable African American migration.[7]

In 1963, the state legislature passed the Rumford Fair Housing Act that outlawed racial discrimination in housing.[8] In response, the California Real Estate Association launched a signature drive for a ballot proposition to repeal the act and entrench the absolute right of property owners to discriminate as they saw fit. Brown staunchly opposed the measure, calling its supporters "the shock troops of bigotry, echoes of Nazi Germany, echoes of another hate binge which began more than thirty years ago in a Munich beer hall."[9] Bowing to pressure from the real estate lobby, the University of California banned campus political advocacy. In November 1964, the measure, Proposition 14, passed with an overwhelming two-thirds majority.[10] Yet nearly 25 percent of the electorate voted for both Proposition 14 *and* Lyndon Johnson.[11] On December 2, 1964, student demonstrators occupied Sproul Hall in protest of the university policy, launching what became known as the "Free Speech Movement." Seven months later, the Watts Riots shook Los Angeles.[12]

At the time, the most politically prominent pension fund in the country was the Central States Pension fund controlled by Teamster president James R. Hoffa. After a dramatic congressional showdown with Attorney General Robert F. Kennedy, Hoffa invested tens of millions of dollars of union pension money into casino projects in Las Vegas.[13] A special in the *New York Times* published on the morning of November 22, 1963, warned of the power of "obscure figures" arising from this nexus of finance, labor, and organized crime extending "from underworld to government" who "poured money into Havana casinos." CalPERS, meanwhile, was quiet. The program included few retirees relative to the number of active workers, and its portfolio was invested in a conservative mix of government and corporate bonds. The discount rate was set at 4.5 percent, corresponding roughly to prevailing long-term interest rates. As a result, the required return to balance assets and liabilities was easily generated by productive investments in utilities, hydropower, municipal bonds, and railroad trust certificates.

In May 1966, the California Supreme Court ruled Proposition 14 unconstitutional, elevating "fair housing" to a prominent issue in the gubernatorial campaign.[14] Pat Brown was challenged by former Screen Actors Guild president, General Electric spokesman, and Federal Bureau of Investigation (FBI) informant Ronald Reagan. Reagan's "A Time for Choosing" speech at the 1964 Republican National Convention catapulted the actor to national political prominence. In the speech, Reagan predicted the end of prosperity and "a thousand years of darkness" if the power of the federal government wasn't curtailed. Reagan's campaign deftly capitalized on the grassroots conservative infrastructure built during the 1964 Goldwater presidential primary campaign. Goldwater's surprise victory over Nelson Rockefeller augured the coming shift in the political winds. Reagan campaigned as an outsider "citizen-politician" crusading against big government overreach and proved adept at attracting wealthy donors and manipulating the increasingly relevant medium of television.

By focusing on Watts, Berkeley, civil rights, and the escalating crisis in Vietnam, Reagan could engage postwar liberalism on its cultural rather than material basis. Advisors tried, somewhat successfully, to shift Reagan from rabid anticommunism to moral panic over campus activism at Berkeley as a way of blunting Brown's charges of unhinged Bircher-ism, thereby exploiting the easy redirection of Cold War anticommunism to anxiety about campus activism.[15] Charges of "extremism" that were so effective against Goldwater in the 1964 campaign were now more readily leveled against the Left in the wake of the unrest in Berkeley and Watts.[16] Consultants from the Behavioral Science Corporation helped the campaign target messages at groups of persuadable voters. For example, campaign strategists devised a "Ya Basta" theme to attract Latino voters away from Brown and discovered the resonance of antiwelfare messages among white Democrats.

Reagan won with a shocking 58 percent of the vote. Support for Reagan in 1966 was tightly correlated with support for Proposition 14 in 1964. Reagan won over the crucial bloc of Johnson/Proposition 14 voters by reframing the "fair housing" issue as one of state overreach rather than racial prejudice.[17] According to one pollster, the top issues for voters after the primary were "crime, drugs, juvenile delinquency, racial problems, state taxes, and welfare programs."[18] In the words of another commentator, "the reason Ronald Reagan was elected governor was because he was Ronald Reagan at a time when the people wanted something like Ronald Reagan."[19] The rebuke of postwar liberalism was unmistakable.

In the same election, voters approved Proposition 1, permitting state pension funds to invest in stocks. The measure was placed on the ballot by a unanimous vote of the state legislature. Supporters argued that California needed to catch up to the majority of states that already permitted such investments. The proposition imposed a 25 percent limit on investment in common stocks and limited eligible investments to companies that paid a dividend in eight of the ten preceding years and possessed at least $100 million in assets. Several years earlier, the Los Angeles County Employees Association pushed for their fund to be allowed to invest in stocks as a hedge against rising inflation.[20] A panel of experts convened by the state legislature agreed that the prohibition on such investments was "outdated" and "prevented pension funds from obtaining the yields and growth to which they should be entitled."[21] Speaking to a state panel, University of California, Los Angeles (UCLA) chancellor Franklin Murphy noted that nearly 40 percent of the University of California retirement fund and 60 percent of its endowment were already invested in stocks. Longer life spans, longer employment tenures, and greater benefits required greater returns. As the secretary of the Ohio School Employees Fund explained, "we are trying to meet demands on our fund without having to increase employer (state and local government) or employee contributions."[22] Stock market investments were widely framed as a commonsense way for benefit levels to keep pace with inflation without requiring increased state contributions.[23]

In his first inauguration speech, Reagan vowed to "squeeze and cut and trim until we reduce the cost of government." Later that year, however, Reagan signed a bill enacting the largest percentage tax increase in the history of California—sales, income, excise, gasoline, and inheritance taxes were all raised in an effort to balance the budget.[24] Despite his constant vilification of overpaid state employees during the campaign, Reagan signed several bills that increased their retirement benefits.[25] In 1968, Reagan also signed a bill establishing a "cost of living" escalator to state pensions. In 1970, he increased the predominant retirement formula to 2 percent at 60, up from 1.43 percent at 65.[26]

Reagan governed California as a relative moderate while playing the archconservative on television. Although he campaigned on repealing the Rumford Fair Housing Act, Reagan opposed similar repeal efforts while in office. Reagan also enacted a 1967 abortion liberalization bill and oversaw both the creation of the California Air Resources Board and the passage of the landmark California Environmental Quality Act. Reagan campaigned in favor of Proposition 20, which created the California Coastal Commission and prohibited most development along the California coastline. Developers, their dreams of seaside master-planned communities dashed by popular referendum despite outspending proponents of the proposition 100-to-1, sold 125,000 acres of coastal land to the state park system.[27] In November 1968, Reagan narrowly lost the Republican presidential nomination to Richard Nixon.

Reagan, however, did deliver on several campaign promises. One signature policy, the sweeping welfare reform bill, imposed residency requirements on welfare recipients and linked provision for indigent children to their father's wages.[28] Reagan also worked with assembly speaker Jesse Unruh to oust University of California chancellor Clark Kerr, after receiving pressure from FBI director J. Edgar Hoover to fire Kerr for his insufficient cooperation with the bureau's anticommunist crusade against student organizers of the Free Speech Movement. Although Reagan was not able to implement his desired program for "vetting" prospective faculty in politically sensitive disciplines, his budget cuts did force the University of California system to begin charging tuition.

In 1970, Reagan defeated Unruh for a second term as governor. In his gubernatorial campaign, Unruh ran to the right of Reagan on a number of key issues. For instance, Unruh called for the complete abolition of property taxes on residential property and decried "pussyfooting" administrators who refused to quell campus unrest. Noting a 57 percent increase in welfare applications, Unruh expressed support for Nixon's national welfare reform plan. Unruh also proposed creating a Reserve Officer Training Corps (ROTC)–like program for aspiring police officers in the University of California system.

In 1974, Reagan championed Proposition 1, a measure that would have capped the state budget at 7 percent of state income. Reagan sought to use Proposition 1 as a springboard back into national politics, one which would outflank his rivals for the 1976 Republican presidential nomination on his fiscal bona fides. The ballot language was drafted by Sacramento lawyer and future Supreme Court justice Anthony Kennedy.[29] The measure was soundly defeated, but luckily for Reagan, the defeat was quickly overshadowed by the spiraling Watergate scandal.[30] In that year's gubernatorial race, Pat Brown's son Jerry narrowly defeated University of Southern California professor and state controller Houston Flournoy.[31] Down ballot, Unruh was elected state treasurer, a position he would occupy until his death in 1987.

FROM TAX REVOLT TO GLOBAL INVESTOR

By the early 1970s, many foresaw a crisis as property tax rates and home values crept higher in Los Angeles and across the state. The modernization of the state property tax system, which Isaac William Martin defined as the "centralization, professionalization, and standardization of property assessment," fundamentally transformed the politics of taxation in California.[32] Previously, assessments were left to the discretion of the county assessor, which in practice produced a patronage system.

In 1966, San Francisco county assessor Russell Wolden was convicted of bribery and conspiracy for running an elaborate scheme whereby businesses would pay artificially inflated property taxes unless they sought out the advice of his network of tax consultants.[33] In response, the California legislature passed a bill requiring property tax assessments to be set at 25 percent of market value. Previous tax privileges were now replaced with a more "objective" measure determined by the market. California homeowners were not pleased; the reforms both deprived them of their particular privileges under the previous system and linked their tax bills to the exploding price of real estate across the state.

Los Angeles was ground zero for the unrest.[34] A general rightward turn had been percolating for some time.[35] During the depression, the city switched to a pay-as-you-go funding model for its pension system, accumulating massive unfunded liabilities. In 1959, the Los Angeles city charter was amended to switch to an "actuarial basis" accounting model that required payments to address this unfunded liability. Rather than absorb the shock of higher contributions immediately, however, the city set a fifty-year amortization schedule for the changes to take effect. In 1961, the city council voted to increase property taxes by 10 percent each year until the full payment amount was reached.

As a result, the city's pension cost doubled between 1970 and 1975. Nearly half of all Los Angeles property taxes funded pension benefits.[36] In the words of one city official, "if we are going to get property tax relief it is necessary for the city to find some other sort of revenue to finance [pension] systems." Between 1970 and 1980, housing prices in Los Angeles increased by a factor of five, an extreme example of the more general increase in housing prices across the country.[37] The local perception was that overpaid public employees were to blame for driving up taxes, rather than the confluence of factors including skyrocketing housing prices, a property tax system based on market valuation, cost-of-living increases, and the hangover from the city's earlier accounting model.

In the 1978 primary election, California voters approved Proposition 13 by a nearly two-to-one margin. Led by area businessman and perennial crank Los Angeles mayoral candidate Howard Jarvis, Proposition 13 kicked off the "tax revolt" that was instrumental in delivering the presidency to Ronald Reagan two years later. Proposition 13 functionally removed local control over government finance. City and state officials could now only recommend taxes for the ballot, which required a two-thirds supermajority to be approved. Neoconservative commentator Irving Kristol hailed Proposition 13 as a decisive answer to the prevailing question of "economic growth in a free society versus the allocation of income and wealth by government in a stagnant economy."[38] Between the primary and the general election, Pat Brown pivoted hard toward Proposition 13, referring to himself as a "born-again tax cutter"; this earned him the endorsement of Howard Jarvis. Many labor leaders were aghast at this switch from stalwart opposition to near-endorsement of Proposition 13.[39] The gambit worked:

opinion polls revealed that the public believed Brown to be a backer of Proposition 13 and his Republican challenger an opponent.

Against the backdrop of the tax revolt, Brown squared off against Republican candidate and California attorney general Evelle Younger. Younger, previously of the FBI and the Office of Strategic Services (OSS), made a name for himself as Los Angeles district attorney by initiating the first felony prosecutions for campus demonstrations at San Fernando Valley State and secretly indicting the East L.A. 13 for leading walkouts in protest of unequal conditions in predominantly Chicano public schools.[40] Younger collected four pensions: one from the military, one from Los Angeles county, and two from the State of California.[41] Brown attacked Younger for benefiting from cost-of-living increases to his pensions while current state workers were forced to forego pay raises, painting Younger as a hypocrite for living off the dole while calling for public spending cuts.[42]

With an eye toward his 1980 run for the Democratic presidential nomination, Brown also scolded President Jimmy Carter for printing money to finance the deficit, decrying the "red machine in Washington" that "prints red ink" and insisting that the "red ink takes money out of your pocket by way of inflation, and therefore in each sector we must tighten down, whether it's in health, education, pensions, government spending of all kinds."[43] Brown's then-singular combination of techno-futurism, Buddhism, and fiscal conservatism was pilloried by San Francisco–based punk rock band Dead Kennedys in their 1979 debut single "California Über Alles," with visions of "suede denim secret police," "organic poison gas," "Zen fascists," and jogging "for the master race."

Conservative columnist George Will applauded Brown's recognition that there was no longer political support in California for "explicit redistribution of income for egalitarian purposes" but noted that "Californians are receptive to a program for more direct government production of 'human capital' (trained manpower) and government 'targeting' of financial capital."[44] In his 1980 presidential campaign, Brown's economic policy called for organized capital investments aimed at "reindustrializing the country to sustain our needs and our competitive position."[45] In Brown's diagnosis, postwar liberalism exceeded its material basis: "the underlying problem is that our economic growth is reaching a plateau." The reason, Brown argued, involved the "rules governing the various biological, personal, political, and economic aspects of the world. It is the task of leadership to find those rules, and to communicate them clearly."[46]

* * *

The annual cost-of-living adjustments approved by Reagan in 1968, and subsequently increased over the next few years, proved extremely costly during the inflationary 1970s. The combination of inflation and Proposition 13 created a serious bind for California public employers. Wage and pension costs were rising at unprecedented rates just as tax revenues were drastically cut. In Los Angeles, for instance, this combination led the city to fire 20 percent of its municipal workforce in order to meet its increased pension obligations.[47] How would California public employers escape this double bind?

Many public employers cut the required employee pension contributions as a cheaper alternative to pay increases. Rather than giving out raises that must be paid every year, the employer could discount their increased contribution to cover the shortfall over many years.[48] Ideally, investment returns would make up the difference and prevent dipping into the general fund. As one retirement system manager explained, "politicians use the retirement system as a means of placating employees because it's a pay-later system."[49] Another widespread adaptation was increasing service and use fees in an effort to offset the decline in property tax revenues. The end result was that public agencies shifted the tax base from encompassing taxation for collective purposes to fee-for-service public goods on the model of a private enterprise.[50]

Increasing investment returns was paramount in this new political landscape. CalPERS head Jim Smith described the pressures now facing public pension funds: "pension fund managers above everything else have to make an adequate yield."[51] Brown made it clear that "pension funds will have to institutionalize an allocation to greater risk."[52] More risk meant more potential return and less state support in a new era of resource constraints. Brown pushed CalPERS toward investments in high-tech California businesses as a means of keeping up with Japanese competitors.[53] In 1978, Jeremy Rifkin and Randy Barber observed how pension funds in search of higher returns were exacerbating the shift of investment capital to the Sun Belt and away from traditional industrial bases in the northeast.[54] In 1982, the CalPERS board increased the discount rate from 6.5 percent to 8.5 percent, which both stabilized funding levels on paper and reflected the new era of higher interest rates.

A new financial asset class offered a seemingly miraculous solution to CalPERS's predicament. Home mortgages were previously unattractive to pension funds because they were not readily marketable and required long-term commitments at fixed rates of return.[55] The advent of the mortgage-backed security (MBS) and the collateralized mortgage obligation (CMO) removed these obstacles.[56] This latter instrument, first sold by Freddie Mac, eliminated the prepayment and duration risk from mortgages by tranching a pool of mortgages into medium- and long-term bonds. These innovations created a self-reinforcing cycle as more entrants into securitized mortgage markets increased their liquidity, drawing further entrants. In the words of Laurence Fink, then a managing director at First Boston and underwriter of an early CMO issue, "I've never seen a more impressive list of pension managers buy mortgage-backed securities."[57] However, Reagan administration Office of Management and Budget (OMB) economist Lawrence Kudlow decried the concentration of the GSEs in the secondary mortgage markets. Speaking of policy changes at the federal level, MBS pioneer Lewis Ranieri said, "Decisions are being made right now that will shape housing for years."

Before the Volcker shock, real estate investments were limited to government-guaranteed mortgage certificates. After the Volcker shock, CalPERS began making direct investments in real estate that promised even higher returns than agency mortgage pools.[58] One emblematic example was its purchase of the U.S. Steel building in Pittsburgh in 1982.[59] Through its real estate portfolio, CalPERS could satisfy rising demands for both "socially responsible" and California-focused investment without making any sacrifice to financial returns.[60] Brown was highly encouraging of efforts to increase investment in the California housing stock via its pension funds.[61] At the same time, pension funds could supplement the sharp declines in mortgage financing from savings and loan institutions.[62] Proposals for CalPERS to begin investing in private-label MBS and direct equity investments were cheered by bankers and developers as a new source of funding in the Volcker era of 20 percent mortgage interest rates.[63] By 1981, 25 percent of the portfolio was invested in mortgages, peaking at 35 percent in the mid-1980s. CalPERS's mortgage book yielded an astounding 14 percent. Increased risk delivered increased rewards, and the political lesson was unmistakable.

In 1984, Proposition 21 removed the 25 percent cap on equity investments. The measure was pushed by CalPERS, California State Teachers' Retirement System (CalSTRS), and Assembly Speaker Willie Brown. CalPERS was now free to invest in the stock market without limit.[64] At the same time, the growing size of its equity portfolio required CalPERS to become more engaged in questions of corporate governance to increase returns. Unruh founded the Council of Institutional Investors in response to the Bass brothers' attempt to take over Texaco in 1984. The council promulgated a "shareholder bill of rights" that called for a principle of "one share one vote" and shareholder approval for significant corporate actions.

In November 1984, Brown lost a Senate race to San Diego mayor Pete Wilson, and Los Angeles mayor Tom Bradley narrowly lost the governor's race to Attorney General George Deukmejian after leading in opinion polling throughout the race.[65] Meanwhile, CalSTRS faced a scandal as Chairman Gilbert Chilton was caught accepting a $1 million bribe for steering a $50 million loan to a shady oil company. Chilton abruptly resigned his post and fled both his family in Fresno and the law with his twenty-four-year-old girlfriend Cheryl "Chicky" Ciccarelli.[66]

For the remainder of the 1980s and 1990s, CalPERS became famous for driving corporate governance reforms at major corporations. "The Board adopted a resolution declaring its intent to seek representation on the boards of directors of companies held in the portfolio. The intent [was] to improve corporate profitability and to stimulate corporate managements to better operate the companies for the shareholders' benefit and increased return."[67] New equity exposure placed CalPERS at the forefront of a broader shift toward "shareholder value" as the dominant ideology of corporate governance became "widely regarded as the leader in shareholder activism in the U.S. equities market."[68] Riding the prevailing financial tailwinds, CalPERS earned double-digit returns throughout the 1980s.

The United States officially entered a recession in July of 1990. The proximate cause was the doubling of global oil prices after the Iraqi invasion of Kuwait. The American economy was further hamstrung by the hangover from the savings and loan crisis and commercial real estate bubble of the late 1980s. The recession hit California especially hard. The end of the Cold War precipitated a wave of layoffs among aerospace and defense contractors disproportionately concentrated in southern California. As a result, state gross domestic product (GDP) contracted by 4 percent between 1990 and 1993. The economic malaise lingered into the mid-1990s, compounded further by the racial unrest of 1992 and the 1994 earthquake in Los Angeles. The recession and ensuing collapse of the commercial real estate bubble weighed heavily on the CalPERS portfolio.[69]

In 1991, newly inaugurated governor Pete Wilson launched the most aggressive political offensive against CalPERS in its history. In response to a $14 billion state deficit, Wilson sought to redirect $1.6 billion from CalPERS and raise the discount rate from 8.5 percent to 9.5 percent to reduce the required state contributions. Perhaps more significantly, Wilson's plan would have also reshaped the CalPERS board by empowering the governor to appoint a majority of its members.[70] State controller and former Jerry Brown chief of staff Gray Davis drew an analogy to foreign affairs: "Hussein wanted Kuwait so he took it. The governor wants CalPERS and he's trying to take it."[71]

Wilson briefly succeeded in appointing a state actuary who dictated a higher discount rate, thus reducing required state contributions. In response to Wilson's attempted takeover, however, public employees organized a drive for Proposition 162, which passed narrowly in 1992. The proposition empowered the CalPERS Board of Administration with the "sole and exclusive power over the management and investment of public pension funds," constitutionally insulating CalPERS from political pressure. With this new political independence, the board increased the equity allocation of the portfolio to a record high of 63 percent and decreased the fixed-income allocation to 30 percent. As the annual report explained, "CalPERS believes the shift into equities is a natural and necessary response to the demographic realities that we face."[72] CalPERS was now fully invested in global capitalism.

Private Equity

In 1990, CalPERS made its first investment—a 2 percent allocation—in a new asset class called "private equity."[73] A few years prior, former Treasury secretary William Simon made national headlines when he netted a $70 million profit in just eighteen months from a leveraged buyout (LBO) of the Gibson greeting card company.[74] In an LBO, a private equity firm acquires a company using a combination of its own capital raised from investors and borrowed money from investment banks and the junk bond market. The profit generated by the acquired business is used to pay down the debt issued to acquire the company.

After a holding period of several years, the private equity firm sells the company, ideally for a handsome profit.[75] The basic principle can be illustrated by the following analogy: in buying a rental property, an investor stakes the down payment for the mortgage and then uses the rental income from the property to pay down the mortgage. When the property is sold, the owner receives the difference between the sale price and the remaining balance on the mortgage. Although the first LBO was completed in the 1950s, the practice exploded in the 1980s. The Kemp-Roth tax cut of 1981 lowered the top capital gains rate from 28 percent to 20 percent, enabling the same capital investment to yield more after-tax profit.

The rise of these new private equity firms reflected the turmoil of the preceding decade. In the aftermath of the oil crises of the 1970s, American producers became flush with cash. In 1980, oil companies alone earned one-third of all corporate profits. Texas oil money looked to expand on its good fortune. Oil barons, including the Bass brothers, T. Boone Pickens, and H. L. Hunt, all founded private equity firms to redeploy their windfalls.[76] Thomas Edsall and Mike Davis argue that this new money from the New Right in the Sun Belt played a crucial role in financing Reagan's presidential campaigns and served more generally as the "financial glue" that fused this emergent faction with the old Republican establishment of the northeast.[77] In 1988, Vice President George H. W. Bush, formerly of the Zapata Petroleum Corporation and son of former Connecticut senator and Brown Brothers Harriman partner Prescott Bush, was elected president. In 1990, Bush's son and campaign advisor George W. Bush was investigated by the Securities and Exchange Commission (SEC) for insider trading stemming from an investment in Harken Energy. Several years prior, Mitt Romney, son of former Michigan governor, Department of Housing and Urban Development secretary, and Packard executive George Romney, founded Bain Capital. Other private equity giants like Blackstone, Apollo, KKR, TPG, and the Carlyle Group were all founded during this period.[78]

State pension funds were important early investors in these new funds. John Hitchman, chief of the Washington state pension fund, justified these investments: "all the squares on the Monopoly board have been taken."[79] The Oregon state pension fund invested 40 percent of the money (8 percent of the fund's assets) for KKR's takeover of Fred Meyer in 1981.[80] Some speculated that "by allying themselves with KKR, the Walter Mitty types who ran big state pension funds could feel that they were players, too."[81] KKR's 1989 buyout of RJR Nabisco was famously chronicled in the book *Barbarians at the Gate* by Bryan Burrough and John Helyar. The state of Iowa invested 5 percent of its pension fund in the RJR deal alone. The generosity from the state pension funds did not go unnoticed. KKR donated to Edward Regan's campaign for New York State comptroller (the position responsible for making decisions on public pension fund investments). New York subsequently invested $55 million in 1986 and $370 million in 1987 with KKR.[82] One 1996 study estimated that nearly 30 percent of all private equity capital came from public pension funds.[83]

Economist Michael Jensen welcomed the private equity boom for solving the "central weakness of the public corporation—the conflict between owners and managers over the control and use of corporate resources."[84] In a public corporation, managers are incentivized to hoard cash rather than distribute it to shareholders in the form of buybacks or dividends. In Jensen's view, takeovers were necessary to disgorge the cash that would otherwise rot in corporate treasury accounts. Furthermore, the debt required to finance a leveraged buyout was a beneficial disciplining device: "debt can force managers to adopt value-creating policies they would otherwise resist." Financial discipline thereby increases financial productivity.[85]

CalPERS, like many other state pension funds, increased its allocation to hedge funds and private equity.[86] Public pension funds were catching up to university endowments that had already made significant allocations to this asset class. At Yale, Chief Investment Officer (CIO) David Swensen pioneered "The Yale Model," in which a significant percentage of the portfolio was held in illiquid "alternative" asset classes like hedge funds, private equity, timberland, and real estate. Yale averaged 34 percent return on its private equity investments between 1997 and 2007, and CalPERS was eager to replicate their success.[87] The vast majority of private equity investments were made in "corporate restructuring" strategies.[88]

In 2001, CalPERS purchased a 5 percent equity stake in the Carlyle Group. Unlike most other major private equity firms, Carlyle was based in Washington, DC, and used its network of well-connected advisors to source deals and bring in investors.[89] Carlyle focused on industries highly sensitive to government policy like defense, banking, and telecommunications. This business model created an uncomfortable scene on September 11, 2001, when Shafiq bin Laden, brother of Osama bin Laden, George H. W. Bush, and James Baker (Bush family consigliere and architect of the *Bush v. Gore* Supreme Court case) were all in attendance at an investment conference near the White House.[90]

In 2004, CalPERS approved a policy restricting private equity investments in "public sector outsourcers" defined as companies that sell goods or services that "might result in the reduction of government jobs."[91] To date, this is the only policy restriction on the fund's private equity investments. Building on the 2001 equity investment in the Carlyle Group, CalPERS bought similar stakes in Apollo Global Management and Silver Lake Partners.[92] As partial owner, CalPERS would earn a share of the firm's total profits in addition to investments in the firm's funds. Another $400 million was invested in a hedge fund led by former SEC chairman Richard Breeden, who helped create the Resolution Trust Corporation under Reagan.[93] From 1990 to 2015, CalPERS paid at least $3.4 billion in fees to its private equity managers.[94]

Shareholder Value

Despite its considerable investments in private equity, CalPERS was better known for its activities in the public equity market.[95]

Beginning in the late 1980s, CalPERS began publishing a "hit list" of underperforming companies in its equity portfolio, naming blue-chip companies like Reebok, American Express, Westinghouse, and IBM as laggards. With accidental help from Michael Moore's debut documentary *Roger & Me*, CalPERS successfully ousted Roger Smith as chief executive officer (CEO) of GM. CalPERS secured a public promise from Kodak CEO Kay Whitmore to make the firm more profitable in exchange for supporting Whitmore's desired slate of directors. For corporate executives, this newfound shareholder activism was an unwelcome development. In 1990, the Business Roundtable organized a series of meetings between CalPERS head Dale Hanson and corporate CEOs at the Treetops mansion in Stamford, Connecticut, to negotiate a detente.[96] The result was a marked softening of the combative tone that dominated Unruh's anti-greenmail campaigns.[97] After these meetings, CalPERS's most common demands shifted to reductions in executive compensation packages and installing more independent directors on corporate boards.[98]

The goal of shareholder activism was to "enhance shareholder value for CalPERS' members" by "positively reforming undervalued companies in the internal portfolio that produce the lowest long-term value relative to peers and lack good governance practices." The fund dubbed the growth in "shareholder value" from corporate governance initiatives as "the CalPERS effect."[99] The first principle of "accountable corporate governance" is "optimizing shareowner return: Corporate governance practices should focus the board's attention on optimizing the company's operating performance, profitability and returns to shareowners."[100] In a similar vein, a report commissioned by New York governor Mario Cuomo argued that "the fiduciaries responsible for today's large pension funds have become, like senior management in the banking, insurance, and security industries, the nation's *capital managers*."[101]

In 1994, CalPERS began sending corporate governance questionnaires to its top two hundred stock holdings and publishing an annual "report card" based on their responses. By 1997, Business Roundtable's

Statement on Corporate Governance recommended CalPERS's most common proxy demands as corporate best practices.[102] By 2003, all companies listed on the NYSE or NASDAQ were required to have majority-"independent" boards of directors. CalPERS launched a similar International Corporate Governance Program to "exercise ownership rights" in Japan, Germany, the United Kingdom, and France.[103]

In 1993, CalPERS made its first direct investment—$250 million—in a partnership with the Houston-based Enron Corporation to invest in natural gas infrastructure.[104] The CalPERS investment was an important vote of confidence for Enron as it transitioned from staid owner of energy infrastructure to high-flying broker profiting from the "financialization of energy."[105] The Joint Energy Development Investments LP (JEDI) would allow CalPERS to reap the benefits of private equity investment without the usual fees. In 1995, CalPERS invested $200 million in Relational Investors, an activist investor founded by alumni of T. Boone Pickens's famous activist hedge fund.[106] CalPERS had become a central protagonist in the transformation of corporate governance wherein the firm was no longer treated as an entity producing goods and services but as a financial asset to be maximized by any means necessary.[107]

Les Cinq Glorieux

In 1994, Pete Wilson rode the national Republican wave to an easy gubernatorial reelection victory over Kathleen Brown, daughter of Pat and sister of Jerry. Wilson was able to deflect the poor economic performance of the previous four years with his advocacy for Proposition 187, a measure that would have required proof of citizenship to access public services. The measure passed but was blocked immediately by the federal courts. Proposition 184, which created California's notorious "three strikes" law, passed overwhelmingly with 72 percent of the vote. In the following years, several other conservative ballot propositions passed with comfortable margins. In 1996, Proposition 209 banned affirmative action and Proposition 218 extended Proposition 13's requirement of voter approval for all taxes and most fees, thereby closing several loopholes public agencies had relied upon. Many California cities responded by pursuing redevelopment projects in an effort to recoup lost revenue. In 1998, Proposition 227 banned most forms of bilingual education in public schools.

A few weeks after the 1994 election, Orange County declared bankruptcy.[108] At the time, it was the largest municipal bankruptcy in American history. The source of the trouble was the Orange County Investment Pool (OCIP), which invested over $7.5 billion on behalf of two hundred public agencies in Orange County. County treasurer Robert Citron generated high returns for members, enabling them to rely on interest income from their investments in the OCIP for an increasing share of their budget. Before the bankruptcy, Orange County believed that earnings from the fund would meet 35 percent of their fiscal year 1995 budget (the state average at the time was just 3 percent).

The secret of OCIP's success lay in the bourgeoning world of "derivatives," which enabled the fund to amass a nearly $20 billion position betting on declining interest rates. However, Federal Reserve chairman Alan Greenspan unexpectedly doubled interest rates over the course of the year to fight inflation, completely wiping out the fund. In the words of one financial adviser describing the county's embrace of speculative finance, "You can pin this almost 100 percent on Proposition 13. The only reason people are out there trying to turn two dimes into a quarter is they can't finance basic needs anyway else. The Music Man comes in and says 'I can get you 10 percent when everyone else gets 5 percent,' and he's a hero."[109] However, Greenspan quickly shot down calls to regulate the nascent derivatives market in light of the bankruptcy.

In 1996, California became one of the first states to "deregulate" its electricity market. Four years prior, the federal Energy Policy Act of 1992 opened the door to such experiments after a decade of political wrangling. The Public Utility Holding Company Act of 1935 created the familiar system of vertically integrated utilities generating and distributing power within a defined service area.[110] The 1992 act opened the door to state-level "unbundling" of generation from distribution, permitting the creation of a "competitive wholesale power market."[111] The California bill was drafted by Assemblyman Jim Brulte and State Senator Steve Peace (the auteur behind the *Attack of the Killer Tomatoes!* tetralogy) and passed the assembly unanimously. As he signed AB1890 into law, Wilson proclaimed: "We've pulled the plug on another outdated monopoly and replaced it with the promise of a new era of competition."[112] The state was tasked with ensuring the proper operation of the new market for electricity dubbed the "California Power Exchange" (CalPX). Utilities were now required to buy and sell power on the state exchange. To prevent favoritism, the law also charged the California Independent System Operator (CalISO) with control over the state's high-voltage distribution system. In this way, the law created a market for electricity and tasked the state with ensuring its proper operation.

After years of economic malaise, an increase in southern California tourism and northern California tech "startups" finally restored healthy growth rates. By the end of the 1990s, CalPERS's funding ratio exceeded 100 percent and the state enjoyed a healthy budget surplus stemming from a wave of tech initial public offerings (IPOs). In 1999, Governor Gray Davis signed SB400 into law, massively expanding retirement benefits for state employees. The California State Employees Association threatened to authorize a strike if Davis did not grant pay raises (state employee compensation had been frozen since the early 1990s).[113] The bill passed both houses of the state legislature with overwhelming bipartisan support. Among other things, the bill allowed California highway patrolmen to retire with a 3 percent pension per year of service at age fifty, reduced the pension calculation window from three years to one, drastically increasing benefits, and gave a 5 percent raise to all state employees. The booming stock market increased these benefits without requiring additional contributions from employees or employers. The good fortune would not last.

FROM DOTCOM TO SUBPRIME

The bull market of the late 1990s ended abruptly in March of 2000, when the tech-heavy NASDAQ index entered a freefall. The collapse of the dot-com bubble resulted in significant reductions to both state income tax revenues and CalPERS's portfolio value. Given restrictions on property taxes, California was heavily reliant on income and sales taxes. Unlike property taxes, however, these taxes were inherently more procyclical and thus responsive to prevailing economic conditions. The result was a massive state budget deficit. Simultaneously, an electricity crisis engulfed the state and led to rolling blackouts, the bankruptcy of a major utility, and the first recall of a sitting governor in state history.

Beginning in 1998, the state's three major "investor-owned utilities," Pacific Gas and Electric (PG&E) in northern California, Southern California Edison (SCE) in the greater Los Angeles region, and San Diego Gas and Electric in San Diego County, were required to buy and sell electricity on the state's new market for electricity—the California Power Exchange (CalPX). Although wholesale electricity prices—those paid by the utilities to generators—were now floating in accordance with the whims of the market, most Californians were protected by a rate freeze that lasted until 2002.

The first sign of trouble presented itself in the summer of 2000 when electricity rates in San Diego quadrupled. While the population of California increased nearly 15 percent during the 1990s, electrical generation capacity remained flat. The state made up the difference by importing power from out of state, particularly from federal hydropower plants in Oregon and Washington. However, widespread drought drastically reduced the availability of hydropower exports from the northwest. Much like the oil crisis two decades prior, a relatively small reduction in the supply of a highly "inelastic" commodity precipitated a sharp increase in prices. By December, wholesale electricity prices on CalPX were eleven times higher than the year before.[114] The state responded by recapping prices. However, utilities were still required to buy power from CalPX. With retail prices set by regulators, utilities were forced to pay skyrocketing wholesale prices and absorb the losses.

On January 17, 2001, a power plant in northern California unexpectedly tripped offline. Grid operators were unable to secure sufficient imports to cover the resulting shortfall and implemented rolling blackouts across a wide swath of the state to prevent a cascading failure of the state grid. The problem was compounded by a bottleneck on "Path 15," the high-voltage transmission corridor connecting California's northern and southern population centers; this prevented small power surpluses in the south from being sent north. Earlier in the week, Southern California Edison defaulted on a payment of hundreds of millions of dollars to its creditors and suppliers. PG&E faced similar financial strains. Generators were increasingly unwilling to sell power to these financially imperiled utilities. Liquidating California's largest utility was not an option.

On February 1, the state assembly authorized the Department of Water Resources to buy power on behalf of its regulated utilities. The State of California thus deployed its "full faith and credit" to bail out the utilities and ensure the continued availability of electricity in the state. Around the same time, the University of California and California State systems sued their power supplier, Enron, for breaking their contract for fixed electricity rates and exposing them to spiraling market rates.[115] On April 6, PG&E declared bankruptcy after burning through its cash reserves. At the time, it was the largest corporate bankruptcy in the history of the United States. It did not hold that title for very long.

On April 30, an Enron energy trader emailed his colleagues a song set to the tune of the famous opening credit sequence from the TV western *Rawhide*:

Rollin', rollin', rollin',
Though the state is golden,
Keep them blackouts rollin', statewide.

A little colder weather,
And we all freeze together,
Wishin' more plants were on the line.
All the things I'm missin',
Like lights and television,
Are waitin' 'til we can pay the price.

Turn 'em on, turn 'em off,
Shut 'em down, block 'em out,
Turn 'em on, turn 'em off, statewide!
Brown 'em out, black 'em out,
Charge 'em more, give 'em less,
Let the pols fix the mess, statewide![116]

In May, the state created a new financing authority for issuing revenue bonds to support power generation. Echoing the Carter administration, the California Energy Commission began offering rebates for households willing to turn in multiple refrigerators in a desperate and inadequate attempt to decrease consumption. The Bush administration firmly rebuffed Davis's entreaties to cap interstate electricity prices. Some attributed the hesitancy to the fact that Enron and its founder Ken Lay were "the top patrons of Mr. Bush's political career since his first campaign for Congress in 1978."[117] Though Davis harbored ambitions of running for the Democratic presidential nomination in 2004, he proved an easy punching bag representing California's kooky environmentalism, conservationism, and free-market-denialism. After more than a year of political wrangling, the state issued its largest-ever municipal debt offering: a $11.3 billion revenue bond to recoup the costs of buying electricity on behalf of the imperiled utilities. To bypass the need for voter approval, the bonds were to be repaid from surcharges on electricity bills, rather than from the state's general fund.[118]

The crisis finally eased when the Federal Energy Regulatory Commission imposed caps on interstate wholesale electricity prices after a rare public rebuke from Alan Greenspan.[119] The caps brought an end to Enron's most profitable trading strategy of buying wholesale power in California at the capped price, moving it out of state, and then reimporting it at uncapped prices. Meanwhile, CalPERS quietly dispatched a delegation led by Willie Brown to visit companies in its energy portfolio to address worries that political backlash to the ongoing energy crisis would imperil CalPERS's investments in these firms.[120]

Enron's gleeful exploitation of the crisis did not last much longer. A few years prior, CalPERS withdrew its investment from the JEDI II vehicle, the successor entity to its original 1993 investment with Enron.[121] Rather than assume CalPERS's share directly, Enron created another off-balance sheet vehicle, Chewco, to hold the investment. This accounting trick allowed Enron to book profits from JEDI II while its debt remained off of Enron's balance sheet. After admitting that Chewco did not qualify as an "independent entity," Enron was forced to restate several years of financial performance. This admission triggered a spiral of related accounting scandals that culminated in the company's collapse and bankruptcy filing on December 2, 2001. At the time, it was the largest corporate bankruptcy in the history of the United States.[122] Again, this title was not held for very long.

TOTAL RECALL

By late 2002, California made national headlines for its $30 billion budget deficit, a sum larger than the budgets of every state except

New York. One-quarter of the state's revenue came from capital gains on stocks and stock options. During the tech bubble, this provided a windfall surplus of $7 billion. However, this funding source had mostly dried up, leaving a massive deficit in its place. The state failed to pass a budget and entered a partial government shutdown. The impasse was eventually resolved with 10 percent across-the-board budget cuts, tripling of vehicle license fees, a 30 percent increase in tuition at state universities, and $11 billion of new borrowing. The state credit rating was downgraded to one notch above junk. The CalPERS board approved a plan to postpone scheduled raises for public employees in exchange for skipping their annual pension contributions.[123]

After the sharp decline in global equity prices in the early 2000s, CalPERS's funding ratio collapsed, leaving the fund desperate for return. In addition to its portfolio losses, CalPERS faced lower prospective returns in the new low interest rate environment, further impairing its funding status. Unlike in decades past when the fund's discount rate approximated prevailing interest rates, economic stagnation had now pushed interest rates chronically below pension funds' discount rate assumptions, forcing CalPERS to consider creative alternatives. For the first time in its history, all thirteen CalPERS board members represented either organized labor or the Democratic Party. Under new CEO Federico Buenrostro and senior investment officer Michael McCook, CalPERS embarked upon a more aggressive investment strategy to increase returns and fend off political pressure.

Despite the precarious fiscal situation, Davis easily defeated Republican challenger Bill Simon, Jr. (son of Nixon and Ford Treasury secretary William E. Simon, Sr.). The press harangued Simon for his failure to disclose holdings in offshore bank accounts and investment vehicles. But by May 2003, Davis's approval rating stood at just 27 percent. Davis could not escape his handling of the electricity crisis and several allegations of ethical improprieties, accusations compounded by his acceptance of campaign contributions from

Worldcom, Enron, and Arthur Andersen. A consortium of Republicans led by Darrell Issa of San Diego began collecting signatures for a recall election.

Qualifying for the recall ballot required collecting just sixty-five signatures and paying a nominal filing fee. Candidates included former child actor Gary Coleman, media figure Arianna Huffington, and porn magnate Larry Flynt. Emerging atop the pileup of 135 candidates, however, was bodybuilder-turned-actor Arnold Schwarzenegger. Schwarzenegger, a wealthy political outsider running a self-funded campaign as a Republican, was initially dismissed by both Democrats and Republicans as an unserious sideshow in an already chaotic race. One strategist said of Schwarzenegger, "Arnold has name recognition—but some polls have found that a big part of the electorate does not take him seriously."[124] Nevertheless, Schwarzenegger won the recall election with nearly 50 percent of the vote.[125]

One of Governor Schwarzenegger's first acts was to oust Michael Harrigan as CalPERS board president. Harrigan speculated his ouster was retaliation for CalPERS withholding votes for board directors, particularly Michael Eisner at Disney and Steve Burd at Safeway.[126] Disney and Safeway, incidentally, are two of the largest corporate taxpayers in California. The Chamber of Commerce accused Harrigan of neglecting his fiduciary duty to beneficiaries, thereby providing Schwarzenegger the necessary political cover. Harrigan, a pugnacious union lawyer, was replaced with a former school maintenance worker.

A crucial plank of Schwarzenegger's fiscal recovery plan was a pair of ballot measures that would authorize $15 billion in general obligation bonds for deficit funding and mandate balanced budgets going forward. Although state payments to CalPERS were drastically reduced during the tech stock bubble, they increased by nearly a factor of ten between 2000 and 2004. An outraged Schwarzenegger pushed to privatize CalPERS and replace defined pension benefits with the 401(k) retirement scheme now common in the private sector. The proposal went nowhere in Sacramento, but CalPERS received the message that higher investment returns were necessary to forestall future blowback from the state.

In late 2005, five members of the San Diego City Employees' Retirement System (unaffiliated with CalPERS) were indicted on federal conspiracy charges stemming from a 2002 deal that greatly increased benefits to plan members while reducing city contributions.[127] Worryingly for CalPERS, federal prosecutors alleged that the board members misled investors about the solvency of the fund in offering memorandums for various debt issues. The lone independent investment advisor on the board was threatened by other board members with "citizen's arrest" when she refused to leave a meeting after raising concerns about the degree of underfunding and lapse of fiduciary care.[128]

Given the backdrop of chronic fiscal crisis and federal scrutiny, CalPERS was under tremendous pressure to increase investment returns. Fortunately for CalPERS, financial markets again emerged from the postcrisis doldrums. International equity, private equity, and real estate led the way, returning an average of 25 percent for each asset class.[129] By the middle of 2007, the fund made over $100 billion and was fully funded once again. In late 2007, the board reduced the allocation to stocks and bonds and increased the allocation to private equity and real estate: the portfolio was allocated 70 percent to equities, 20 percent to real estate, and 10 percent to corporate and government debt.[130]

Pension funds like CalPERS were principal investors in the collateralized debt obligation (CDO) craze sweeping Wall Street and fueling the ongoing boom in subprime lending. Given the macroeconomic and political pressures facing funds like CalPERS, CDOs—like MBSs two decades prior—appeared to be manna from heaven. Investment banks like Bear Stearns dangled the prospect of 20 percent returns with an investment-grade risk profile. Though mostly invested in the AAA-rated tranches, CalPERS invested at least $140 million in the unrated equity tranches.[131] These securities, also known as the "toxic waste" tranche, were the first to absorb losses from the CDO's portfolio of lower-rated MBSs. CalPERS also held at least $2.5 billion in subprime MBSs directly.[132] When asked about CalPERS's exposure to the developing crisis in the subprime housing market, spokesman Clark McKinley assured reporters that their holdings were all "triple-A rated, the safest to hold."[133]

2008 CRISIS

The global financial crisis of 2007–2008 precipitated widespread declines across every major asset class. In a little less than a year, CalPERS lost nearly $100 billion, reducing its funded status to 60 percent. In response, the board adopted several changes to the "smoothing" policy that phased in the impact of these investment losses over three years.[134] These changes were designed to soften the impact of investment losses on the required contributions of employers, who now faced the prospect of increased pension contributions in tandem with sharp revenue declines from the crisis and ensuing recession.

Several major losses stand out. CalPERS lost $1.3 billion on AAA-rated investments in the Cheyne structured investment vehicle (SIV). Cheyne was one of the first major SIVs to be liquidated in the summer of 2007, a move that marked a significant development in the escalating subprime crisis. CalPERS eventually recouped several hundred million dollars in a settlement with the rating agencies responsible for rating Cheyne's offerings. According to the lawsuit, one Standard & Poor's executive wrote to a colleague: "Lord help our fucking scam."[135]

CalPERS lost another billion dollars on an investment in Mountain House, a master-planned community twenty miles southwest of Stockton. In the depths of the crisis, Mountain House was the most underwater zip code in America; its average homeowner owed $122,000 more than the value of their property.[136] In an effort to boost the attractiveness of Mountain House to potential homebuyers, CalPERS contributed $52 million to build a local high school (the CIO attended the ribbon-cutting ceremony).[137] Mountain House was not unique: CalPERS accumulated nearly 300,000 homes and lots concentrated in California, Florida, and Arizona, which had all plummeted in value. As delinquencies mounted, CalPERS discontinued the Member Home Loan Program established in 1982. Over the life of the program, CalPERS originated 130,000 loans totaling over $21 billion for its members. As recently as 2005, members received a "paycheck stuffer" advertising the program. The fund held $500 million in member home loans. As part of the program, members could borrow against their pensions for no-money-down jumbo loans.[138]

Yet another billion evaporated on a 15,000-acre parcel of undeveloped land in Santa Clarita, thirty miles north of Los Angeles.[139] Five hundred million dollars on Stuyvesant Town apartments in New York City and $100 million on a project to replace 1,800 rent-subsidized tenants in East Palo Alto with luxury condominiums also disappeared. According to the offering memorandum, East Palo Alto was "poised for growth and gentrification." The project was mired in tenant lawsuits, and the investment vehicle defaulted in 2008.[140] Another $1.5 billion was lost on industrial properties in Chicago.[141] Yet another $1 billion was wiped out in a failed attempt to save Washington Mutual through an investment with private equity firm TPG.[142]

In 2009, voters rejected a series of propositions that would have extended emergency tax cuts, sold lottery bonds, freed certain state revenues for other purposes, and shored up education funding. Instead, voters approved a proposition prohibiting raises for legislators in years with budget deficits. In 2010, Attorney General Jerry Brown sued former CalPERS CEO Buenrostro and Alfred Villalobos for fraudulently concealing their financial relationship with Apollo Global Management, one of CalPERS's largest private equity managers. Villalobos, a former CalPERS board member and official in the Los Angeles city economic development office, was a "placement agent" who was paid commissions for securing investments in Villalobos's clients' funds.

Apollo paid Villalobos nearly $50 million over several years for securing several billion dollars in investment from CalPERS. Among other things, Villalobos arranged for the CalPERS investment officer responsible for private equity investments to fly by private jet from Sacramento to New York to attend a fundraiser hosted by Apollo founder Leon Black at the Museum of Modern Art.[143] Villalobos conspired with Buenrostro to secure allocations to Apollo funds and channel kickbacks to Buenrostro. In 2014, Buenrostro pleaded guilty to a federal conspiracy charge and was sentenced to five years in prison. Villalobos died by suicide at a gun range in Reno shortly before his trial was set to begin in 2015.[144]

Soon after, the state of California was investigated by the SEC for possible securities fraud over its disclosure of pension fund risks in its debt issuances.[145] The SEC brought an enforcement action against New Jersey for similar reasons the previous year. The state responded by suing Wall Street banks and the rating agencies. Jerry Brown's replacement as attorney general, former San Francisco district attorney Kamala Harris, secured $300 million from JP Morgan for misrepresentations in the prospectuses for various mortgage investments.[146] Moody's paid CalPERS another $130 million on CDOs it rated AAA. CalPERS had at least $2.5 billion invested in these products.[147]

As governor, Jerry Brown orchestrated the passage of the Public Employees' Pension Reform Act (PEPRA). As part of the act, state employees hired after January 1, 2013, are subject to lower benefit formulas, higher contribution rates, and caps on total "pensionable compensation."[148] The act also prohibits certain forms of pay from counting toward this number ("spiking") and empowers the state to revoke pensions for retirees convicted of certain felonies. The 1955 California Supreme Court decision *Allen v. City of Long Beach* created the "California Rule," which stipulates that a worker's pension benefits accrue in the terms set on date of hire and cannot be retroactively altered. The California Supreme Court ruled that PEPRA's prohibition on service credit buying and pension spiking was indeed constitutional.[149]

In late 2014, a new residential skyscraper at 432 Park Avenue in Manhattan was completed. Inspired by a *fin de siècle* Viennese trash can, 432 Park is a perfect 93-foot by 93-foot square rising 1,400 feet above New York City.[150] At the time, it was the tallest residential building in the world. In the United States, only the Freedom Tower and Chicago's Willis Tower stood taller. One-quarter of the building's floors were designed to be empty, in order to circumvent height restrictions and maximize the value of its units. The penthouse sold to a Saudi retail magnate for nearly $100 million. Architectural critics likened the building to a "middle finger" for its shocking proportions and the shadows it casts over Central Park. The project was led by developer CIM Group, of which CalPERS was the single largest investor.[151] The flagship of "Billionaire's Row" on Central Park South was partially financed with the pension funds of millions of California public employees.

In November 2014, Jerry Brown soundly defeated former treasury undersecretary for financial stability and Troubled Asset Relief Program (TARP) architect Neel Kashkari to win yet another term as governor.[152] In a televised debate, Brown rebuked the doubters: "they were calling California a failed state—another Greece—[the budget] is now in surplus."[153]

* * *

The recent history of CalPERS reveals how a para-state financial entity created to ease distributive conflict enacted a number of significant neoliberal transformations. By a financial sleight of hand, Richard Walker explains, "Californians have been fooled into thinking they could have both low taxes and high quality public infrastructure."[154] Private equity, shareholder value, labor-disciplining mobile international capital, subprime CDOs, and a range of other financial innovations were all partially seeded by the imperative of generating the required rates of financial return. Beyond CalPERS, there is a clear correlation across public pension funds between funding ratios and allocation to risky assets.[155] An anonymous source close to the fund explained the dilemma:

> If they stuck with a 7.75 percent return target and stretched for yield and then the portfolio got hammered by the volatility that comes with that riskier territory, they'd be blamed by beneficiaries and voters alike, no matter how many consultants told them it was okay. If they backed off to a lower, safer number in expectation that the world was likely to be less benign for investors, they'd be vilified by Sacramento for sending much bigger bills to government employer units throughout the state, which was already in a pitched budget battle over scarce resources.[156]

As a result, Michael McCarthy summarizes, "pension fund investment practices are now driven almost solely by capitalist market imperatives."[157] In late 2021, the CalPERS board increased the private equity allocation to 13 percent and added 5 percent of leverage to the portfolio.[158]

6

THE CRISIS OF FINANCE

Is there a greater tragedy imaginable than that, in our endeavor consciously to shape our future in accordance with high ideals, we should in fact unwittingly produce the very opposite of what we have been striving for?
—F. A. Hayek

As long as the music is playing, you've got to get up and dance.
—Chuck Prince

Isn't it wonderful? I'm going to jail!
—George Bailey

In 2004, Federal Reserve Board member Ben Bernanke delivered a speech praising the decline in macroeconomic volatility since the mid-1980s. Although Bernanke listed a number of possible explanations, including changing structural features of the global economy and simple good luck, he insisted that monetary policy "deserves more credit than it has received in the literature." Bernanke thereby placed the wreath on the head of then–Federal Reserve chairman Alan Greenspan for achieving the macroeconomists' holy grail of prolonged growth, low unemployment, and low inflation.

In the 1970s, Bernanke argued, monetary policymakers mistakenly believed that monetary policy could "offset shocks to output" and "underestimate[d] their own contributions to the inflationary problems of the time. . . . Several years passed before policymakers were finally persuaded by the evidence that sustained anti-inflationary monetary policies would actually work. As you know, these policies were implemented successfully after 1979, beginning under Fed Chairman Volcker."[1]

Four years later, as the worst financial crisis since the Great Depression unfolded, Greenspan faced the House Committee on Oversight and Government Reform. The committee was pursuing the question of whether or not Greenspan's resistance to regulation had contributed to the spiraling crisis. Chairman Henry Waxman (a Democrat from California) had the floor.

> WAXMAN: Do you feel that your ideology pushed you to make decisions that you wish you had not made?
>
> GREENSPAN: Well, remember what an ideology is, is a conceptual framework with the way people deal with reality. Everyone has one. You have to—to exist, you need an ideology. The question is whether it is accurate or not. And what I'm saying to you is, yes, I've found a flaw. I don't know how significant or permanent it is. But I've been very distressed by that fact.
>
> WAXMAN: You found a flaw in the reality . . .
>
> GREENSPAN: Flaw in the model that I perceived as the critical functioning structure that defines how the world works so to speak.
>
> WAXMAN: In other words, you found that your view of the world, your ideology was not right. It was not working.
>
> GREENSPAN: Precisely. That's precisely the reason I was shocked, because I had been going for 40 years or more with very considerable evidence that it was working exceptionally well.[2]

What should we make of Greenspan's confession?

For nearly twenty years, Greenspan governed global monetary policy in accordance with the basic tenets of neoliberalism: markets are efficient and self-correcting, governments are inefficient and distorting, and the role of the Federal Reserve is to actively serve the needs of financial market participants. In his early years, Greenspan was a member of Ayn Rand's ironically named "Collective" of misfit libertarians in New York City.[3] Rand dubbed Greenspan "the Undertaker" for his preference for dark suits and ties. After rising through the policymaking ranks, the Undertaker was nominated by Reagan to replace Paul Volcker in 1987 as chairman of the Federal Reserve. Volcker's departure was triggered by his disagreement with Reagan over a proposal to allow commercial banks to engage in investment banking activities.[4] Rand joined Greenspan and his mother at the swearing-in ceremony in the Oval Office.[5]

Greenspan's tenure seemed to validate neoliberal ideology: small government, balanced budgets, and financial deregulation delivered high growth rates while unemployment and inflation remained low. Political apathy reigned as Americans gorged themselves on the spoils of financialization and globalization.[6] Greenspan was eventually rebranded "the Oracle" and "the Maestro" for his cryptic, withholding public persona, apparent mastery of financial market arcana, and steady hand at the monetary helm.[7]

But shortly after his departure from the Federal Reserve in 2006, the mighty dynamo began to sputter. Home prices peaked then fell, mortgage default rates rose, and strip mall mortgage brokers and high-yield credit hedge funds collapsed. The contagion spread rapidly throughout the financial system: greed turned to panic, credit markets froze, and the global financial system teetered on the edge of collapse. The ensuing rescue required jettisoning every tenet of neoliberalism to stave off financial Armageddon. The financial crisis precipitated the worst recession since the Great Depression and ushered in a prolonged period of political unrest.

A composite, if contested, account of the crisis goes something like this: regulators and politicians held in the thrall of neoliberal ideology, claiming the supremacy and efficiency of unfettered markets, did not recognize a housing bubble until it was too late and failed to see the link between the housing market and the global financial system. When they finally acted, they emptied the public treasury to bail out those responsible for the crisis, ensuring the financial system would be made whole while millions lost their jobs, homes, and retirement savings. Neoliberalism's nominal commitment to efficient and self-regulating markets allowed financial sector greed to metastasize into system-jeopardizing fraud with catastrophic consequences for the real economy. However, policymakers readily embraced statism to protect financial sector bonuses and portfolios, revealing neoliberal ideology to be thin cover for the interests of capital.

Initially, many believed that the financial crisis created openings for "alternatives" to neoliberalism to finally take root. The catastrophic failure of neoliberal ideology and policymaking seemed to vindicate critics and call out for a radically new way of thinking and being. The contradiction between neoliberalism's faith in the power of unregulated markets and trillion-dollar state bailouts was unmistakable. After being forcibly disabused of the neoliberal conceit that markets are efficient and self-regulating, policymakers would have no choice but to rediscover the virtues of regulation and redistribution.

These hopes did not last long. Although the crisis was widely considered to be an invalidation of neoliberal ideology and policymaking, as Greenspan reluctantly admitted to Congress, neoliberalism easily survived. Colin Crouch canonically characterized the immediate aftermath of the crisis as the "strange non-death of neoliberalism."[8] Jamie Peck similarly argued that neoliberalism merely lost "another of its nine lives."[9] Barack Obama, an African American born of 1960s academia turned community organizer and professor of constitutional law, seemed to similarly find no alternative. The conflicts of an earlier political era roared back to life.

This chapter demonstrates how the "shadow banking system" in which the 2008 financial crisis originated was created by the political response to inflation in the early 1980s. My purpose is to supplement existing accounts of the crisis with an explanation of the *political* dynamic driving the evolution of shadow banking. The specific instruments and institutions of the shadow banking system were enabled by the response to this earlier crisis. Accordingly, the 2008 financial crisis was not only the result of free market ideology, gross capture, and malign neglect but also of the foundational imperative for depoliticization at the heart of liberal government. For this reason, the financial crisis cannot be explained *solely* as a textbook crisis of capitalism enabled by an ideologically captured regulatory apparatus. Rather, the crisis originated in a bipartisan political response to the earlier crisis of inflation.

This account does not deny the role of particular political and social interests in shaping the trajectory of financialization. There can be no doubt that Greenspan, Washington, and Wall Street all wanted and actively promoted financial liberalization. Rather, my purpose is to explain how these interests coincided with the default path of liberal depoliticization. To this end, this chapter rearranges the existing set of facts about the financial crisis to explain why the American federal government found itself in roughly the same position as the Stockton city council and the CalPERS board: with no alternative to capitulating to the demands of finance, sacrificing the needs and wants of its constituents along the way.[10]

THE FINANCIAL GROWTH REGIME

Under the Fordist growth regime of embedded liberalism, the state managed the domestic cycle between mass production and mass consumption by finessing the level of aggregate demand, driving public investment, and generating mass consumption norms.[11] Steel, cars, semiconductors, media, machine tools, pharmaceuticals, and weapons poured out of American factories and onto world markets. Cookie-cutter Levittowns sprung up around the eastern industrial centers as the budding white middle class fled cities for the suburbs. The white middle class prospered, and the income distribution compressed. However, as chapter 2 charted, shocks emanating from within and without threw the whole regime into confusion and disarray. Fordism gave way to a "post-Fordist" or "financial" growth regime in which the state actively supported the development and extension of financial markets to supplement stagnant incomes and the retrenchment of public provision.[12]

After a decade of turmoil, the good times returned once again: from 1982 to 2007, real gross domestic product (GDP) growth approached the peak of the postwar Golden Era (3.5 percent versus 3.9 percent). For the better part of three decades and four presidencies, cheap oil, cheap credit, cheap consumer goods, and rising home prices fueled the American economy, supplementing stagnant real incomes and the end of the Fordist family wage.[13] Lizabeth Cohen observes that postwar suburban consumerism "promised the socially progressive end of economic equality without requiring politically progressive means of redistributing existing wealth."[14] Financialization offered something similar: rising living standards and distributive depoliticization were achieved through the wealth effect of rising financial asset prices combined with lower consumer prices from globalization and consumer credit access rather than rising incomes.[15] Under this new growth regime, lower prices and lower taxes would boost household purchasing power as real household income remained stagnant.[16] Though steel mills would close and their well-paying union jobs would vanish, the American consumer would recoup some of this lost income in the form of lower prices on imported steel. A rising tide of financial asset prices would lift the most electorally important boats without requiring overt redistribution, binding the interests of the white middle class with the interests of big business.

Paradoxically, the remission of inflation and return of growth were accompanied by a steady decline of the American industrial base. Deregulation and globalization generated unprecedented profits for the financial sector while goods-producing industries fled overseas. Over the course of the 1980s, 1.5 million manufacturing jobs, 300,000 steel jobs, 260,000 railroad jobs, and 120,000 coal mining jobs evaporated into the new circuits of global capital. As the American economy "de-industrialized," its employment base shifted to healthcare, business services, retail, finance, and education. The factories that closed in Bethlehem, Youngstown, Hamtramck, and St. Louis were replaced with office parks in Sandy Springs, Plano, Scottsdale, and Sunnyvale. Chinos replaced hardhats as the totem of the American worker.[17] A booming "service sector" provided outsourced business services such as consulting, accounting, legal services, advertising, public relations, and information technology (IT) to globalizing American multinationals.[18] Much remaining job growth was concentrated in low-wage restaurant, hospitality, and social service jobs; these employees, tasked with serving the ascendant professional class, were disproportionately female and nonwhite.[19]

Reagan's great "discovery" was that cutting taxes did not also require cutting spending: a voracious appetite for treasury bonds filled the gap.[20] Who wouldn't want a risk-free asset yielding 10 percent? As a result, public debt as a percentage of GDP doubled from 30 percent in 1981 to 60 percent in 1991 (where it would more or less remain until 2008). The Volcker shock drove up the value of the dollar as foreign investors sought to capitalize on sky-high American interest rates. As a result, imports became comparatively cheaper, and exports more expensive. In material terms, these yawning trade deficits allowed Americans to consume 3–5 percent more than what they produced in aggregate, financed with capital account inflows. In 1986, America became the largest national debtor.[21] The "exorbitant privilege" of printing the world's reserve currency meant that the United

States never faced the balance of payments crisis such imbalances would otherwise precipitate.[22]

The composition of public spending shifted dramatically over the course of the 1980s. Reagan showered tax expenditures on his voters (disproportionately white homeowners) while enacting brutal austerity for nonvoters and Democratic voters (disproportionately nonwhite renters), all under the heading of fiscal propriety. The operative distributive principle was something like the inverse of Rawls's difference principle, where inequalities are arranged to the least benefit for the least advantaged. Or, as one headline summarized Reagan's 1982 budget proposal, "Benefits for Poor People Face Deepest Cuts."[23] Spending cuts were concentrated in employment training, low-income energy assistance, food stamps, student loan guarantees, welfare, and Medicaid, while federal funding was lavished on marquee defense projects like the B-2 Spirit, Arleigh Burke-class guided missile destroyers, and the Strategic Defense Initiative (also known as, "Star Wars").

Credit access generally replaced welfare spending over this period as public debt loads increased in lockstep with the decline of social spending.[24] Goods once provisioned collectively were now accessed financially. Sarah Quinn shows how "the use of state-promoted financial development and risk redistribution [served] as an alternative to more direct forms of wealth redistribution."[25] From 1980 to 2007, household debt as a percentage of disposable income more than doubled from 60 percent to 130 percent. Households borrowed heavily to preserve their social position amid stagnant incomes and rising precarity.[26] One result was the notion of a "citizen-debtor" replacing the more familiar figure of the "citizen-worker" in sociological studies of economic citizenship.[27] A "finance culture" took root among American households, where different socioeconomic strata were differentially incorporated into the financialized economy.[28]

The single-family home, as repository for consumption goods and nexus of traditional morality, remained the foundation of the post-Fordist financial growth regime, but it now also served as a financial asset to be maximized. In this new regime of "mortgage Keynesianism," rising financial asset prices provided a further supplement to stagnant real wages.[29] New financial products like home equity loans enabled households to transmute rising home prices into disposable income. Household stock portfolios extended the logic of home-ownership society to retirement.[30] Eventually, this phenomenon would be termed the "wealth effect" of rising financial asset prices and an integral component of Federal Reserve policymaking.[31] The wealth effect of rising stock portfolios was buoyed by a dramatic transformation in corporate behavior, which prioritized quarterly financial results and shareholders over all else.[32]

The Financialized Corporation

Over the same period, "shareholder value" became the predominant corporate governance paradigm, shifting the dominant model of corporate governance from "retain and reinvest" to "downsize and distribute."[33] Milton Friedman expressed the ethos in a famous *New York Times Magazine* essay entitled "The Social Responsibility of Business Is to Increase Its Profits." The threat of private equity takeovers and the rise of institutional investors (related developments charted in chapter 5) empowered a cadre of professional managers and devolved corporate decision-making from a business's centralized headquarters to its units responsible for profit and loss targets. Private equity giants like KKR and Forstmann Little were donors to the Council of Institutional Investors, which spearheaded shareholder-friendly corporate governance reforms.[34]

The supremacy of shareholder profits entailed changing employment relations, suppressing wages, increasing worker precarity, the decline of unions, and a general wealth transfer from workers to financial rentiers. Shareholder value can be understood as a solution to the political problem of control among the competing groups—workers, managers, shareholders, bondholders, and customers—that comprise a firm.[35] The sole objective of the corporation is to maximize returns for shareholders. All else is secondary. A standard corporate finance textbook explains the basic political logic of shareholder value:

> Wal-Mart has over 300,000 shareholders. There is no way that Wal-Mart's shareholders can be actively involved in management; it would be like trying to run New York City by town meetings. Authority has to be delegated to professional managers. But how can Wal-Mart's managers make decisions that satisfy all the shareholders? No two shareholders are exactly the same. They differ in age, tastes, wealth, time horizon, risk tolerance, and investment strategy. Delegating the operation of the firm to professional managers can work only if the shareholders have a common objective. Fortunately there is a natural financial objective on which almost all shareholders agree: Maximize the current market value of shareholders' investment in the firm.[36]

In 1982, the Securities and Exchange Commission (SEC) adopted Rule 10b-18, allowing corporations to buy back their own stock on the open market. Stock buybacks became an attractive alternative to dividends because they were not subject to the usual tax and inflated a corporation's earnings per share (EPS) by reducing the number of outstanding shares.

The Rise of Shadow Banking

Inflation, the Volcker shock, and the ensuing waves of financial liberalization fundamentally transformed American housing finance. The bedrock of the old regime was the savings and loan association ("thrift") that transmuted local savings into local mortgages.[37] This conventional form of banking involved borrowing short term (deposits), lending long term (mortgages and commercial loans), and collecting the difference between these two interest rates. This bank-based model of housing finance, in which a single institution originates and holds a portfolio of thirty-year fixed-rate mortgages to maturity, was imperiled by gyrating short-term interest rates. The result was a shift to capital market–based housing finance or, as it would come to be known after the 2008 crisis, "shadow banking."[38] A combination of state and para-state infrastructure supported this new regime, mirroring original codification of the thirty-year fixed-rate mortgage, transforming a "spatially fixed and opaque commodity" into a globalized financial product.[39] By the end of the decade, the New Deal reforms to the financial system generally and to mortgage finance specifically had been largely dismantled; only half of all outstanding mortgage debt was held by thrifts.[40]

When interest rates rose above their statutory maximums, savers would move deposits out of thrifts and into money market funds that offered higher rates. In 1978, the Supreme Court ruled unanimously in *Marquette National Bank of Minneapolis v. First of Omaha* that state anti-usury laws capping interest rates did not apply to nationally chartered banks, effectively eliminating state interest rate caps. In response to this dynamic of "disintermediation," Congress deregulated interest rates to stem the flow of funds from thrifts into other investment vehicles.[41] The repeal of Regulation Q allowed thrifts total autonomy in setting their deposit interest rates. The result was a bidding war among thrifts for deposits.

Paying above-market rates on deposits necessitated earning above-market rate returns on assets. Thrifts shifted away from the traditional business of home mortgages and toward commercial real estate as the market boomed in the early 1980s. The first Reagan tax cut in 1981 introduced the accelerated cost recovery system (ACRS), which drastically shortened the timeline for recognizing capital asset depreciation, thereby boosting the resulting tax deduction.[42] Combined with the reduction in the capital gains tax rate, the rate of return on commercial real estate projects increased significantly.[43] The commercial real estate market was further buoyed by the secular shift in employment toward the service sector and the geographic shift toward the Sun Belt. However, the second Reagan tax cut in 1986 removed the most important provisions of the ACRS and helped pop the commercial real estate bubble.[44]

In 1984, Continental Illinois Bank was on the verge of collapse as a result of oil and gas loans accumulated during the energy crisis that had soured during the subsequent "oil glut." Regulators deemed Continental Illinois "too big to fail," as nearly two hundred other banks had more than half of their equity capital in exposure to the bank.[45] The collapse of Continental Illinois, although an extreme case, was emblematic of the general decline in the commercial banking industry during the 1980s.[46] Like thrifts, commercial banks were similarly disintermediated, as corporations and other borrowers could now raise money directly on capital markets rather than rely on traditional forms of bank lending.

What the thrifts lost on margins they compounded by volume: between 1980 and 1987, total thrift assets doubled while net income turned negative. Roughly 20 percent of these were classified as "zombie" thrifts; they were insolvent but still liquid. Dozens failed every year. The crisis precipitated several scandals among prominent politicians including John McCain and Neil Bush.[47] The single largest failure was American Savings and Loan headquartered in Stockton, California. News of a $1.1 billion loss on commercial real estate led to a $7 billion deposit run—the largest in history—and a $5.4 billion bailout.[48] The remnants of American Savings and Loan were eventually acquired by Washington Mutual. By 1992, commercial real estate prices had fallen nearly 50 percent from their peak. Over one thousand thrifts failed, and the federal government contributed nearly $130 billion to a bailout. Alongside the oil shock from the Gulf War, the crisis was an important contributor to the early 1990s recession.[49]

The savings and loan crisis further accelerated the transformation of American housing finance toward a market-based system.[50] Mortgages were progressively "vertically disintegrated" into their component elements of origination, brokerage, warehousing, credit risk, and servicing; each of these elements was performed by different entities along the housing "value chain" rather than by one entity under a single corporate roof.[51] This transformation created a huge market opportunity for government-sponsored enterprises (GSEs). By 1987, nearly half of all mortgages were securitized. By 1990, GSEs either guaranteed or directly held 60 percent of all mortgages. Thrifts, meanwhile, held only 15 percent, down from nearly half of all mortgages in the early 1970s.[52] Institutional investors like endowments, insurance funds, mutual funds, and pension funds acquired roughly half of the increase in mortgage debt over the course of the 1980s.[53]

Despite their rapid growth, the business model of the GSEs and their role in the American housing market remained largely unchanged. Although Fannie Mae, Freddie Mac, and Ginnie Mae focus on different segments of the housing market, their business models are the same. Mortgage lenders deliver a pool of eligible loans to a GSE. In return, lenders receive a mortgage-backed security (MBS) collateralized by these loans that can then be sold on the secondary market. The ultimate holder of the MBS receives payments collected from the underlying mortgages. In exchange for a "guarantee fee," the GSE guarantees the principal and interest payments on the underlying mortgages. The MBS investors are thereby assured that they will be paid as agreed, so long as the GSE remains solvent. GSE revenues are determined by their share of mortgage securitizations. As long as the mortgages perform as expected, the GSEs could make fabulous amounts of money. However, the business model is predicated on a massive unhedged exposure to the housing market with an implicit state backstop.[54]

The shift to market-based housing finance required further regulatory overhauls.[55] The SEC created the official designation of "nationally recognized statistical rating organization" (NRSRO) to specify which ratings were valid for the purposes of calculating regulatory capital requirements. Rather than rating issuers itself, the federal government deputized a handful of ratings agencies, whose determinations would be ensconced in law. Rather than state governments deciding which assets qualify as "safe" or "risky," a process that would pose immeasurable political obstacles, these governments could instead rely on the ratings of para-state agencies presumed to be run by apolitical technocrats. The "opinions" of the big three rating agencies were thus blessed with the imprimatur of the federal government. In 1984, the Secondary Mortgage Market Enhancement Act allowed nationally chartered banks to invest in MBS, provided the securities carried one of the two highest ratings from a ratings agency.

As both for-profit corporations and para-state agencies, the GSEs enjoyed significant structural advantages. First, they had much looser capital requirements (nearly ten times) than their bank counterparts, allowing them to take on more risk at lower cost. Unlike a bank that funds its mortgage book with insured deposits, the GSEs used funds raised on capital markets to fund their holdings of MBSs. Investors rightly assumed that the GSEs carried an implicit government guarantee and thus a similar risk profile to Treasury bonds. Fannie and Freddie spent significantly on lobbying and helped draft the financial reform bills of 1989 and 1992, entrenching major structural advantages in the mortgage markets for the GSEs. As a result, GSE assets swelled from $759 billion in 1990 to $2.4 trillion in 2000.[56] Between 1980 and 2007, GSE assets grew at a 16 percent compounded annual rate.[57]

The rapid growth of the GSEs contributed to the creation of the shadow banking system.[58] The shadow banking system is often defined as the "money market funding of capital market lending."[59] Rather than regulated and insured deposits funding mortgages held to maturity by the issuing bank, large institutional investors invest cash in short-term debt obligations issued by entities holding pools of mortgage-backed securities. A shadow banking entity, like a regular bank, borrows short to lend long and profits from the spread between the rate it earns on its assets and the rate it pays on its liabilities. However, the credit, liquidity, and maturity transformation of short-term borrowing into long-term lending is accomplished by separate entities along the "securitization food chain." A shadow banking entity, like a regular bank, fails when investors withdraw their money from the system (not renewing their short-term lending) faster than the bank can convert its assets into cash. The shadow banking system replicates the regulated and insured banking system by using AAA-rated collateral as insurance against counterparty default.[60] However, shadow banking entities do not have any form of public "liquidity enhancements" such as deposit insurance, discount window access, or loan guarantees, making them vulnerable to sudden shifts in investor sentiment.[61]

During the 1990s and early 2000s, the global rate of saving climbed steadily higher. Much of savings was recycled into safe, liquid assets in the United States.[62] Ben Bernanke blamed this "global savings glut" for the increased capital inflows into the United States from emerging markets flush with dollars (particularly China), driving interest rates below where macroeconomists thought they ought to have been given prevailing conditions. These inflows pushed up the value of the dollar, contributing to record trade deficits and demand for highly rated dollar-denominated assets.

The imbalances resulting from twenty-five years of financial globalization and stagnant growth created huge institutional cash pools existing outside the regulated banking system, cash pools in need of safe return. The shadow banking system replicated the regulated banking system for these investors. Shadow bank liabilities such as money market mutual funds and asset-backed commercial paper were attractive to large institutional investors who could not deposit their cash in Federal Deposit Insurance Corporation (FDIC)-insured savings accounts. The American housing market served as an attractive forum for domestic and global investors seeking safe returns in a low-interest-rate environment. Thus, the global demand for dollar-denominated safe assets was directly linked to the increasingly precarious state of the American middle class.[63]

Financial Consolidation

In 1992, a man from a little town in Arkansas called Hope won the presidency. In his speech accepting the Democratic nomination for president, Bill Clinton summarized his platform: "The most important family policy, urban policy, labor policy, minority policy and foreign policy America can have is an expanding, entrepreneurial economy of high-wage, high-skill jobs." During the Clinton era, competitiveness and economic growth solidified as the self-evident objective of governmental policy. Many commentators hailed Clinton's program as a pragmatic synthesis of liberalism and conservatism.[64] The strategy was to pivot to the suburbs in order to reclaim segments of the electorate lost in the Reagan revolution.

The political situation was at an impasse: the political foundation of the New Deal order had crumbled, but its universal welfare programs proved surprisingly durable. Consequently, Republicans could not fully dismantle the New Deal, but neither could Democrats shore it up.[65] Two of Clinton's main advisors, Rahm Emanuel and Bruce Reed, pushed Democrats away from the New Deal and toward "updating it for a mobile society," arguing that "citizenship is a responsibility not an entitlement program."[66] For James Carville, the formula was simple: "It's the economy, stupid!" The solution was to embrace the economic orthodoxy of the preceding administrations.[67] An increasing reliance on "expertise" would help keep economic policy questions depoliticized.[68]

On September 14, 1993, President Clinton, flanked by Vice President Gore and former presidents Carter, Ford, and Bush, signed the

North American Free Trade Agreement (NAFTA). During the 1992 campaign, Independent candidate and Texas billionaire Ross Perot had warned of a "giant sucking sound" drawing jobs to Mexico. But, in the words of Vice President Al Gore, "there are some issues that transcend ideology." The passage of NAFTA set the stage for the Uruguay Round of General Agreement on Tariffs and Trade (GATT) negotiations and the creation of the World Trade Organization the following year. Scholars describe this paradigm as the "new constitutionalism," in which international rules would "lock in" neoliberal reforms.[69] Clinton's treasury secretary Robert Rubin, former cochairman of Goldman Sachs, championed the Deficit Reduction Act of 1993, aiming to reverse the deficits of previous administrations and finally implement real "fiscal responsibility." The act's mix of tax hikes and spending cuts received no Republican support, narrowly passed the House, and required Vice President Gore's vote to break a 50–50 tie in the Senate.

Shortly thereafter, unemployment fell below what the Federal Reserve believed to be the nonaccelerating inflation rate of unemployment (NAIRU), a threshold coined and popularized by Milton Friedman. This is the level of unemployment below which incremental job gains are imagined to be inflationary.[70] In response, Greenspan raised interest rates to forestall inflation, triggering a massive wipeout in global bond markets.[71] The resulting sovereign debt crises conjured the figure of the "bond vigilante" punishing recalcitrant states for their fiscal impropriety.

In November 1994, Republicans captured the House of Representatives for the first time since 1955 and the South for the first time since Reconstruction.[72] The following year, Speaker of the House Newt Gingrich engineered a government shutdown after President Clinton vetoed a Republican-led spending bill.[73] For the first time, the government's ability to pay its debts was seriously questioned, as Congress and the White House could not agree on a proposal to raise the federal debt ceiling and avert default. After Moody's threatened to cut the credit rating of nearly $400 billion in Treasury securities and polling indicated the public largely blamed the GOP for the shutdown, Gingrich and Senate Majority Leader Bob Dole relented.[74]

In 1999, Clinton signed the Financial Services Modernization Act, repealing Glass-Steagall and creating a new category of "financial holding company" that allowed well-capitalized financial conglomerates to offer depository banking, as well as previously prohibited financial services such as underwriting, brokerage, insurance, and advisory services. Citigroup chairman Sandy Weill recruited both Gerald Ford and Robert Rubin to steer the bill through Congress. The act permitted the formation of universal financial services firms; banks like JP Morgan, Bank of America, Wells Fargo, and Citi could now offer everything from retail checking accounts and home mortgages to investment banking and prime brokerage under one corporate roof.[75] Employment growth in the 1990s continued the trend of the previous decade, with business services, healthcare, and restaurants dominating employment growth.[76]

The Commodity Futures Modernization Act (CFMA) of 2000 shepherded by Treasury secretary Larry Summers and Greenspan exempted "over-the-counter" (i.e., non–exchange-traded) derivatives from regulation as either "futures" or "securities" and thus from the regulatory authority of the Commodity Futures Trading Commission (CFTC) and SEC. A principal beneficiary of this legislation was the American International Group (AIG). AIG began as American Asiatic Underwriters, a small concern in East Asia that became a front company for "Wild" Bill Donovan's Office of Strategic Services (the company's property records were used to identify bombing targets during World War II).[77] Passage of the CFMA ensured that AIG could write increasingly popular credit default swap (CDS) contracts without hedging or meeting capital reserve requirements to cover potential losses, as a regulated insurer would. Unlike regulated insurers that only pay out when losses actually occur, AIG's CDS contracts triggered collateral calls when the value of underlying assets dropped.

In the span of two decades, the American financial system was dramatically transformed. Before the 1980s, corporate finance was dominated by large commercial banks with stable relationships to a class of blue-chip companies. Similarly, housing finance was dominated by local savings and loan associations ("thrifts"). The political response to inflation charted in chapter 2 seeded the shift from a bank-based to a market-based system alluded to earlier.[78] The effects of this transformation were profound, both to the process of market "plumbing," through which investment is provisioned, and in the effects it induced in borrowers. Attracting investment on the open market now required generating market returns. No more three-martini lunches. Bank-like functions such as credit, liquidity, and duration transformation were now performed by nonbank entities not subject to the same regulations and without access to the same public liquidity guarantees as banks.[79] These changes, in sum, created a financial system beyond the reach and comprehension of any single financial regulator.

THE HOUSING BUBBLE

After the collapse of the tech bubble in the early 2000s, interest rates were slashed to historic lows in an effort to stimulate the economy and soften the ensuing recession. The Fed hoped to spur households to refinance their mortgages at lower interest rates, freeing up disposable income and thus speeding the recovery. The Bush tax cuts of 2001 were pitched as a fiscal antidote to the slowdown.[80] One investment manager noted at the time that "there is room for the Fed to create a bubble in housing prices, if necessary, to sustain American hedonism."[81] The Oracle's monkey paw curled.

In Charles Kindleberger's anatomy of financial bubbles, monetary policy during this period created a "displacement" in the form of a self-reinforcing upward price spiral in the housing market.[82] Between 2001 and 2006, home price increases averaged 11 percent per year; as mortgage rates collapsed to record lows, homebuyers could afford more expensive houses for the same monthly payment. Total mortgage debt doubled (in Stockton, home prices quadrupled over this same period). Rising home prices also enabled households to cash out equity through home equity loans and second mortgages. Roughly $2 trillion of home equity was extracted between 2000 and 2007, providing a significant tailwind to consumer spending. The housing boom created jobs in construction, finance, and insurance, as other sectors lagged behind.

Beginning around 2002, investment banks began securitizing "nonconforming" mortgages into their own "private-label" MBS. Nonconforming mortgages are those that do not meet the minimum GSE purchase requirements (e.g., FICO score too low, loan-to-value ratio too high, missing or no documentation). "Subprime" mortgages are those with FICO scores of 500–660, higher loan-to-value ratios, credit "derogatories" (e.g., bankruptcies and repossessions), and high debt service–to–income ratios.[83] Between 2000 and 2006, the number of outstanding subprime mortgages increased by a factor of ten, with most destined for private-label MBS pools. Unlike "conforming" mortgages, the vast majority of subprime financing came from private-label securitizations.[84] Subprime origination exploded after the prime market was exhausted.[85]

Unlike standard fixed-rate mortgages, subprime mortgages were generally structured as either a "2/28" or "3/27," where the interest rate is fixed for two or three years and then "adjusts" to a higher rate. This structure is intended to induce borrowers to refinance at the end of the initial fixed-rate period to capitalize on the home price appreciation of the intervening years. The resulting increase in homeowner equity allows borrowers to refinance and replace their floating-rate mortgage with a more standard fixed-rate structure.[86] The performance of subprime mortgages is therefore uniquely sensitive to continued home price appreciation.

Securitization allowed subprime mortgages to spread widely throughout the shadow banking system. Money market mutual funds held short-term exposure in the form of investment banks' commercial paper and their structured investment vehicles (SIVs). These latter entities were legal pass-throughs that allowed assets to be held "off the balance sheet" while retaining the imprimatur of the sponsoring bank. These issues were often sweetened with "liquidity puts" that obligated the sponsoring bank to buy the SIV's short-term paper if no other buyers were available. Like a regular bank, SIVs earn income on the spread between the interest paid on their liabilities—usually asset-backed commercial paper—and the interest rates earned on their assets—usually a portfolio of MBSs and collateralized debt obligations (CDOs). Long-term investors included pension funds and insurance companies with fixed liabilities who held MBS and CDO tranches directly.[87]

Building on the success of the collateralized mortgage obligation, Wall Street created CDOs that transmuted the lower-rated tranches of MBSs into AAA securities. The crucial innovation was the "Gaussian copula" formula for elegantly estimating joint default probabilities from CDS prices.[88] Because the CDO held a diversified pool of mezzanine MBS tranches, the senior tranches of the CDO were believed to have the risk profile of a single AAA-rated issuer (somewhere between zero and twenty basis point probability of default per year).[89] The sponsoring entity, usually a large investment bank, would pay for a rating. These ratings, at base, were estimations of the default rates and correlations on the underlying mortgages. CDO ratings increased by a factor of seven while staff barely increased.[90] This arrangement created a clear moral hazard: ratings are purchased by the security issuer, creating a financial incentive for rating agencies to cave to issuer demands less they defect to another ratings agency.

In 2005, AIG paid the SEC and New York State over $1.6 billion as part of a settlement stemming from a variety of fraudulent accounting and business practices.[91] As part of the settlement, AIG agreed to "cooperate on all examinations and regulatory requests." A similar accounting scandal engulfed Fannie Mae. The White House formed a taskforce nicknamed "Operation Noriega" to rein in the GSEs.[92] The business-friendly Bush administration did not want another Enron on its hands. Fannie Mae chief executive officer (CEO) Franklin Raines was ousted, and the company agreed to a $400 million settlement for not abiding by generally accepted accounting principles (GAAP). Freddie Mac preemptively switched accountants; the new ones promptly discovered that the company had overstated its earnings by $5 billion, going back several years.

Home prices kept climbing higher and the fees kept rolling in. By 2008, AIG's infamous "financial products" division had written nearly half a trillion dollars in protection on CDOs. Their AAA credit rating enabled AIG to insure at lower costs, owing to its reduced collateral requirements; this allowed AIG to dominate the market. Meanwhile, mortgage underwriting standards deteriorated markedly. The end of the refinancing boom in 2003 pushed mortgage originators increasingly into subprime.[93] In 2004, Countrywide surpassed Wells Fargo as the largest originator of mortgages in the United States.[94] Unlike Wells Fargo, Countrywide was an exemplar of the "originate-to-distribute" model, wherein its mortgages were sold to other investors down the securitization pipeline.[95] If there were problems with their mortgages, it would not be their problem. By the end of 2005, housing starts approached the all-time peak reached in 1973.

In 2004, for example, 40 percent of private-label subprime MBSs were ultimately purchased by a GSE. In 2006, Fannie Mae's board approved a plan to "increase [their] penetration into subprime," thereby increasing exposure as the housing market crested in the second quarter of 2006.[96] Fannie Mae also charged lower guarantee fees than their models recommended in order to grow their market share in Alt-A MBSs (and lowered their underwriting standards accordingly). These efforts were designed to recoup lost market share to private-label MBSs. In total, the GSEs acquired nearly $700 billion of subprime and Alt-A securities over the course of the housing boom.[97]

The Enron and Worldcom scandals prompted a regulatory response from both Congress and the Financial Accounting Standards Board (FASB). The FASB is a private organization recognized by the SEC that sets the accounting standards (GAAP) for publicly traded companies. These standards are especially impactful for banks whose required regulatory capital is calculated as a percentage of the value of their assets.[98] After several years of bureaucratic wrangling, FASB Directive 157 came into effect on November 15, 2007.

This directive stipulated the methodology for measuring the "fair value" of financial assets held on banks' balance sheets. Enron, for example, had used dubious mark-to-market accounting practices to recognize $110 million in profits from a pilot project with Blockbuster Video for home media streaming.[99] FASB 157 was designed to prevent such abuses by specifying exactly how fair value would be determined. Simultaneously, the ABX—a new financial index that tracks the prices of subprime MBSs—began trading. Like the familiar S&P500 index of the stock market, the ABX references a portfolio of twenty residential MBSs (RMBSs) deals intended to be representative of the broader subprime market. Introduction of the ABX created a market price for subprime risk, just as the housing market peaked. The timing could not have been worse.

Despite these regulatory developments, the Fed remained primarily concerned with inflation, which was approaching 5 percent. Shelter, commodity, and energy prices were all increasing, rendering inflation "uncomfortably high."[100] In response, the Federal Open Market Committee raised the federal funds rate by twenty-five basis points at seventeen consecutive meetings between June 2004 to June 2006, from 1 percent to 5.25 percent. This marked the most significant tightening of American monetary policy since 1994. The Fed funds rate remained at 5.25 percent for another year. Blinded by orthodox macroeconomics, the Fed missed the linkages connecting the subprime market to the rest of the financial system.[101] Raising interest rates to combat inflation, just like in the late 1970s, popped the housing bubble and took the rest of the global economy down with it.

CRISIS

The housing market peaked sometime in the first half of 2006. Delinquencies on subprime mortgages began rising shortly thereafter. Subprime mortgages are uniquely sensitive to home price appreciation: after an initial "teaser" period, the interest rate increases to incentivize refinancing based on the accrued equity. However, falling home prices prevented subprime borrowers from refinancing and paying the "step up" interest rate, which by design is prohibitively expensive, as a means to incentivize refinancing. The result in 2006 was a sharp increase in delinquencies. The largest increases in delinquencies were among subprime borrowers in the "sand states" of California, Nevada, Arizona, and Florida—states that had experienced the sharpest run-up in prices. The realized default rates were one hundred times higher than those predicted by the models governing the packaging, pricing, and rating of these securities. In absolute terms, subprime mortgage delinquencies increased by about seven percentage points between 2004 and 2007, concentrated in the vintages that were now hitting their resets.

The unexpected and widespread increase in delinquencies upended the structure of subprime MBSs, one that depended on cash flows from refinancing to pay investors. The sensitivity of subprime mortgages to housing prices was further compounded by the "thin" tranching of subprime MBSs.[102] In other words, the design of these securities meant that small increases in default rates would result in total wipeouts. As a result, the price of AAA-rated MBS tranches plunged in value. These price declines imperiled CDOs, which had become disproportionately invested in subprime MBSs. CDO investors had no way of "looking through" to the individual mortgages they were ultimately funding to determine their exposure to subprime mortgages in Nevada or Florida. Furthermore, most CDOs could be liquidated by the senior investors if the value of the CDO's assets fell below certain thresholds, leaving junior investors with nothing.[103]

Greed turned to fear. The run on the shadow banking system began in early 2007.[104] Unlike Depression-era bank runs where depositors lined up outside a bank to withdraw their money, shadow bank "deposits" were withdrawn when investors did not renew ("roll" in industry parlance) their short-term loans to shadow banking entities. The two primary forms of shadow bank deposits were asset-backed commercial paper (ABCP) and repurchase agreements using asset-backed securities (ABSs) as collateral. These investors withdrew, or stopped rolling, their "deposits" because, like with a traditional bank run, they were concerned about the value of the shadow bank's assets and could not determine which entities were exposed to subprime risk.

Over the next few months, outstanding ABCP declined by nearly 50 percent and repo "haircuts" (the difference between the market value of the collateral and the amount of the loan) began rising.[105] However, the turmoil was not limited to subprime MBSs. Other ABS asset classes began suffering similar runs, as investors worried that unrelated market participants would be forced to liquidate these assets and thus further impair prices. Rising haircuts meant less liquidity, further amplifying price declines as ABS holdings were further marked down.[106] This combination produced a self-reinforcing spiral of price declines and asset fire sales: price declines prompted redemption requests from investors and collateral calls from lenders.

The ensuing rating downgrades of subprime MBSs and CDOs further compounded the price declines, as investors with strict ratings minimums (like pension and insurance funds) were forced to sell and realize significant losses. The downgrades also rendered many of these securities ineligible as repo collateral. Additionally, FASB 157 accelerated the asset impairment from this cycle of price declines, spreading developing panic in ABS markets to financial entities of all kinds; these entities were obligated to mark their holdings of ABSs to rapidly collapsing prices. The crisis bore all the hallmarks of a pre–Federal Reserve era banking panic.

In early 2007, subprime mortgage originators began filing for bankruptcy en masse. Subprime originations were largely funded through the securitization pipeline, which had now shut off. Without the ability to sell its mortgages or use them as collateral for repurchase agreements to generate cash, Countrywide and other originators faced a severe liquidity crunch. At the other end of the pipeline, the leveraged investors in subprime RMBSs and CDOs faced a similar crisis. In June 2007, two credit hedge funds at Bear Stearns collapsed. These funds used a combination of investor and borrowed money to invest in AAA- and AA-rated CDOs, earning "carry" on the difference between the interest earned on the CDOs and the interest owed on the borrowed money. The return generated by these strategies is determined by the degree of leverage. Accordingly, the funds were highly levered, so a small price decline in the value of the funds' assets was sufficient to wipe them out. Bear Stearns was forced to pay $3 billion to meet the funds' obligations to its creditors and prevent foreclosure. For the rest of Wall Street, the collapse of these funds was tantamount to a dead canary in the subprime coal mine.

In June 2007, the Las Vegas Sands Corporation was in the final stages of converting the massive husk of the shuttered Bethlehem Steel Works into the Sands Casino Resort Bethlehem. The Bethlehem Steel Works manufactured the artillery shells, naval guns, armor plates, and aircraft parts used to win World War II; it produced the continuously rolled steel used to build iconic American landmarks including the Golden Gate Bridge, the George Washington Bridge, the Chrysler Building, the World Trade Center, the United Nations headquarters, and the Hoover Dam. It was in the Works' No. 2 machine shop that superintendent Frederick Taylor devised his revolutionary *Principles of Scientific Management*.

Construction stalled because the contractors couldn't procure enough structural steel—this in the city that was once the world's largest steel producer.[107] Would Bethlehem Steel Works, paragon of twentieth-century American industry, and now on its way to becoming a casino, be just another half-finished real estate project on the eve of the worst financial crisis since the Great Depression? In an ironic twist, contractors for the Sands Corporation were able to order the necessary steel from Charlotte, North Carolina–based Nucor. Nucor revolutionized the steel industry with the introduction of "mini mills" in 1966, a development that sealed the demise of Bethlehem Steel. Thousands of unionized steel jobs that provided generous pay and benefits at the Bethlehem Works were replaced with low-paying service jobs paying a fraction of what its predecessors on the same site once offered.[108]

On July 26, 2007, Goldman Sachs made its first collateral call to AIG. Goldman began reducing its exposure to subprime mortgages and to financial counterparties with significant exposure to subprime. In August 2007, the panic spread to the interbank markets.[109] IKB Deutsche Industriebank, a midsize German bank headquartered in Dusseldorf, was both heavily reliant on wholesale funding and exposed to subprime CDOs. In April, IKB invested in Goldman's infamous Abacus 2007-AC1 deal. Abacus was a "synthetic" CDO referencing a portfolio of subprime MBSs.[110] Unbeknownst to investors like IKB, the bonds referenced by Abacus were selected by hedge fund manager John Paulson who, anticipating a collapse in subprime, intended to bet against Abacus using credit default swaps.[111]

By August, IKB lost its entire investment in Abacus. IKB was dependent on wholesale funding, particularly asset-backed commercial paper. Holders of IKB commercial paper included the City of Oakland, a school district in Minneapolis, and the Montana Board of Investments.[112] By late July, Goldman Sachs and Deutsche Bank refused to sell any more of IKB's paper. On August 7, IKB was bailed out by state-owned KfW Bankengruppe. On August 9, BNP Paribas announced it was suspending redemptions from three of its credit hedge funds. The panic had spread to the regulated banking system, and it was impossible to tell where other pockets of subprime losses might be lurking.

One hundred miles above the Arctic Circle in Norway, the little town of Narvik faced at least a $60 million loss—one-third of its annual budget—on an investment in a Citigroup CDO.[113] In Jackson Hole, Bernanke argued that "it is not the responsibility of the Federal Reserve—nor would it be appropriate—to protect lenders and investors from the consequences of their financial decisions. But developments in financial markets can have broad economic effects felt by many outside the markets, and the Federal Reserve must take those effects into account when determining policy."[114] The Fed subsequently cut interest rates by two percentage points between September 2007 and January 2008 owing to the "considerable worsening of the economic outlook."[115] Consumer spending began to slow as oil prices crept above $100.

On September 14, a run on Northern Rock led to the first bank failure in the United Kingdom in 150 years. Wall Street banks reported huge losses from write-downs on their holdings of "super-senior" CDO tranches and the liquidity puts (obligations to buy commercial paper if no one else would) sold to their SIV conduits. Like the Bear Stearns hedge fund, a thirty-to-one leverage ratio meant that small declines in asset values would lead to insolvency. In 2007 alone, losses on direct subprime RMBS and ABS CDO holdings wiped out two-thirds of Merrill Lynch's capital.[116] Banks warehoused large volumes of MBSs on their balance sheets during the securitization process. On the eve of crisis, banks held $1.2 trillion in subprime mortgages funded by ABCP.[117] By comparison, this amount eclipsed that of the entire Treasury bill market. This is the key mechanism that radiated the crisis outward from the subprime housing market.

The shadow banking run continued to accelerate. The proximate cause of both the Northern Rock and Bear Stearns failures was not asset write-downs but, instead, a sudden loss of funding from shadow bank "depositors." Countrywide was locked out of wholesale funding markets and acquired by Bank of America in January 2008. AIG faced billions in collateral calls from counterparties of its credit default swaps. Bear Stearns was similarly locked out of commercial paper markets and forced to shift its funding base to overnight repo.[118]

On March 11, the Federal Reserve announced that it would invoke the "unusual and exigent circumstance" authority under the Federal Reserve Act to create a Term Securities Lending Facility (TSLF). This facility would allow primary dealers to swap eligible collateral for treasuries. Importantly, the TSLF was open to nonbank institutions previously ineligible for Fed support. However, the TSLF was not established in time to save Bear Stearns. Counterparties increasingly refused to lend to Bear, and by the end of the week, the firm's cash reserves were depleted. To stave off a potential bankruptcy, the New York Fed engineered a sale of Bear Stearns to JP Morgan. The Fed created a special vehicle—"Maiden Laine LLC"—to purchase $30 billion of Bear's most impaired assets to sweeten the deal for JP Morgan. When Bear Stearns collapsed, it had $12 billion in equity supporting $363 billion in liabilities and relied on $70 billion in overnight wholesale funding. Shortly after Bear's demise, the Fed created the Primary Dealer Credit Facility (PDCF), which extended overnight loans to primary dealers. In effect, the PDCF extended unlimited discount window borrowing to nondepository financial institutions. The PDCF would prove to be one of the most important of the Fed's interventions during the crisis. By the time the facility closed on February 1, 2010, it had lent nearly *$10 trillion*, much of it to foreign institutions.

On July 11, IndyMac—a thrift spun off from Countrywide in the early 2000s—was placed into conservatorship by the FDIC. The failure of IndyMac marked yet another phase of the crisis. The bank's primary business was originating Alt-A mortgages, those in the category between prime and subprime, one believed to be safe from the turmoil in the subprime market.[119] However, the market for Alt-A securitizations was also weakening. In late June, Senator Chuck Schumer released a letter he had written to the FDIC, Office of Thrift Supervision (OTS), and Federal Home Loan Bank (FHLB), expressing concerns about IndyMac's health. The letter precipitated a bank run on IndyMac: $1.3 billion in deposits were withdrawn in the span of ten days, rapidly accelerating what the Office of the Inspector General characterized as IndyMac's "course for probable failure."[120] With nearly $40 billion in assets, IndyMac was the largest bank failure since Continental Illinois in 1984. Though the IndyMac failure consumed a significant percentage of the FDIC deposit insurance fund, that figure would soon be dwarfed by the "probable failure" of the GSEs.

At this point, the GSEs owned or guaranteed half of the residential mortgages in the United States. Combined, they held approximately $5.5 trillion in assets at a leverage ratio of 75 to 1.[121] The spread between GSE debt and treasuries began rising, increasing funding pressure and the threat of insolvency. A series of regulatory examinations over the course of the summer made clear that nationalization was the only option. On March 10, *Barron's* warned that "any realistic assessment of Fannie Mae's capital position would show the company is currently insolvent."[122] On September 7, the Federal Housing Finance Agency—created two months earlier—placed Fannie Mae and Freddie Mac into conservatorship.

On September 15, Lehman Brothers filed for bankruptcy. Unlike Bear Stearns, the Fed could not find a buyer for Lehman and was unwilling to provide the necessary guarantees. Treasury Chief of Staff Jim Wilkinson emailed, "I just can't stomach us bailing out Lehman. . . . Will be horrible in the press don't u think."[123] Lehman's bankruptcy shocked the market consensus that the government would not allow a major investment bank to fail. One immediate consequence of the bankruptcy was that the Reserve Primary Fund, the oldest money market mutual fund, "broke the buck." The fund held a significant amount of Lehman's now worthless commercial paper, leading to runs on other money market funds and spiking borrowing costs dramatically. Due to bankruptcy law in the United Kingdom, Lehman was forced to freeze all of its prime brokerage accounts. As a result, clients could no longer access their funds. Immediately, the catastrophic consequences of this decision became clear. The neoliberal regulatory apparatus realized it must rescue the financial system by any means necessary, shifting decision-maker consensus overnight from market fundamentalism to unlimited taxpayer support and state intervention.

On September 16, the Fed effectively nationalized AIG.[124] From 2000 to 2007, AIG's cumulative profits were $66 billion. In 2008, AIG lost $100 billion. On September 18, Federal Reserve Chairman Ben Bernanke and Treasury Secretary Hank Paulson met congressional leaders in the office of House Speaker Nancy Pelosi. According to Pelosi, Bernanke told those present, "If we do not act immediately we will not have an economy by Monday." Two weeks later, Congress passed the $700 billion Troubled Asset Relief Program (TARP), which enabled the Treasury to recapitalize troubled financial institutions. The House of Representatives initially voted down the bill, and stock markets reacted with one of the largest percentage point drops ever. The House quickly reversed course and passed the bill: a majority of House Democrats sided with a Republican president to bail out the financial system weeks before an election.

On September 25, the Office of Thrift Supervision seized Washington Mutual, after the firm suffered a $17 billion run. The remnants of the firm subsequently sold to JP Morgan for a paltry $1.9 billion.[125] In late November, the government injected $45 billion into Citigroup and provided guarantees for over $300 billion in other troubled assets. The Lehman Brothers episode demonstrated that preventing cascading failure required transferring private financial risk onto the public balance sheet. However, the perilous passage of TARP revealed that this necessary risk transfer could not be accomplished through fiscal policy alone.

The technocratic fixes offered by the Obama administration were no match for the scale of the crisis.[126] Instead, decisive policy action came largely from the Fed, which acted aggressively to preserve financial order and to partially offset political gridlock. Bernanke, a student of the Great Depression, actively applied the lesson that monetary policy could be used to support financial asset prices and prevent deflationary spirals. Interventions like lending programs, swap lines, and asset purchases were widely hailed as preventing the Great Recession from turning into another Great Depression. The Fed saved the global financial system by injecting it with upward of $15 trillion through asset purchases, discount window lending, central bank swap lines, and other rescue facilities. Through the emergency powers granted to the Fed under Section 13(c) of the Federal Reserve Act, the Fed acted decisively to backstop the shadow banking system, transforming itself from lender of last resort to domestic commercial banks to the dealer of last resort to the global dollar system, by providing unlimited liquidity secured by the imperiled collateral.[127]

The federal funds rate—the usual tool of monetary policy—only influences short-term interest rates and could not be lowered below zero. The Fed launched several rounds of asset-buying programs called "quantitative easing" to aid economic recovery in late 2008. Quantitative easing allowed the Fed to inject money into the financial system by adding cash to dealer balance sheets and lowering long-term interest rates. By driving up bond prices (thereby pushing down yields), the Fed hoped to both lower long-term borrowing costs and move investors out of cash and into riskier assets.

Although the Fed was careful to frame its "unconventional" activities strictly as an employment policy in order to not run afoul of its constitutional mandate, their interventions can be considered through the lens of financial depoliticization. The continued public support for financial risk helped restore a version of the financial growth regime after the crisis. Large-scale asset purchases were designed to lower long-term interest rates and force investors into riskier assets to earn the same returns. However, investors saw fewer and fewer opportunities to deploy capital at attractive rates of return. By injecting liquidity into the financial system, the Fed could blow air into financial markets faster than the real economy could deflate.[128]

In addition to causing massive losses in the financial system, the crisis spilled over into the real economy, inducing the sharpest and most prolonged recession since the Great Depression. As with the recession of the early 1980s, job losses were concentrated in goods-producing sectors such as construction and manufacturing. In 2008, 3.6 million jobs were lost, and another 4.7 million went away in 2009. Roughly ten million families lost their homes to foreclosure. In 2010, one in five working-age men were unemployed. Similar to the recession of the early 1990s, the exit from recession was marked by a "jobless recovery," in which GDP growth vastly outpaced job growth. Crabgrass crept back across the frontier. Public budgets were slashed. In every state except Vermont, the combination of substantial revenue declines and constitutional balanced budget requirements mandated brutal austerity and dramatic cuts to public employment, further compounding the crisis.[129]

* * *

As far as Lehman's structured finance division knew, subprime CDOs were a good business, offering hefty fees and fat bonuses. Traders demanded more subprime mortgages for the securitization pipeline while Lehman's treasury department believed it was sitting on a pile of AAA-rated repo collateral. A less ideologically captured regulatory apparatus might have saved Lehman to forestall the obvious consequences of an uncontrolled bankruptcy or even the subprime housing bubble itself. In either case, the financial growth regime would have remained. Even if financial regulators noticed the rampant fraud in the subprime housing market, they wouldn't have wanted to kill the golden goose: an immensely profitable business serving an established policy goal. Meaningful intervention would have required cutting against the political grain. As Bernanke said himself, policymakers believed that any problems in the subprime housing market would be contained. They did not understand the linkages that allowed a meltdown in the subprime market to radiate outward.[130]

Put differently, the financial growth regime underlying neoliberalism contained a fatal flaw: neoliberal elites believed that markets actually operated according to the neoliberal theoretical model.[131] On September 14, 2008, former Goldman Sachs CEO and incumbent Treasury secretary Hank Paulson believed allowing Lehman Brothers to fail was in the best interest of financial stability. He was wrong. Even among the true believers, the cost of faith in the power of omniscient and self-correcting markets—global financial Armageddon—became apparent. On September 15, Paulson realized that unprecedented state intervention was required. Over that fateful weekend in September 2008, neoliberal ideology and the power of finance came into violent contradiction. Finance triumphed.

The 2008 financial crisis marked an inflection point, not the total defeat, of the financial growth regime. Interventions by the Fed succeeded in restoring financial asset price appreciation. Just as Fordism required constant wage growth, the financial growth regime required constantly rising asset prices.[132] However, the postcrisis political economy was defined by sluggish growth, uneven recovery, wage stagnation, and another explosion of income inequality.[133] Between 2008 and 2020, total public debt quadrupled. Of the $15 trillion increase, nearly one-third was monetized by the Fed. From housing to corporate investment, many have observed a breakdown in the transmission mechanism between financial asset prices and real investment.[134] The "exorbitant privilege" of the United States was now its ability to use monetary means to avoid the distributive crisis that would otherwise result if postcrisis adjustment were to be managed fiscally.[135] However, these financial interventions were insufficient to sweep the underlying social conflicts back under the rug.

At one level, the crisis manifested years of a self-serving elite ideology that allowed the financial system to metastasize beyond control and tank the global economy. But at another, the crisis revealed the neoliberal state to be at the mercy of financial imperatives it could shape but not radically alter. Bailouts and austerity were the other half of the financial Faustian bargain: there is no contradiction between an ideology that trumpets the virtues of unregulated markets and demands for trillion-dollar state bailouts of the financial system. Both sustain the regime of distributive depoliticization. From the standpoint of distributive conflict, the apparent contradiction between a governing ideology that stresses both free markets and massive state bailouts of the financial system at taxpayers' expense melts away: it was not permissible to let the financial system, as the enforcer of the regime of depoliticized distribution, fail. In the aftermath of the crisis, finance was deployed yet again to contain distributive conflict as the Federal Reserve filled the void created by the inability to govern distribution politically. It was not entirely successful.

The immediate financial crisis was resolved when the shadow banking system was absorbed onto public balance sheets. The political crisis was just beginning.

THE RETURN OF DISTRIBUTIVE CONFLICT

In the aftermath of the financial crisis, distributive conflict reemerged along similar fault lines as in the 1960s and 1970s. On February 19, 2009, Rick Santelli, a former commodity trader at defunct investment bank Drexel Burnham Lambert turned CNBC contributor, stood in front of the trading pits at the Chicago Board of Trade. In a fiery televised rant, Santelli decried President Obama's program, announced the previous day, that would allow homeowners to refinance distressed mortgages and stave off foreclosure. The first Black president threatened to encourage private mortgage lenders to modify mortgages to aid struggling homeowners. He called for a "Chicago Tea Party" to protest Obama's policy of "subsidizing the losers." The traders assembled behind him whistled and applauded. In the months that followed, a grassroots movement fertilized with piles of megadonor cash swept American politics. Across the country, local "Tea Party" chapters sprung up in opposition to the new administration.

Former vice-presidential nominee Sarah Palin matter-of-factly stated that "the Tea Party movement wouldn't exist without Barack Obama."[136] A common complaint was that Obama was an "elitist" bent on destroying America. Claims of Obama's elitism were, at least in part, thinly veiled euphemisms for Obama's violation of the incumbent racial hierarchy in American political life. In the America known by the Tea Party, African Americans did not golf, take private jets to Broadway shows, or sign bills into law. The only explanation for this violation of the natural order was that Obama was not in fact an American, but a Muslim, communist, foreigner, homosexual, or some combination thereof.

The mortal fear motivating the Tea Party was that Obama and the Democrats would raise taxes on them (patriotic hard-working everyday Americans) to bail out their sworn enemies (college students and racial minorities), as Obama had done for Wall Street. This fear was seemingly confirmed when Obama's signature legislative push—the Affordable Care Act (ACA)—threatened to expand health insurance access to the poor and the infirmed via modest government subsidies for private health insurance. Responding to the financial crisis with a modicum of solidarity augured a potentially more inclusive and egalitarian future. Thus, Obama was viewed widely by Tea Party activists as a "liberal elitist working in the interests of the undeserving."[137]

One early sign of the changing political climate presented itself during a presidential address to a joint session of Congress that September.[138] Obama was interrupted mid-speech by Representative Joe Wilson of South Carolina shouting "You lie!" after Obama stated that benefits from the ACA would be limited to lawful residents and citizens. Three days later, a crowd of at least 75,000 people, organized and funded by a confederation of conservative groups, descended on Washington. The crowd's signs and slogans captured the litany of grievances against the new administration: "YOUR MORTGAGE IS NOT MY PROBLEM," "TAXED ENOUGH ALREADY," and "YOUR 'FAIR SHARE' IS NOT IN MY WALLET."

Theda Skocpol and Vanessa Williamson explain that the Tea Party worldview is organized around "a well-marked distinction between workers and nonworkers—between productive citizens and freeloaders."[139] Tea Party supporters asserted the prerogatives of individual license against a rising tide of social demands. Much like the tax revolt of the late 1970s, Tea Party supporters felt "put upon by the governmental process—and [saw] themselves as losing out to others profiting unfairly from government spending."[140] Obama, a Harvard-educated Black man, was the ultimate avatar of this broader anxiety about declining status in the face of the pincer of global economic competition and domestic political competition. Before long, the Republican base began denying Obama's legitimacy as president. Skocpol and Williamson observed: "Stoked by demagogues like Donald Trump, the claim about President Obama's otherness and illegitimacy reached its apogee in 'Birtherist' claims that Obama was not really born in the United States."[141] For the Tea Party, all matters of public policy became increasingly cast in racialized terms.

In January 2010, political unknown and former *Cosmopolitan Magazine* nude model Scott Brown defeated Massachusetts Attorney General Martha Coakley in a special election to fill the Senate seat vacated by the death of Ted Kennedy.[142] One political commentator attributed the surprise victory to the fact that "people were hoping for some economic relief from Obama and the Democrats and they didn't get it."[143] In February, Obama issued an executive order creating the National Commission on Fiscal Responsibility and Reform.[144] The commission, led by bipartisan cochairs Alan Simpson and Erskine Bowles, recommended a predictable slate of entitlement cuts and tax increases.[145] The commission fell short of its required supermajority threshold to submit these recommendations to Congress for a vote. In March, the ACA was signed into law.

That November, Republicans swept the midterm elections, winning sixty-three House seats, establishing trifectas in the crucial presidential swing states of Wisconsin, Michigan, Ohio, Pennsylvania, and Florida, and inaugurating a condition of political gridlock that would define the remainder of Obama's presidency.

Four months into the new congressional term, the federal government reached the statutory debt ceiling. The newly empowered Tea Party Republicans were eager to flex their political muscle. After several months of political brinksmanship and "extraordinary measures" from the Department of the Treasury to forestall a default, House Republicans passed the Budget Control Act of 2011, which raised the debt ceiling by $2.1 trillion in exchange for $1 trillion of future spending cuts.[146] The act also created the Joint Select Committee on Deficit Reduction (also known as the "Supercommittee"), which was charged with developing a plan for reducing the deficit by a further $1.5 trillion over ten years. The Supercommittee concluded its work in November with a terse press release reading, "We have come to the conclusion today that it will not be possible to make any bipartisan agreement available to the public before the committee's deadline."[147] The Budget Control Act also contained automatic spending cuts that would take effect in 2013 if an agreement on the deficit was not reached.

A few days after the debt ceiling deal was signed into law, Standard & Poor's (S&P) downgraded the credit rating of the United States to AA+ from AAA. In their memorandum justifying the rating change, S&P analysts wrote, "The political brinksmanship of recent months highlights what we see as America's governance and policymaking becoming less stable, less effective, and less predictable than what we previously believed." In September, "Occupy Wall Street" took over Zuccotti Park in lower Manhattan. Alan Greenspan noted that "in a democratic society, such a stark bifurcation of wealth and income trends among large segments of the population can fuel resentment and political polarization."

In 2012, Senate Majority Leader Harry Reid claimed that "the Tea Party will disappear as soon as the economy gets better."[148] By that point, however, "polarization" had already become a dominant theme in commentary and scholarship on American politics.[149] The same year, economist Robert Gordon asked if U.S. economic growth was over.[150] Gordon, arguing against the received orthodoxy of limitless growth, claimed that economic growth was largely driven by "one-time-only" transformations: once the benefits of innovations like steam power, indoor plumbing, electricity, and computers are realized, they do not contribute further to growth. Furthermore, newer advancements in information technology and telecommunications had much less impact than, for example, the shift from animal to machine power, on overall levels of productivity. Once these benefits are realized, growth is only realized from smaller incremental improvements.

Gordon's argument would come to be known as the "secular stagnation" hypothesis; many realized that the housing boom obscured otherwise lackluster growth rates in the 2000s. Federal Reserve economist Zoltan Pozsar explained the rise of the shadow banking system as an attractive venue for parking the financial surpluses generated through financialization. In the absence of investment opportunities yielding an attractive rate of return, investors parked their money in safe, liquid, short-term assets. The shadow banking system, as Pozsar explained, is the "financial economy reflection of the very same real economy imbalances that are behind the recently revived concept of secular stagnation."[151] Former Treasury secretary Larry Summers argued that "it appears that the difficulty that has arisen in recent years in achieving adequate growth has been present for a long time, but has been masked by unsustainable finances."[152] The ability of the American economy to generate sufficient growth was widely questioned.

At the end of 2012, the Fed launched another round of its quantitative easing program. The Fed was concerned that unemployment would remain too high and inflation would remain too low "without sufficient policy accommodation."[153] The Fed would eventually buy $1.75 trillion of Treasury and mortgage bonds through this program. At the same time, the federal government reached the "fiscal cliff" established by the previous debt ceiling deal and breached the debt ceiling once more. This impasse coincided with the expiration of the 2001 and 2003 Bush tax cuts. Both laws contained sunset provisions that permitted their passage via reconciliation, avoiding the de facto sixty-vote threshold in the Senate. The American Taxpayer Relief Act of 2012, passed in the early morning hours of January 1, 2013, extended all but the highest bracket of Bush tax cuts and temporarily avoided triggering the automatic spending cuts built into the previous debt ceiling deal.

In October 2013, an agreement on the continuing resolution could not be reached, and the federal government shut down. This was the first shutdown since the Clinton/Gingrich showdown over the 1996 budget. Tea Party–affiliated Republicans sought to defund the implementation of the ACA. Their plan was masterminded by Edwin Meese, who in 1964, as deputy district attorney of Alameda County, California, requested permission from Pat Brown to arrest the student demonstrators occupying Sproul Hall. Experts debated a number of procedural workarounds, including minting a trillion-dollar platinum coin or invoking the Fourteenth Amendment's dictum that "the validity of the public debt of the United States . . . shall not be questioned."[154] A deal to fund the government through 2015 was reached in mid-December.[155] The debt limit was subsequently "suspended" several times over the next few years attached to continuing resolutions or Bipartisan Budget Acts.

Only 36 percent of eligible voters cast ballots in the 2014 midterm elections.[156] Republicans gained nine seats in the Senate and increased their margin to fifty-nine seats in the House. Former

Arthur Andersen consultant, economics professor, and chairman of the BB&T Moral Foundations of Capitalism program at Randolph-Macon College, Dave Brat, upset incumbent House majority leader Eric Cantor in the Republican primary. Despite being outspent nearly 27 to 1, Brat won by running to Cantor's right on immigration and against the phantom "Obama amnesty program." The following year, a group of House Republicans including Jim Jordan, Mark Meadows, and Ron DeSantis founded the Freedom Caucus. The group succeeded in ousting John Boehner as speaker, which one political scientist characterized as "a virtually unprecedented feat in the modern Congress."[157] However, they lacked support among the rest of the Republican conference to install their preferred candidate: former vice-presidential candidate Paul Ryan was elected speaker in October 2015.

On November 8, 2016, Donald J. Trump was elected president of the United States. This event was alternatively hailed as the death or ultimate victory of neoliberalism.

EPILOGUE

Finance or Democracy?

He will take a tenth of your flocks, and you yourselves will become his slaves. When that day comes, you will cry out for relief from the king you have chosen, but the Lord will not answer you on that day.

—1 Samuel 8:17–18

The word "finance" is the word of a slave; it is unknown in the true republic. In a genuinely free state, the citizens do everything with their own hands and nothing by means of money.

—Jean Jacques Rousseau

Pay no attention to that man behind the curtain.

—*The Wizard of Oz*

In the aftermath of the 2008 financial crisis, "democratizing" or "socializing" finance emerged as a popular program for opposing neoliberalism. As the site of the latest meltdown, the financial system is an obvious venue for piloting a more general democratization of the economy.[1] By increasing the interfaces between democracy and policymaking, economic outcomes could be yoked to popular demands rather than shareholder profits. Against the neoliberal orthodoxy of free markets and the unlimited license of capital, a reinvigorated state empowered by an organized, mobilized, and energized citizenry would regulate and decarbonize the economy, set industrial policy, reduce economic inequalities, bust monopolies, tame speculation, redress patterns of historical underinvestment and inequality, and chart a path of "inclusive and sustainable growth."

The basic idea is that democratic control would correct the inequalities arising out of the financial system, which, as presently constituted, "works to reinforce the disproportionate political power of the wealthy" and "can be mobilized to block egalitarian reforms."[2] More concretely, a democratized financial system would equalize the power wielded by financial elites and the interest rates paid by rich and poor and incorporate popular input into investment decisions.[3] How might this work? Proposals for democratizing finance take several forms.

The first genre calls for the creation of new public financial entities like postal banks, investment banks, and sovereign wealth funds that replicate the functions of existing financial institutions on a more democratic basis. The principal benefits of these institutions would be to reduce the gap between the financial terms offered to the rich and poor, increasing local control of financial resources and channeling investment to infrastructure and clean energy. In this model, one proponent argues, "large-scale investments . . . would be financed by a network of nonprofit financial entities structured to be responsive to public input."[4] A democratized financial system would also move beyond the restrictive and discriminatory aspects of the existing credit rating system.[5]

In a democratized financial system, a decentralized confederation of financial nonprofits would finance projects in their particular area of expertise. These entities would help shift to "productive investment in infrastructure, multifamily housing, clean energy, conservation, and small business" and reduce the political influence of large financial institutions.[6] Capital would thus be redeployed toward "equitable growth" and investment in high-wage industries rather than maximizing financial profits. As Michael McCarthy explains, "with greater public control over lending and flows of finance, the reallocation of credit might not only help stabilize financial turbulence but also could redirect capitalist societies towards new forms of social egalitarianism and more ecologically sustainable modes of organizing life."[7] More radically, some see the creation of a parallel public and nonprofit financial system as softening the "transition trough" between the election of a socialist government and the actual implementation of a socialist agenda wherein capital fights and flights.

The second genre calls for increasing political participation in economic policymaking and, hence, to limit the phenomenon of captured regulators seeking incremental benefits for their future employers. More public participation is expected to generate more egalitarian policy outcomes. Advocates point to participatory budgeting in cities like Porto Alegre, Brazil, as models for how ordinary citizens can shape policymaking priorities.[8] Some hope an extension of public participation in the world of financial policymaking can serve as a possible counterweight to "shareholder value" ideology.[9]

The third genre seeks to deploy central banks to de-commodify capitalist social relations and renew national welfare states for an age of financialization. At the level of the international monetary system, John Ruggie and Rawi Abdelal call for "re-embedding liberalism" and a return to the principles undergirding the Bretton Woods international monetary system.[10] Domestically, advocates of modern monetary theory (MMT)—a macroeconomic framework arguing governments that issue their own fiat currencies can print money freely to finance public spending—see monetary policy as a key avenue for reform.[11] Although not framed in opposition to neoliberalism per se, MMT provides an economic rationality directly counter to the reigning orthodoxy of austerity and fiscal constraint.[12] MMT provides a theoretical justification for public spending unrestrained by deficits and can be read as an alternative to monetarism as a thin ideological cover for easy money. An embrace of MMT would, some proponents claim, enable programs like the Green New Deal or a universal basic income to be implemented by circumventing a terminally deadlocked Congress.[13]

As a political program, democratizing finance logically follows from the explanation of neoliberalism by design: a new policymaking orthodoxy is consolidated and disseminated among sympathetic policymakers, politicians are elected who share this expansive vision of renewal, and a new political economic order is gradually built from the ruins of the old. If neoliberalism was in fact the product of a successful implementation of a coherent ideological program, then a post-neoliberal social democracy might be won in a similar manner. Neoliberalism by design is an attractive account of the contemporary predicament because it suggests that neoliberalism can be reversed in the same manner it was deployed. Reversing neoliberalism would simply require new policymakers and politicians guided by new ideology, a possibility lying in the grasp of electoral majorities in the North Atlantic world.

However, the Stockton redevelopment agency, CalPERS, and the shadow banking system were all created by liberal democratic bodies trying to resolve the problem of distributive conflict without redistribution or taxation.[14] In other words, democratic creation or control does not necessarily oppose financial logic and imperatives, even if it opposes the effects or the most obvious beneficiaries of privatized finance. The combination of plebiscitary democracy and union control in California did not produce encouraging results. Mike Davis observes that "the vaunted Progressive system of 'direct democracy' proved in practice to be an almost ideal instrument for the perpetuation of California's ruling groups."[15] Democracy is not necessarily a counterweight to antidemocratic forces.

There is little reason to expect the results would be different when "democracy" is applied to different types of financial institutions under prevailing circumstances. Publicly run financial institutions might redistribute some surplus currently captured by the financial system or subsidize credit-starved sectors of the economy, but such reforms do not alter the operative form of monetary valuation. "Democratizing finance," in short, does not challenge the logic of liberal depoliticization.[16] The political aspiration of "democratizing finance" is limited to restoring liberal depoliticization on a slightly greener and more egalitarian basis.

Without engaging these deeper inheritances of liberalism, democracy can only be a thin legitimating wrapper around a largely fixed set of imperatives.[17] Democracy must be able to restrain and redirect social forces prior to the outbreak of a crisis if it is to have any independent value as a rival or antidote to the privately deployed forms of social power that structure the world. For this reason, neoliberalism cannot be reversed by simply reintroducing "the reality of society" into the prevailing policymaking calculus, containing the worst excesses of financial capitalism, or more effectively titrating levels of taxation and social spending to ameliorate the resulting inequalities. The problem goes much deeper.

If, following from the argument of chapter 1, "the economy" is a construct of liberal depoliticization, it cannot simply be "re-politicized" under liberalism. Instead, we must consider what liberal obstacles impede democratic self-governance. The political task would be to create the conditions under which democratic agency and popular sovereignty can be reclaimed from their liberal and financial strictures.

LIBERALISM VERSUS DEMOCRACY

Chapter 1 charted how liberalism naturalizes and sequesters the political problem of distribution in "the economy" to preempt and neutralize otherwise destabilizing political conflicts. Liberal depoliticization transubstantiates "definite social relations" into "relations between things," which, orthodox economics assures us, are spontaneously efficient and unimprovable.[18] Through this transubstantiation, social processes are recast as natural ones obeying innate laws beyond human design. Accordingly, there is no need or ability for the public to access substantive knowledge about the workings of the economy.[19] The actual structure of most human activity is preemptively declared to be unknowable and therefore politically off-limits.

However, the effects of collectively generated powers continue to be felt as liberal civil society remains in the grip of mystified social powers. These collective powers are not simply hidden but projected onto external entities. This is why critics argue that liberal political consciousness is inherently religious despite being formally secular: liberal depoliticization generates a distinctively *religious* mystification of actual social relations. We are separated from one another and the effects of our collective powers and capacities.[20] In this condition, we confront ourselves as something alien: we don't see our face on the cross or the dollar. For this reason, Marx argues, money "is only the illusory sun about which man revolves so long as he does not revolve about himself."[21] Distributive conflict behind the monetary veil assumes the character and intensity of religious conflict because it is mystified in exactly the same way. Mystification cannot be resolved or undone by setting an ideological inversion right side up. Instead, a less mystified political condition would require a public perspective from which these collectively generated powers might be apprehended and governed.

It is no coincidence that liberals from John Locke to Friedrich Hayek deny the possibility of such a public perspective and the possibility of altering social relations in accordance with public values. Michel Foucault reminds us that "the basic function or role of the theory of the invisible hand is to disqualify the political sovereign."[22] Liberalism, in Foucault's telling, is premised on denying the existence of political sovereignty over the economy. Without such a public perspective, political claims are parsed as claims of private interest and therefore ineligible from governing publicly. Instead, the only legitimate public actions are those that contribute to economic growth.[23] Growth thus serves as a universalizable normative principle: it is compatible with all possible private ends and avoids subjecting private property to public valuation or control.[24]

The growth imperative is a constraint on democracy that often doesn't feel like one. Growth enables us to be interconnected yet unattached.[25] With no other tie to bind liberal subjects in a mystified social condition, they will only agree to collective action that increases the value of their property. Liberalism narrows the basis for social cooperation to relations among self-interested proprietors: liberal subjects can only ask for more. Sheldon Wolin characterizes the contemporary subject as unsuited to the rigors of democratic self-governance: "self-interested, exploitative, competitive, striving for inequalities, fearful of downward mobility."[26] How often does one see free and equal citizens in the rare public spaces that still endure, such as malls, airports, and sporting events?

Pierre Rosanvallon argues that Marxists, economists, liberals, and communitarians alike share the same vision of the unified, happy society free from conflicts. These positions all aim at becoming emancipated from a certain kind of conflict, not from the condition of social mystification itself.[27] Although utopian liberals lament the solipsistic and consumeristic productions of a market society and the corrosive concentration of economic and political power, they cannot reject the necessary depoliticizing role of the market within liberalism. In Rosanvallon's formulation, "the liberal economic utopia and the socialist political utopia are two distinct faces of the same representation of society."[28] The liberal state, contrary to its self-presentation, is not a neutral apparatus into which different political ideologies can be slotted. Its very constitution forecloses much of what proponents of "democratizing finance" would hope to achieve. Consequently, meaningful concessions or transformations cannot be "won" at the ballot box no matter how urgently they are needed.[29] Liberalism is fully invested in the market and the property of its subjects: there is currently no alternative mechanism capable of replicating the same depoliticizing or governing functions.

Moving beyond neoliberalism requires exiting the sterilized political world of liberalism. Instead, we must return to politics and squarely confront the conflicts liberalism is premised on avoiding. We must attack what Rosanvallon terms the "common soil of utopian liberalism" and break free from liberal fictions however hopeful and comforting they might be. Emancipation cannot come from the implementation of a "truer" policy orthodoxy by the liberal state, but from a demystification and collectivization of the alienated social powers that govern and dominate us under liberalism. Distributive conflicts cannot be abolished, but they can be set in a political framework that makes democratic resolution possible. It would be naive to think full transparency is possible, but we can achieve more than what finance offers. Resisting financial power requires democratic institutions capable of governing distributive conflict in accordance with a shared reality and shared values, exactly what neoliberal theorists like Hayek believe to be impossible.[30]

Constructing an alternative to neoliberalism would require exactly such an epistemic perspective and normative consensus capable of governing the powers and structures currently tasked to "the market." Democracy, understood as the exercise of meaningful collective self-determination based on political equality, is not possible when most of human life lies outside the legitimate bounds of liberal politics. Democratically resisting and altering the default path of liberal depoliticization requires that collective powers are, to some minimal degree, collectively tractable. The shared governance of collective powers and conditions is not possible without some common basis for political action and the exercise of political power.

A first theoretical task is to appropriate what travels now as "the economy" as an object of political thought—not "the economy" as the abstract mechanism described in and by liberal theory, but the definite material and ideological configuration of the human system being studied.[31] Democratic publics must be able to see themselves behind the monetary veil, to grasp the concrete social relations governing their lives, and to comprehend the decisions made on their behalf. As Marx explained, "the religious reflex of the real world [will] . . . only then finally vanish, when the practical relations of everyday life offer to man none but perfectly intelligible and reasonable relations with regard to his fellow men and to Nature."[32]

If the problem is "capitalism," it can be overcome by placing the economy under political control. If the problem is liberalism, then the problem is the possibility of political control itself. Establishing political control would require confronting the problem of distributive conflict. A political confrontation with the problem of distributive conflict would require a fundamental reorientation such that people do not confront one another as hostile self-interested proprietors but as modestly self-governing conduits of social power. This task goes well beyond policymaking ideologies.

Liberalism and democracy were sutured together under specific historical conditions that no longer prevail. They will part ways. Financial power, however, will long outlive its liberal democratic husk. Accordingly, the question is not whether financial power will endure, but what form it will take. We already have clear models of what happens when the state dissolves and the power of money remains: cartels, client states, mercenary armies, captive populations of customers and workers—property and inequality unbounded by the need for legitimacy.

Liberal democracies are at the mercy of depoliticizing imperatives they cannot deny or radically alter. In the pairing of liberal democracy, democratic control is always subordinate to the liberal imperative of depoliticizing distributive conflict. From cities to pension funds to states, democratic bodies must respond to distributive conflict under the terms imposed by liberalism. Accordingly, the reach of democracy is inherently constrained. Without breaking free from these deeper liberal structures, the emancipatory potential of democracy is seriously limited. Like the old joke about an economist on a desert island "assuming a can opener," calls to democratize finance and the economy assume to already possess that which can only be generated through fundamental transformation. In other words, these perspectives start at the end rather than at the beginning, presuming a solution to the very problem to be solved. Opponents of neoliberalism cannot assume that after nearly four hundred years of liberalism we already possess an alternative.

NOTES

INTRODUCTION

1. In 2002, Margaret Thatcher was asked what she saw as her greatest achievement. She replied: "Tony Blair and New Labour." See Gary Gerstle, *The Rise and Fall of the Neoliberal Order* (New York: Oxford University Press, 2022).
2. See Timothy P. R. Weaver, "By Design or by Default: Varieties of Neoliberal Urban Development," *Urban Affairs Review* 54, no. 2 (2018): 234–66.
3. Jamie Peck, *Constructions of Neoliberal Reason* (New York: Oxford University Press, 2010); Angus Burgin, *The Great Persuasion* (Cambridge, MA: Harvard University Press, 2015); Daniel Stedman Jones, *Masters of the Universe* (Princeton, NJ: Princeton University Press, 2012); and Philip Mirowski and Dieter Plehwe, *The Road from Mont Pèlerin* (Cambridge, MA: Harvard University Press, 2009).
4. As Mark Blyth explains, "The point of economic ideas is not merely to diagnose the economy but is also to win the polity." Mark Blyth, *Great Transformations* (Cambridge: Cambridge University Press, 2002), 194.
5. David Harvey, *A Brief History of Neoliberalism* (New York: Oxford University Press, 2005), 19.
6. Harvey, *A Brief History of Neoliberalism*, 19–20. Also see James Ferguson, "The Uses of Neoliberalism," *Antipode* 41 (2009): 166–84, 170–71.
7. Quinn Slobodian, *Globalists* (Cambridge, MA: Harvard University Press, 2018). Also see Werner Bonefeld, *The Strong State and the Free Economy* (London: Rowman & Littlefield, 2017).
8. Brenner, Peck, and Theodore define neoliberalism as the "tendenc[y] of regulatory change that has been unleashed across the global capitalist system since

the 1970s." Neil Brenner, Jamie Peck, and Nik Theodore, "After Neoliberalization?," *Globalizations* 7, no. 3 (2010): 327–45, 329. Duménil and Lévy similarly define neoliberalism as "the term now used to describe the transformations capitalism underwent at the turning point of the 1970s and 1980s." See Gérard Duménil and Dominique Lévy, *Capital Resurgent* (Cambridge, MA: Harvard University Press, 2004), 1.

9. Gérard Duménil and Dominique Lévy, *The Crisis of Neoliberalism* (Cambridge, MA: Harvard University Press, 2011); Philip Mirowski, *Never Let a Serious Crisis Go to Waste: How Neoliberalism Survived the Financial Meltdown* (London: Verso, 2013); and Cédric Durand, *Fictitious Capital* (London: Verso, 2017).

10. Harvey, *A Brief History of Neoliberalism*, 156. Wolfgang Streeck also suggests that inflation was a "trick . . . to [make] the cake seem larger. But that illusion faded over time and finally disappeared when the declining value of money induced its owners either to stop investing or to seek safety in other currencies." Wolfgang Streeck, *Buying Time: The Delayed Crisis of Democratic Capitalism* (New York: Verso, 2017), 33. Martijn Konings helpfully disconnects the presumed causal mechanism linking the Volcker shock to the subsequent decline in inflation: "In an important sense, the Federal Reserve's turn to monetarism was highly successful: Interest rate levels skyrocketed to historic levels and over the next few years inflation came down." Martijn Konings, *The Development of American Finance* (Cambridge: Cambridge University Press, 2014), 136.

11. Recent work in economics contests the false premises of Reaganomics, particularly the assumed trade-off between growth and equity. See Heather Boushey, *Unbound: How Inequality Constricts Our Economy and What We Can Do About It* (Cambridge, MA: Harvard University Press, 2019).

12. Gerald Epstein, *Financialization and the World Economy* (London: Edward Elgar, 2005); Greta Krippner, "The Financialization of the American Economy," *Socio-Economic Review* 3 (2005): 173–208; Thomas Palley, *Financialization* (London: Palgrave Macmillan, 2013); Englebert Stockhammer, "Financialization and the Slowdown of Accumulation," *Cambridge Journal of Economics* 28, no. 5 (2004): 719–41; Robin Greenwood and David Scharfstein, "The Growth of Finance," *Journal of Economic Perspectives* 27, no. 2 (2013): 3–28; Natascha van der Zwan, "Making Sense of Financialization," *Socio-Economic Review* 12 (2014): 99–129; Randy Martin, *Financialization of Daily Life* (Philadelphia: Temple University Press, 2002); Gerald Davis, *Managed by the Markets: How Finance Re-Shaped America* (New York: Oxford University Press,

2009); Neil Fligstein and Adam Goldstein, "The Emergence of a Finance Culture in American Households, 1989–2007," *Socio-Economic Review* 13, no. 3 (2015): 575–601; and Ivan Ascher, *Portfolio Society: On the Capitalist Mode of Prediction* (New York: Zone Books, 2016).
13. Michel Feher, *Rated Agency: Investee Politics in a Speculative Age* (New York: Zone Books, 2018), introduction.
14. Wendy Brown, *Undoing the Demos* (New York: Zone Books, 2016).
15. Wendy Brown, *In the Ruins of Neoliberalism: The Rise of Antidemocratic Politics in the West* (New York: Columbia University Press, 2019), 163.
16. For emblematic statements of the neoliberal-skeptical position, see Taylor Boas and Jordan Gans-Morse, "Neoliberalism: From New Liberal Philosophy to Anti-Liberal Slogan," *Studies in Comparative International Development* 44, no. 2 (2009): 137–61; and Rajesh Venugopal, "Neoliberalism as Concept," *Economy and Society* 44, no. 2 (2015): 165–87.
17. Fred Block, "The Ruling Class Does Not Rule: Notes on the Marxist Theory of the State," *Socialist Revolution* 33 (1977): 6–28.
18. See Rick Perlstein's monumental trilogy: *Nixonland: The Rise of a President and the Fracturing of America* (New York: Scribner, 2009), *The Invisible Bridge: The Fall of Nixon and the Rise of Reagan* (New York: Simon & Schuster, 2015), and *Reaganland: America's Right Turn 1976–1980* (New York: Simon & Schuster, 2020).
19. Wolfgang Streeck, *How Will Capitalism End?* (New York: Verso, 2016), 16.
20. David Roediger, *The Wages of Whiteness: Race and the Making of the American Working Class* (New York: Verso, 1991).
21. Colin Crouch, *The Strange Non-Death of Neoliberalism* (Cambridge: Polity, 2011).
22. Jonathan Hopkin, *Anti-System Politics: The Crisis of Market Liberalism in Rich Democracies* (New York: Oxford University Press, 2020).
23. However, as innumerable memoirs attest, the cabal of state and capital who met in the wood-paneled conference rooms of the New York Fed and the Capitol building in the fall of 2008 did not form a coherent executive committee of class power singing from the same ideological songbook (however much they all agreed the circumstances required a blank check from the government). See Timothy Geithner, *Stress Test* (New York: Crown, 2015); Ben Bernanke, Timothy Geithner, and Henry Paulson, *Firefighting: The Financial Crisis and Its Lessons* (New York: Penguin, 2019); Ben Bernanke, *The Courage to Act* (New York: W. W. Norton, 2015); and Andrew Ross Sorkin, *Too Big to Fail* (New York: Penguin, 2010). Also see Geoff Mann, *In the Long Run We Are All Dead* (New York: Verso, 2022).

24. Dieter Plehwe, Quinn Slobodian, and Philip Mirowski, eds., *Nine Lives of Neoliberalism* (London: Verso, 2020).
25. The core argument reverses Harvey's dictum of "neoliberalism entails the financialization of everything" to "financialization entails the neoliberalization of everything." Harvey, *A Brief History of Neoliberalism*, 33.
26. The point is not to deny that throughout the relevant period private owners of the major means of production appropriate surplus value from wage laborers who in turn invest that surplus with no democratic input (as a basic definition of "capitalism" adapted from Dylan Riley). Rather, the point is that these dynamics do not explain the transformation in the American political economy from the late 1970s to the present.
27. Duncan Bell, "What Is Liberalism?," *Political Theory* 42, no. 6 (2014): 1–34.
28. Graham Burchell notes the following: "Liberal government is far from being the perfect realization of an idea or doctrine called liberalism. The invention and assembly of particular techniques into an art of government might answer to the liberal definition of the problem of how to govern, but it takes place through particular attempts to resolve diverse local problems and difficulties, through the need to address unforeseen consequences or the effects of the 'failure' of previous actions and always under uncertain conditions." Graham Burchell, "Liberal Government and Techniques of the Self," *Economy & Society* 22, no. 3 (1993): 267–82, 273.
29. Michael Walzer, "Liberalism and the Art of Separation," *Political Theory* 12, no. 3 (1984): 315–30, 315. But also see Michael Walzer, *The Struggle for a Decent Politics: On 'Liberal' as an Adjective* (New Haven, CT: Yale University Press, 2023).
30. Walzer, "Liberalism," 315.
31. See David Leopold, *The Young Karl Marx: German Philosophy, Modern Politics, and Human Flourishing* (Cambridge: Cambridge University Press, 2009).
32. Karl Marx, "On the Jewish Question," in *The Marx-Engels Reader*, 2nd edition, ed. Robert C. Tucker (New York: W. W. Norton, 1978), 33–45, 33.
33. Judith Miller, *Mastering the Market: The State and the Grain Trade in Northern France, 1700–1860* (Cambridge: Cambridge University Press, 1998).
34. Karl Marx, *Capital: A Critique of Political Economy* (Chicago: Charles H. Kerr, 1912), 195–96.
35. Joyce Appleby argues that "men believed in natural economic laws not because the facts led them to that conclusion but because of the social, political and intellectual implications of their possible existence." Joyce Appleby, "Locke, Liberalism and the Natural Law of Money," *Past & Present* 71 (1976): 43–69, 69.

36. As Wendy Brown explains, this is the heart of the "ruse" through which the liberal state self-legitimizes its claim to "universality" while "reinstantiating the 'particularity' of civil society through this depoliticization." The avowed neutrality of the liberal state amounts to a backdoor legitimation of these forces. The forces remain, still particular in their effects, and now without any kind of public standing. Thus, Marx writes, "man was not liberated from religion; he received religious liberty. He was not liberated from property; he received the liberty to own property." Marx exposes the fundamentally chimeric nature of liberalism: its imaginary freedom and illusory equality cannot deliver mankind from what actually makes us unfree and unequal because it is premised on depoliticizing rather than abolishing these forces. Liberal freedom is a chimera in both senses: an illusion and a monstrous hybrid. Wendy Brown, "Rights and Identity in Late Modernity: Revisiting the 'Jewish Question,'" in *Identities, Politics, and Rights*, ed. Austin Sarat and Thomas R. Kearns (Ann Arbor: Michigan University Press, 1995), 85–130, 101.

37. It is commonly accepted among scholars of critical macrofinance that the "de-risking" state "changes the relationship between state and citizen further away from collective provision of public goods." See Daniela Gabor, "The Wall Street Consensus," *Development and Change* 52, no. 3 (2021): 429–59.

38. There is considerable ambiguity in the literature on this point. Jamie Peck argues neoliberalism is not simply a matter of imposing a "Hayekian blueprint" from on high. See Jamie Peck, *Constructions of Neoliberal Reason* (New York: Oxford University Press, 2010). Yet precise mechanisms are rarely specified.

39. See Daniel Rodgers, *Age of Fracture* (Cambridge, MA: Belknap, 2011), chap. 2.

40. Greta Krippner, *Capitalizing on Crisis: The Political Origins of the Rise of Finance* (Cambridge, MA: Harvard University Press), 144.

41. Krippner, *Capitalizing on Crisis*, 22.

42. Streeck, *Buying Time*, 4.

43. Lester Thurow, *The Zero Sum Society* (New York: Basic Books, 1980); and Daniel Bell, *The Cultural Contradictions of Capitalism* (New York: Basic Books, 1976).

44. See Juan Gabriel Valdes, *Pinochet's Economists: The Chicago School in Chile* (Cambridge: Cambridge University Press, 1995); James Ferguson, *Global Shadows: Africa in the Neoliberal World Order* (Durham, NC: Duke University Press, 2006); and Aihwa Ong, *Neoliberalism as Exception* (Durham, NC: Duke University Press, 2006).

1. LIBERALISM AND DISTRIBUTIVE CONFLICT

1. Kinch Hoekstra, "Hobbes on the Natural Condition of Mankind," in *The Cambridge Companion to Hobbes's Leviathan* (Cambridge: Cambridge University Press, 2007), 122.
2. Thomas Hobbes, *Leviathan*, ed. Richard Flathman and David Johnston (New York: W. W. Norton, 1997), chap. 18, 102.
3. John Locke, *Political Writings* (Indianapolis, IN: Hackett, 1993), 325.
4. John Rawls, *Political Liberalism* (New York: Columbia University Press, 1993), xxiv. Also see Charles Larmore, "Political Liberalism," *Political Theory* 18, no. 3 (1990): 339–60.
5. See Rainer Forst, *Toleration in Conflict* (Cambridge: Cambridge University Press, 2013).
6. Secularism did not achieve its stated objective—leaving us with closeted Christian states and marginalized and stigmatized religions.
7. Pierre Rosanvallon, *Democracy Past and Future* (New York: Columbia University Press, 2007), 153.
8. For a representative account, see Russell Hardin, *Liberalism, Constitutionalism, and Democracy* (Oxford: Oxford University Press, 1999), chap. 2.
9. Physical markets and decentralized exchange long predate liberalism. See Moses Finley, *The Ancient Economy* (Berkeley: University of California Press, 1973), and Karl Polanyi, *Trade and Market in the Early Empires* (Glencoe, IL: Free Press, 1957) for discussions of the distinction between "the market" as a physical location in which commerce and exchange takes place versus an abstract regulatory mechanism.
10. Richard Dees, "Establishing Toleration," *Political Theory* 27, no. 5 (1999): 667–93, 672. However, tolerance eventually took root in England after 1689. It has been argued that the decentralization of economic power in protocapitalist England encouraged subjects to interact as buyer and seller rather than as Catholic or Anglican, indicating a complementarity between these two aspects.
11. "Restoring the American Dream: Bob Dole's Pro-Growth Plan for American Families," The Dole Kemp 96 Web Site, http://www.dolekemp96.org/agenda/economics/theplan.html.
12. Felix Rohatyn, "Recipe for Growth," *Wall Street Journal*, April 11, 1996.
13. Walter Lippmann, "The War on Poverty," *Washington Post*, March 19, 1964, A19.
14. Daniel Bell, *The Cultural Contradictions of Capitalism* (New York: Basic Books, 1976), 276.

1. LIBERALISM AND DISTRIBUTIVE CONFLICT • 259

15. William Ophuls, *Ecology and the Politics of Scarcity* (New York: W. H. Freeman, 1977), 185.
16. Adam Smith, *Wealth of Nations*, book V, chap. 1, part 2.
17. Ellen Meiksins Wood, "The Separation of the Economic and the Political in Capitalism," *New Left Review* I, no. 127 (1981): 66–95, 67.
18. See Stefan Eich, "John Locke and the Politics of Monetary Depoliticization," *Modern Intellectual History* 17, no. 1 (2020): 1–28.
19. The preface to the *Second Treatise* dedicates that work to King William as England's "Great Restorer."
20. See David Kynaston, *Till Time's Last Sand: A History of the Bank of England* (London: Bloomsbury, 2017).
21. See Richard Ashcraft, *Revolutionary Politics and Locke's Two Treatises of Government* (Princeton, NJ: Princeton University Press, 1986).
22. Sheldon Wolin argues, "To the extent that modern liberalism can be said to be inspired by any one writer, Locke is undoubtedly the leading candidate." Sheldon Wolin, *Politics and Vision* (Boston: Little Brown, 1960), 263.
23. See John Dunn, *The Political Thought of John Locke* (London: Cambridge University Press, 1969); A. John Simmons, *Lockean Theory of Rights* (Princeton, NJ: Princeton University Press, 1992); James Tully, *An Approach to Political Philosophy: Locke in Contexts* (Cambridge: Cambridge University Press, 1993); and Jeremy Waldron, *The Right to Private Property* (Oxford: Clarendon, 1988).
24. Locke, *Political Writings*, 394.
25. Locke, *Political Writings*, 396.
26. Locke, *Political Writings*, 394.
27. This is the core of Friedrich Hayek's argument against state intervention in *The Road to Serfdom* (London: Routledge, 1944).
28. Locke, *Political Writings*, 394–95.
29. Locke, *Political Writings*, 420.
30. Locke, *Political Writings*, 406.
31. Locke, *Political Writings*, 424.
32. See C. B. Macpherson, *The Political Theory of Possessive Individualism* (Oxford: Oxford University Press, 1962), chap. 5.
33. Locke, *Political Writings*, 274.
34. Locke, *Political Writings*, 274. This restriction is logically required by the premise that "each man has a right to his preservation." See Macpherson, *Possessive Individualism*, 201.
35. Locke, *Political Writings*, 275.
36. Locke, *Political Writings*, 277.

37. Locke, *Political Writings*, 276.
38. Locke, *Political Writings*, 278.
39. Locke, *Political Writings*, 275.
40. John Rundin, "A Politics of Eating: Feasting in Early Greek Society," *American Journal of Philology* 117, no. 2 (1996): 179–215.
41. Marek Wecowski, *The Rise of the Greek Aristocratic Banquet* (Oxford: Oxford University Press, 2013).
42. Plato, *Laws*, 757b–c.
43. Locke, *Political Writings*, 279.
44. Locke, *Political Writings*, 286.
45. Macpherson, *Possessive Individualism*, 210.
46. Locke, *Political Writings*, 270.
47. Pierre Rosanvallon argues that economic theory should be understood "as a response to problems left unresolved by the political theorists of the social contract." See Rosanvallon, *Democracy Past and Future*, 148.
48. The life and work of John Locke are indeed a testament to the foundational interdependence between liberalism and money. The ensuing "financial revolution," as historian John Miller observes, "was accompanied with no great statements of political philosophy." Innovations included fractional reserve banking, circulating credit instruments, permanent national debt, and the rise of the city of London as a global financial center. While the British merchant classes were in a position to capitalize on the political crisis, their interests did not drive the revolution itself. From the beginning, liberalism and finance have been deeply intertwined, but their relationship has not been straightforwardly encapsulated in canonical liberal theory. John Miller, *The Glorious Revolution* (London: Longman, 1983), 50. Similarly, Steven Pincus summarizes that "the Financial Revolution was the result of foreign imposition rather than domestic ideological debate." Steven Pincus, *1688: The First Modern Revolution* (New Haven, CT: Yale University Press, 2009), 367. Also see Stefan Eich, *The Currency of Politics* (Princeton, NJ: Princeton University Press, 2021).
49. Also see Albert Hirschman, *The Rhetoric of Reaction* (Cambridge, MA: Harvard University Press, 1991).
50. Karl Olivecrona, "Appropriation in the State of Nature: Locke on the Origin of Property," *Journal of the History of Ideas* 35, no. 2 (1974): 211–30, 223.
51. Compare Locke's formulation to the introductory chapter of any economics textbook.

I. LIBERALISM AND DISTRIBUTIVE CONFLICT • 261

52. Notably, however, the conception of democracy employed in these conventional formulations is generally an interest-based conception of democracy and not a more capacious conception of democracy as collective self-rule.
53. What one commentator aptly describes as Mill's "Hamlet-like quality" derives from this condition.
54. Pedro Schwartz, *The New Political Economy of John Stuart Mill* (London: London School of Economics, 1968).
55. Severing the link to social philosophy will later transmute "political economy" as a branch of moral philosophy into "economics" as an abstract science. In tandem, the object of study shifts from "wealth" to "the market." Whereas political economy studied the production, distribution, and exchange of societal wealth, economics studies the imagined qualities of "the market" as an abstract mechanism. Henry Spiegel observes that after Marx, "economics became the science of treating the allocation of a given quantum of total resources, which meant that little attention continued to be devoted to the question of how this quantum was determined and how it could be increased." Henry Spiegel, *The Growth of Economic Thought* (Durham, NC: Duke University Press, 1991), 505. Through utilitarianism, moral theory is fully incorporated into "scientific" economics.
56. John Stuart Mill, *Principles of Political Economy and Some of Their Applications to Social Philosophy* (Indianapolis, IN: Hackett, 2004), 85.
57. Mill, *Principles of Political Economy*, 92.
58. Mill, *Principles of Political Economy*, 167.
59. Mill, *Principles of Political Economy*, 142. Also see Michael Kalecki, "Political Aspects of Full Employment," *Political Quarterly* 14, no. 4 (1943): 322–31.
60. Mill, *Principles of Political Economy*, 98.
61. Mill, *Principles of Political Economy*, 101.
62. Mill, *Principles of Political Economy*, 92.
63. Mill, *Principles of Political Economy*, 92.
64. Mill, *Principles of Political Economy*, 93.
65. Mill, *Principles of Political Economy*, 93.
66. Mill, *Principles of Political Economy*, 113.
67. Mill, *Principles of Political Economy*, 167.
68. Commodification, dispossession, and fetishism remain missing.
69. Mill, *Principles of Political Economy*, book 4, chap. 7, §6.
70. Mill, *Principles of Political Economy*, book 4, chap. 7, §6.
71. Mill, *Principles of Political Economy*, 277.

72. Mill, *Principles of Political Economy*, 279.
73. Mill, *Principles of Political Economy*, 285.
74. John Stuart Mill, *On Liberty* (New York: Penguin, 2007), 13.
75. Mill, *On Liberty*, 96. Mill never explains these different grounds.
76. Mill, *On Liberty*, 96.
77. Mill, *On Liberty*, 96.
78. Mill, *On Liberty*, 99. Mill uses the language of tolerance to describe the relationship between the state and these personally injurious habits: "fornication, for example, must be tolerated, and so must gambling."
79. Mill, *On Liberty*, 102.
80. Mill, *On Liberty*, 102.
81. Mill, *On Liberty*, 226.
82. John Stuart Mill, "Chapters on Socialism," in *On Liberty and Other Writings*, ed. Stefan Collini (Cambridge: Cambridge University Press, 1989), 222.
83. Mill, "Chapters on Socialism," 222.
84. Mill, "Chapters on Socialism," 261.
85. Mill, "Chapters on Socialism," 231.
86. Mill, "Chapters on Socialism," 259.
87. Joseph Persky, *The Political Economy of Progress: John Stuart Mill and Modern Radicalism* (Oxford: Oxford University Press, 2016), 72.
88. Mill, *Principles of Political Economy*, 86.
89. David Brink, *Mill's Progressive Principles* (Oxford: Oxford University Press, 2013).
90. Hence, Mill's liberalism is "progressive," while Locke's liberalism is "conservative"—liberalism aimed at maintaining a particular set of arrangements.
91. Mill, "Chapters on Socialism," 276.
92. Mill, "Chapters on Socialism," 279.
93. Mill, "Chapters on Socialism," 279.
94. Mill, "Chapters on Socialism," 279.
95. Karl Marx, *Capital*, trans. David Fernbach (New York: Penguin, 1993).
96. Rawls, *Political Liberalism*, 47.
97. Rawls, *Political Liberalism*, 441.
98. John Rawls, "Kantian Constructivism in Moral Theory," *Journal of Philosophy* 77, no. 9 (1980): 515–72, 542.
99. John Rawls, "The Domain of the Political and Overlapping Consensus," *New York University Law Review* 64 (1989): 233–55, 235.
100. John Rawls, "Justice as Fairness: Political Not Metaphysical," *Philosophy & Public Affairs* 14, no. 3 (1985): 223–51, 223.

1. LIBERALISM AND DISTRIBUTIVE CONFLICT • 263

101. Rawls, "Justice as Fairness," 231.
102. John Rawls, *A Theory of Justice* (Cambridge, MA: Belknap, 1971), 6.
103. Rawls, *A Theory of Justice*, 25.
104. Rawls, *A Theory of Justice*, 242.
105. Rawls, *A Theory of Justice*, 242.
106. Rawls, *A Theory of Justice*, 76.
107. Rawls, *A Theory of Justice*, 316.
108. Kenneth Arrow, *Social Choice and Individual Values* (New York: Wiley, 1951).
109. E. Roy Weintraub, *General Equilibrium Analysis* (Ann Arbor: University of Michigan Press, 1993).
110. Allan Feldman, "Welfare Economics," in *The New Palgrave Dictionary of Economics*, ed. John Eatwell, Murray Milgate, and Peter Newman (London: Palgrave, 2008).
111. The dividing line between "orthodox" and "heterodox" economics is the assumption of equilibrium. See J. Green and Colin Hay, "Towards a New Political Economy of the Crisis," *New Political Economy* 20, no. 3 (2015): 331–41.
112. Kenneth Arrow and Gérard Debreau, "Existence of an Equilibrium for a Competitive Economy," *Econometrica* 22, no. 1 (1954): 265–90.
113. See Brian Judge, "The Impossibility of a Rawlsian Liberal," *Cambridge Journal of Economics* 45 (2021): 195–208.
114. Rawls, "Justice as Fairness," 231–33.
115. Two contemporary libertarian theorists write: "As much or more than any other issue, the problem of economic liberty also divides liberal citizens into rival and contending groups." Jeppe von Platz and John Tomasi, "Liberalism and Economic Liberty," in *The Cambridge Companion to Liberalism*, ed. Steven Wall (Cambridge: Cambridge University Press, 2015), 278.
116. Joseph Raz, "Facing Diversity: The Case of Epistemic Abstinence," *Philosophy and Public Affairs* 19, no. 1 (1990): 3–46, 9.
117. Rawls, *A Theory of Justice*, 76.
118. Rawls, *Political Liberalism*, 69.
119. Rawls, *A Theory of Justice*, 54.
120. Katrina Forrester, *In the Shadow of Justice* (Princeton, NJ: Princeton University Press, 2019).
121. This is the historical dividing line between "orthodox" and "heterodox" political economy.
122. Marx, *Capital*, vol. 1, chap. 6.
123. People are assumed to operate according to "stable, well-behaved preference functions" that are "exogenous" from the standpoint of economic analysis.

Thus, there is no structural unemployment or poverty wages but only individuals who prefer leisure to labor. George Stigler and Gary Becker, "De Gustibus Non Est Disputandum," *American Economic Review* 62, no. 2 (1977): 76–90. Also see Samuel Bowles, "Endogenous Preferences: The Cultural Consequences of Markets and Other Economic Institutions," *Journal of Economic Literature* 3 (1998): 75–111.

124. This paradoxically amplifies the importance of these privatized identities as the political claims emanating from them are banished from liberal discourse.

125. Jürgen Habermas, *The Structural Transformation of the Public Sphere*, trans. Thomas Burger (Cambridge, MA: MIT Press, 1991), 56.

126. F. A. Hayek, *The Constitution of Liberty* (Chicago: University of Chicago Press, 1960).

127. Mill, *Principles of Political Economy*, book IV, chap. 1, §1.

128. Gareth Dale, "Critiques of Growth in Classical Political Economy: Mill's Stationary State and a Marxian Response," *New Political Economy* 18, no. 3 (2013): 431–57.

129. Hannah Arendt explains: "This process of never-ending accumulation of power necessary for the protection of a never-ending accumulation of capital determined the 'progressive' ideology of the late nineteenth century that foreshadowed the rise of imperialism. Not the naive delusion of a limitless growth of property, but the realization that power accumulation was the only guarantee for the stability of so-called economic laws, made progress irresistible." Hannah Arendt, *The Origins of Totalitarianism* (New York: Harcourt and Brace, 1973), 143.

130. Rawls, *Political Liberalism*, 7. Rawls notes elsewhere that the difference principle "does not require continual economic growth over generations to maximize upward indefinitely the expectations of the least advantaged." John Rawls, *Justice as Fairness: A Restatement* (Cambridge, MA: Belknap, 2001), 63.

131. Samuel Freeman, "Illiberal Libertarians: Why Libertarianism Is Not a Liberal View," *Philosophy and Public Affairs* 30, no. 2 (2002): 105–51.

132. Freeman, "Illiberal Libertarians."

133. David Hume, *Writings on Economics*, ed. Eugene Rotwein (Madison: University of Wisconsin Press, 1970).

134. See Dominic Losurdo, *Liberalism: A Counter-History* (New York: Verso, 2005), and Karuna Mantena, *Alibis of Empire* (Princeton, NJ: Princeton University Press, 2010).

135. Milton Friedman, "The Methodology of Positive Economics," in *Essays in Positive Economics* (Chicago: University of Chicago Press, 1966), 41.

136. Milton Friedman, *Capitalism and Freedom* (Chicago: University of Chicago Press, 2002), 23–24.
137. Bell, *The Cultural Contradictions of Capitalism*, 235.

2. THE CRISIS OF INFLATION

1. For an extended discussion of this order, see Steve Fraser and Gary Gerstle, *The Rise and Fall of the New Deal Order* (Princeton, NJ: Princeton University Press, 1990).
2. Karl Polanyi, *The Great Transformation* (Boston: Beacon, 2001).
3. Dudley Dillard, *The Economics of J.M. Keynes* (London: Prentice Hall, 1948).
4. John Ruggie, "International Regimes, Transactions, and Change: Embedded Liberalism in the Postwar Economic Order," *International Organization* 36 (1982): 379–415, 415.
5. Mark Blyth, *Great Transformations* (New York: Cambridge University Press, 2002).
6. Paul Samuelson, "Worldwide Stagflation," in *The Collected Scientific Papers of Paul A. Samuelson*, vol. 4 (Cambridge, MA: MIT Press, 1977).
7. Blyth, *Great Transformations*, 150. For intellectual histories, see Jamie Peck, *Constructions of Neoliberal Reason* (Oxford: Oxford University Press, 2010); Daniel Rodgers, *Age of Fracture* (Cambridge, MA: Belknap, 2011); and Angus Burgin, *The Great Persuasion* (Cambridge, MA: Harvard University Press, 2012).
8. Wendy Brown, *Undoing the Demos: Neoliberalism's Stealth Revolution* (Princeton, NJ: Princeton University Press, 2017), 51.
9. James Buchanan and Richard Wagner, *Democracy in Deficit: The Political Legacy of Lord Keynes* (New York: Academic Press, 1977). Also see Melinda Cooper, *Family Values: Between Neoliberalism and Social Conservatism* (New York: Zone Books, 2017), chap. 2.
10. See Lawrence Glickman, *Free Enterprise: An American History* (New Haven, CT: Yale University Press, 2019).
11. See *America's New Beginning: A Program for Economic Recovery* (Washington, DC: Office of the Press Secretary, 1981).
12. Philip Mirowski and Dieter Plehwe, *The Road from Mont Pèlerin* (Cambridge, MA: Harvard University Press, 2009).
13. Brad Delong observes that "arithmetic decompositions of the rise in inflation into upward jumps in the prices of special commodities were never convincing to those working in the monetarist tradition." See Bradford Delong,

"America's Peacetime Inflation," in *Reducing Inflation: Motivation and Strategy*, ed. Christina D. Romer and David H. Romer (Chicago: University of Chicago Press, 1997), 267.

14. Rick Perlstein, *The Invisible Bridge: The Fall of Nixon and the Rise of Reagan* (New York: Simon and Schuster, 2014).

15. In the context of the Tony Blair government in the United Kingdom, Peter Burnham defined the "politics of depoliticization" as "placing at one remove the political character of decision-making." Governing is done indirectly through financial markets rather than directly through state policy. Rules replace political discretion. Peter Burnham, "New Labour and the Politics of Depoliticization," *British Journal of Politics and International Relations* 3, no. 2 (2001): 127–49.

16. See Brian Judge, "Piercing the Veil of Monetarism: A Decomposition of American Inflation, 1970–1985," *New Political Economy* (2023): https://doi.org/10.1080/13563467.2023.2200243.

17. See Alan Blinder, *Economic Policy and the Great Stagflation* (New York: Academic Press, 1979).

18. This process is not limited to neoliberalism. Polanyi explained how commodification of land, labor, and capital was a crucial precondition for the rise of capitalism and classical liberalism.

19. Blyth, *Great Transformations*, 144.

20. Robert Gordon explained that "economic research on the causes of inflation has been primarily devoted to the theoretical and empirical study of the links between government policy variables and the rate of inflation." Robert Gordon, "The Demand for and Supply of Inflation," *Journal of Law & Economics* 18 (1975): 807–836, 807.

21. Jonathan Kirshner, "Money Is Politics," *Review of International Political Economy* 10, no. 4 (2003): 645–60, 655.

22. William Simon, *A Time for Truth* (New York: Readers Digest, 1978), 91. See also Jude Wanniski, *The Way the World Works* (New York: Basic Books, 1978); and Henry Hazlitt, *The Inflation Crisis and How to Resolve It* (New Rochelle, NY: Arlington House, 1978).

23. Buchanan and Wagner, *Democracy in Deficit*, 24. Also see Nancy MacLean, *Democracy in Chains: The Deep History of the Radical Right's Stealth Plan for America* (New York: Viking, 2017).

24. Buchanan and Wagner, *Democracy in Deficit*, 64.

25. William Nordhaus, "The Political Business Cycle," *Review of Economic Studies* 42 (1975): 169–90, 185.

26. Samuel Huntington, "The Democratic Distemper," *Public Interest* (1975): 9–38, 11, 30.
27. Milton Friedman, "Answering the Big Questions," *Newsweek*, May 29, 1978, 80–81.
28. Daniel Bell, *The Cultural Contradictions of Capitalism* (New York: Basic Books, 1976), 239.
29. John Kenneth Galbraith, "Recession Economics," *New York Review of Books*, February 4, 1982.
30. Arthur Burns, "The Anguish of Central Banking," Per Jacobsson Lecture, Sava Center Complex, Belgrade, Yugoslavia, September 30, 1979.
31. "Nixon's Program—'I Am Now a Keynesian,'" *New York Times*, January 10, 1971, D1.
32. *1968 Economic Report of the President*, 3–20.
33. *1970 Economic Report of the President*, 5.
34. Jimmy Carter, "Address to the Nation on Energy and National Goals," July 15, 1979.
35. *1982 Economic Report of the President*, 4.
36. *America's New Beginning: A Program for Economic Recovery*, February 18, 1981, 4.
37. *1985 Economic Report of the President*, 3.
38. Ronald Reagan's comprehension of monetary policy was limited to two levers: "zooming the money" and "pulling the string." See William Greider, *Secrets of the Temple: How the Federal Reserve Runs the Country* (New York: Simon and Schuster, 1989), 541.
39. "Presidential Debate," October 28, 1980.
40. William Greider, "The Education of David Stockman," *Atlantic*, December 1981.
41. William Niskanen, *Reaganomics: An Insider's Account of the Policies and the People* (New York: Oxford University Press, 1988).
42. See Milton Friedman, "The Role of Monetary Policy," *American Economic Review* 58 (1963): 1–17; Martin Feldstein, "The Retreat from Keynesian Economics," *Public Interest* 64 (1981): 92–105; David Laidler, "Monetarism: An Interpretation and Assessment," *Economic Journal* 91 (1981): 1–28; Phillip Cagan, "Monetarism," in *The New Palgrave Dictionary of Economics*, ed. Steven N. Durlauf and Lawrence E. Blume (London: Palgrave Macmillan, 2008).
43. Milton Friedman, "The Counter-Revolution in Monetary Theory," Wincott Memorial Lecture, Institute of Economic Affairs, Occasional paper 33 (1970). For the expectations view of monetarism, see Thomas Sargent, "The Ends

of Four Big Inflations," in *Inflation: Causes and Effects*, ed. Robert E. Hall (Chicago: University of Chicago Press, 1982). Also see Thomas Sargent and Neil Wallace, "'Rational' Expectations, the Optimal Monetary Instrument, and the Optimal Money Supply Rule," *Journal of Political Economy* 83 (1975): 241–54; and Robert Hall and Thomas Sargent, "Short-Run and Long-Run Effects of Milton Friedman's Presidential Address," *Journal of Economic Perspectives* 32 (2018): 121–34.

44. Paul Volcker, *Changing Fortunes* (New York: New York Times Books, 1992), 167.
45. N. Gregory Mankiw, *Principles of Economics* (Boston: Cengage Learning, 2012), 15.
46. Michael Bordo and Athanasios Orphanides, "Introduction," in *The Great Inflation: The Rebirth of Modern Central Banking*, ed. Michael D. Bordo and Athanasios Orphanides (Chicago: University of Chicago Press, 2013), 8; Miguel Centeno and Joseph Cohen, "The Arc of Neoliberalism," *Annual Review of Sociology* 38 (2012): 317–40; John Woolley, *Monetary Politics: The Federal Reserve and the Politics of Monetary Policy* (New York: Cambridge University Press, 1984); Iwan Morgan, "Monetary Metamorphosis: The Volcker Fed and Inflation," *Journal of Policy History* 24 (2012): 545–71. Also see Peter Hall, "Policy Paradigms, Social Learning, and the State: The Case of Economy Policymaking in Britain," *Comparative Politics* 25 (1993): 275–96.
47. Nevertheless, the defeat of monetarism as a policymaking paradigm helped consolidate neoliberalism as a broader (and not entirely compatible) set of theories and understandings. See Marion Fourcade and Sarah Babb, "The Rebirth of the Liberal Creed: Paths to Neoliberalism in Four Countries," *American Journal of Sociology* 108, no. 3 (2002): 533–79.
48. See Greta Krippner, *Capitalizing on Crisis: The Political Origins of the Rise of Finance* (Cambridge, MA: Harvard University Press), 119–20; and Blyth, *Great Transformations*, 171–72.
49. Thomas J. Sargent, *The Conquest of American Inflation* (Princeton, NJ: Princeton University Press, 1999), 1.
50. Gérard Duménil and Dominique Lévy, *Capital Resurgent: Roots of the Neoliberal Revolution* (Cambridge, MA: Harvard University Press, 2004), 14.
51. Witold Kula, *Measures and Men* (Princeton, NJ: Princeton University Press, 1986); Giovanni Sartori, "Concept Misinformation in Comparative Politics," *American Political Science Review* 64 (1970): 1033–53; Robert Adcock and David Collier, "Measurement Validity: A Shared Standard for Qualitative

2. THE CRISIS OF INFLATION • 269

and Quantitative Research," *American Political Science Review* 95 (2001): 529–46.

52. James Tobin, "The Monetarist Counter-Revolution Today—An Appraisal," *Economic Journal* 91 (1981): 29–42, 33.
53. As quoted in Gordon, "The Demand for and Supply of Inflation," 809.
54. The definitive statement can be found in James O'Connor, *The Fiscal Crisis of the State* (London: Transaction, 1973). For a comprehensive review of the various positions, see Ian Gough, "State Expenditure in Advanced Capitalism," *New Left Review* 92 (1975): 53–92; and George Thomas and John Meyer, "The Expansion of the State," *Annual Review of Sociology* 10 (1984): 461–82.
55. Krippner, *Capitalizing on Crisis*, 140.
56. Fred Block, "The Fiscal Crisis of the Capitalist State," *Annual Review of Sociology* 7 (1981): 1–27, 1.
57. Block, "Fiscal Crisis," 2.
58. O'Connor, *The Fiscal Crisis of the State*, 6.
59. The Regulation School likewise theorized inflation as marking a crisis of capitalist productivity. See Michel Aglietta, *A Theory of Capitalist Regulation* (New York: Penguin Random House, 2015).
60. Albert Hirschman, *Essays in Trespassing* (Cambridge: Cambridge University Press, 1981), 202.
61. Hirschman, *Essays in Trespassing*, 194.
62. Albert M. Wojnilower, "The Central Role of Credit Crunches in Recent Financial History," *Brookings Papers on Economic Activity, Economic Studies Program, the Brookings Institution* 11, no. 2 (1980): 277–340, 325–26.
63. David Harvey, *Limits to Capital* (London: Verso, 2007), 311.
64. Harvey, *Limits to Capital*, 314.
65. Harvey, *Limits to Capital*, 280.
66. Harvey, *Limits to Capital*, 296.
67. Harvey, *Limits to Capital*, 315.
68. Harvey, *Limits to Capital*, 314.
69. David Harvey, *A Brief History of Neoliberalism* (New York: Oxford University Press, 2005), 23.
70. For a detailed description of methodology, see the "The Consumer Price Index" in the Bureau of Labor Statistics, *Handbook of Methods*, available at https://www.bls.gov/cpi/methodology.htm.
71. Robert Collins, *More: The Politics of Economic Growth in Postwar America* (New York: Oxford University Press, 2000). Also see Charles Maier, "The Politics of

Productivity: Foundations of American International Economic Policy After World War II," *International Organization* 31, no. 4 (1977): 607–33.
72. Robert Caro, *The Power Broker* (New York: Alfred Knopf, 1974).
73. Douglas Massey and Nancy Denton, *American Apartheid: Segregation and the Making of the Underclass* (Cambridge, MA: Harvard University Press, 1998).
74. John Mollenkopf, *The Contested City* (Princeton, NJ: Princeton University Press, 1983), 41.
75. Mark Reisner, *Cadillac Desert* (New York: Penguin, 1986).
76. Kenneth Jackson, *Crabgrass Frontier* (New York: Oxford University Press, 1985).
77. "State Motor Vehicle Registrations, by Years, 1900-1995," https://www.fhwa.dot.gov/ohim/summary95/mv200.pdf.
78. Lizabeth Cohen, *A Consumers' Republic: The Politics of Consumption in Postwar America* (New York: Penguin Random House, 2003), chap. 3.
79. Rob Kling, Spencer Olin, and Mark Poster, *Postsuburban California: The Transformation of Orange County Since World War II* (Berkeley: University of California Press, 1995).
80. Lisa McGirr, *Suburban Warriors* (Princeton, NJ: Princeton University Press, 2015).
81. Becky Nicolaides, *My Blue Heaven: Life and Politics in the Working-Class Suburbs of Los Angeles, 1920–1965* (Chicago: University of Chicago Press, 2002).
82. M. P. Baumgartner, *The Moral Order of a Suburb* (New York: Oxford University Press, 1988).
83. Lewis Mumford, *The City in History: Its Origin, Its Transformation, and Its Prospects* (New York: Hougton Mifflin, 1961), 494.
84. C. Wright Mills, *White Collar* (New York: Oxford University Press, 1951).
85. David Riesman, *The Lonely Crowd* (New Haven, CT: Yale University Press, 2020).
86. See Herbert Marcuse, *One-Dimensional Man* (Boston: Beacon, 1965).
87. Two economists observe that "the entry of the Baby Boom generation into its house-buying years is found to be a major cause of the increase in real housing prices in the 1970s." N. Gregory Mankiw and David Weil, "The Baby Boom, the Baby Bust, and the Housing Market," *Regional Science and Urban Economics* 19 (1989): 235–58.
88. Federal Reserve Bank of New York, *Monthly Review*, September 1966, 209.
89. Federal Reserve Bank of New York, *Monthly Review*, 215.
90. Donald Foley, "The Sociology of Housing," *Annual Review of Sociology* 6 (1980): 457–78.

2. THE CRISIS OF INFLATION • 271

91. Barbara Miles and Thomas Robinson, "Residential Construction Boom, 1970–1973," *Bureau of Economic Analysis Survey of Current Business* May (1973): 14–22.
92. Federal Home Loan Mortgage Corporation, *Annual Report* (Washington, DC: Government Printing Office, 1972), 2.
93. Suzanne Mettler, *The Submerged State: How Invisible Government Policies Undermine American Democracy* (Chicago: University of Chicago Press, 2011).
94. Sarah Quinn, "'The Miracles of Bookkeeping': How Budget Politics Link Fiscal Policies and Financial Markets," *American Journal of Sociology* 123 (2017): 48–85.
95. Richard Nixon, "Statement on Signing the Emergency Home Finance Act of 1970," July 24, 1970.
96. For a comprehensive narration of the government-sponsored enterprise policy changes during this period and their estimated financial impact, see Andrew Fieldhouse and Karel Mertens, "A Narrative Analysis of Asset Purchases by Federal Agencies," *National Bureau of Economic Research*, Working Paper no. 23165 (2017).
97. Sarah Quinn, *American Bonds: How Credit Markets Shaped a Nation* (Princeton, NJ: Princeton University Press, 2019), chap. 9.
98. Nancy Saltojanes, "Inflation in Housing Costs," *Congressional Research Service* 3854 (1983), 43.
99. Morton Schussheim, "Housing: An Overview," in *Housing: A Reader* (Washington, DC: U.S. Government Printing Office, 1983), 15.
100. Isaac William Martin, *The Permanent Tax Revolt: How the Property Tax Transformed American Politics* (Stanford, CA: Stanford University Press, 2008).
101. Martin, *Tax Revolt*, chap. 2.
102. Benjamin Stein, "Housing Boom Goes Bust in Los Angeles," *New York Times*, August 17, 1981, A15.
103. Thomas Byrne Edsall and Mary D. Edsall, *Chain Reaction: The Impact of Race Rights and Taxes on American Politics* (New York: W. W. Norton, 1991), 13.
104. Martin, *Tax Revolt*, 127.
105. See Matthew Dallek, *The Right Moment: Ronald Reagan's First Victory and the Decisive Turning Point in American Politics* (New York: Oxford University Press, 2004); and Sean Wilentz, *The Age of Reagan: A History, 1974–2008* (New York: Harper, 2009).
106. Clifton Luttrell, "The Russian Wheat Deal—Hindsight vs. Foresight," *Federal Reserve Bank of St. Louis Report* 81 (1973): 2–9.
107. William Safire, "El Nino," *New York Times*, August 30, 1973, 33.

108. Department of Agriculture, *Russian Wheat Sales and Weaknesses in Agriculture's Management of Wheat Export Subsidy Program* (Washington, DC: Government Printing Office, 1973).
109. Joseph Albright, "The Full Story of How America Got Burned and Russia Got Bread," *New York Times*, November 25, 1973, 36.
110. John Schnittker, "The 1972–1973 Food Price Spiral," *Brookings Papers on Economic Activity* 2 (1973): 498–507.
111. Yvonne Davies, "Fewer Cattle = Less Beef = Higher Prices," *Federal Reserve Bank of Atlanta Economic Review*, May/June 1978.
112. Marlyn Shelton, "The 1967 and 1977 Drought in California: Extent and Severity," *Weatherwise* 30, no. 4 (2010): 139–54.
113. M. King Hubbert, "Nuclear Energy and the Fossil Fuels," *Presentation to the American Petroleum Institute*, San Antonio, TX, March 1956, 8.
114. Charles Issawi, "The 1973 Oil Crisis and After," *Journal of Post Keynesian Economics* 1 (1978): 3–26.
115. Timothy Mitchell, *Carbon Democracy: Political Power in the Age of Oil* (London: Verso, 2011).
116. Mitchell, *Carbon Democracy*, 142.
117. Department of State Memorandum, "Meeting with Oil Company Executives," October 26, 1973, 7.
118. Timothy Mitchell denies that the trajectory of oil prices in the 1970s can be described as a "supply shock." Far from a "textbook case of the law of supply and demand," the "energy crisis" was instead a complex political invention. Mitchell argues that the Arab members of OPEC were trying to link "the price of oil and the policy of the United States regarding the Palestine question." The oil shock is only "exogenous" from the standpoint of macroeconomic models that must ignore such political linkages. See Timothy Mitchell, "The Resources of Economics: Making the 1973 Oil Crisis," *Journal of Cultural Economy* 3 (2010): 189–204. Also see Alan Blinder, *Economic Policy and the Great Stagflation* (New York: Academic Press, 1979); and James Hamilton, "Oil and the Macroeconomy Since World War II," *Journal of Political Economy* 91 (1983): 228–48.
119. Henry Kissinger, *Years of Upheaval* (Boston: Little and Brown, 1982). Nixon fired Special Prosecutor Archibald Cox three days later on October 20, 1973.
120. Meg Jacobs, *Panic at the Pump: The Energy Crisis and Transformation of American Politics in the 1970s* (New York: Hill and Wang, 2016), 39.
121. Victor McFarland, "Living in Never-Never Land: The United States, Saudi Arabia, and Oil in the 1970s" (PhD diss., Yale University, 2014).

122. Paul Sabin, "Crisis and Continuity in US Oil Politics, 1965–1980," *Journal of American History* 99 (2012): 177–86.
123. In 1978, SPR imports represented nearly 1 percent of total crude oil consumption. Energy Information Administration, *Annual Energy Review*, 2012, https://www.eia.gov/totalenergy/data/annual/showtext.php?t=ptb0517.
124. Energy Information Administration, table 5.7, available at https://www.eia.gov/totalenergy/data/annual/showtext.php?t=ptb0507.
125. Daniel Yergin, *The Prize: The Epic Quest for Oil, Money, and Power* (New York: Free Press, 2009), 667–69.
126. Jacobs, *Panic at the Pump*, 36–37.
127. Shane Hamilton, "The Populist Appeal of Deregulation: Independent Truckers and the Politics of Free Enterprise, 1935–1980," *Enterprise & Society* 10 (2009): 137–77.
128. Nixon commuted Hoffa's federal prison sentence for jury tampering on Christmas Eve 1971, and the Teamsters Union endorsed Nixon in the 1972 presidential election. See Fred Graham, "Nixon Commutes Hoffa Sentence, Curbs Union Role," *New York Times* December 24, 1971, A1.
129. As quoted in Hamilton, "The Populist Appeal of Deregulation," 151.
130. Hamilton, "The Populist Appeal of Deregulation," 159.
131. Another presidential hopeful, Governor Jerry Brown of California, riding his implementation of Proposition 13, advocated a balanced-budget constitutional amendment, free trade, and alternatives to fossil fuels.
132. Shane Hamilton, *Trucking Country: The Road to America's Wal-Mart Economy* (Princeton, NJ: Princeton University Press, 2014), 231.
133. Michel Foucault, *The Birth of Biopolitics* (New York: Palgrave, 2008), 196.
134. David Spiro, *The Hidden Hand of American Hegemony* (Ithaca, NY: Cornell University Press, 1998).
135. William Seidman, *Full Faith and Credit* (New York: Random House, 1993), 38.
136. The Abu Dhabi Investment Authority, for instance, was founded in 1976 and now manages nearly $700 billion. See Gawdat Bahgat, "Sovereign Wealth Funds in the Persian Gulf States," in *The Oxford Handbook of Sovereign Wealth Funds* (Oxford: Oxford University Press, 2017).
137. Many commentators link lower oil prices to the collapse of the USSR in 1989 and the Iraqi invasion of Kuwait in 1990. The resulting oil price spike (doubling from $17 to $36 per barrel) and mild recession helped secure Bill Clinton's victory over George H. W. Bush in the 1992 presidential election. Recently, historians have also emphasized the role of North Sea oil

production in enabling Margaret Thatcher's agenda in the United Kingdom. See Giuliano Garavini, "Thatcher's North Sea: The Return of Cheap Oil and the 'Neo-Liberalisation' of European Energy," *Contemporary European History*, https://doi.org/10.1017/S0960777322000686.
138. See Kimberly Phillips-Fein, *Fear City: New York's Fiscal Crisis and the Rise of Austerity Politics* (New York: Metropolitan, 2017).
139. Frances Cerra, "Car Insurance Fees Are Called Inflated," *New York Times*, September 14, 1976, A1.
140. A. W. Phillips, "The Relation Between Unemployment and the Rate of Change of Money Wage Rates in the United Kingdom, 1861–1957," *Economica* 25, no. 100 (1958): 283–99.
141. Michal Kalecki, "Political Aspects of Full Employment," in *The Political Economy: Readings in the Politics and Economics of American Public Policy*, ed. Thomas Ferguson and Joel Rogers (New York: Routledge, 1984).
142. Phillips, "Relation," 299.
143. Notably, they convert Phillips's dependent variable of "money wages" into "inflation" without explanation. Paul Samuelson and Robert Solow, "Problem of Achieving and Maintaining a Stable Price Level: Analytical Aspects of Anti-Inflation Policy," *American Economic Review* 50, no. 2 (1960): 177–94, 192.
144. Harry Johnson, "The Keynesian Revolution and the Monetarist Counter-Revolution," *American Economic Review* 61, no. 2 (1971): 1–14.
145. Foucault, *The Birth of Biopolitics*, 79. For an explanation of the technical contradictions among these positions, see Conrad Waligorski, *The Political Theory of Conservative Economics* (Lawrence: University Press of Kansas, 1990). Also see Steven K. Vogel, "Neoliberal Ideology and the Myth of the Self-Made Entrepreneur," *Entrepreneurialism and Society: New Theoretical Perspectives* 81 (2022): 77–99.
146. Greider, *Secrets of the Temple*.
147. Stacey Schreft, "Credit Controls: 1980," *Economic Review of the Federal Reserve Bank of Richmond* (November/December 1990): 25–55.
148. Bureau of Labor Statistics, *CPI Detailed Report 1980*, 2.
149. Freddie Mac, 30-year fixed rate mortgage average in the United States.
150. Bureau of Labor Statistics, *CPI Detailed Report—December 1981*.
151. Wojnilower, "The Central Role of Credit Crunches," 278.
152. Craig Howell and Jesse Thomas, "Price Changes in 1981: Widespread Slowing of Inflation," *Monthly Labor Review* April (1982): 3–14, 5.
153. Robert Gillingham and Walter Lane, "Changing the Treatment for Shelter Costs for Homeowners in the CPI," *Monthly Labor Review* (June 1982): 9–14.

154. Gillingham and Lane, "Shelter Costs for Homeowners," 10.
155. The Consumer Price Index's (CPI) role in inflating tax brackets and setting Social Security cost-of-living-adjustment payments during this period further complicates the politics of this change. For a related example with the calculation of unemployment, see Bruce Western and Katherine Beckett, "How Unregulated Is the U.S. Labor Market?," *American Journal of Sociology* 104 (1999): 1030–60.
156. Bureau of Labor Statistics, *CPI Detailed Report—December 1981*, 4. These changes in the CPI would later obscure the inflation of the housing market before the 2008 financial crisis.
157. "Transcript of Reagan Address Reporting on the State of the Nation's Economy," *New York Times*, February 6, 1981.
158. John Cassidy, "Taxing," *New Yorker*, January 26, 2004.
159. Christina Romer and David Romer, "Institutions for Monetary Stability," in *Reducing Inflation: Motivation and Strategy*, ed. Christina D. Romer and David H. Romer (Chicago: University of Chicago Press, 1997), 314.
160. Romer and Romer, "Institutions for Monetary Stability," 327. See also Alan Blinder, "Is Government Too Political?," *Foreign Affairs* 76 (1997): 115–26.
161. Krippner, *Capitalizing on Crisis*, chap. 2.
162. For the financialized corporation, production became a necessary evil in the pursuit of profit. See Jonathan Levy, "Accounting for Profit and the History of Capital," *Critical Historical Studies* 1, no. 2 (2014): 171–214, 211.
163. PL 97-320, Title VIII.
164. Leigh Clare La Berge, *Scandals and Abstractions: Financial Fiction of the Long 1980s* (New York: Oxford University Press, 2014). Also see Mary Poovey, *Genres of the Credit Economy* (Chicago: University of Chicago Press, 2008); and John Kenneth Galbraith, "Big Shots," *New York Review of Books*, May 12, 1988.
165. Zoltan Pozsar, Tobias Adrian, Adam Ashcraft, and Hayley Boesky, "Shadow Banking," *FRBNY Policy Review* 458 (2012): 1–16.
166. Annelise Riles, *Collateral Knowledge: Legal Reasoning in the Global Financial Markets* (Chicago: University of Chicago Press, 2011).
167. Kenneth Garbede, "The Evolution of Repo Contracting Conventions in the 1980s," *FRBNY Economic Policy Review* (May 2006): 27–42.
168. See Greta Krippner, "Democracy of Credit: Ownership and the Politics of Credit Access in Late Twentieth-Century America," *American Journal of Sociology* 123 (2017): 1–47. These policy changes also served to rejuvenate the social primacy of the heterosexual, male-dominated family unit. See Cooper, *Family Values*, 315.

169. Gary Gorton, *Slapped by the Invisible Hand* (New York: Oxford University Press, 2009).
170. John Zysman, *Governments, Markets, Growth* (Ithaca, NY: Cornell University Press, 1983); Peter Hall and David Soskice, *The Varieties of Capitalism* (New York: Oxford University Press, 2001); Iain Hardie et al., "Banks and the False Dichotomy in the Comparative Political Economy of Finance," *World Politics* 65, no. 4 (2013): 691–728.
171. David Harvey approvingly summarizes Gérard Duménil and Dominique Lévy as arguing that neoliberalism "was from the very beginning a project to achieve the restoration of class power." Harvey, *A Brief History of Neoliberalism*, 57.
172. Milton Friedman's riposte to the "oil and food" counterargument was that price increases in specific markets affect "relative" but not "absolute" price levels. As Friedman explains, "the special conditions that drove up the prices of oil and food required purchasers to spend more on them, leaving less to spend on other items. . . . In the main, however, [oil and food] have been convenient excuses for besieged government officials and harried journalists rather than reasons for the price explosion." This argument assumes that the quantity of money in circulation is fixed and cannot expand endogenously in response to price increases. Friedman thereby creates a tautological loop in which price increases can only result from expansions of an otherwise fixed money supply. See Milton Friedman, "Perspective on Inflation," *Newsweek*, June 24, 1974, 73.
173. See Kevin Boyle, *The Shattering: America in the 1960s* (New York: Norton, 2021).
174. Robert Self describes related "ostensible signifiers" of a broader transformation like "white flight" or "urban decline." See Robert Self, *American Babylon* (Princeton, NJ: Princeton University Press, 2003).
175. See Martha Derthick and Paul Quirk, *The Politics of Deregulation* (Washington, DC: Brookings Institution, 1985).
176. Monica Prasad has shown how access to credit is negatively correlated with growth in welfare spending. See Monica Prasad, *The Land of Too Much* (Cambridge, MA: Harvard University Press, 2012), chap. 9.
177. Alan Greenspan, "Opening Remarks," *Federal Reserve Bank of Kansas City Jackson Hole Symposium*, August 31, 2001.
178. Herman Schwartz, *Subprime Nation* (Ithaca, NY: Cornell University Press, 2009).
179. Dr. Gingrich's doctoral dissertation, "Belgian Education Policy in the Congo, 1945–1960," asks, "Did the colonial powers perform a painful but positive

function in disrupting traditional society and so paving the way for more rapid modernization? Even if they did, was the price of colonial exploitation too high?"
180. See George Packer, *The Unwinding: An Inner History of the New America* (New York: Farrar, Straus and Giroux, 2011).
181. Michel Foucault, *Society Must Be Defended* (New York: Picador, 2003), 15.

3. THE FINANCIALIZATION OF LIBERALISM

1. Quinn Slobodian and Dieter Plehwe observe the following: "It would be ironic, as some have noted, if leftist critics became fixated on the realm of ideas while the right adopted materialist explanations of the present." Quinn Slobodian and Dieter Plehwe, *Nine Lives of Neoliberalism* (New York: Verso, 2021), 2.
2. Walzer writes, "I want to say again that the limitation of power is liberalism's historic achievement." Or, "the liberal achievement has been to . . . limit the reach of government." Walzer, expressing skepticism of Foucault, writes, "It is only in authoritarian states, which systematically violate institutional integrity, that Foucault's 'disciplinary society' is likely to be realized in anything like the form he describes." Michael Walzer, "Liberalism and the Art of Separation," *Political Theory* 12 (1984): 315–30.
3. Walzer, "Liberalism and the Art of Separation," 322.
4. A standard economics textbook defines "monetary neutrality" as "the proposition that changes in the money supply do not affect real variables." When the supply of money changes, "real variables, such as production, employment, real wages, and real interest rates, are unchanged." See N. Gregory Mankiw, *Principles of Economics*, 6th ed. (Boston: Cengage Learning, 2012), 650.
5. Michel Aglietta and André Orléan, *La Violance de la Monnaie* (Paris: Presses Universitaires de France, 1982).
6. Charles Mills, "Ideal Theory as Ideology," *Hypatia* 20, no. 3 (2005): 165–84.
7. David Harvey, *Marx, Capital, and the Madness of Economic Reason* (New York: Oxford University Press, 2017), 2.
8. Michel Foucault, *The Birth of Biopolitics* (New York: Palgrave, 2008), 94, 131.
9. See Wendy Brown, *Undoing the Demos: Neoliberalism's Stealth Revolution* (Princeton, NJ: Princeton University Press, 2017), chap. 2.
10. Foucault, *The Birth of Biopolitics*, 2.
11. My purpose is not to present a comprehensive alternative to the conventional wisdom but rather to use Foucault to help identify key features neoliberalism by design misses.

278 • 3. THE FINANCIALIZATION OF LIBERALISM

12. Michel Foucault, *Society Must Be Defended* (New York: Picador, 2003), 33.
13. Michel Foucault, *Security, Territory, Population* (New York: Springer, 2009), 33.
14. Thomas Biebricher, "Disciplining Europe—The Production of Economic Delinquency," *Foucault Studies* 23 (2017): 63–85.
15. Mankiw, *Principles of Economics*, 556.
16. As elsewhere, the fit between "theory" and "practice" is imperfect. My purpose is to sketch such a vocabulary and suggest its relevance for comprehending the effect of finance on liberalism. However, because it is a sketch, it cannot claim to be comprehensive or exhaustive.
17. Foucault, *Security, Territory, Population*, 247.
18. Foucault, *The Birth of Biopolitics*, 20.
19. Wendy Brown, "Power After Foucault," in *The Oxford Handbook of Political Theory*, ed. John S. Dryzek, Bonnie Honig, and Anne Phillips (Oxford: Oxford University Press, 2008).
20. Michel Foucault, *History of Sexuality* (New York: Knopf Doubleday, 1990), 97.
21. Brown, "Power After Foucault," 72. Also see Nikolas Rose, Pat O'Malley, and Mariana Valverde, "Governmentality," *Annual Review of Sociology* 2 (2006): 83–104; Peter Miller and Nikolas Rose, "Governing Economic Life," *Economy & Society* 19 (1990): 1–31; Mike Gane, "Foucault on Governmentality and Liberalism," *Theory, Culture & Society* 25 (2008): 353–63; Mitchell Dean, *Governmentality* (London: Sage, 2009); and William Walters, *Governmentality* (London: Routledge, 2012).
22. Foucault, *Security, Territory, Population*, 8.
23. Foucault, *Security, Territory, Population*, 103.
24. See Bernard Harcourt, *The Illusion of Free Markets* (Cambridge, MA: Harvard University Press, 2012).
25. Foucault, *Security, Territory, Population*, 34.
26. Michel Foucault, *Discipline & Punish* (New York: Penguin Random House, 1995), 201.
27. Foucault, *Discipline & Punish*, 216.
28. Foucault, *Discipline & Punish*, 219.
29. Foucault, *Discipline & Punish*, 220.
30. Paul Rabinow, *The Foucault Reader* (New York: Pantheon, 1984), 207.
31. Rabinow, *The Foucault Reader*, 205.
32. Foucault, *Society Must Be Defended*, 36.
33. Foucault, *Society Must Be Defended*, 36.
34. Foucault, *Society Must Be Defended*, 249–50.

3. THE FINANCIALIZATION OF LIBERALISM • 279

35. Foucault, *Society Must Be Defended*, 6, 23.
36. Foucault, *Society Must Be Defended*, 35.
37. Foucault, *Society Must Be Defended*, 95.
38. Foucault, *The Birth of Biopolitics*, 67.
39. Foucault, *The Birth of Biopolitics*, 20.
40. Foucault, *The Birth of Biopolitics*, 69.
41. Foucault, *The Birth of Biopolitics*, 69.
42. Foucault, *The Birth of Biopolitics*, 70.
43. Foucault offers a schematic account of the stagflationary crisis within which neoliberalism was able to take hold in France and Germany. It appeared as a crisis of investment resulting from "errors in investment policy" that was compounded by the oil crisis "formation of a market price for both oil and energy generally." Economic liberalism appeared as "the only solution" because it alone could take "into account" the new price of energy.
44. Foucault, *The Birth of Biopolitics*, 243.
45. Foucault does not engage Gary Becker because he is "correct" about punishment or childrearing, but because Becker's theory of human capital marks a new way of dividing the world into an imagined regime of true and false.
46. Graham Burchell, "Liberal Government and Techniques of the Self," *Economy and Society* 22 (1993): 267–282, 274.
47. Foucault, *The Birth of Biopolitics*, 247.
48. Michel Foucault, "The Confession of the Flesh," in *Power/Knowledge* (New York: Pantheon, 1977), 194.
49. Foucault, "The Confession of the Flesh," 195.
50. Foucault, *The Birth of Biopolitics*, 19.
51. Francois Ewald, "Insurance and Risk," in *The Foucault Effect*, ed. Graham Burchell, Colin Gordon, and Peter Miller (Chicago: University of Chicago Press, 1991), 206. Also see Francois Ewald, *L'Etat Providence* (Paris: Bernard Grasset, 1986).
52. Ewald, "Insurance and Risk," 211.
53. Daniel Defert, "Popular Life and Insurance Technology," in *The Foucault Effect*, ed. Graham Burchell, Colin Gordon, and Peter Miller (Chicago: University of Chicago Press, 1991), 215.
54. Ewald, "Insurance and Risk," 210.
55. Michel Foucault, "The Political Technology of Individuals," in *Power: The Essential Works of Foucault 1954–1984* (New York: The New Press, 2000), 153.
56. A mortgage is the canonical example of collateralization: if payments are not made, then the lender takes possession of ("repossesses") the house.

57. Saskia Sassen, *Expulsions* (Cambridge, MA: Harvard University Press, 2014), 87.
58. Return on investment is a looser rubric than cost-benefit analysis because the ends are not predetermined.
59. Higher interest rate loans are inherently riskier: the increased rate is compensation to the lender for the elevated risk of default by the borrower.
60. See Daniela Gabor, "Wall Street Consensus," *Development and Change* 52 (2021): 429–59.
61. See Michel Feher, *Rated Agency* (Princeton, NJ: Princeton University Press, 2018).
62. Jacob Hacker has shown how policymakers deliberately prevented the existing welfare state apparatus from adapting to the changing structure of the American economy as a result of these changes. See Jacob Hacker, "Privatizing Risk Without Privatizing the Welfare State: The Hidden Politics of Social Policy Retrenchment in the United States," *American Political Science Review* 98, no. 2 (2004): 243–60.
63. See Melinda Cooper, *Family Values: Between Neoliberalism and Social Conservatism* (New York: Zone Books, 2017), chap. 6.
64. T. H. Marshall, "Citizenship and Social Class," in *Class, Citizenship, and Social Development*, ed. Ricardo Blaug and John Schwarzmantel (Garden City, NY: Doubleday, 1963).
65. Susan Strange, *The Retreat of the State* (Cambridge: Cambridge University Press, 1996); Benjamin Cohen, *The Geography of Money* (Ithaca, NY: Cornell University Press, 1998); Stephen Krasner, *Sovereignty: Organized Hypocrisy* (Princeton, NJ: Princeton University Press, 1999); Robert Gilpin, *The Political Economy of International Relations* (Princeton, NJ: Princeton University Press, 1987); Susan Strange, "Finance, Information and Power," *Review of International Studies* 16 (1990): 259–74; Eric Helleiner, *States and the Emergence of Global Finance* (Ithaca, NY: Cornell University Press, 1994); Wendy Brown, *Walled States, Waning Sovereignty* (New York: Zone Books, 2010); Thomas Biebricher, "Sovereignty, Norms, and Exception in Neoliberalism," *Qui Parle* 23 (2014): 77–107.
66. Joseph Vogl and Christine Desan both chart a genealogy of the financial aspects of sovereignty from the Roman *fiscus* to Jean Bodin to seigniorage, and both conclude that sovereignty has always had an important financial dimension and that finance has always been a product of sovereign power. See Joseph Vogl, *The Ascendancy of Finance* (London: Polity, 2017); and Christine Desan, *Making Money: Coin, Currency, and the Coming of Capitalism* (Oxford: Oxford University Press, 2014), chap. 4.

67. Bruce Carruthers, *City of Capital: Politics and Markets in the English Financial Revolution* (Princeton, NJ: Princeton University Press, 1999); Aihwa Ong, *Neoliberalism as Exception: Mutations in Citizenship and* Sovereignty (Durham, NC: Duke University Press, 2006); Narcis Serra and Joseph Stiglitz, eds., *The Washington Consensus Reconsidered: Towards a New Global Governance* (Oxford: Oxford University Press, 2008); Odette Lienau, *Rethinking Sovereign Debt* (Cambridge, MA: Harvard University Press, 2014); Marion Fourcade, "State Metrology: The Rating and Judgment of Nations," in *The Many Hands of the State*, ed. Kimberly Morgan and Ann Orloff (New York: Cambridge University Press, 2017); Yanis Varoufakis, *Adults in the Room* (New York: Farrar, Strauss, and Giroux, 2017).
68. Regardless of their origin or intention, state practices such as mass incarceration bolster the political project of neoliberalism by confining the unprofitable at the taxpayer's expense, further squeezing public finances.
69. Thomas Friedman, *The Lexus and the Olive Tree* (New York: Farrar, Strauss, and Giroux, 1999), 87–88.
70. Andreas Kruck, *Private Ratings, Public Regulations* (London: Palgrave, 2011).
71. Roi Livne and Yuval Yonay, "Performing Neoliberal Governmentality," *Socio-Economic Review* 14 (2016): 339–62. Benjamin Lemoine, "L'Etat estratège pris dans les taux," *Revue Française de Science Politique* 66 (2016): 435–59.
72. For an extended intellectual genealogy of the conception of the fine in penal discourse, see Patricia Faralda-Cabana, *Money and the Governance of Punishment* (London: Routledge, 2017), chap. 2.
73. Marion Fourcade, "The Fly and the Cookie: Alignment and Unhingement in 21st-Century Capitalism," *Socio-Economic Review* 15 (2017): 661–78; Frank Pasquale, *The Black Box Society* (Cambridge, MA: Harvard University Press, 2015).
74. Foucault, *Security, Territory, Population*, 46.
75. Brian Scudamore, "Here's What Happened When I Started Running My Life Like a Business," *Inc.*, February 13, 2018, https://www.inc.com/brian-scudamore/heres-what-happened-when-i-started-running-my-life-like-a-business.html.
76. "What Is Financial Discipline?," Quicken, https://web.archive.org/web/20201210132153/https://www.quicken.com/what-financial-discipline.
77. Len Penzo, "50 Personal Finance Habits Everyone Should Follow," *Money*, https://web.archive.org/web/20180806040026/http://time.com/money/collection-post/4023439/personal-finance-habits.

78. Frank Dobbin et al., "Managing Investors: How Financial Markets Reshaped the American Firm," in *The Sociology of Financial Markets*, ed. K. K. Cetina and A. Preda (London: Oxford University Press, 2004), 269–89.
79. Foucault, *Discipline & Punish*, 202.
80. Justin Fox, "Learn to Play the Earnings Game," *Fortune*, March 31, 1997.
81. Ford Credit, *Series 2013–1 Asset Backed Notes Prospectus*, 26.
82. Jonathan Simon, "The Ideological Effects of Actuarial Practices," *Law & Society Review* 771 (1988): 771–800, 773.
83. Simon, "The Ideological Effects of Actuarial Practices," 772.
84. See Carol Heimer, *Reactive Risk and Rational Action* (Berkeley: University of California Press, 1989); Martha Poon, "Scorecards as Devices for Consumer Credit: The Case of Fair, Isaac & Company Incorporated," *Sociological Review* 55 (2007): 284–306; Sarah Quinn, "The Transformations of Morals and Markets: Death, Benefits, and the Exchange of Life Insurance Policies," *American Journal of Sociology* 114 (2008): 738–80; Bruce Carruthers, "From Uncertainty Toward Risk: The Case of Credit Ratings," *Socio-Economic Review* 11 (2013): 525–51; Tom Baker and Jonathan Simon, eds., *Embracing Risk: The Changing Culture of Insurance and Responsibility* (Berkeley: University of California Press, 2014); Viviana Zelizer, *Morals and Markets* (New York: Columbia University Press, 2017); Ivan Ascher, *Portfolio Society: On the Capitalist Mode of Prediction* (Cambridge, MA: MIT Press, 2016); Josh Lauer, *Creditworthy: A History of Consumer Surveillance and Financial Identity in America*, (New York: Columbia University Press, 2017); Julie Froud et al., "Shareholder Value and Financialization," *Economy and Society* 29 (2000): 80–110.
85. Modern portfolio theory (MPT) attempts to maximize the return of a financial portfolio for a given level of risk. MPT requires only three inputs to calculate the optimal portfolio: risk, return, and correlation. Now, any array of income streams, whether produced by a multinational corporation, subprime borrower, or small city, can be assimilated into the same portfolio in an optimal manner. The investor is now indifferent to the source of these cash flows: MPT endows each with equal standing. Of course, as Marx makes clear, the substantive effects of reducing every financialized entity—be it a multinational corporation or municipal government—to risk, return, and correlation are far from egalitarian.
86. Moody's, "Rating Methodology: US Local Government General Obligation Debt," January 2014, 24. See also Marion Fourcade, "State Metrology: The Rating of Sovereigns and the Judgment of Nations," in *The Many Hands of the*

State: Theorizing Political Authority and Social Control, ed. Kimberly J. Morgan and Ann Shola Orloff (New York: Cambridge University Press, 2017), 112.
87. Jason Read, "A Genealogy of Homo-Economicus: Neoliberalism and the Production of Subjectivity," *Foucault Studies* 6 (2009): 25–36.
88. Foucault, *The Birth of Biopolitics*, 147.
89. Foucault, *The Birth of Biopolitics*, 226, 147.
90. Foucault, *The Birth of Biopolitics*, 269.
91. Foucault, *The Birth of Biopolitics*, 252.
92. Michel Feher, "Self-Appreciation," *Public Culture* 21 (2009): 21–41, 27.
93. Stephen Gill, "Globalisation, Market Civilisation, and Disciplinary Neoliberalism," *Millennium* 24 (1995): 169–99.
94. Louis Pauly, *Who Elected the Bankers? Surveillance and Control in the World Economy* (Ithaca, NY: Cornell University Press, 1998), chap. 6.
95. Much in the same way Foucault describes the prisoner confessing to his crimes or the psychiatrist seeking a therapeutic confession of illicit sexual desire, corporations must periodically confess their financial position in the form of financial statements. In the United States, the Securities and Exchange Commission requires publicly traded companies to maintain and disseminate timely and accurate financial statements, including a balance sheet, an income statement, and a cash flow statement that jointly reveal the entity's financial position.
96. Neil Fligstein and Adam Goldstein, "The Emergence of a Finance Culture in American Households, 1989–2007," *Socio-Economic Review* 13 (2015): 575–601; and Gerald Davis, *Managed by the Market* (New York: Oxford University Press, 2009), 6.
97. Ivan Ascher, *Portfolio Society* (New York: MIT Press, 2016).
98. Brown, *Undoing the Demos*, 39.

4. GROWTH MACHINE POLITICS

1. Stockton is a city of 300,000 people in the heart of the San Joaquin river delta, roughly sixty miles east of the San Francisco Bay Area. Founded during the 1849 Gold Rush, Stockton was named in honor of Commodore Robert Stockton who captured California the previous year during the Mexican-American War. Stockton was the first major city in the new state of California with neither a native nor Spanish name.
2. Detroit surpassed Stockton for the largest municipal bankruptcy the following year.

3. This puzzle does not only apply to Stockton: Chicago has consistently been at the forefront of urban financialization while remaining a Democratic stronghold. See Amanda Kass, Martin Luby, and Rachel Weber, "Taking a Risk: Explaining the Use of Complex Debt Finance by the Chicago Public Schools," *Urban Affairs Review* 55, no. 4 (2018): 1–35; Philip Ashton, Marc Doussard, and Rachel Weber, "Reconstituting the State: City Powers and Exposures in Chicago's Infrastructure Leases," *Urban Studies* 53, no. 7 (2016): 1384–400; and Larry Bennett, Roberta Garner, and Euan Hague, eds., *Neoliberal Chicago* (Bloomington: University of Illinois Press, 2016). For the case of Jefferson County, Alabama, see Michael Howell-Maroney and Jeremy Hall, "Waste in the Sewer: The Collapse of Accountability and Transparency in Public Finance in Jefferson County, Alabama," *Public Administration Review* 71, no. 3 (2011): 232–42.
4. Neil Brenner and Nik Theodore, "Cities and the Geographies of 'Actually Existing Neoliberalism,'" *Antipode* 34, no. 3 (2002): 349–79; Jamie Peck, "Austerity Urbanism," *City* 16, no. 6 (2012): 626–55; Jamie Peck, Nik Theodore, and Neil Brenner, "Neoliberal Urbanism: Models, Moments, Mutations," *SAIS Review* 29, no. 1 (2009): 49–66; and Roi Livne and Yuval Yonay, "Performing Neoliberal Governmentality: An Ethnography of Financialized Sovereign Debt Management Practices," *Socio-Economic Review* 14, no. 2 (2016): 339–62.
5. Michelle Anderson, "The New Minimal Cities," *Yale Law Journal* 123, no. 5 (2014): 1118–227.
6. David Harvey, "From Managerialism to Entrepreneurialism: The Transformation in Urban Governance in Late Capitalism," *Geografiska Annaler* 71, no. 1 (1989): 3–17; and Jamie Peck, "Pushing Austerity: State Failure, Municipal Bankruptcy and the Crises of Fiscal Federalism in the USA," *Cambridge Journal of Regions, Economy and Society* 7 (2014): 17–44.
7. Rachel Weber, "Selling City Futures: The Financialization of Urban Redevelopment Policy," *Economic Geography* 86, no. 3 (2010): 251–74.
8. Sean Safford, *Why the Garden Club Couldn't Save Youngstown* (Cambridge, MA: Harvard University Press, 2009); Jamie Peck and Heather Whiteside, "Financializing Detroit," *Economic Geography* 92, no. 3 (2015): 235–68; Seth Schindler, "Detroit After Bankruptcy: A Case of Degrowth Machine Politics," *Urban Studies* 53, no. 4 (2016): 818–36; and Charlie LeDuff, *Detroit: An American Autopsy* (New York: Penguin, 2013).
9. Within the study of urban politics, the centrality of growth has long been recognized. Harvey Molotch, "The City as a Growth Machine: Toward a

Political Economy of Place," *American Journal of Sociology* 82, no. 2 (1976): 309–32; and John Mollenkopf, *The Contested City* (Princeton, NJ: Princeton University Press, 1983).
10. John Logan and Harvey Molotch, *Urban Fortunes: The Political Economy of Place* (Berkeley: University of California Press, 1987), 87.
11. As Rachel Weber observes, "During the Millennial boom of the late 1990s and the first decade of the 2000s, many U.S. municipal governments acted as the kind of innovators that we associate with private market actors. They assisted capital in finding profitable investment outlets by devising new ways to monetize their own assets and create new securities. They turned income streams from their existing and future tax bases, infrastructure, and pension funds into fungible securities and helped build secondary markets for their exchange, both of which momentarily took some pressure off of the global capital glut." Weber, "Selling City Futures," 270.
12. David Schattschneider, *The Semisovereign People: A Realist's View of Democracy in America* (Boston: Wadsworth, 1960); Robert Dahl, *Who Governs? Democracy and Power in an American City* (New Haven, CT: Yale University Press, 1961); Theodore Lowi, *The End of Liberalism* (New York: W. W. Norton, 1969); and Phillippe Schmitter, "Still the Century of Corporatism?," *Review of Politics* 36, no. 1 (1973): 85–131.
13. Katharina Pistor, *The Code of Capital: How the Law Creates Wealth and Inequality* (Princeton, NJ: Princeton University Press, 2019).
14. Wolfgang Streeck, *Buying Time: The Delayed Crisis of Democratic Capitalism* (London: Verso, 2014); and Armin Schäfer and Wolfgang Streeck, *Politics in the Age of Austerity* (Cambridge: Polity, 2013).
15. John Hurst, "Stockton: An Inferiority Complex on a Rampage," *Los Angeles Times*, September 26, 1986.
16. Michelle Conlin and Jim Christie, "Stockton, California: The Town the Housing Boom Broke," *Reuters*, March 19, 2012.
17. Ashok Bardhan and Richard Walker, "California Shrugged: Fountainhead of the Great Recession," *Cambridge Journal of Regions, Economy and Society* 4 (2011): 303–22.
18. Casey Blount et al., "Redevelopment Agencies in California: History, Benefits, Excesses, and Closure," Working Paper 2014-01, U.S. Department of Housing and Urban Development.
19. George Lefcoe and Charles Swenson, "Redevelopment in California: The Demise of TIF-Funded Redevelopment in California and Its Aftermath," *National Tax Journal* 67, no. 3 (2014): 719–44.

20. Josh Pacewicz, "Tax Increment Financing, Economic Development Professionals and the Financialization of Urban Politics," *Socio-Economic Review* 11, no. 3 (2013): 413–40.
21. L. Owen Kirkpatrick and Michael Smith, "The Infrastructural Limits to Growth: Rethinking the Urban Growth Machine in Times of Fiscal Crisis," *International Journal of Urban and Regional Research* 35, no. 3 (2011): 477–503; and Mark Davidson and William Kutz, "Grassroots Austerity: Municipal Bankruptcy from Below in Vallejo, California," *Environment and Planning* 47 (2015): 1440–59.
22. City of Stockton, *2004–2005 Annual Budget*, 219.
23. Stockton City Council meeting, February 17, 2004.
24. Stockton City Council meeting, February 17, 2004.
25. Stockton City Council meeting, March 2, 2004.
26. The city manager was fired a week later after the cost of the concert ($1 million) became public.
27. Stockton City Council meeting, August 31, 2006.
28. Interest rates would fall to zero eighteen months later, meaning Stockton locked in their borrowing rate at the worst possible time.
29. David Siders, "City Owes Retirees $152m," *Stockton Record*, September 1, 2006.
30. Stockton City Council meeting, November 6, 2007.
31. Immediately after the pension obligation bonds (POBs) were approved by the council, there was a discussion of a city ordinance banning Walmart. A parade of blue-vested workers who had been sitting silently during the discussion of the POBs approached the lectern to deliver messages of support. A Walmart vice president who had flown in from Boise carried a large bag of "supporter cards" to the lectern. She began, "Regulating consumer choice is short sighted. We have collected over 1,500 supporter cards. These folks support Walmart and consumer choice and oppose outright bans on big boxes. It would be discriminatory for people who depend on convenience and low prices our stores offer . . . [to] ban discount stores in under-served areas where Walmart is trying to locate." Next, a lawyer for Walmart explained that "reports have shown that fears of negative economic impacts are unfounded."
32. Stockton City Council Resolution 07-0206.
33. Stockton City Council meeting, April 10, 2007, Agenda Item 6.03.
34. City of Stockton, Fire Unit Memorandum of Understanding, December 11, 2007.
35. Stockton City Council, Budget Study Session, May 8, 2008.
36. Davidson and Kutz, "Grassroots Austerity."

4. GROWTH MACHINE POLITICS • 287

37. Stockton City Council, Budget Study Session, August 28, 2008.
38. Sara Hinkley, "Structurally Adjusting: Narratives of Fiscal Crisis in Four US Cities," *Urban Studies* 54, no. 9 (2017): 2123–38.
39. Stockton City Council, Budget Study Session, August 28, 2008.
40. Lawrence White, "Credit Rating Agencies: An Overview," *Annual Review of Sociology* 5 (2013): 93–122.
41. David Siders, "Chavez a Step from Condo Foreclosure," *Stockton Record*, January 29, 2009.
42. Kim Phillips-Fein, *Fear City: New York's Fiscal Crisis and the Rise of Austerity Politics* (New York: Metropolitan, 2017).
43. David Siders and Ian Hill, "A Sign of the Crimes," *Stockton Record*, May 30, 2010.
44. Stockton City Council meeting, January 27, 2010.
45. Stockton City Council meeting, February 17, 2010.
46. David Siders, "Stockton Officials' Message Is Dire," *Stockton Record*, May 6, 2010.
47. Stockton City Council meeting, April 10, 2010.
48. Daniel Thigpen, "Labor Ballot Measure Inflames City, Fire Tensions," *Stockton Record*, September 6, 2010.
49. Moody's Investor Service, "Rating Update: Moody's Downgrades to A1 from Aa3 City of Stockton, CA," January 20, 2011.
50. Jason Hackworth, *The Neoliberal City: Governance, Ideology, and Development in American Urbanism* (Ithaca, NY: Cornell University Press, 2007).
51. Stockton City Council meeting, March 22, 2011.
52. Moody's Investor Service, "Rating Update: Moody's Downgrades to A3 from A1 City of Stockton, CA," June 28, 2011.
53. David Siders, "Stockton Will Transfer $34m to Settle Suit," *Stockton Record*, March 25, 2009.
54. Bob Deis, "Fiscal Condition Update for Fiscal Years 2010–11, 2011–12 and 2012–13," memorandum, February 28, 2012, 5.
55. Deis, "Fiscal Condition Update," 3.
56. Deis, "Fiscal Condition Update," 4.
57. Deis, "Fiscal Condition Update," 32.
58. Michael Fitzgerald, "City Hall on Road to Repo," *Stockton Record*, May 11, 2012.
59. City of Stockton, Special Budget Study Session, June 11, 2012.
60. A pendency plan outlines the operating budget of the city while in bankruptcy. Malia Wollan, "Mediation Fails, Pushing Stockton Toward Bankruptcy," *New York Times*, June 27, 2012.

61. City of Stockton, *Pendency Plan*, June 26, 2012, 207.
62. City of Stockton, *Plan of Adjustment*, 19.
63. City of Stockton, *Employee Letter*, June 20, 2012.
64. City of Stockton, *Application for Preliminary Injunction*, 41.
65. Case 12–02302, 3.
66. See In re: City of Stockton, CA, Debtor, United States Bankruptcy Court Eastern District of California, 12-32118-C-9.
67. Bob Deis, "A Message from the City That Went Bankrupt," *Wall Street Journal*, September 27, 2012; and Bob Deis, "Stockton's Bankruptcy and Pension Reform," *Sacramento Bee*, August 4, 2014.
68. Randy Diamond, "CalPERS Will Get Its Due from Bankrupt Cities," *Pensions and Investments*, July 23, 2012.
69. City of Stockton, *Pendency Plan*.
70. Scott Smith, "Mayor's Race Is Wide Open," *Stockton Record*, May 6, 2012.
71. Michael Winter, "Bloody 2 Days Sets Killing Record in Stockton, Calif," *USA Today*, October 23, 2012.
72. Donald Blount, "Bankruptcy Plus Violence Equals Upset," *Stockton Record*, November 12, 2012.
73. David Siders, "Mayor of Bankrupt Stockton Isolated, Under Investigation," *Sacramento Bee*, July 21, 2013.
74. Alex Breitler, "Stockton Mayor Floats an Idea: Bring in Manatees," *Stockton Record*, November 8, 2014.
75. Scott Smith, "Silva Pleads for Support Ahead of Censure Vote," *Stockton Record*, December 3, 2013.
76. City of Stockton, *Plan of Adjustment*, 183.
77. City of Stockton, *Stockton FY2017–18 Annual Budget*, A-27.
78. In early 2019, Stockton began the largest universal basic income pilot in the United States. The program was spearheaded by Michael Tubbs, the youngest mayor of a major American city. Tubbs's campaign was seeded by a $50,000 donation from Evan Spiegel, founder of Snapchat and Tubbs's Stanford classmate. Other large donors to Tubbs's campaign included Steven Denning, chairman of both the Stanford board of trustees and General Atlantic Partners (a Connecticut-based private equity firm), and Jerry Yang, founder of Yahoo. Oprah Winfrey contributed $10,000 to Tubbs's first city council race. One of Tubbs's signature achievements as mayor was securing $20 million from Spiegel to finance a college fund grant for low-income Stockton students. In the 2020 election, Tubbs decisively lost his reelection bid to political newcomer Kevin Lincoln. According to his LinkedIn profile, Lincoln began

his career as a military police officer in the Marine One unit during the Bush administration. After the Marines, he became a district manager for a private security company in Silicon Valley (acquired by Blackstone in 2008). Lincoln earned a bachelor's degree from Grand Canyon University in 2015 and a master's degree in executive leadership from Liberty University in 2019. From 2013 through the end of 2020, he was an associate pastor at a nondenominational evangelical church in Stockton. Despite being outraised three to one, Lincoln capitalized on the perception among residents that Tubbs was primarily concerned with raising his national political profile. See David Siders, "The Fall of Michael Tubbs," *Politico*, December 23, 2020; and Dana Davidsen, "Oprah Gives to Young Stockton Campaign," *CNN*, July 6, 2012.

79. Jessica Hice, "Former Stockton Mayor Arrested at San Francisco Airport," *Sacramento Bee*, March 5, 2017.
80. Michael Fitzgerald, "Report Details Costly Issues with New City Hall," *Stockton Record*, June 28, 2018.
81. Aaron Leathley, "Moving Stockton City Hall to Waterfront Towers Will Likely Cost $63.3 Million," *Stockton Record*, November 4, 2021.
82. Nina Eliasoph, *Avoiding Politics: How Americans Produce Apathy in Everyday Life* (Cambridge: Cambridge University Press, 1998).

5. DEMOCRACY AND FINANCE IN CALIFORNIA

1. The California Public Employees Retirement System (CalPERS) does not cover all public employees in the state. Public school teachers' pensions are managed by the California State Teachers Retirement System (CalSTRS), the second largest pension plan in the country. Some cities and counties, most notably San Francisco, Los Angeles, and San Diego, run their own pension systems for their employees and retirees. In total, there are more than eighty pension systems in the state.
2. Some use the term "asset manager capitalism" or "asset manager society" to capture these and related developments. See Benjamin Braun, "Asset Manager Capitalism as a Corporate Governance Regime," in *The American Political Economy*, ed. Jacob S. Hacker, Alexander Hertel-Fernandez, Paul Pierson, and Kathleen Thelen (Cambridge: Cambridge University Press, 2021); and Brett Christophers, *Our Lives in Their Portfolios* (New York: Verso, 2023).
3. See Miriam Pawel, *The Browns of California* (New York: Bloomsbury, 2018).
4. Edmund G. "Pat" Brown, "First Inaugural Address," January 5, 1959.

5. See Andrea Gibbons, *City of Segregation* (New York: Verso, 2018). For the story of Detroit, see Thomas Sugrue, *The Origins of the Urban Crisis* (Princeton, NJ: Princeton University Press, 1996).
6. James Loewen, *Sundown Towns: A Hidden Dimension of American Racism* (New York: The New Press, 2018).
7. Tyler Reny and Benjamin Newman, "Protecting the Right to Discriminate," *American Political Science Review* 112, no. 4 (2018): 1104–10.
8. Peter Radkowski, "Managing the Invisible Hand of the California Housing Market, 1942–1967," *California Legal History Journal* (2006): 7–71.
9. "Brown Likens Rumford Act Foes to Nazis," *Los Angeles Times*, August 20, 1964, B8.
10. Daniel HoSang argues that the identity position of the homeowner was crucial in the political mobilization against civil rights. HoSang writes: "'Homeowner' became a social and political identity animated by particular normative race, class, and gendered assumptions: a white nuclear family headed by a breadwinning father, a homemaking mother, and their immediate children—the home serving as both the foundation and index of this condition." Daniel HoSang, *Racial Propositions: Ballot Initiatives and the Making of Postwar California* (Berkeley: University of California Press, 2010), 53.
11. Lisa McGirr, *Suburban Warriors* (Princeton, NJ: Princeton University Press, 2015), 133–36.
12. See Mike Davis and Jon Wiener, *Set the Night on Fire: L.A. in the Sixties* (New York: Verso, 2020).
13. Wallace Turner, "Las Vegas: Casinos Get Millions in Loans from Teamsters' Fund," *New York Times*, November 22, 1963.
14. In 1967, the Supreme Court, led by chief justice and former governor of California Earl Warren, ruled 5–4 in *Reitman v. Mulkey*, agreeing with the California Supreme Court that Proposition 14 violated the Fourteenth Amendment's equal protection clause. The crux of the ruling was that Proposition 14 required the state to take "affirmative action of a legislative nature designed to make possible private discriminatory practices which previously were legally restricted." See Reitman v. Mulkey, 387 US 369 (1967).
15. Matthew Dallek, *The Right Moment: Ronald Reagan's First Victory and the Decisive Turning Point in American Politics* (New York: Oxford University Press, 2004), 192.
16. McGirr, *Suburban Warriors*, 207.

17. Mark Brilliant, *The Color of America Has Changed: How Racial Diversity Shaped Civil Rights Reform in California, 1941–1978* (New York: Oxford University Press, 2010), 222.
18. McGirr, *Suburban Warriors*, 209.
19. Gerrard De Groot, "A Goddamned Electable Person: The 1966 California Gubernatorial Campaign of Ronald Reagan," *History* 82, no. 267 (1997): 429–48, 446.
20. Maury Beam, "Pension Fund Use for Stock Buying Studied," *Los Angeles Times*, September 18, 1961, B1.
21. Arelo Sederberg, "Stock Purchases by State Pension Funds Supported," *Los Angeles Times*, October 11, 1966, B7.
22. David Smith, "Shifting Investments: State Pension Funds Seek Higher Returns in Stock, Real Estate," *Wall Street Journal*, July 20, 1962, 1.
23. Ernest Schonberger, "Government Pension Funds: Market Windfall in California," *Los Angeles Times*, September 17, 1967.
24. The bill was steered through Sacramento by assembly speaker and Inglewood representative Jesse "Big Daddy" Unruh. Unruh was something like Willy Stark in Sacramento: an imposing figure at three hundred and fifty pounds, Unruh escaped crushing poverty in his native Texas where he had grown up sleeping in a chicken coop.
25. Jackson Putnam, "Governor Reagan: A Reappraisal," *California History* 83, no. 4 (2006): 24–45.
26. Under a "2 percent at 50" formula, a retiree would earn 2 percent of their final year compensation multiplied by their years of service credit as a pension.
27. David Helvarg, "The Savior of California's Coast," *Los Angeles Times*, April 8, 2012.
28. "California Legislature Approves Welfare Reform Bill After Compromise with Reagan," *New York Times*, August 12, 1972.
29. At Reagan's suggestion, Gerald Ford nominated Anthony Kennedy to the Ninth Circuit Court. Kennedy was later nominated by Reagan in 1987 to replace Lewis Powell on the Supreme Court after the defeat of the Robert Bork and Douglas Ginsburg nominations.
30. Garin Burbank, "Governor Reagan's Only Defeat," *California History* (1993): 361–73.
31. Presumptive Republican nominee and Reagan lieutenant governor Ed Reinecke was forced to withdraw after being indicted for perjury during the Watergate investigation.

32. Isaac William Martin, *The Permanent Tax Revolt: How the Property Tax Transformed American Politics* (Stanford, CA: Stanford University Press, 2008), 57.
33. Martin, *Tax Revolt*, 45.
34. For a general history of postwar Los Angeles, see Mike Davis, *City of Quartz* (New York: Verso, 1990).
35. Becky Nicolaides, *My Blue Heaven: Life and Politics in the Working-Class Suburbs of Los Angeles, 1920–1965* (Chicago: University of Chicago Press, 2002).
36. John Kendall, "Public Pension Plans: A Bottomless Morass?," *Los Angeles Times*, March 13, 1972, A1.
37. This period inaugurated the chronic housing shortage that has plagued California ever since. Since the 1970s, California has consistently ranked at the bottom of states in terms of housing units per resident.
38. Irving Kristol, "The Meaning of Proposition 13," *Wall Street Journal*, June 28, 1978, A14.
39. Harry Bernstein, "Brown Runs Into Problem with Labor," *Los Angeles Times*, September 14, 1978, A12.
40. Judith Michaelson, "Younger's Walk Between the Raindrops," *Los Angeles Times*, October 10, 1978, C1.
41. Scott Austin, "Angry Mrs. Younger Lashes Out at Brown," *Los Angeles Times*, September 28, 1978, B3.
42. Lou Cannon, "With Week to Go, California's Governor Brown Is Showing His Heels," *Washington Post*, November 1, 1978, A2.
43. Nancy Skelton, "Brown Pitches for Pollution Cleanup, Inflation Control," *Los Angeles Times*, September 15, 1978, A1.
44. George Will, "Jerry Brown's Serious Ideas," *Atlanta Constitution*, December 6, 1981, D3.
45. "Jerry Brown on the 'Reindustrialization of America,'" *Washington Post*, January 14, 1980, A23.
46. Orville Schell, "The Tail of the Donkey, the Trunk of the Elephant," *Rolling Stone*, October 18, 1979, 66.
47. The $56 million increase in pension costs roughly equaled the salary of the fired workers. Robert Lindsey, "Los Angeles Plans Layoffs Next Year," *New York Times*, December 27, 1981, 23.
48. Dan Fisher, "LA Pension Plans: Public's Achilles Heel?," *Los Angeles Times*, November 27, 1975, A1.
49. Craig Turner and Patrick Boyle, "Pension Plan Growth May Burst Bubble," *Los Angeles Times*, September 10, 1978, A1.

50. Roger Kemp, "California's Proposition 13: A One-Year Assessment," *State & Local Government Review* 14, no. 1 (1982): 44–47.
51. Debra Whitefield, "Pension Funds: The Last, Best Hope for 'Rescue' of Housing," *Los Angeles Times*, March 15, 1981, G1.
52. Roger Smith, "Brown Urges Pension Investment Changes," *Los Angeles Times*, July 31, 1980, A26.
53. Mitchell Lynch and Daniel Hertzberg, "Restrictions on Public Pension Funds Ease as States and Cities Seek Greater Returns," *Wall Street Journal*, April 13, 1981, 21.
54. Jeremy Rifkin and Randy Barber, *The North Will Rise Again: Pensions, Politics and Power in the 1980s* (Boston: Beacon, 1978).
55. Debra Whitefield, "Pension Funds: The New Mortgage Bankers," *Washington Post*, March 21, 1981, E28.
56. California briefly flirted with a plan to create "Callie Mae" to guarantee California-specific mortgage pools. John Jones, "Fannie, Freddie May Get Cousin," *Los Angeles Times*, January 13, 1981, E1.
57. Christopher Conte, "Home Economics: Big Secondary Market in Mortgages Smooths Flow of Housing Funds," *Wall Street Journal*, July 11, 1983, A1.
58. Cary Lowe, "Pension Funds Could Aid State Economy," *Los Angeles Times*, February 15, 1982, B5.
59. Herbert Vida, "Pension System Buys U.S. Steel Offices," *Los Angeles Times*, October 1, 1982, E1.
60. Nancy Ross, "The Pension Funds Answer: Increase Mortgage-Related Investments," *Washington Post*, May 5, 1980, WB20.
61. Smith, "Brown Urges Pension Investment Changes."
62. Kenneth Harney, "Pensions Provide Mortgage Money," *Washington Post*, January 2, 1982, D1.
63. Douglas Shuit, "Real Estate Deals Attract State Pension Fund Money," *Los Angeles Times*, November 7, 1983, A23.
64. In 1982, Proposition 6 was defeated. It would have raised the cap to 60 percent.
65. This phenomenon of African American candidates underperforming relative to opinion polling became known as the "Bradley effect." Deukmejian campaign manager Bill Roberts resigned after (correctly) predicting that "up to 5 percent of the voters who were polled would conceal racial prejudice when asked if they would support Mayor Tom Bradley." Or, as Roberts stated, "If we are down only 5 points or less in the polls at election time, we're going to win. It's just a fact of life." "Aide to Coast GOP Candidate Resigns After Remarks on Racism," *New York Times*, October 13, 1982, B6.

294 • 5. DEMOCRACY AND FINANCE IN CALIFORNIA

66. Douglas Shuit, "Ex-Teachers Pension Chief Pleads Guilty in Loan Case," *Los Angeles Times*, September 25, 1987.
67. CalPERS, *1982 Annual Report*, 47–48.
68. Michael Smith, "Shareholder Activism by Institutional Investors: Evidence from CalPERS," *Journal of Finance* 51, no. 1 (1996): 227–52, 230.
69. James White, "Pension Funds Crowd Real Estate Pools' Exits," *Wall Street Journal*, September 13, 1990, C1.
70. John Myers, "How a Governor's Bid to Exert Control Over California Public Pensions Backfired," *Los Angeles Times*, October 7, 2016.
71. Scot Paltrow, "Pension Experts Troubled by Plan to Tap CalPERS," *Los Angeles Times*, June 19, 1991, D1.
72. CalPERS, "1995–6 Comprehensive Annual Financial Report: Operations Summary," 26.
73. James White, "Pension Cash Fuels Growth of New Funds," *Wall Street Journal*, July 17, 1990, C1.
74. Ann Crittenden, "Reaping the Big Profits from a Fat Cat," *New York Times*, August 7, 1983, C6.
75. Generally speaking, private equity firms look for three- to seven-year investment periods and a 20 percent internal rate of return.
76. Peter Elkind, "The Breakup of the Bass Brothers," *New York Times*, November 24, 1991, F35. Ed Bass financed the Biosphere 2 project in Arizona. Robert Bass founded private equity firm Oak Hill Capital Partners in 1986 and sold the Plaza Hotel in Manhattan to Donald Trump in 1988.
77. Thomas Edsall, *The New Politics of Inequality* (New York: W. W. Norton, 1985), 93–94; and Mike Davis, *Prisoners of the American Dream: Politics and Economy in the History of the US Working Class* (New York: Verso, 2000), 246.
78. "C for Capitalism," *Economist*, June 26, 2003
79. George Anders, *Merchants of Debt: KKR and the Mortgaging of American Business* (New York: Basic Books, 1992), 54.
80. Anders, *Merchants of Debt*, 43.
81. Anders, *Merchants of Debt*, 44.
82. Sarah Bartlett, "Gambling with the Big Boys," *New York Times*, May 5, 1991, F38.
83. Steven Lipin, "Pension Funds Target Buyout Funds' Big Fees," *Wall Street Journal*, October 23, 1996, C1.
84. Michael Jensen, "Eclipse of the Public Corporation," *Harvard Business Review*, September–October 1989.
85. Marion Fourcade and Rakesh Khurana, "The Social Trajectory of a Finance Professor and the Common Sense of Capital," *History of Political Economy* 49, no. 2 (2017): 347–81.

5. DEMOCRACY AND FINANCE IN CALIFORNIA • 295

86. Allison Colter and Arden Dale, "States Are Moving to Diversify Retirement Plans with Hedge Funds," *Wall Street Journal*, July 9, 2003, B11.
87. Yale University, "Endowment Update," 2007.
88. CalPERS, "AIM Quarterly Review," June 30, 2008.
89. Leslie Wayne, "Elder Bush in Big GOP Cast Toiling for Top Equity Firm," *New York Times*, March 5, 2001, A1. The Carlyle Group's first big break came in the late 1980s when cofounder David Rubenstein pulled off what became known internally as "The Great Eskimo Tax Scam of 1987." For a brief period of time, Native Alaskan companies were allowed to sell their losses to other corporations for tax write-offs. Rubenstein, like any good financial intermediary, orchestrated the purchase and sale of these credits, generating massive returns in the process. Michael Lewis, "The Access Capitalists," *New Republic*, October 17, 1993. Rubenstein also owns a copy of the Magna Carta, bought at auction from Ross Perot, who in turn had acquired it from the family of James Brudenell, Seventh Earl of Cardigan and cavalry commander who led the Charge of the Light Brigade during the Crimean War, which is memorialized in the eponymous Alfred Tennyson poem.
90. "C for Capitalism," *Economist*, June 28, 2003.
91. CalPERS, "Statement of Investment Policy: Restricting AIM Investments in Public Sector Outsourcers," December 13, 2004.
92. "CalPERS Buys Stake in Apollo," *Pensions & Investments*, September 7, 2007.
93. H&R Block, "Richard C. Breeden to Step Down as Chairman," March 17, 2011.
94. Alexandra Stevenson, "Calpers Paid $3.4 Billion to Private Equity Firms," *New York Times*, November 25, 2015, B3.
95. For a more detailed history of CalPERS's shareholder activism, see Sanford Jacoby, *Labor in the Age of Finance* (Princeton, NJ: Princeton University Press, 2021), chap. 2.
96. The mansion was built by Broadway star Libby Holman in the 1930s. Holman was accused of murdering her first husband Zachary Smith Reynolds, heir to the R. J. Reynolds tobacco company. Reynolds died of a gunshot wound under mysterious circumstances in 1932. Holman later helped finance Martin Luther King Jr.'s trip to India in 1959.
97. George Anders, "While Head of Calpers Lectures Other Firms, His Own Board Frets," *Wall Street Journal*, January 29, 1993, A1.
98. See Neil Fligstein, *The Transformation of Corporate Control* (Cambridge, MA: Harvard University Press, 1993).
99. Mark Anson, Ted White, and Ho Ho, "Good Corporate Governance Works: More Evidence from CalPERS," *Journal of Asset Management* 5, no. 3 (2004): 149–56.

100. CalPERS, "Global Principles of Accountable Corporate Governance," August 18, 2008, 7.
101. Bill Taylor, "Can Big Owners Make a Big Difference?," *Harvard Business Review*, September–October 1990.
102. Diane del Guerico and Jennifer Hawkins, "The Motivation and Impact of Pension Fund Activism," *Journal of Financial Economics* 52, no. 3 (1999): 293–340.
103. Sanford Jacoby, "Convergence by Design: The Case of CalPERS in Japan," *American Journal of Comparative Law* 55, no. 2 (2007): 239–93.
104. Donald Woutat, "State Pension Fund Will Invest Directly," *Los Angeles Times*, July 1, 1993, A2.
105. Bethany MacLean, "Is Enron Overpriced?," *Fortune Magazine*, March 5, 2001.
106. "CalPERS to Invest $200 Million in New Fund," *New York Times*, June 23, 1995, D6. CalPERS added another $275 million two years later.
107. Brian Cheffins, "Corporate Governance Since the Managerial Capitalism Era," *Business History Review* 89 (2015): 714–44.
108. For a comprehensive account of the Orange County affair, see Mark Baldassare, *When Government Fails: The Orange County Bankruptcy* (Berkeley: University of California Press, 1998).
109. Floyd Norris, "Orange County Crisis Jolts Bond Market," *New York Times*, December 8, 1994, D1.
110. The law required regulated utilities to divest from their nonutility businesses. Electric streetcars were one such business. General Motors, Standard Oil, Phillips Petroleum, and Firestone Tire jointly established National City Lines in 1936 to buy up as many of these newly available streetcar systems as possible and replace them with buses. In 1946, former Navy officer and inventor E. Edward Quinby self-published an expose on the conspiracy. Nearly a decade prior, Quinby delivered the radio equipment on behalf of his employer, Western Electric, to Amelia Earhart for her ill-fated 1937 flight across the Pacific. After a brief congressional inquiry, General Motors was ultimately fined $5,000. A version of the streetcar conspiracy serves as the plot of the 1988 film *Who Framed Roger Rabbit?*
111. Jeffrey Watkiss and Douglas Smith, "The Energy Policy Act of 1992—A Watershed for Competition in the Wholesale Power Market," *Yale Journal on Regulation* 10 (1993): 447–92.
112. Dan Morain, "Deregulation Bill Signed by Wilson," *Los Angeles Times*, September 24, 1996.

113. Dan Morain and Dave Lesher, "State Workers Union Raises Strike Threat," *Los Angeles Times*, January 26, 1999.
114. "California's Energy Crisis," U.S. Energy Information Administration, https://www.eia.gov/electricity/policies/legislation/california/subsequentevents.html.
115. Massie Ritsch, "UC, Cal State Systems Sue Power Seller," *Los Angeles Times*, March 13, 2001, A3.
116. "A Law Enforcement Perspective on the California Energy Crisis," *Attorney General's Working Paper*, April 2004, 22.
117. John Broder and Don van Natta, "The 2000 Campaign: The Money," *New York Times*, July 30, 2000, A1.
118. Debora Vrana, "State Sells Nearly All of Power Bonds," *Los Angeles Times*, November 6, 2002, C4.
119. John Berry, "Greenspan Unafraid of Energy Price Caps," *Washington Post*, June 29, 2001.
120. Jerry Hirsch, "CalPERS to Press Power Firms About Investment," *Los Angeles Times*, June 19, 2001.
121. Cathy Booth Thomas, "California' Prescient Brush with Enron," *Time Magazine*, February 11, 2002.
122. One of the more explosive revelations from the government's autopsy of Enron was a series of recorded phone calls between Enron traders that provided an unvarnished look at the "animal spirits" empowered by Mr. Market:

> KEVIN: So the rumor's true? They're fucking taking all the money back from you guys? All the money you guys stole from those poor grandmothers in California?
> BOB: Yeah, Grandma Millie, man. But she's the one who couldn't figure out how to fucking vote on the butterfly ballot. Yeah, now she wants her fucking money back for all the power you've charged right up, jammed right up her ass for fucking $250 a megawatt hour. You know, Grandma Millie, she's the one Al Gore's fighting for, you know?
> KEVIN: Something's wrong with the country.

Richard Oppel, "Enron Traders on Grandma Millie," *New York Times*, June 13, 2004.
123. Evan Halper, "Pension Board Oks Davis Plan on Pay Hikes," *Los Angeles Times*, September 18, 2003, B8.
124. Rene Sanchez, "Schwarzenegger to Run for Governor," *Washington Post*, August 7, 2003.

125. Arnold Schwarzenegger later recalled that Richard Nixon originally encouraged him to run for governor.
126. Jim Wasserman, "CalPERS President Gets Heave-Ho," *Associated Press*, December 2, 2004.
127. John Broder, "Five Officials in San Diego Are Indicted Over Pensions," *New York Times*, January 7, 2006.
128. The pension system was previously scrutinized by the Fed in 1996 when the city used pension returns to help fund the Republican National Convention.
129. As part of a program to increase economic development in underserved areas of California, CalPERS invested in a TV venture led by Joel Hyatt and Al Gore. INdTV was intended to engage an audience of young voters interested in progressive issues. The investment was made through a private equity fund led by Richard Blum, husband of senator Dianne Feinstein and University of California regent. State Treasurer Phillip Angelides championed a push to divest from tobacco stocks and emerging markets with dubious labor practices and reinvest the proceeds in real estate. He introduced several resolutions calling for limits on executive compensation and golden parachutes. Indonesia, Malaysia, the Philippines, and Thailand were all dropped from CalPERS's international equity portfolio. In response, the consulates organized busloads of local residents to protest at the CalPERS headquarters in Sacramento. Ron Russell, "Looking Inside INdTV," *S.F. Weekly*, July 28, 2004.
130. CalPERS, "CIO's Consolidated Investment Activity Report," August 31, 2008, 4.
131. David Evans, "US Pension Funds Are Big Buyers of Riskiest Debt," *Bloomberg*, June 4, 2007.
132. Maria Cometto, "Toxic Waste in Pension Funds," *Investments & Pensions Europe*, September 2007.
133. Daisy Maxey, "Pension Funds May Feel Little Subprime Strain; Conservative Picks, Diversity Should Keep Any Contagion at Bay," *Wall Street Journal*, April 2, 2007, C15.
134. CalPERS Board of Administration, "Agenda Item #14: Impact of Employer Rates and Possible Smoothing Modifications," June 17, 2009.
135. As quoted in Matt Taibbi, "The Last Mystery of the Financial Crisis," *Rolling Stone*, June 19, 2013.
136. David Streitfeld, "A Town Drowns in Debt as Home Values Plunge," *New York Times*, November 10, 2008.
137. Dale Kasler, "Drought Trips Up Real Estate Development Backed by CalPERS," *Sacramento Bee*, June 15, 2015.

5. DEMOCRACY AND FINANCE IN CALIFORNIA

138. In 2016, Mountain House was hit with a record $1.5 million fine from the State Water Resources Board for ignoring a curtailment order. Bettina Boxall, "Record Fine May Be Tossed," *Los Angeles Times*, May 27, 2016, B1.
139. Michael Corkery et al., "Risky, Ill-Timed Land Deals Hit Calpers," *Wall Street Journal*, December 17, 2008. CalPERS invested in similar deals in Phoenix, Arizona, and Jacksonville, Florida.
140. Gennady Sheyner, "Documents: CalPERS' $100 Million Page Mill Loss," *Palo Alto Online*, September 28, 2010.
141. Zoe Hughes, "LaSalle Loses $1.9bn CalPERS Industrial Portfolio," *PERE News*, December 2, 2010.
142. Stephen Taub, "WaMU Raises $7 Billion," *CFO Magazine*, April 8, 2008; and Arleen Jacobius, "WaMu Failure Costs TPG Fund $2 Billion," *Pensions & Investments*, September 26, 2008.
143. Marc Lifsher, "Alfred Villalobos Strongly Denies Wrongdoing in CalPERS Fraud Case," *Los Angeles Times*, May 28, 2010.
144. Ted Rohrlich, "Official's Past Includes Lawsuits, Bankruptcy," *Los Angeles Times*, October 24, 1993.
145. Mary Williams Walsh and Louise Story, "S.E.C. Said to Scrutinize California Fund," *New York Times*, January 8, 2011.
146. Office of the California Attorney General, "AG Kamala Harris Announces $300 million Settlement with JP Morgan Chase," November 19, 2013, https://oag.ca.gov/news/press-releases/attorney-general-kamala-d-harris-announces-300-million-settlement-jp-morgan.
147. James Koren, "Moody's to Pay CalPERS $130 Million to Settle Suit," *Los Angeles Times*, March 10, 2016, C2.
148. CalPERS, "Summary of PEPRA Act of 2013," November 27, 2012.
149. During the Stockton bankruptcy proceedings, a federal judge ruled that pension obligations can indeed be impaired during bankruptcy. Sarah Anzia summarizes the postcrisis pension landscape: "the picture that emerges is one of rising local pension spending and cities and counties cutting back the size of their workforces in response." Sarah Anzia, "Pensions in the Trenches: How Pension Spending Is Affecting U.S. Local Government," *Urban Affairs Review* 58, no. 1 (2022): 3–32, 6.
150. Margaret Rhodes, "NYC's $1.3B Supertall Skyscraper Was Inspired by a Trash Can," *Wired Magazine*, June 2, 2015.
151. Craig Karmin, "New York Placing Tallest Order," *Wall Street Journal*, October 19, 2011.

152. Despite her hardline stance on immigration, Meg Whitman admitted employing an undocumented housekeeper. Whitman spent nearly $140 million of her own money on advertisements.
153. C-SPAN, "Political Response to 2008 Financial Crisis," October 29, 2013, https://www.c-span.org/video/?315930-3/political-response-2008-financial-crisis.
154. Dick Walker, "Golden State Adrift," *New Left Review* 66 (2010): 28.
155. Alice Munnell, "The Miracle of Funding by State and Local Pension Plans," *Center for Retirement Research at Boston College*, Working Paper no. 5 (2008).
156. James Shinn, "CIO, Board Struggle to Fix CalPERS," *Institutional Investor*, March 13, 2012.
157. Michael McCarthy, *Dismantling Solidarity: Capitalist Politics and American Pensions since the New Deal* (Ithaca, NY: Cornell University Press, 2017), 125.
158. Alicia McElhaney, "CalPERS Is Turning to Private Equity and Leverage to Boost Returns and Reduce Risk. Will It Work?," *Institutional Investor*, December 6, 2021.

6. THE CRISIS OF FINANCE

1. Ben Bernanke, "The Great Moderation," speech to the Eastern Economic Association, February 20, 2004, Washington, DC.
2. "The Financial Crisis and the Role of Federal Regulators," Hearing before the Committee on Oversight and Government Reform, October 23, 2008, https://www.govinfo.gov/content/pkg/CHRG-110hhrg55764/html/CHRG-110hhrg55764.htm.
3. See Jennifer Burns, *Goddess of the Market: Ayn Rand and the American Right* (New York: Oxford University Press, 2009).
4. "Internal Battle Changes Tone of Federal Reserve," *New York Times*, March 24, 1986, A1, https://www.nytimes.com/1986/03/24/business/internal-battle-changes-tone-of-federal-reserve.html.
5. Christopher Hitchens, "Greenspan Shrugged," *Vanity Fair*, December 6, 2000.
6. See Haynes Johnson, *Sleepwalking Through History: America in the Reagan Years* (New York: W. W. Norton, 1991).
7. See Bob Woodward, *Maestro: Greenspan's Fed and the American Boom* (New York: Simon and Schuster, 2001).
8. Colin Crouch, *The Strange Non-Death of Neoliberalism* (Cambridge: Polity, 2011).
9. Jamie Peck, *Constructions of Neoliberal Reason* (Oxford: Oxford University Press, 2010), 277. Also see Philip Mirowski, Dieter Plehwe, and Quinn Slobodian, *Nine Lives of Neoliberalism* (London: Verso, 2020).

6. THE CRISIS OF FINANCE • 301

10. For the definitive history of the crisis, see Adam Tooze, *Crashed: How a Decade of Financial Crises Changed the World* (New York: Viking, 2018).
11. Robert Antonio and Alessandro Bonanno, "A New Global Capitalism? From 'American and Fordism' to 'Americanization-Globalization,'" *American Studies* 41, no. 2/3 (2000): 33–77.
12. Robert Boyer, "Is a Finance-Led Growth Regime a Viable Alternative to Fordism? A Preliminary Analysis," *Economy and Society* 29, no. 1 (2000): 111–45.
13. Melinda Cooper, *Family Values* (New York: Zone Books, 2017).
14. Lizabeth Cohen, *A Consumers' Republic* (New York: Penguin Random House, 2003), 133.
15. Mike Davis termed this regime "overconsumptionism." See Mike Davis, *Prisoners of the American Dream* (New York: Verso, 1993), chap. 7.
16. In 1988, Walmart opened its first "supercenter" in Washington, Missouri. As Walmart's corporate slogan once described the political economy of neoliberalism: "Save Money. Live Better." See Bethany Moreton, *To Serve God and Wal-Mart: The Making of Christian Free Enterprise* (Cambridge, MA: Harvard University Press, 2009).
17. David Brooks, *Bobos in Paradise* (New York: Simon and Schuster, 2000). Also see Gabriel Winant, *The Next Shift: The Fall of Industry and the Rise of Health Care in Rust Belt America* (Cambridge, MA: Harvard University Press, 2021).
18. Lois Plunkert, "The 1980s: A Decade of Job Growth and Industry Shifts," *Monthly Labor Review* (September 1990): 3–16.
19. See Emma Rothschild, "The Reagan Economic Legacy," *New York Review of Books*, July 21, 1988.
20. See Greta Krippner, *Capitalizing on Crisis: The Political Origins of the Rise of Finance* (Cambridge, MA: Harvard University Press), chap. 4.
21. Stuart Auerbach, "U.S. Becomes World's No. 1 Debtor Nation," *Washington Post*, June 25, 1986.
22. See Barry Eichengreen, *Exorbitant Privilege* (New York: Oxford University Press, 2012).
23. Robert Pear, "Benefits for Poor People Face Deepest Cuts," *New York Times*, February 14, 1982, A1.
24. Monica Prasad has shown how access to credit is negatively correlated with growth in welfare spending. See Monica Prasad, *The Land of Too Much* (Cambridge, MA: Harvard University Press, 2012), chap. 9.
25. Sarah Quinn, *American Bonds: How Credit Markets Shaped a Nation* (Princeton, NJ: Princeton University Press, 2019), 175.

26. Louis Hyman, *Debtor Nation* (Princeton, NJ: Princeton University Press, 2011), chap. 7.
27. Greta Krippner, "Democracy of Credit: Ownership and the Politics of Credit Access in Late Twentieth-Century America," *American Journal of Sociology* 123, no. 1 (2017): 1–47.
28. Neil Fligstein and Adam Goldstein, "The Emergence of a Finance Culture in American Households, 1989–2007," *Socio-Economic Review* 13, no. 3 (2015): 575–601.
29. Prasad, *The Land of Too Much*, chap. 10.
30. Michael McCarthy, *Dismantling Solidarity: Capitalist Politics and American Pensions since the New Deal* (Ithaca, NY: Cornell University Press, 2017), chap. 5.
31. Alan Greenspan, "Opening Remarks," *Federal Reserve Bank of Kansas City Jackson Hole Symposium*, August 31, 2001.
32. Bennett Harrison and Barry Bluestone, *The Great U-Turn: Corporate Restructuring and the Polarizing of America* (New York: Basic Books, 1990).
33. William Lazonick and Mary O'Sullivan, "Maximizing Shareholder Value: A New Ideology for Corporate Governance," *Economy and Society* 29, no. 1 (2000): 13–35.
34. Michael Useem, *Executive Defense* (Cambridge, MA: Harvard University Press, 1993).
35. See Neil Fligstein, *The Architecture of Markets* (Ithaca, NY: Cornell University Press, 2001).
36. Richard Brealey, Stewart Myers, and Franklin Allen, *Principles of Corporate Finance*, 10th ed. (London: McGraw-Hill, 2011), 9.
37. A thrift is an FDIC-insured savings bank that focuses on mortgage lending funded by retail deposits.
38. John Zysman, *Governments, Markets, Growth* (Ithaca, NY: Cornell University Press, 1983). Also see Iain Hardie, David Howarth, Sylvia Maxfield, and Amy Verdun, "Banks and the False Dichotomy in the Comparative Political Economy of Finance," *World Politics* 65, no. 4 (2013): 691–728.
39. Kevin Fox Gotham, "The Secondary Circuit of Capital Reconsidered: Globalization and the U.S. Real Estate Sector," *American Journal of Sociology* 112, no. 1 (2006): 231–75, 235.
40. Neil Fligstein, *The Banks Did It* (Cambridge, MA: Harvard University Press, 2021), 61.
41. Eric Helleiner, *States and the Emergence of Global Finance* (Ithaca, NY: Cornell University Press, 1994).

42. Hans-Werner Sinn, "Why Taxes Matter: Reagan's Accelerated Cost Recover System and the US Trade Deficit," *Economic Policy* 1, no. 1 (1985): 239–50.
43. Federal Deposit Insurance Corporation, *History of the Eighties: Lessons for the Future* (Washington, DC: FDIC, 1997).
44. Jeffrey Birnbaum, *Showdown at Gucci Gulch* (New York: Knopf, 1987).
45. Renee Haltom, "Failure of Continental Illinois," Federal Reserve History.
46. Gerald Davis and Mark Mizruchi, "The Money Center Cannot Hold: Commercial Banks in the U.S. System of Corporate Governance," *Administrative Science Quarterly* 44, no. 2 (1999): 215–39, 219.
47. In 1984, Greenspan was hired by a law firm representing Charles Keating's Lincoln Savings and Loan to write a letter to the Federal Home Loan Bank of San Francisco. Greenspan wrote in support of Keating's ultimately unsuccessful request for an exemption from a rule prohibiting thrifts such as Lincoln from "direct investments" into real estate projects—essentially asking to be exempted from regulations capping the amount of risk Lincoln could take on. In 1989, Lincoln went bankrupt, prompting a famous corruption scandal implicating five U.S. senators including John Glenn and John McCain. Another notable failure was Silverado, a thrift in Denver run by Neil M. Bush, son of President George H. W. Bush and brother of Bush 1992 campaign advisor George W. Bush. Although Neil Bush faced a civil action brought by the FDIC for several breaches of fiduciary duty, the case was ultimately settled out of court and the $50,000 fine was paid with Bush campaign funds. In 1990, Keating was indicted by the State of California for fraud. Mother Teresa pleaded with the trial judge to be merciful with Keating, a devout Catholic and major contributor to her charities. Los Angeles County Superior Court Judge Lance Ito was unmoved and sentenced Keating to ten years in prison. Five years later, Judge Ito presided over the O. J. Simpson murder trial.
48. Bill Cook, "Stockton Thrifts Wild Ride," *Stockton Record*, July 23, 1996.
49. Carol Loomis, "Victims of the Real Estate Crash," *Fortune Magazine*, May 18, 1992.
50. Gerald Davis and Mark Mizruchi, "The Money Center Cannot Hold: Commercial Banks in the U.S. System of Corporate Governance," *Administrative Science Quarterly* 44, no. 2 (1999): 215–39.
51. Michael Jacobides, "Industry Change Through Vertical Disintegration: How and Why Markets Emerged in Mortgage Banking," *Academy of Management Journal* 48, no. 3 (2005): 465–98.

52. Adam Goldstein and Neil Fligstein, "Financial Markets as Production Markets: The Industrial Roots of the Mortgage Meltdown," *Socio-Economic Review* 15, no. 3 (2017): 483–510.
53. Douglas Diamond and Michael Lea, "United States," *Journal of Housing Research* 3, no. 1 (1992): 145–70.
54. John McConnell and Stephen Buser, "The Origins and Evolution of the Market for Mortgage-Backed Securities," *Annual Review of Financial Economics* 3 (2011): 173–92. Freddie Mac issued the first collateralized mortgage obligation (CMO) in 1983. This new product was designed to entice investors who would otherwise avoid mortgage-backed securities (MBSs) because of the prepayment risk. A CMO structures a portfolio of MBSs into safer and riskier tranches according to investor preference. The first "private label" (i.e., nonguaranteed) CMOs were issued in the mid-1990s.
55. Steven Vogel, *Freer Markets, More Rules* (Ithaca, NY: Cornell University Press, 1996).
56. Financial Crisis Inquiry Commission, "Final Report," 40.
57. Viral V. Acharya, Matthew Richardson, Stijn van Nieuwerburgh, and Lawrence J. White, *Guaranteed to Fail: Fannie Mae, Freddie Mac, and the Debacle of Mortgage Finance* (Princeton, NJ: Princeton University Press, 2011).
58. The term "shadow banking" itself was coined by Paul McCulley of investment manager PIMCO in a speech at the 2007 annual Jackson Hole Economic Policy Symposium. John McCulley, "Teton Reflections," Pacific Investment Management Company LLC, 2007, accessed December 18, 2015, https://www.pimco.com/insights/economic-and-market-commentary/global-central-bank-focus/teton-reflections.
59. Zoltan Pozsar, "Shadow Banking: The Money View," Office of Financial Research Working Paper 14–04, July 2, 2014, 6.
60. Gary B. Gorton, *Slapped by the Invisible Hand: The Panic of 2007* (Oxford: Oxford University Press, 2010), 27.
61. Zoltan Pozsar, Tobias Adrian, Adam Ashcraft, and Hayley Boesky, "Shadow Banking," Federal Reserve Bank of New York Staff Reports No. 458, February 2012, 7.
62. Ben Bernanke et al., "International Capital Flows and the Returns to Safe Assets in the United States, 2003–2007," Board of Governors of the Federal Reserve System Finance Discussion Papers 1014, February 2011.
63. Melinda Cooper, "Shadow Money and the Shadow Workforce: Rethinking Labor and Liquidity," *South Atlantic Quarterly* 114, no. 2 (2015): 395–423.

64. In 2002, Margaret Thatcher said that Tony Blair and New Labour were her greatest accomplishments. See Colin Hay, *The Political Economy of New Labour* (Manchester: Manchester University Press, 1999).
65. "Governments confronting the electoral imperatives of modern democracy will undertake retrenchment only when they discover ways to minimize the political costs involved." Paul Pierson, "The New Politics of the Welfare State," *World Politics* 48, no. 2 (1996): 143–79, 179.
66. Rahm Emanuel and Bruce Reed, *The Plan: Big Ideas for America* (New York: Public Affairs, 2006).
67. Ed Burmila, *Chaotic Neutral: How the Democrats Lost Their Soul in the Center* (New York: Bold Type, 2022).
68. Stephanie Mudge, *Leftism Reinvented: Western Parties from Socialism to Neoliberalism* (Cambridge, MA: Harvard University Press, 2018), chap. 7.
69. Stephen Gill, "New Constitutionalism, Democratization and Global Political Economy," *Pacifica Review* 10, no. 1 (1998): 23–38.
70. For an orthodox discussion of NAIRU, see Laurence Ball and N. Gregory Mankiw, "The NAIRU in Theory and Practice," *Journal of Economic Perspectives* 16, no. 4 (2002): 115–36. Ball and Mankiw theorize inflation as inflation expectations plus deviation below the nonaccelerating inflation rate of unemployment (NAIRU) plus a "supply shock": $[\Pi = \Pi e - a(U - U^*) + v]$.
71. James Risen, "Anatomy of a Rate Hike: How Greenspan Got the Fed to Change Course," *Los Angeles Times*, May 11, 1994.
72. That same year, JP Morgan sold the first credit default swap to sell some of its credit risk to outside investors. Patrick Augustin et al., "Credit Default Swaps: Past, Present, and Future," *Annual Review of Financial Economics* 8 (2016): 10.1–10.22.
73. Some speculated that Gingrich committed to the shutdown after Clinton forced him to sit in the back of the plane when returning from Yitzhak Rabin's funeral in Israel. Steven Gillon, *The Pact: Bill Clinton, Newt Gingrich, and the Rivalry That Defined a Generation* (Norman: University of Oklahoma Press, 1999).
74. The *New York Times* noted that "the pressure from Wall Street may be exactly what Mr. Rubin hoped would happen once he declared on Monday that at the end of February he would be out of legal options to keep the country from defaulting." David Sanger, "Moody's Says It Is Considering Lowering U.S. Credit Rating," *New York Times*, January 25, 1996, A16.
75. Fligstein, *The Banks Did It*, chap. 3.

76. Julie Hatch and Angela Clinton, "Job Growth in the 1990s: A Retrospect," *Monthly Labor Review* (December 2000): 3–18. Real wages in all sectors except FIRE (finance, insurance, and real estate) were either lower or flat.
77. Barry Eichengreen, *Hall of Mirrors: The Great Depression, the Great Recession, and the Uses and Misuses of History* (New York: Oxford University Press, 2015), 203.
78. John Zysman, *Governments, Markets, Growth* (Ithaca, NY: Cornell University Press, 1983).
79. Quinn, *American Bonds*, 181.
80. Frank Bruni, "Bush Defends Size of Surplus and Tax Cuts," *New York Times*, August 22, 2001, A1.
81. Paul McCulley, "Show a Little Passion, Baby," *PIMCO Central Bank Focus*, July 1, 2001.
82. Charles Kindleberger, *Manias, Panics, and Crashes* (New York: Basic Books, 1978).
83. Alt-A is the category between prime and subprime.
84. Gorton, *Slapped*, 66–83.
85. Neil Fligstein and Adam Goldstein, "A Long Strange Trip: The State and Mortgage Securitization, 1968–2010," in *The Oxford Handbook of the Sociology of Finance*, ed. Karin Knorr Cetina and Alex Preda (New York: Oxford University Press, 2012), 339–56, 352.
86. Marvin Smith and Christy Hevener, "Subprime Lending Over Time: The Role of Race," *Journal of Economics and Finance* 38 (2014): 321–44.
87. See Pozsar, Adrian, Ashcraft, and Boesky, "Shadow Banking."
88. Felix Salmon, "Recipe for Disaster: The Formula That Killed Wall Street," *Wired Magazine*, February 23, 2009.
89. On the eve of the financial crisis, the only AAA-rated corporations were Exxon, Johnson & Johnson, Microsoft, Pfizer, General Electric, Berkshire Hathaway, and ADP.
90. Financial Crisis Inquiry Commission, "Final Report," 206.
91. Gretchen Morgenson, "AIG Apologizes and Agrees to $1.64 Billion Settlement," *New York Times*, February 10, 2006, C1.
92. Bethany McLean, "The Fall of Fannie Mae," *Fortune Magazine*, January 24, 2005.
93. Tooze, *Crashed*, 57.
94. Connie Bruck, "Angelo's Ashes," *New Yorker*, June 22, 2009.
95. Countrywide also ran a "Friends of Angelo" program that extended mortgages to prominent politicians including Senate Banking Chairman Christopher

Dodd and Senate Budget Committee Chairman Kent Conrad. See Conde Nast Portfolio, June 12, 2008.
96. Financial Crisis Inquiry Commission, "Final Report," 181.
97. Financial Crisis Inquiry Commission, "Final Report," 225.
98. Bank capital is not a reserve fund stashed at the Fed, but the difference between the value of a bank's assets and liabilities. In other words, bank capital represents the residual value of the firm if all assets were liquidated and all liabilities repaid. Capital is therefore a buffer for absorbing losses on the bank's assets.
99. Paul Healy and Krishna Palepu, "The Fall of Enron," *Journal of Economic Perspectives* 17, no. 2 (2003): 3–26, 10.
100. Minutes of the Federal Open Market Committee, October 24–25, 2006. Measured inflation would have been markedly higher with the pre-1982 Consumer Price Index (CPI) calculation explored in chapter 2.
101. Neil Fligstein, Jonah Brundage, and Michael Schultz, "Seeing Like the Fed: Culture, Cognition, and Framing in the Failure to Anticipate the Financial Crisis of 2008," *American Sociological Review* 82, no. 5 (2017): 879–909.
102. For a detailed account see Gorton, *Slapped*, chap. 3.
103. Gorton, *Slapped*, 99.
104. Vikas Bajaj and Julie Creswell, "Bear Stearns Staves Off Collapse of 2 Hedge Funds," *New York Times*, June 21, 2007,
105. Gorton, *Slapped*, 117–27.
106. Gorton, *Slapped*, 134.
107. Matt Assad, "BethWorks Says Beam Me Up," *Morning Call Allentown*, June 22, 2007, https://www.redorbit.com/news/business/977537/bethworks_says_beam_me_up_project_officials_scurrying_to_get/index.html.
108. When the Bethlehem Steel Corporation was finally liquidated in 2001, a reporter asked corporate icon and General Electric Chairman Jack Welch if he could have saved the company. Welch replied, "I don't think Christ could have done it." Carol Loomis, "The Sinking of Bethlehem Steel," *Fortune*, April 5, 2004, http://archive.fortune.com/magazines/fortune/fortune_archive/2004/04/05/366339/index.htm.
109. London Inter-Bank Offered Rate (LIBOR) is the rate at which banks lend to one another on an unsecured basis. An overnight indexed swap (OIS) is an interest rate swap. No exchange of principal occurs, so there is less credit risk. Both measure the perceived credit risk in interbank markets.
110. As the available pool of subprime mortgages dried up, Goldman Sachs and other banks began creating "synthetic" collateralized debt obligations

(CDOs) constructed from credit default swaps that referenced other CDOs and mortgage-backed securities (MBSs). These synthetic CDOs also enabled hedge funds to short the housing market. In many cases, a single tranche of a CDO was referenced many times over via synthetic exposure. Hedge funds were shorting mezzanine MBS tranches, and banks were packaging synthetic CDOs on the other side, unknowingly amplifying risk by holding the highest tranches even as they sold off riskier pieces. For a detailed description of synthetic CDOs, see Financial Crisis Inquiry Commission, "Final Report," 144.

111. See Securities and Exchange Commission, "Goldman Sachs to Pay Record $550 Million to Settle SEC Charges Related to Subprime Mortgage CDO," July 15, 2010, https://www.sec.gov/news/press/2010/2010-123.htm. Goldman Sachs was eventually fined $550 million by the SEC for not disclosing Paulson & Company's role in selecting the assets in the Abacus portfolio. In 2013, Fabrice Tourre was found liable for fraud and was ordered to pay $825,000. In 2018, Tourre was hired as an assistant professor of finance at Copenhagen Business School.

112. Financial Crisis Inquiry Commission, "Final Report," 247.

113. Mark Landler, "U.S. Credit Crisis Adds to Gloom in Norway," *New York Times*, December 2, 2007.

114. Ben Bernanke, "Keynote Speech," Jackson Hole Symposium, August 16, 2007.

115. Federal Open Market Committee Minutes, January 29–30, 2008.

116. Merrill Lynch, *2008 Annual Report*.

117. Tooze, *Crashed*, 66.

118. Financial Crisis Inquiry Commission, "Final Report," 283.

119. Jason Moran-Bates, "The Decline and Fall of IndyMac," *North Carolina Banking Institute* 13, no. 1 (2009): 515–40.

120. Office of the Inspector General Department of the Treasury, "Safety and Soundness: Material Loss Review of IndyMac Bank," OIG-09-32, February 26, 2009.

121. Helen Thompson, "The Political Origins of the Financial Crisis: The Domestic and International Politics of Fannie Mae and Freddie Mac," *Political Quarterly* 80, no. 1 (2009): 17–24.

122. As quoted in Financial Crisis Inquiry Commission, "Final Report," 314.

123. Financial Crisis Inquiry Commission, "Final Report," 330.

124. William Sjostrom, "The AIG Bailout," *Washington & Lee Law Review* 66 (2009): 943–91.

125. JP Morgan had been eyeing a potential acquisition of WaMu for at least a year. See Eric Dash, "A Banker Embraces WaMu's Challenge," *New York Times*, October 6, 2008.
126. Tooze, *Crashed*, 395.
127. Perry Mehrling, *The New Lombard Street* (Princeton, NJ: Princeton University Press, 2010).
128. For an extended discussion of the transformation in the Federal Reserve's remit after the financial crisis, see Lev Menand, *The Fed Unbound* (New York: Columbia University Press, 2022).
129. U.S. Census Bureau, Press Release #CB11-179, October 31, 2011.
130. Neil Fligstein, Jonah Brundage, and Michael Schultz, "Seeing Like the Fed: Culture, Cognition, and Framing in the Failure to Anticipate the Financial Crisis of 2008," *American Sociological Review* 82, no. 5 (2017): 879–909.
131. The reigning economic commonsense exhibited remarkably little change after the crisis, evolving gradually into a "depoliticized Keynesianism." See Oliver Levingston, "Minsky's Moment? The Rise of Depoliticized Keynesianism and Ideational Change at the Federal Reserve After the Financial Crisis of 2007/8," *Review of International Political Economy* 28, no. 6 (2021): 1459–86. On the remarkable impermeability of orthodox economics to the lessons of the financial crisis, see Philip Mirowski, *Never Let a Serious Crisis Go to Waste* (New York: Penguin Random House, 2014), chap. 4.
132. Lisa Adkins, Melinda Cooper, and Martijn Konings, *The Asset Economy* (Cambridge: Polity, 2022); and Simon Clarke, "Crisis of Fordism or Crisis of Capitalism?," *Telos* 83 (1990): 71–98.
133. Ken-Hou Lin and Donald Tomskovic-Devey, "Financialization and U.S. Income Inequality, 1970–2008," *American Journal of Sociology* 118, no. 5 (2013): 1284–329.
134. Sebastian Kohl, "Too Much Mortgage Debt? The Effect of Housing Financialization on Housing Supply and Residential Capital Formation," *Socio-Economic Review* 19, no. 2 (2021): 413–40.
135. The European Union briefly flirted with this option during the sovereign debt crisis before Mario Draghi declared that the European Central Bank would do "whatever it takes" to maintain financial order.
136. CNN, "Wildfires & Tornadoes; New Rules for Air Controllers; Serial Killer Investigation," April 18, 2011, http://www.cnn.com/TRANSCRIPTS/1104/18/cnr.02.html.
137. Theda Skocpol and Vanessa Williamson, *The Tea Party and the Remaking of Republican Conservatism* (New York: Oxford University Press, 2012), 81.

310 • 6. THE CRISIS OF FINANCE

138. During the Obama years, political scientists became increasingly interested in "polarization"—Why was there such fierce opposition to incremental reform in the collective interest?
139. Skocpol and Williamson, *The Tea Party*, 65.
140. Skocpol and Williamson, *The Tea Party*, 66.
141. Skocpol and Williamson, *The Tea Party*, 78.
142. Frank Bruni, "Where Scott Brown Is Coming From," *New York Times*, February 28, 2010, M24.
143. Mo Cunningham, as quoted in Ben Schreckinger, "Martha Chokeley," *Politico*, October 15, 2014.
144. Executive Order 13531, February 18, 2010.
145. Jackie Calmes, "Panel Seeks Social Security Cuts and Higher Taxes," *New York Times*, November 10, 2010, A1.
146. "The Budget Control Act: Frequently Asked Questions," Congressional Research Service R44874.
147. "Statement from Co-Chairs of the Joint Select Committee on Deficit Reduction," November 21, 2011, http://www.deficitreduction.gov/public/index.cfm/2011/11/statement-from-co-chairs-of-the-joint-select-committee-on-deficit-reduction.
148. As quoted in Skocpol and Williamson, *The Tea Party*, 189.
149. Laura Meckler, "Vow to Tame Partisan Rancor Eludes Obama Four Years In," *Wall Street Journal*, August 22, 2012.
150. Robert Gordon, "Is U.S. Economic Growth Over? Faltering Innovation Confronts the Six Headwinds," *NBER Working Papers Series*, No. 18315, 2012. Also see Robert Gordon, *The Rise and Fall of American Growth* (Princeton, NJ: Princeton University Press, 2016).
151. See Pozsar, Adrian, Ashcraft, and Boesky, "Shadow Banking," 23.
152. This point was echoed by the Bank of International Settlements: "debt has been acting as a political and social substitute for income growth for far too long." Bank of International Settlements, *2016 Annual Report*, 8.
153. Minutes of the Federal Open Market Committee, October 23–24, 2012, https://www.federalreserve.gov/monetarypolicy/fomcminutes20121024.htm.
154. Adam Liptak, "Experts See Potential Ways Out for Obama in Debt Ceiling Maze," *New York Times*, October 4, 2013, A26.
155. Lori Montgomery, "Senate Passes Bipartisan Budget Agreement," *Washington Post*, December 18, 2013.
156. Peter Mair, *Ruling the Void* (New York: Verso, 2013).
157. Matthew Green, *Legislative Hardball: The House Freedom Caucus and the Power of Threat-Making in Congress* (Cambridge: Cambridge University Press, 2019), 47.

EPILOGUE: FINANCE OR DEMOCRACY?

1. Fred Block defines democratic socialism as "simply the extension of democracy to include the economy." Fred Block, "Financial Democratization and the Transition to Socialism," *Politics & Society* 47, no. 4 (2019): 529–56, 550.
2. Fred Block, "Introduction to the Special Issue," *Politics & Society* 47, no. 4 (2019): 483–89, 485.
3. Block, "Introduction," 485–86.
4. Block, "Financial Democratization," 530.
5. Fred Block, "Democratizing Finance," *Politics & Society* 42, no. 1 (2014): 3–28.
6. Block, "Financial Democratization," 547.
7. Michael McCarthy, "Three Modes of Democratic Participation in Finance," in *Democratizing Finance: Restructuring Credit to Transform Society*, ed. Erik Olin Wright, Fred Block, and Robert Hockett (New York: Verso, 2022).
8. Gianpaolo Baiocchi and Ernesto Ganuza, *Popular Democracy: The Paradox of Participation* (Stanford, CA: Stanford University Press, 2016).
9. K. Sabeel Rahman, *Democracy Against Domination* (New York: Oxford University Press, 2017).
10. Rawi Abdelal and John Ruggie, "The Principles of Embedded Liberalism: Social Legitimacy and Global Capitalism," in *New Perspectives on Regulation*, ed. David Moss and John Cisternino (Cambridge, MA: Tobin Project, 2009), 151–62.
11. For a critique from the standpoint of orthodox macroeconomics, see N. Gregory Mankiw, "A Skeptic's Guide to Modern Monetary Theory," *AEA Papers and Proceedings* 110 (2020): 141–44. For a neo-Keynesian critique, see Thomas Palley, "Money, Fiscal Policy, and Interest Rates: A Critique of Modern Monetary Theory," *Review of Political Economy* 27, no. 1 (2015): 1–23.
12. In orthodox macroeconomics, government deficits are problematic because they "crowd out" private borrowing and drive up interest rates. Deficits are believed to cause interest rates to rise, thereby lowering investment and economic growth as more efficient private investment is instead rerouted to less efficient public spending.
13. Annie Lowrey, *Give People Money* (New York: Crown, 2018); Andrew Yang, *The War on Normal People* (New York: Hachette, 2018); and Andy Stern, *Raising the Floor* (New York: PublicAffairs, 2016).
14. In the words of one anonymous observer: "Fannie has this grandmotherly image, but they will castrate you, decapitate you, tie you up, and throw you in the Potomac. They are absolutely ruthless." As quoted in Bethany McLean, *Shaky Ground: The Strange Saga of the U.S. Mortgage Giants* (New York: Columbia Global Reports, 2015), 61.

15. Mike Davis, *Prisoners of the American Dream: Politics and Economy in the History of the US Working Class* (New York: Verso, 2018), 159.
16. The history of the California ballot proposition illustrates the point beyond financial institutions. The citizens of California have the ability to enact their political will by referendum. In practice, however, the ballot proposition has served as a tool of concentrated interests for extending markets and conservative morality with substantial majorities.
17. Jodi Dean, *Democracy and Other Neoliberal Fantasies* (Durham, NC: Duke University Press, 2009).
18. Karl Marx, *Capital*, trans. David Fernbach (New York: Penguin, 1993), 320–21.
19. Hayek called for the complete abolition of government-collected economic data on the grounds that it tempts freedom-destroying interventions in the "spontaneous order" of the market.
20. Wendy Brown, "Is Capital Secular?," *Qui Parle* 23, no. 1 (2013): 109–22, 115.
21. Karl Marx, "Economic and Philosophical Manuscripts of 1844," in *The Marx-Engels Reader*, 2nd edition, ed. Robert C. Tucker (New York: W. W. Norton, 1978), 54.
22. Michel Foucault, *The Birth of Biopolitics* (New York: Palgrave, 2008), 283.
23. Foucault, *The Birth of Biopolitics*, 144.
24. Timothy Mitchell, "Uber Eats: How Capitalism Consumes the Future," in *Critical Zones: The Science and Politics of Landing on Earth*, ed. Bruno Latour and Peter Weibel (Cambridge, MA: MIT Press, 2020).
25. Michael Sandel, "The Procedural Republic and the Unencumbered Self," *Political Theory* 12, no. 1 (1984): 81–96.
26. Sheldon Wolin, *Politics and Vision: Continuity and Innovation in Western Political Thought* (Princeton, NJ: Princeton University Press, 2004), 597.
27. See Daniel Rodgers, *Age of Fracture* (Cambridge, MA: Harvard University Press, 2012), chap. 4.
28. Pierre Rosanvallon, *Le Capitalisme utopique. Critique de l'idéologie économique* (Paris: Le Seuil, 1979).
29. Kate Aronoff, Alyssa Battistoni, Daniel Aldana Cohen, and Thea Riofrancos, *A Planet to Win: Why We Need a Green New Deal* (New York: Verso, 2019).
30. F. A. Hayek, "The Use of Knowledge in Society," *American Economic Review* 35, no. 4 (1945): 519–30.
31. Greta Krippner and Anthony Alvarez, "Embeddedness and the Intellectual Projects of Economic Sociology," *Annual Review of Sociology* 33 (2007): 219–40.
32. Karl Marx, *The German Ideology* (Buffalo, NY: Prometheus, 1988).

INDEX

AAA-rated securities, of CDOs, 221, 222, 224–25
Abacus of Goldman Sachs, IKB investment loss in, 227
ABCP. *See* asset-backed commercial paper
absolutism, 9, 116, 120; Locke resistance to, 29, 49; *raison d'état* corresponding to era of, 115; religion and property under, 22, 29
ABSs. *See* asset-backed securities
Abu Dhabi Investment Authority, 273n136
ABX financial index, on subprime MBSs, 223, 225
ACA. *See* Affordable Care Act
accelerated cost recovery system (ACRS), Reagan tax cut and, 211–12
Affordable Care Act (ACA), of Obama, 236–37, 238
Aglietta, Michel, 109
AIG. *See* American International Group
Allen v. City of Long Beach (1955), California Rule of, 198–99

Alt-A securitizations, 230, 306n83
American International Group (AIG): CDS contracts of, 218–19; as CFMA beneficiary, 218–19; Fed nationalization of, 231; Goldman Sachs, IKB and, 227; SEC and New York settlement by, 221–22
American Taxpayer Relief Act (2012), 240
Appleby, Joyce, 256n35
appropriation of property: Locke on individual, 33–37; Mill on, 42; money and unlimited, 37–38; private right of, 26, 39
Arendt, Hannah, 264n129
asset-backed commercial paper (ABCP), in shadow bank deposits, 225, 228
asset-backed securities (ABSs), in shadow bank deposits, 225, 228
asset manager capitalism, 289n2
Assured Guaranty, 400 East Main repossession by, 162–63
austerity and market-oriented reorganization, in Stockton, California, 19, 138, 153–55

Baby Boomers, demand for housing by, 83, 270n87
bank capital, 307n98
Bank of International Settlements, on debt, 310n152
bankruptcy: Bethlehem Steel Works, 226, 307n108; Detroit, Michigan, 283n2; Enron Corporation, 191, 297n122; Lehman Brothers, 135, 230; Orange County, California, 187; PG&E, 190; to populism, in Stockton, 159–62; Stockton, California, 17–19, 136, 155–63, 299n149; subprime mortgage investment filings for, 226; Vallejo, California, 151, 155–57; Washington Mutual, 135–36
banks: democratized financial system through central, 245–46; Fed 1979 policy of targeting reserves of, 96; Fed and capital of, 307n98. *See also* savings and loan association; shadow banking system
Barbarians at the Gate (Burrough and Helyar), 183
Baumgartner, M. P., 83
Bear Stearns investment bank: collapse of, 226, 228; Fed arrangements of JP Morgan sale of, 229, 230; subprime lending of, 195
Becker, Gary, 118–19, 279n45
Bell, Daniel, 16; on economic growth, 25; on market, 65
Bentham, Jeremy, 11, 60, 115; panopticon of, 128
Bernanke, Ben, 228, 231–32; on global savings, 215; on monetary policy, 201–2; on subprime housing market, 234
Bethlehem Steel Works bankruptcy, 226, 307n108
biopower, 116–17
Birth of Biopolitics, The, Foucault lecture series, 111, 118, 274n145
Blair, Tony, 3, 266n15, 305n64
Block, Fred, 311n1
BLS. *See* Bureau of Labor Statistics
Bradley, Tom, 293n65
Bradley effect, 293n65
Bretton Woods system, 66, 245
Brown, Jerry: as California Attorney General, 197; California governor 2014 election win, 199; PEPRA passage by, 198–99; Proposition 13 implementation by, 86, 175–76, 273n131
Brown, Pat, 165, 167; California liberalism from 1958-1966, 168; Nixon 1962 loss to, 168; presidential campaign, 176–77
Brown, Scott, 237
Budget Control Act (2011), 238
Burchell, Graham, 256n28
Bureau of Labor Statistics (BLS): CPI-U of, 78–103, 79, 80, 275n155; on inflation and interest rates, 98
Burnham, Peter, 266n15
Burrough, Bryan, 183
Bush, George H. W., 182, 273n137, 303n47
Bush, George W., SEC investigation of, 182, 303n47
Bush, Neil M., 303n47
Bush v. Gore (2001), 184

business, 209; discipline and financial surveillance of, 129; Friedman on social responsibility to increase profits of, 124

Business Roundtable *Statement on Corporate Governance*, on CalPERS, 185–86

California: ballot proposition history, 312n16; budget deficit of 2002, 192–93; electricity market deregulation in, 187–88; Free Speech Movement of 1964 in, 169, 173; housing price increase in, 175; housing shortage in, 292n37; Orange County bankruptcy, 187; Reagan political rise in, 167–74; recall ballot for 2002 election, 192–96; recession of 1990 impact on, 168, 180; Republican 1930 elected offices in, 165–66; SEC investigation for securities fraud, 198; state property tax revolt in, 86, 87, 176; suburbanization growth in southern, 82–83; wave of tech startups IPOs, 188; Wolden bribery and conspiracy conviction, 174. *See also* Stockton, California; *specific Propositions*

California Environmental Quality Act (CEQA), 141, 172

California Power Exchange (CalPX), electricity market of, 189, 190

California Public Employees' Retirement System (CalPERS), 165, 289n1; Business Roundtable *Statement on Corporate Governance* on, 185–86; as CDO principal investor, 195–96; corporate governance reforms of 1980s and 1990s, 180; discount rate and funding ratio of, 166–67, 178, 180–81, 188, 193; dot-com collapse and subprime mortgage investment, 189–92; Enron Corporation partnership with, 186; financial crisis of 2008 and, 196–99; fiscal crisis and federal scrutiny of, 195; INdTV investment by, 298n129; investment strategy, 17, 193–94; large financial capital portfolio of, 166; MBS and CMOs purchased by, 178–79, 196; normal cost and UAL components of, 146; private equity and, 19, 167, 168, 179, 181–84, 197–98, 298n129; Proposition 21 support by, 179; public employee compensation supplemented, 19; public sector outsourcers policy of, 184; real estate allocations and, 167, 168, 178–79, 196–97; Schwarzenegger ousting of Harrigan of, 194; shareholder value and, 19, 167, 179–80, 184–86; SIV and, 196; stock market investments of, 171–72; Stockton pension payments to, 161; subprime mortgage investment and, 19, 178–79; Walker on, 199–200; P. Wilson attempted takeover of, 180–81

California Rule, of *Allen v. City of Long Beach*, 198–99

California State Teachers' Retirement System (CalSTRS), 289n1; Chilton scandal at, 180; Proposition 21 support by, 179

CalPERS. *See* California Public Employees' Retirement System
CalPX. *See* California Power Exchange
CalSTRS. *See* California State Teachers' Retirement System
capital, 18, 44, 50; in autonomous domain of economy, 109; bank, 307n98; equitable growth and, 244–45; Fed and bank, 307n98; human, 118–19, 127; neoliberalism intensification of, 3; sovereignty and globalized, 126; Streeck on abandonment of, 6
Capital (Marx), 44, 50
capitalism, 3, 16, 25, 44–45, 256n26, 266n18; asset manager, 289n2
capital market-based housing finance, of shadow banking, 211, 214
Carlyle Group, CalPERS private equity purchase of, 184
Carter, Jimmy, 67, 176; Credit Control Act of, 97; deregulation as inflation response, 105; domestic oil prices decontrol by, 94; inflation struggles of, 110; Motor Carrier Act and, 93
CDO. *See* collateralized debt obligation
CDS. *See* credit default swap
central banks, democratized financial system through, 245–46
CEQA. *See* California Environmental Quality Act
CFMA. *See* Commodity Futures Modernization Act
CFTC. *See* Commodity Futures Trading Commission
Chapters on Socialism (Mill), 47–50

Chilton, Gilbert, 180
Citigroup CDO, Arctic Circle town investment loss, 228
Clinton, Bill, 3, 216–18, 273n137
CMO. *See* collateralized mortgage obligation
Cohen, Lizabeth, 206
collateralized debt obligation (CDO): AAA-rated securities of, 221, 222, 224–25; CalPERS as principal investor of, 195–96; Goldman Sachs and, 307n110; pension funds investment in, 221
collateralized mortgage obligation (CMO), 279n56; CalPERS purchase of, 178–79; Freddie Mac sale of, 178, 304n54
commercial real estate: project increase in 1981, 211–12; thrift move to, 211
Commodity Futures Modernization Act (CFMA) (2000): AIG as beneficiary of, 218–19; CFTC and SEC regulation removal, 218; on over-the-counter derivatives regulation exemption, 218
Commodity Futures Trading Commission (CFTC), 218
competition, Mill on distribution and, 43–44
competitive markets, Rawlsian liberalism on, 52–53
Concerned Citizens Coalition, of Stockton, 141–42
conservatism, suburbanization and, 83
Consumer Price Index for Urban Consumers (CPI-U), of BLS: on apparel, 79; decomposition

of, 78–103, 79, 80, 275n155; on entertainment, 79; on housing, 79, 80–87, 275n156; on medical care, 79; subcategories of, 79; on transportation, 79, 89–95
Continental Illinois Bank collapse, of 1984, 212
corporate governance, 185–86; CalPERS and reforms of 1980s and 1990s, 180; shareholder value in, 209
corporation: EPS of, 210; financial crisis of 2008 financialized, 209–10; G. Romney on Fannie Mae as private, 85
Countrywide, 222, 226, 229, 306n95
CPI-U. *See* Consumer Price Index for Urban Consumers
CRAs. *See* credit rating agencies
credit, 238; access increase in financial growth regime, 208; crunch for housing, 83–84; democracy of, 101; Fed on growth restraints, 97, 100; Krippner on, 275n168; Prasad on access to, 276n176, 301n24
Credit Control Act (1980), 97
credit default swap (CDS), 20; of AIG, 218–19; of JP Morgan, 305n72
credit rating agencies (CRAs), as product of sovereignty, 126
crime rate, Stockton, California escalated, 161–62
Crouch, Colin, 6; on neoliberalism, 204
Cultural Contradictions of Capitalism, The (Bell), 25

Davis, Mike, 135
debt: Bank of International Settlements on, 310n152; Budget Control Act raising of ceiling for, 238; financial growth regime and household, 208; GDP as share of, 99, 207; housing bubble and doubling of mortgage, 220; security in repayments of, 159. *See also* collateralized debt obligation
decentralized markets, neoclassical economics on, 55–56
Defert, Daniel, 111, 119–20
Deficit Reduction Act (1993), 217
de-industrialization, of economy, 207
Delong, Brad, 265n13
demand management, Keynesian, 4
democracy: conception of, 261n52; of credit, 101; liberal, 7, 9–10, 14, 20; liberalism compared to, 247–52; Mill resistance to, 49; neoliberalism agenda support by, 5
democratic socialism, Block definition of, 311n1
democratized financial system, 244–46
Department of Agriculture, U.S. (USDA), 93
depoliticization, 205, 247; of distribution, 9, 13, 39–40, 52, 105; financial, 120–25; financialization as political strategy for re-, 14, 106, 125; Friedman on market and distributive conflict, 64–65; liberal democracy and, 7, 9–10, 20; as liberalism and distributive conflict solution, 26, 112; of private property from state, 23; Rawls on growth and, 61–63; of religion, 8, 57–59, 58; of rule of finance, 103
Depository Institutions Act (1980), 100

deregulation: by Carter as inflation response, 105; of economics, 14; of electricity market in California, 187–88; in financial depoliticization, 122–23; globalization and, 207; interest financial, 100; of trucking industry, 93–94
derivatives market, 187, 218
Desan, Christine, 280n66
Detroit, Michigan bankruptcy, 283n2
Deutsche Industriebank (IKB), Goldman Sachs Abacus investment by, 227
difference principle, of Rawls, 208, 264n130
direct financial risk-taking, in financial depoliticization, 122, 123–24
Directive 157, of FASB, 223, 225
disciplinary power, 115–16
discipline: business financial surveillance and, 129; components of, 127; human capital maximization with, 127; neoliberalism and, 127–29; panopticon of Bentham and, 128; Quicken software company definition of, 127–28
Discipline & Punish (Foucault), 115–16
discount rate and funding ratio, of CalPERS, 166–67, 178, 180–81, 188, 193
distribution: depoliticization of, 9, 13; financialization and re-depoliticization of, 14, 105; Locke on depoliticization of, 39–40; Mill on competition in, 43–44; political governing of, 20; political management inability for, 28; Rawls on depoliticization of, 52; Rawls rejection of, 57
distributive conflict, 248, 250; during crisis of 1970s inflation, 68–69, 103–6; definition and examples, 10–11; finance as depoliticization response to, 26, 112; financial crisis of 2008 return of, 235–41; financialization as political reaction to, 14, 106, 125; financialization link to, 15–16, 103–6; laissez-faire, 58; Marx on, 10, 12. *See also* liberalism and distributive conflict
distributive depoliticization, of Fordism, 106
Donahoe Higher Education Act (1960), of P. Brown, 168
dot-com collapse, CalPERS and, 189–92
Drucker, Peter, 165
Drysdale Securities, 1982 collapse of, 101

earnings per share (EPS), of corporation, 210
economic growth, 25–26, 239
economic liberty, 263n115
economics, 263n111; Appleby on laws of, 256n35; decentralization of power of, 258n10; deregulation of, 14; policies to maximize growth, 25; political participation in policies of, 245; Rosanvallon on theory of, 206, 260n47. *See also* neoclassical economics model
economy: capital as autonomous domain of, 109; de-industrialization of, 207; liberal depoliticization and, 247; liberalism relocation

of distributive conflict to, 11;
as political thought, 250–51;
suburbanization and postwar mass
consumption, 82
Edsall, Mary, 86–87
Edsall, Thomas, 86–87, 182
efficiency and equality trade-offs, in
neoclassical economics, 55–56
electricity market: California
deregulation of, 187–88; of CalPX,
189, 190; Federal Energy Regulatory
Commission on, 192
Emanuel, Rahm, 216
embedded liberalism, 103; Fordist
growth regime of, 205; free trade,
market and, 66; neoliberalism
dismantling of, 104; Ruggie on,
66–67; state blame for threats to, 106
Emergency Home Finance Act (1970),
Freddie Mac creation by, 85
Energy Policy Act (1992), 187–88
Enron Corporation: California
bankruptcy of, 191, 297n122;
CalPERS partnership with, 186;
FASB regulatory response to, 223
enterprise policy changes, of
government, 271n96
entertainment, CPI-U on, 79
EPS. *See* earnings per share
equitable growth, capital and, 244–45
equity investments, Proposition 21 on,
179
Ewald, Francois, 111, 119–20

fact of reasonable pluralism, of Rawls, 51
Fannie Mae. *See* Federal National
Mortgage Association

FASB. *See* Financial Accounting
Standards Board
FDIC. *See* Federal Deposit Insurance
Corporation
Fed. *See* Federal Reserve
Federal Deposit Insurance Corporation
(FDIC)-insured savings accounts,
215
Federal Energy Regulatory
Commission, electricity price caps
by, 192
Federal Home Loan Mortgage
Corporation (Freddie Mac), 84,
85, 213; CMOs sold by, 178, 304n54;
Federal Housing Finance Agency
conservatorship of, 230; GAAP
and, 222
Federal Housing Administration, 99
Federal Housing Finance Agency,
Fannie Mae and Freddie Mac
conservatorship by, 230
Federal National Mortgage
Association (Fannie Mae), 84, 213,
311n14; Federal Housing Finance
Agency on conservatorship of,
230; Raines ousted from, 222; G.
Romney declaration of private
corporation of, 85
Federal Open Market Committee,
federal funds rate increase by, 223
Federal Reserve (Fed): AIG
nationalization by, 231; bank
capital and, 307n98; Bear Stearns
engineered sale to JP Morgan by,
229, 230; on credit growth restraints,
97, 100; federal funds rate target set
by, 95; financial growth regime

Federal Reserve (Fed) (*continued*)
and, 234; financial system liquidity
and, 233; Greenspan nomination by
Reagan to, 203; housing bubble and,
219; inflation as primary concern
of, 223; interest rate cuts in 2007
and 2008, 228; Lehman Brothers
bankruptcy and, 230; monetarism
and, 97; PDCF creation by, 229;
pension system scrutiny in 1996
of, 298n128; quantitative easing
asset-buying programs of, 232, 240;
shadow banking system backstop
by, 232; TSLF and, 229; Volcker
position at, 203

Feher, Michel, 132

finance: Aglietta and Orléan on, 109;
basic structure of, 121; capital,
inflation during crisis of 1970s and,
18; as depoliticization response, to
distributive conflict, 112; financial
contracts in, 121–22; liberal
democracy empowerment of, 7,
14; liberalism impacted by, 278n16;
neoliberalism deployed by, 13, 125;
political power operated by, 18;
social power and, 110; theorizing of,
112–20

Financial Accounting Standards Board
(FASB): Directive 157 of, 223, 225;
Enron Corporation regulatory
response from, 223; GAAP
standards set by, 223

financial consolidation, in financial
crisis of 2008: CFMA and, 218–19;
Clinton presidency and, 216–17;
Financial Services Modernization
Act and, 218; Gingrich government
shutdown, 217, 305n73; NAFTA,
GATT, WTO and, 216–17;
unemployment fall with NAIRU,
217, 305n70

financial contracts, in finance, 121–22

financial crisis of 2008, 17; bipartisan
political response to inflation
impact on, 204; CalPERS and,
196–99; CDS and, 20; Crouch on
non-death of neoliberalism after,
6; depoliticization impact on, 205;
distributive conflict return, 235–41;
financial consolidation, 216–19,
305n73; financial growth regime
and, 205–24, 234; financialized
corporation and, 209–10; financial
reforms for social conflict, 19; free
market ideology impact on, 19,
205; Greenspan and, 201–2, 203;
housing bubble, 219–24; losses
from, 233; MBS and, 19, 178–79,
196, 213–14, 221–23, 307n110;
neoliberalism survival in, 204;
populism and social unrest
after, 4; shadow banking system
and, 20, 205, 210–20; subprime
MBSs structure impact on, 19,
178, 224–25; subprime mortgage
delinquencies, 224

financial depoliticization, 120–21, 125;
deregulation in, 122–23; direct
financial risk-taking in, 122, 123–24;
subsides in, 122, 123

financial growth regime, 205, 216–24;
breakdown during crisis of 1970s
inflation, 18, 68; de-industrialization

of economy in, 207; Fed and, 234; flaw in, 234; GDP growth in postwar Golden Era, 206; GSEs and, 213–15, 222; household debt and credit access increase in, 208; service sector and IT growth in, 207; shareholder value in, 209; thrift in, 210–11; wealth effect and, 105, 209

financialization: crisis of 1970s and, 16, 104–5; distributive conflict link to, 15–16, 103–6; inflation link to, 104–5; link to growth machine politics, 139–50; money and monetary maximization in, 122; neoliberalism by design and, 5; political strategies for, 14, 15, 125; re-depoliticization of distribution and, 105; as re-depoliticizing distributive conflict political strategy, 14, 106, 125; security in, 130–31; social powers and, 133; transformations from, 12–13; urban, 284n3

financialization of liberalism, 108–9; financial crisis of 2008 and, 205; financial depoliticization, 120–25; Foucault on power and, 18, 110–11; liberalism and finance theorizing, 112–20; Marx thesis of liberal depoliticization and, 18; neoliberalism and, 125–34; reconfiguration of, 18

financial nonprofits, decentralized confederation of, 244

financial political rule, inflation during crisis of 1970s and, 18, 67–68

Financial Revolution, Pincus on, 260n48

Financial Services Modernization Act (1999), 218

First Treatise of Government (Locke), 33

fiscal and monetary policies, Keynesian, 78

fiscal federalism, Keynesian, 137

food and beverages: CPI-U on, 79, 87–89; factors for price spike, 88–89; Nixon grain sale to Soviet Union, 88; oil embargo of 1973 fertilizer shortages, 87–88

Fordism, 105, 206, 243; distributive depoliticization of, 106; growth regime of embedded liberalism and, 205

foreclosures, Stockton leading per capita, 136

Foucault, Michel, 94, 96, 115, 277n11; *The Birth of Biopolitics* lecture series, 111, 118, 274n145; on liberalism, 110, 112–14, 118, 248; on liberal order of power, 18, 110–11; on neoliberalism, 112, 114, 118; on politics, 107; on regimes of veridiction, 117–18; on sovereign power, 114, 116; on stagflation, 279n43; Walzer on, 277n2

400 East Main building (Stockton, California): Assured Guaranty repossession of, 162–63; Stockton purchase for city office of, 148–49, 156, 158–59, 162; Washington Mutual office at, 135–36, 148; Wells Fargo repossession of, 158

Freddie Mac. *See* Federal Home Loan Mortgage Corporation
Freedom Caucus, 241
free enterprise, 93; Reagan on, 67–68
Freeman, Samuel, 62–63
free market conservatism, 243; financial crisis of 2008 impacted by, 19, 205; Reagan and, 2
Free Speech Movement of 1964, in California, 169, 173
free trade: embedded liberalism and, 66; Mill on, 46
Friedman, Milton, 3, 93, 108, 209; on business social responsibility to increase profits, 124; on monetarism, 63, 96–97; NAIRU and, 217; on neoliberalism, 63, 64; on oil and food counterargument, 276n172
Friends of Angelo program, of Countrywide, 306n95
funding ratio. *See* discount rate and funding ratio

GAAP. *See* generally accepted accounting principles
Garn-St. Germain Act (1982), 100
GATT. *See* General Agreement on Tariffs and Trade
GDP. *See* gross domestic product
General Agreement on Tariffs and Trade (GATT), 216–17
general equilibrium theory, neoclassical economics and, 54
generally accepted accounting principles (GAAP): FASB establishment of, 223; Freddie Mac and, 222

GI Bill. *See* Servicemen's Readjustment Act
Gingrich, Newt, 5, 106; government shutdown in 1994, 217, 305n73; on politics as war for power, 107
Ginnie Mae. *See* Government National Mortgage Association
globalization, deregulation and, 207
globalized capital, sovereignty and, 126
global savings: during 1990s and early 2000s, 215; Bernanke on, 215
Goldman Sachs: AIG, IKB and, 227; CDOs and, 307n110; IKB investment loss in Abacus of, 227; SEC fine of, 308n111
Goldstein, Adam, 133
goods-producing industries move overseas, 207
Gordon, Robert: on economic research on inflation, 266n20; secular stagnation hypothesis of, 239
Gore, Al, 25, 216, 217
government: bailouts to thrifts, 212; enterprise policy changes of, 271n96; Mill on power of, 45; shut down of 2013, 240; Weber on municipal market actors, 285n11
governmentality: Foucault on liberalism and neoliberalism history of, 112; regimes of veridiction of Foucault and, 117–18. *See also* history of governmentality
Government National Mortgage Association (Ginnie Mae), 84, 213
government-sponsored enterprises (GSEs): for housing, 84–85; Kudlow on secondary mortgage markets

concentration of, 178; MBSs and, 213–14, 222; mortgage opportunity for, 213; non-conforming mortgages and, 220; Operation Noriega to rein in, 222; probable failure of, 230; rapid growth and shadow banking system creation, 214–15; structural advantages of, 214

Great Recession, 136, 159, 203, 232–33

Greenspan, Alan, 187, 192, 303n47; financial crisis of 2008 and, 201–2, 203; House Committee on Oversight and Government Reform interrogation of, 202; neoliberalism policy of, 203; Reagan nomination to Federal Reserve, 203; on wealth and political polarization, 238–39

gross domestic product (GDP), 92, 180, 233; federal debt as share of, 99, 207; growth in postwar Golden Era, 206

growth: economic, 25–26, 239; of GDP in postwar Golden Era, 206; inflation, post war remission and return of, 207; of IT, 207; liberalism and distributive conflict requirement of, 28; Mill on liberalism of, 41–50; politics, 135–64; Rawls on depoliticization and, 61–63; Reagan on, 165; service sector, 207. *See also* financial growth regime

growth machine politics: financialization link to, 139–50; in Stockton, California, 135–63

GSEs. *See* government-sponsored enterprises

Habermas, Jürgen, 60
Hacker, Jacob, 280n62
Hamilton, Shane, 93–94
harm principle, of Mill, 45–46
Harrigan, Michael, 194
Harvey, David: on hydrological cycle, 109–10; on neoliberalism, 3, 4, 256n25
Hayek, Friedrich A., 3, 201, 248, 259n27, 312n19
Helyar, John, 183
history of governmentality: Foucault on critical junctures in, 114–15; liberalism as form of, 113, 114; *raison d'état* form of, 114, 115
Hitchman, John, 183
Hobbes, Thomas, 8, 11; on absolute sovereign for security, 21–22; on political order, 21–22
Hoffa, James R., 169–70, 273n128
Hollande, Francois, 108
Homo economicus figure: Feher on, 132; financial conduct of, 132–33; neoliberalism and, 131–34; portfolio society of, 133
HoSang, Daniel, 290n10
House Committee on Oversight and Government Reform, Greenspan interrogation by, 202
household debt increase, 208
housing: Baby Boomers demand for, 83, 270n87; California price increase for, 175; California Proposition 13 tax cuts, 86–87, 107, 139–40, 175–77, 187, 273n131; California shortage of, 292n37; CPI-U on, 79, 80–87, 275n156; credit crunch for, 83–84;

housing (*continued*)
  GI Bill response to undersupply of, 81; GSEs for availability of, 84–85; Housing and Urban Development Act for, 84; R. Moses redevelopment of, 81; price of, 85–86; racialized housing discrimination, 81, 169; response to unprecedented demand for, 102; G. Romney on declaration of Fannie Mae as private corporation, 85; suburbanization in, 81–83, 206; Truman Fair Deal and, 81
Housing Act (1949), 81
Housing and Urban Development Act (1968), 84
housing bubble: Fed and, 219; in financial crisis of 2008, 219–24; housing market peak in 2006, 224; Kindleberger on, 219; market-based system for, 213; mortgage debt doubling in, 220; non-conforming mortgages in, 220; upward price spiral in housing market, 219–20
Hubbert, M. King, 89–90
human capital: Becker theory of, 118–19, 279n45; discipline maximization of, 127; theory of, 118–19
Hume, David, 63

ICC. *See* Interstate Commerce Commission
IKB. *See* Deutsche Industriebank
individual autonomy, state noninterference and, 23
Industrial Revolution, disciplinary power and, 116
IndyMac, 229–30
inflation: Carter on struggles of, 110; as Fed primary concern, 223; Gordon on economic research of, 266n20; interest rates raise to combat, 223–24; post war remission and growth return, 207; Regulation School on, 269n59; Volcker shock and, 254n10
inflation, during crisis of 1970s, 2, 66, 107; breakdown of financial growth regime and, 18, 68; CPI-U decomposition on, 78–103, 79, 80, 275n155; distributive conflict and financialization in, 103–6; distributive crises intersections in, 69; finance capital and, 18; financialization link to, 16, 104–5; financial political rule and, 18, 67–68; on interest, 95–103; monetarism and, 17–18; as monetary manifestation of distributive conflict, 68–69; neoliberalism and, 4, 17–18, 69; new common sense in, 69–78; oil company profit after, 182; Ruggie on embedded liberalism, 66–67; Samuelson on stagflation in, 67; social conflicts and, 18, 68; unemployment trade-off and, 2, 95–96
information technology (IT): collapse of bubble in early 2000s, 219; growth of, 207
initial public offerings (IPOs), California tech startups wave of, 188

interest: democracy of credit for, 101; Depository Institutions Act and, 100; direct and indirect costs for consumers of, 97–98; Drysdale Securities and Lombard-Wall collapse, 101; financial deregulation in, 100; Garn-St. Germain Act and, 100; inflation of 1970s and, 95–103; repurchase agreements and, 101; shadow banking system and, 100–101; stagflation and, 96; state financial markets and, 102–3

interest rates, 280n59, 311n12; BLS on inflation and, 98; Fed 2007 and 2008 cuts in, 228; inflation combat by raise of, 223–24; LIBOR and OIS for, 307n109; state cap on, 211

Interstate Commerce Commission (ICC), 93

Interstate Highway System, suburbanization impacted by, 81

interventionism, Keynesian, 118

investment strategy, of CalPERS, 17, 193–94

Invisible Hand theory, of Smith, 54

IPOs. *See* initial public offerings

Iraqi invasion, oil and, 273n137

Islamic Revolution, oil prices and, 91–92

IT. *See* information technology

Ito, Lance, 303n47

Jackson, Kenneth, 81
Jamieson, Kenneth, 90–91
Jensen, Michael, 183
Johnson, Harry, 96
Johnson, Lyndon B., 72

Johnston, Ann, 152, 154
Joint Select Committee on Deficit Reduction (Supercommittee), 238
JP Morgan, CDS of, 305n73

Keating, Charles, 303n47
Kennedy, Anthony, 291n29
Kennedy, John F., 25, 168
Keynes, John Maynard, 67, 70
Keynesian orthodoxy, 67, 101, 309n131; demand management in, 4; fiscal and monetary policies, 78; fiscal federalism in, 137; Foucault on, 96; interventionism, 118; Nixon on, 72; policymaking, 70
Kindleberger, Charles, 219
Kissinger, Henry, 90–91
Krippner, Greta, 275n168
Kristol, Irving, 21, 175
Kudlow, Lawrence, 178

labor theory of value, of Mill, 50
laissez-faire system, 66, 115; distributive conflict and, 58; Mill on, 42, 45–46, 49
Las Vegas Sands Corporation: Bethlehem Steel Works conversion to Sands Casino Resort Bethlehem by, 226; stalled construction on, 227
Laws (Plato), 36–37
LBO. *See* leveraged buyout
legislation: ACA, of Obama, 236–37, 238; American Taxpayer Relief Act, 240; Budget Control Act, 238; CEQA, 141, 172; CFMA, 218–19; Credit Control Act, 97; Deficit Reduction Act, 217; Depository

legislation (*continued*)
  Institutions Act, 100; Donahoe
  Higher Education Act, 168;
  Emergency Home Finance Act,
  85; Energy Policy Act, 187–88;
  Financial Services Modernization
  Act, 218; Garn-St. Germain Act,
  100; Housing Act, 81; Housing
  and Urban Development Act,
  84; Motor Carrier Act, 93–94;
  National Environmental Policy
  Act, 89; PEPRA, 198–99; Public
  Utility Holding Company Act,
  187; Rumford Fair Housing Act,
  169, 172; Secondary Mortgage
  Market Enhancement Act, 214;
  Servicemen's Readjustment Act, 81;
  Toleration Act, 29; Tonnage Act, 29
Lehman Brothers: bankruptcy of, 135,
  230; POB offering of, 147
Letter on Toleration (Locke), 29, 30
leveraged buyout (LBO), 181–82
Leviathan (Hobbes), 8
liberal democracy: depoliticization and,
  7, 9–10, 20; finance empowerment
  by, 7, 14
liberalism: P. Brown and California,
  168; Burchell on, 256n28; defining
  features of, 8; democracy
  compared to, 247–52; finance
  impact on, 278n16; financialization
  reconfiguration of, 18; as form of
  history of governmentality, 113,
  114; forms of social power and, 113;
  Foucault on, 110, 112–14, 118, 248;
  inflation and breakdown of regime
  of, 18; Locke on importance of
  money and, 38, 260n48; market
  within, 24–25; postwar, 170–71, 177;
  Rawls on, 8; Rawls on origin of, 22;
  religious conflict response from, 22;
  theorizing of, 112–20; Walzer on, 8,
  9, 109, 277n2
liberalism and distributive conflict,
  8–11, 21–22; depoliticization as
  solution to, 26, 112; distribution
  political management inability,
  28; economic policy to maximize
  growth, 25; growth requirement, 28;
  Locke on liberalism before market,
  24, 28–41; market and, 24–25, 28;
  Mill on, 17, 41–50; personal property
  privatization and, 23–24; political
  economy, 24; Rawls on, 17, 50–65;
  secularism and, 24; wealth effect
  and, 105, 209
liberal order, Foucault and power in,
  18, 110–11
liberal state: depoliticized social power
  and, 11, 109; Marx on, 11, 257n36
LIBOR. *See* London Inter-Bank
  Offered Rate
Lincoln, Kevin, 288n78
Lincoln Savings and Loan, 303n47
loan, security of, 101
Locke, John, 17, 21, 248; absolutism
  resistance from, 29, 49; on
  depoliticization of distribution,
  39–40; on individual appropriation
  of property, 33–37; on liberalism
  and market, 24, 28–41; on market
  price interference, 40; on money
  impact on liberalism, 38, 260n48;
  on noninterference by state, 31,

32; on political order, 22; on poor law reform, 42; on possessive individualism, 34–35; on private property, 33–38, 61; on property, 29, 33–41; on religion, 29, 30–33; on resources, 40–41; on secularism analogy to wealth, 30–31; Wolin on, 259n22

Lombard-Wall, 1982 collapse of, 101

London Inter-Bank Offered Rate (LIBOR), 307n109

lump-sum transfers, 54–55

market, 258n9, 261n55; Bell on, 65; derivatives, 187, 218; embedded liberalism and, 66; financial power and conduct of, 133; Friedman on depoliticization of distributive conflict and, 64–65; governing by, 11; imperatives, 1, 6; within liberalism and distributive conflict, 24–25, 28; Locke on liberalism and, 24, 28–41; neoclassical economics model and competitive, 53; Rawls on depoliticization of, 59–61; religion compared to, 27; upward price spiral in housing, 219–20

market-based housing finance, 213–14

Marquette National Bank of Minneapolis v. First of Omaha (1978), 211

Martin, Isaac William, 86, 87, 174

Marx, Karl, 9, 15, 44, 50, 108, 251, 261n55; on distributive conflict, 10, 12; on liberal state, 11, 257n36

mass incarceration practice, neoliberalism and, 281n68

MBS. *See* mortgage-backed securities

McCarthy, Michael, 200; on public control over lending and finance, 245

McCulley, Paul, 304n58

medical care, CPI-U on, 79

Meese, Edwin, 240

Meir, Golda, 90

middle class, 6, 216; Mills on marketing mentality of, 83; suburbanization and, 83, 206

Mill, John Stuart, 17, 261n53, 262n78; on appropriation of property, 42; *Chapters on Socialism* of, 47–50; democracy resistance from, 49; on economic growth, 62; harm principle of, 45–46; on labor theory of value, 50; on laissez-faire system, 42, 45–46, 49; on liberalism of growth, 41–50; *On Liberty* of, 45–47; *Principles of Political Economy* of, 41–45, 62–64; on private property justification, 43; on property, 42–43, 48–50, 61, 62; on state of society, 62; on vice taxes, 47; on working class, 42, 44–45, 48–49

Mills, C. Wright, 83

Mitchell, Timothy, 90; on supply shock, 272n118

modern monetary theory (MMT), democratized financial system and, 245–46

modern portfolio theory (MPT), 282n85

Mollenkopf, John, 81

monetarism, 17–18; defeat of, 268n47; Delong on, 265n13; Fed and, 97; Friedman on, 63, 96–97

monetary maximization, in financialization, 122
monetary neutrality, 277n4
monetary policy: Bernanke on, 201–2; Reagan on, 267n38
money: in financialization, 122; Hume quantity theory of, 63; Locke on liberalism and, 38, 260n48; Locke on private property impacted by, 37–38; tacit consent to, 38–39; and unlimited appropriation of property, 37–38
money market mutual funds, in shadow banking, 215, 220; SIVs and, 221
Mont Pèlerin Society, neoliberalism and, 2, 3, 13
mortgage-backed securities (MBS), 19, 307n110; ABX financial index on subprime, 223; CalPERS purchase of, 178–79, 196; GSEs and, 213–14, 222; pension fund investment in, 221; Ranieri on, 178; RMBSs and, 223, 226, 230
mortgages: CMOs and, 178–79, 279n56, 304n54; GSEs market opportunity for, 213; non-conforming, in housing bubble, 220; thrift transmuting of local savings in local, 210–11. *See also* subprime mortgages
Moses, Mark, 148
Moses, Robert, 81
Mother Teresa, 303n47
Motor Carrier Act (1980), 93–94
MPT. *See* modern portfolio theory
municipal market actors, Weber on, 285n11

NAFTA. *See* North American Free Trade Agreement
NAIRU. *See* nonaccelerating inflation rate of unemployment
National Commission on Fiscal Responsibility and Reform, of Obama, 237
National Environmental Policy Act, 89
nationally recognized statistical rating organization (NRSRO), of SEC, 213–14
National Maximum Speed Limit Law (1974), 91
National Security Council, NSC-68 report of, 80
NATO. *See* North Atlantic Treaty Organization
neoclassical economics model, Rawls on, 57–58; competitive markets and, 53; decentralized markets distributive efficiency in, 55–56; on efficiency and equality trade-offs, 55–56; general equilibrium theory and, 54; procedural justice and, 54; welfare economics, 53
neoliberalism: capital intensified by, 3; Defert and Ewald on insurance and, 119–20; definition of, 253n8; democracy support of agenda of, 6; discipline and, 127–29; embedded liberalism dismantling of, 104; faith in power unregulated markets in, 204; faith in state bailouts in, 204; finance deployment of, 13, 125; financialization coincidence with, 5, 13; financialization of liberalism and, 125–34; financialized subject

and polity, 131–34; Foucault on, 112, 114, 118; Friedman on, 63, 64; Greenspan policy of, 203; Harvey on, 3, 4, 256n25; *Homo economicus* figure and, 131–34; inflation during crisis of 1970s and, 4, 17–18, 69; mass incarceration practice and, 281n68; Mont Pèlerin Society and, 2, 3, 13; Peck on, 257n38; political rationality of, 5; political struggle against, 20; security and, 130–31; set of practices in, 119; state measures in strength of, 3–4; on strength of state, 3–4

New York, AIG settlement with, 221–22

Nixon, Richard, 6, 272n119, 273n128; on economic growth, 25; grain sale to Soviet Union, 88; Hoffa sentence commuted by, 273n128; on Keynesian economics, 72; loss in 1962 to P. Brown by, 168; National Maximum Speed Limit Law of, 91; on oil embargo, 91; Operation Nickel Grass of, 90; on recession, 72–73

nonaccelerating inflation rate of unemployment (NAIRU), 217, 305n70

non-conforming mortgages, in housing bubble, 220

normal cost component, of CalPERS, 146

North American Free Trade Agreement (NAFTA), 216–17

North Atlantic Treaty Organization (NATO), 90

NRSRO. *See* nationally recognized statistical rating organization

NSC-68. *See United States Objectives and Programs for National Security* report

Obama, Barack, 204, 232; ACA of, 236–37, 238; elitism complaint against, 236; National Commission on Fiscal Responsibility and Reform of, 237; polarization and, 310n138; Santelli criticism of, 235–36; Tea Party movement and, 236

Occupy Wall Street, 238

OCIP. *See* Orange County Investment Pool

Office of Thrift Supervision (OTS), 229; Washington Mutual seizure of, 231

oil, 273n137; Abu Dhabi Investment Authority and, 273n136; Carter domestic oil prices decontrol, 94; companies profit after crisis of 1970s, 182; imports, 273n123; increased dependence on imports of, 102; independent trucking and price spike for, 93; Iraqi invasion and, 273n137; Islamic Revolution and prices of, 91–92; Union Oil Santa Barbara 1969 spill, 89

oil and food counterargument, Friedman on, 276n172

oil embargo (1973): fertilizer shortages from, 87–88; Nixon on, 91; OPEC and, 90–91, 272n118

On Liberty (Mill), 45–47

OPEC. *See* Organization of the Petroleum Exporting Countries

Operation Nickel Grass, 90

Operation Noriega, to control GSEs, 222
Orange County, California bankruptcy, 187
Orange County Investment Pool (OCIP), Orange County bankruptcy and, 187
Organization of the Petroleum Exporting Countries (OPEC), oil embargo and, 90–91, 272n118
Orléan, André, 109
orthodox macroeconomics, 311n12
OTS. *See* Office of Thrift Supervision
overnight indexed swap (OIS), interest rates and, 307n109

Pacific Gas and Electric (PG&E) bankruptcy, 190
panopticon, of Bentham, 128
Pareto-efficient distribution, in welfare economics, 54
PDCF. *See* Primary Dealer Credit Facility
Peck, Jamie, 257n38
Pelosi, Nancy, 231
pendency plan, Stockton, California adoption of, 158, 187n60
pension fund investment practices: Hitchman on, 183; of MBS and CDOs, 221; McCarthy on, 200
pension obligation bond (POB), 286n31; Lehman Brothers offering of, 147; M. Moses support of, 148; Stockton, California and, 146–48
pension system, 291n26; Fed scrutiny in 1996 of, 298n128; pension costs increase, 292n47; Proposition 5 on, 165–66
PEPRA. *See* Public Employees' Pension Reform Act
personal property, privatization of, 23–24
PG&E. *See* Pacific Gas and Electric
Pincus, Steven, 260n48
Plehwe, Dieter, 277n1
POB. *See* pension obligation bond
polarization, Obama and, 310n138
policymaking, Keynesian, 70
political correlates, with suburbanization, 83
political economy, 261n55; liberalism and distribution, 24; Mill on competition and, 43–44
political governing, of distribution, 20
Political Liberalism (Rawls), 62
political order, 21–22
political thought, economy as, 250–51
politics: Foucault on, 107; Gingrich on war for power of, 107; growth in, 135–64; Marx on, 108; neoliberalism and rationality of, 5; program of, 108, 246; strategies for financialization, 14, 15, 125; struggle against neoliberalism, 20
polity, financialized subject and, 131–34
populism: financial crisis of 2008 and backlash of, 4; Stockton, California from bankruptcy to, 159–62
portfolio society, of *Homo economicus*, 133
possessive individualism, Locke on, 34–35
postwar Golden Era, GPD growth in, 206

postwar liberalism: P. Brown on, 177; of
    Reagan, 170–71
power: Arendt on, 264n129;
    biopower, 116–17; class, 255n23;
    decentralization of economic,
    258n10; disciplinary, 115–16; Foucault
    on liberal order of, 18, 110–11;
    Foucault on sovereign, 114, 116;
    market conduct for financial, 133;
    social, 11, 109, 110, 113, 133
Pozsar, Zoltan, 239
Prasad, Monica, 276n176, 301n24
Primary Dealer Credit Facility
    (PDCF), Fed creation of, 229
principle of toleration, of Rawls, 51
Principles of Political Economy (Mill),
    41–45, 62–64
Principles of Scientific Management, of
    Taylor, 226
private equity: CalPERS and, 19,
    167, 168, 179, 181–84, 197–98,
    298n129; Hitchman on pension
    fund investments in, 183; LBO
    and, 181–82; Swensen Yale Model
    and, 183–84; threat of takeovers
    in, 209
private property, 256n26;
    depoliticization from state of,
    23; Locke on, 33–38, 61; Mill on
    justification for, 43, 61; Rawls on, 61
private right, of appropriation of
    property, 26, 39
privatization: of personal
    property, 23–24; of religion,
    23; Schwarzenegger push for
    CalPERS, 194–95; Washington
    Consensus program of, 126

procedural justice: in neoclassical
    economics, 54; Rawlsian liberalism
    on, 52, 57
property: under absolutism,
    22, 29; appropriation of, 26,
    33–39, 42; Locke on, 29, 33–41;
    Mill on, 42–43, 48–50, 61, 62;
    Rawlsian liberalism on basic
    ownership of, 57, 62. *See also*
    private property
Proposition 1, on pension funds stock
    investment, 171–73
Proposition 5, on pension system,
    165–66
Proposition 6, defeat of, 293n64
Proposition 13, on property tax cuts,
    107; J. Brown and, 86, 175–76,
    273n131; T. Edsall and M. Edsall on,
    86–87; Kristol on, 175; Proposition
    218 extension of, 187; public
    employers impacted by, 177; Reagan
    and, 86–87; Stockton impact from,
    139–40
Proposition 14, on property owners and
    discrimination, 169, 170, 290n14
Proposition 18, on TIF funding, 140
Proposition 20, on California Coastal
    Commission creation, 172–73
Proposition 21, on equity investments,
    179
Proposition 184: on public services and
    proof of citizenship, 186–87; three
    strikes law, 186–87
Proposition 218, extension of
    Proposition 13, 187
Proposition 227, on bilingual education
    in public schools ban, 187

public control with lending and financing, in democratized financial system, 245
Public Employees' Pension Reform Act (PEPRA), 198–99
public employment and spending: Proposition 13 impact on, 177; Stockton, California and, 18, 19, 136, 149–50
public financial entities, democratized financial system through new, 244
Public Utility Holding Company Act (1935), 187

quantitative easing asset-buying programs, of Fed, 232, 240
quantity theory of money, of Hume, 63

racialized housing discrimination, 81, 169
Raines, Franklin, 222
raison d'état form, of history of governmentality, 114; absolutism era corresponding to, 115
Ranieri, Lewis, 178
Rawls, John, 8, 17, 50, 64–65; difference principle of, 208, 264n130; on fact of reasonable pluralism, 51; on growth and depoliticization, 61–63; on liberal depoliticization, 58–59; on liberalism origin, 22; on market and depoliticization, 59–61; on neoclassical economics model, 53–58; on principle of toleration, 51; on state of society, 62
Rawlsian liberalism: on basic ownership of property, 57, 62; on competitive markets, 52–53; on procedural justice, 52, 57; reasonable pluralism in, 55; religion and distribution depoliticization, 57–59, 58
Reagan, Ronald, 6, 16, 108, 203; ACRS and, 211–12; T. Edsall and Davis on oil profit finances for, 182; on free enterprise, 67–68; free market conservatism of, 2; on growth, 165; gubernatorial defeat of Unruh in 1970, 173; monetary policy, 267n38; political rise in California of, 167–74; postwar liberalism of, 170–71; Proposition 13 and, 86–87; Proposition 20 support by, 172; on reduced deficits and lower inflation, 99; on Rumford Fair Housing Act repeal, 169, 172; spending cuts and tax expenditures of, 208; tax cuts of, 14, 86–87, 207, 211–12; victory over P. Brown in 1966, 171
Reagan Revolution, 19, 68, 105, 168, 174; cost-of-living adjustments of, 177; enactments of, 172–73; Proposition 1 support in, 173; Proposition 14 and, 169, 170, 290n14; Rumford Fair Housing Act and, 169, 172; welfare reform bill of, 173
real estate: CalPERS and allocations of, 167, 168, 178–79, 196–97; commercial, 211–12; Volcker shock and investments in, 179
reasonable pluralism, in Rawlsian liberalism, 55
recall ballot: in California 2002 election, 192–96; Schwarzenegger win in, 194

recession, 70, 212, 219; California and impact of July 1990, 168, 180; Great Recession, 136, 159, 203, 232–33; L. Johnson on, 72; of July 1981 to November 1982, 97; Nixon on, 72–73; Volcker on inflation and, 97
Reed, Bruce, 216
regimes of veridiction, of Foucault, 117–18
Regulation School, on inflation, 268n59
Reid, Harry, 239
Reinecke, Ed, 291n31
Reitman v. Mulkey (1967), 290n14
religion: under absolutism, 22, 29; depoliticization of, 8, 57–59, 58; Locke on, 29, 30–33; market compared to, 27; privatization of, 23; secularism as depoliticization of, 27; state freedom from, 22–23
religious conflict: liberalism response to, 22; secularism and, 8, 23
repo haircuts, 225
repurchase agreements, 101
residential MBSs (RMBSs), 223, 226, 230
resources, Locke on, 40–41
return on investment, 280n58
RMBSs. *See* residential MBSs
Romney, George, 85, 182
Romney, Mitt, 182
Rosanvallon, Pierre, 20, 206, 249–50, 260n47
Rousseau, Jean Jacques, 243
Ruggie, John, 66–67
Rule 10b-18, of SEC, 210
rule of finance, depoliticization of, 103

Rumford Fair Housing Act (1963), 169, 172
run, on shadow banking system in 2007, 225, 228–29

Samuelson, Paul, 67, 96
Santelli, Rick, 235–36
savings and loan association (thrift): American Savings and Loan failure, 212; assets increase between 1980 and 1987, 212; commercial real estate and, 211; crisis and shadow banking system, 211–13; failures and government bailouts to, 212; local savings transmuted into local mortgages by, 210–11; OTS and, 229, 231
SCEA. *See* Stockton City Employees' Association
Schumer, Chuck, 230
Schwarzenegger, Arnold: California recall ballot win of, 194; CalPERS Harrigan ousted by, 194; fiscal recovery plan of, 194–95; privatization of CalPERS push by, 194–95
SEC. *See* Securities and Exchange Commission
Secondary Mortgage Market Enhancement Act (1984), 214
Second Treatise of Government (Locke), 29, 33
secularism, 24, 258n6; as depoliticization of religion, 27; Locke on analogy to wealth and, 30–31; religious conflict response from, 8, 23

secular stagnation hypothesis, of Gordon, 239
Securities and Exchange Commission (SEC), 218, 283n95; AIG settlement with, 221–22; G. W. Bush investigation by, 182; California investigation for securities fraud by, 198; Godman Sachs fined by, 308n111; NRSROs of, 213–14; Rule 10b-18 of, 210
securitization, 215, 228; subprime mortgages in shadow banking system and, 220, 222, 226, 233; weakening of market for Alt-A, 230, 306n83
security: in debt repayments, 159; Hobbes on absolute sovereign for, 21–22; of loan, 101; neoliberalism and, 130–31. *See also* mortgage-backed securities
Seidman, William, 94
Self, Robert, 276n174
Servicemen's Readjustment Act (1944) (GI Bill), housing undersupply response of, 81
service sector growth, 207
shadow banking system: McCulley on, 304n58; ABCP and ABSs in, 225, 228; of capital market-based housing finance, 211, 214; Fed backstop of, 232; financial crisis of 2008 and, 20, 205, 210–20; GSEs rapid growth contribution to, 214–15; interest and, 100–101; money market mutual funds in, 215, 220–21; Pozsar on, 239; public liquidity enhancements absence in, 215; run on in 2007, 225, 228–29; securitization of subprime mortgages in, 220, 222, 226, 233; short-term borrowing into long-term lending in, 215; subprime mortgages throughout, 220; thrifts crisis and, 211–13
shareholder activism, CalPERS and, 185
shareholder value: in CalPERS, 19, 167, 179–80, 184–86; corporate finance description of, 210; in corporate governance, 209; EPS and, 210
Shelley v. Kraemer, on racist housing covenants, 169
Silva, Anthony, 161–62; embezzlement and money laundering charge against, 163
Simon, William, 181
Simpson, Alan, 237
SIV. *See* structured investment vehicle
Skocpol, Theda, 237
Slobodian, Quinn, 277n1
Smith, Adam, 26, 66; Invisible Hand of, 54
social contract theory, 23
socialism: Block definition of democratic, 311n1; Drucker on, 165; Mill on, 47–50
social power: finance and, 110; financialization and, 133; liberalism and forms of, 113; liberal state and depoliticized, 11, 109
"Social Responsibility of Business Is to Increase Its Profits, The" (Friedman), 209

social unrest, financial crisis of 2008 and, 4
society, Mill and Rawls on state of, 62
Solow, Robert, 96
"Some Considerations of the Consequences of the Lowering of Interest and the Raising the Value of Money" (Locke), 39
sovereignty: CRAs as product of, 126; Foucault on, 114, 116; globalized capital and, 126; neoliberalism and, 125–26; Vogl and Desan on, 280n66
Soviet Union, Nixon grain sale to, 88
Spiegel, Evan, 288n78
Spiegel, Henry, 261n55
stagflation, 67; Foucault on, 279n43; interest and, 96
Standard & Poor (S&P), U.S. credit rating change by, 238
state: embedded liberalism threat from, 106; financial markets and interest, 102–3; individual autonomy and noninterference of, 23; interest rate caps by, 211; Locke on noninterference by, 31, 32; Locke on private property protection by, 33; Mill defense of individual against, 46; neoliberalism on strength of, 3–4; political emancipation of, 10; private property depoliticization from, 23; religion freedom from, 22–23
state property tax, California: modernization of, 174; pension benefits funded from, 175; tax revolt on, 86, 87, 176

stock market investments, of CalPERS, 171–72
Stockton, California: austerity and market-oriented reorganizations in, 19, 138, 153–55; background on, 283n1; bankruptcy of, 17–19, 136, 155–63, 299n149; from bankruptcy to populism, 159–62; budget cut attempts, 155–57; budgets and revenue projections in, 137–38; CalPERS pension payments from, 161; Concerned Citizens Coalition of, 141–42; employee contracts in, 149–50; escalated crime rate in, 161–62; Expected Core Revenues for, 162–63; financial creditors concern and, 19; financialization political origins in, 139–50; financial risk assumption, 19; general fund as backup security for repayments, 159; growth machine politics in, 135–63; Johnston as mayor of, 152, 154; leading foreclosures per capita in, 136; pendency plan adoption, 158, 287n60; POBs and, 146–48; political consequences of finalization in, 150–63; Proposition 13 impact on, 139–40; Proposition 18 TIF impact on, 140; public employment and spending in, 18, 19, 136, 149–50; redevelopment projects of, 140–41; retired employees health insurance discontinuance, 159–60; revenue maximization attempts, 151–53; severe public employee understaffing in, 153–54; Silva as 2012 mayor to, 161–62; state of fiscal

Stockton, California (*continued*)
emergency declaration, 154, 156;
Stockton Arena redevelopment
effort, 142–46; Tubbs as mayo of,
288n78; Washington Mutual 400
East Main building, 135–36, 148–49,
156, 158–59, 162; Washington Mutual
subprime mortgage investment
in, 135; K. Wilson on 2017 fiscal
stability of, 163
Stockton Arena redevelopment project,
142–46
Stockton City Employees' Association
(SCEA), 149–50
Streeck, Wolfgang, 254n10; on capital
abandonment, 6; on financialization
and distributive conflict, 15
structured investment vehicle (SIV),
228; CalPERS loss in, 196; money
market mutual funds and, 221
subprime MBSs structure: ABX
financial index on, 223, 225; financial
crisis of 2008 impacted by, 19, 178,
224–25
subprime mortgage investment:
ABX financial index for, 223, 225;
bankruptcy filings for, 226; by
Bear Stearns investment bank, 195;
CalPERS and, 19, 178–79, 189–92;
increase between 2000 and 2006,
220; throughout shadow banking
system, 220; of Washington
Mutual, 135
subprime mortgages: Bernanke on,
234; delinquencies on, 224; shadow
banking system securitization of,
220, 222, 226, 233

subsidies, in financial depoliticization,
122, 123
suburbanization: Baumgartner on
moral minimalism of, 83; Cohen on
consumerism and, 206; commercial
homebuilders and, 82; conservatism
and, 83; Interstate Highway System
impact on, 81; middle class and,
83, 206; political correlates of,
83; postindustrializing economy
transformed by, 82; postwar mass
consumption economy for, 82;
southern California growth of,
82–83
Supercommittee. *See* Joint Select
Committee on Deficit Reduction
supply shock, Mitchell on, 272n118
Supreme Court cases: *Allen v. City of
Long Beach*, 198–99; *Bush v. Gore*,
184; *Marquette National Bank of
Minneapolis v. First of Omaha*, 211;
Reitman v. Mulkey, 290n14; *Shelley
v. Kraemer*, 169
Swensen, David, 183–84

tacit consent, to money, 38–39
TARP. *See* Troubled Asset Relief
Program
tax cuts: ACRS and, 211–12; California
Proposition 13 on, 86–87, 107,
139–40, 175–77, 187, 273n131; of
Reagan, 14, 86–87, 207, 211–12
tax-increment financing (TIF), of
California Proposition 18, 140
tax revolt, on California state property
tax, 86, 87, 176
Taylor, Frederick, 226

Tea Party movement, 238; Obama and, 236; Reid on, 239
Term Securities Lending Facility (TSLF), Fed creation of, 229
Thatcher, Margaret, 273n137, 305n64
theory of human capital, Becker on, 118–19, 279n45
Theory of Justice, A (Rawls): on basic property rights, 62; on competitive markets, 52
three strikes law, of Proposition 184, 186–87
thrift. *See* savings and loan association
TIF. *See* tax-increment financing
Toleration Act (1689), 29
Tomasi, John, 263n115
Tonnage Act (1694), 29
transportation: CPI-U on, 79, 89–95; Hubbert on, 89–90; ICC and agricultural commodities exemption, 93; independent trucking and oil price spike, 93; Islamic Revolution and oil prices, 91–92; national gas price controls and, 92–93; oil embargo and, 87–88, 90–91; Union Oil Santa Barbara oil spill, 89
Troubled Asset Relief Program (TARP), 231
trucking industry, Hamilton on deregulation of, 93–94
Truman Fair Deal, housing and, 81
Trump, Donald J., 241
TSLF. *See* Term Securities Lending Facility
Tubbs, Michael, 288n78

UAL. *See* unfunded accrued liability
unemployment, 263n123; fall with NAIRU, 217, 305n70; inflation trade-off with, 2, 95–96
unfunded accrued liability (UAL) component, of CalPERS, 146
Union Oil Santa Barbara oil spill (1969), 89
United States Objectives and Programs for National Security (NSC-68) report, 80
universal financial services firms, Financial Services Modernization Act formation of, 218
Unruh, Jesse "Big Daddy," 173–74, 179, 291n24
urban decline, Self on, 276n174
urban financialization, 284n3
USDA. *See* Department of Agriculture, U.S.

Vallejo, California bankruptcy, 151, 155–57
Vogl, Joseph, 280n66
"Voice of the American Trucker, The" (Friedman), 93
Volcker, Paul, 203; on recession and inflation, 97
Volcker shock, 14, 96–97, 99–100, 207; inflation decline and, 254n10; real estate investments and, 179

Walker, Richard, 199–200
Walzer, Michael, 112; on liberalism, 8, 9, 109, 277n2
Washington Consensus program, of privatization of public enterprises, 126

Washington Mutual: bankruptcy of, 135–36; 400 East Main building of, 135–36, 148; OTS seizure of, 231; subprime mortgage investment of, 135
wealth: Greenspan on political polarization and, 238–39; Locke on secularism analogy to, 30–31
wealth effect, 105, 209
Wealth of Nations (Smith), 66
Weber, Rachel, 285n11
welfare economics, 56; Invisible Hand of Smith and, 54; lump-sum transfers, 54–55; neoclassical economics model on, 53; Pareto-efficient distribution in, 54
welfare reform bill, in Reagan Revolution, 173
welfare state, Hacker on, 280n62
Wells Fargo, repossession of 400 East Main building, 158
Wilson, Kurt, 163
Wilson, Peter: California reelection in 1994, 186; CalPERS attempted takeover by, 180–81; senate election of 1984 for, 179
Wojnilower, Albert, 98
Wolden, Russell, 174
Wolin, Sheldon, 259n22
working class, Mill on, 42, 44–45, 48–49
World Trade Organization (WTO), 216–17

www.ingramcontent.com/pod-product-compliance
Ingram Content Group Australia Pty Ltd
76 Discovery Rd, Dandenong South VIC 3175, AU
AUHW022045060125
405158AU00002B/4